CREATING CISTERCIAN NUNS

CREATING CISTERCIAN NUNS

THE WOMEN'S RELIGIOUS MOVEMENT AND ITS REFORM IN THIRTEENTH-CENTURY CHAMPAGNE

ANNE E. LESTER

CORNELL UNIVERSITY PRESS
Ithaca and London

Copyright © 2011 by Cornell University

All rights reserved. Except for brief quotations in a review, this book, or parts thereof, must not be reproduced in any form without permission in writing from the publisher. For information, address Cornell University Press, Sage House, 512 East State Street, Ithaca, New York 14850.

First published 2011 by Cornell University Press
First printing, Cornell Paperbacks, 2017

Library of Congress Cataloging-in-Publication Data

Lester, Anne Elisabeth, 1974–
 Creating Cistercian nuns : the women's religious movement and its reform in thirteenth-century Champagne / Anne E. Lester.
  p. cm.
 Includes bibliographical references and index.
 ISBN 978-0-8014-4989-5 (cloth : alk. paper)
 ISBN 978-1-5017-1349-1 (pbk. : alk. paper)
 1. Cistercian nuns—France—Champagne-Ardenne—History—To 1500. 2. Monastic and religious life of women—France—Champagne-Ardenne—History—To 1500. 3. Champagne-Ardenne (France)—Religious life and customs. I. Title.
 BX4328.Z5F75 2011
 271'.97—dc23   2011022953

Cornell University Press strives to use environmentally responsible suppliers and materials to the fullest extent possible in the publishing of its books. Such materials include vegetable-based, low-VOC inks and acid-free papers that are recycled, totally chlorine-free, or partly composed of nonwood fibers. For further information, visit our website at www.cornellpress.cornell.edu.

*In memory of my grandparents
Maurine Powell Lester
and
Thomas William Lester
storytellers in their own right*

The inferno of the living is not something that will be; if there is one, it is what is already here, the inferno where we live every day, that we form by being together. There are two ways to escape suffering it. The first is easy for many: accept the inferno and become such a part of it that you can no longer see it. The second is risky and demands constant vigilance and apprehension: seek and learn to recognize who and what, in the midst of the inferno, are not inferno, then make them endure, give them space.
—Italo Calvino, *Invisible Cities*

The order was founded for anyone, lettered or unlettered, who needed a city of refuge.
—*The Chronicle of Villers*

Contents

List of Illustrations ix
Preface xi
Acknowledgments xv
On Currencies, Names, and Transcriptions xix
List of Abbreviations and Short Titles xxi

Introduction: Written Fragments and
Living Parts   1

1. Concerning Certain Women:
The Women's Religious Movement
in Champagne   15

2. Cities of Refuge: The Social World
of Religious Women   45

3. Under the Religious Life: Reform and
the Cistercian Order   78

4. The Bonds of Charity: The Special
Cares of Cistercian Nuns   117

5. One and the Same Passion: Convents
and Crusaders   147

6. A Space Apart: Gender and
Administration in a New Social Landscape   171

Epilogue: A Deplorable and Dangerous
State: Crisis, Consolidation, and Collapse   201

*Appendix: Cistercian Convents and
Domus-Dei of Champagne* 211
Bibliography 217
Index 251

Illustrations

1. Playing card, jack of diamonds (undated, ca. late seventeenth century) — xii
2. Donation charter from Beatrix of St.-Rémy for the nuns of Clairmarais outside Reims, October 1224 — 2
3. Detail, plan of Notre-Dame-des-Prés, Troyes, 1772 — 16
4. L'Amour-Dieu, exterior of abbey church, east end of nave — 98
5. La Cour Notre-Dame-de-Michery, exterior of the abbey church, east end of nave — 99
6. Charter from Abbess Isabelle of Notre-Dame-des-Prés, granting permission to the *conversus* John to swear to an agreement in her place, 1251 — 176
7. Detail, rental list (*censive*) from Clairmarais for properties in Reims, undated, ca. thirteenth century — 179
8. Charter officiated by the dean of Christianity of Bar-sur-Aube, 1242 — 183
9. Charter displaying seals of Alice of Jaucourt, the dean of Christianity, and the *prévôt* of Bar-sur-Aube, 1272 — 184
10. Amortization for Val-des-Vignes from Thibaut V, count of Champagne, king of Navarre, 1269 — 198
11. Charter from the abbot of Clairvaux to the nuns of Val-des-Vignes concerning Boniface VIII's *Periculoso,* 1298 — 205

Map 1. Sites of Cistercian convents in Champagne and the neighboring provinces during the thirteenth century — 20

Preface

In the episcopal archives of Troyes, among layers of crumbling paper and yellowing parchments, every now and again there is a flash of color. A small hand-painted playing card appears, folded in half with a hole in the center held by a piece of cotton string (fig. 1). The card—probably painted and played in the late seventeenth century—anchors in place bundles of carefully ordered twelfth- and thirteenth-century charters, which are likewise punctured and connected by the same string. Quite at odds with its original purpose, the card now functions to secure the past in place. Such painted cards come to light throughout the departmental archives of the Aube and Marne. From time to time they surface among the documents of the bishops of Châlons. Another card with a hasty note scribbled on its reverse migrated to Paris and is now tucked inside the last folio of volume 151 of the Collection Champagne in the Bibliothèque nationale de France. An archivist charged with organizing these episcopal records, most likely working in the first half of the eighteenth century, made the cards the guardians of the medieval past: a knave, his pike in hand; a queen, smiling slyly; a complicit four of clubs. The cards hold together groups of charters, some pertaining to the same religious institution, or a plot of contested ground, or the gifts of a particular family, sometimes disputed over generations. These groupings echo the structure of medieval monastic cartularies and administrative registers, which often used the geography of rural estates or social status as organizing principles. Indeed the original documents may have been stored in the very same bundles in chests or armoires before they were tied up and assigned their playing cards.

As entertaining as it is to find a card, it is the medieval charters they secure that beckon, first in the names of the officials who drew them up, and then farther down the page in the names of men and women who paid to have them made to record their gifts, sales, disputes, charity, and prayers. Many of these charters have been read and studied before, but many more persist, overlooked as unremarkable or insignificant, or simply too difficult to read. This is particularly true of several groups of charters related to the Cistercian nuns of Champagne. In some cases convent documents have been

xii **PREFACE**

FIGURE 1. Playing card, jack of diamonds, in the episcopal collection in Troyes (undated, ca. late seventeenth century). AD Aube, G 3101 (May 1242). Photo by the author.

catalogued together as a clearly conceived archive. But several collections of charters for Cistercian convents were subsumed within the archives of male abbeys, making them harder to find and to identify. This has all but erased the archival presence of some Cistercian nuns, leaving historians to assume that no records exist and therefore that nothing can be said about these women and their history. Those who did know of these houses often deemed them too small and insignificant to warrant serious attention. Yet all told, when ferreted out, hundreds of medieval parchment records inhabit the archives of northern France, revealing a women's religious movement and its institutional reform.

Within the monastic history of a great order like the Cistercians, these convents are unusual for they boast no formal medieval cartularies, that is, no bound copies of original texts made during the thirteenth century. Occasionally, selected charters were copied into small paper books in the crabbed hands of fifteenth-century monks or in the careful cursive and classicizing Latin of seventeenth- or eighteenth-century antiquarians. The charters in their bundles and folders form a fragmentary archive that reveals the religious and social worlds that fostered the women's religious movement in northern France. They evoke the men and women, many of whom were local townsmen, burghers, mothers, and widows, who supported the ideals of apostolic poverty and active charity that the nuns embraced. The nunneries' charters also have much to say about the Cistercian order, its relationship with women, and the acceptance and administration of female convents during the 1220s and 1230s. In some cases the conspicuous absence of written records and visitation documents is more telling of how some Cistercian monks viewed their obligations to women under their spiritual care. Certainly those charters appended with silk threads carrying the wax seals of the counts of Champagne and his knights or those with thin strips of parchment folded over and made official by the seal of a *prévôt* or mayor have much to say about the connections between the Cistercian convents and the broader religious currents animating the thirteenth century. They speak of an aristocratic compulsion for provisioning the poor and sick and of an almost pauperizing commitment to crusading and its ideals, of the growing presence and influence of the urban bourgeoisie, of hopes of salvation and remembrance, and of the simple if mundane need for credit in the failing economy that strained secular and religious institutions alike at the turn of the fourteenth century. The convents' charters expose the religious practices and pious intentions of the society of Champagne during the thirteenth century and record how men and women conceived of and crafted the institutionalization of a spiritual ideal. These are the texts that form the backbone of this book.

❧ Acknowledgments

Like the women at the end of this book, I have come to the close of this endeavor deeply in debt, benefiting from the intellectual generosity of many people and places. It is a joy to render account now. This book took shape under the patient teaching and advice of William Chester Jordan. His most challenging questions, often posed casually outside the classroom, became the subjects of chapters and shaped their arguments in critical ways. I am unspeakably grateful for Bill's guidance, support, and friendship and am delighted to remain always his student. This book in its substance began, however, with the gift of an archive, or at least its suggestion. On a small index card over ten years ago, Theodore Evergates wrote "Notre-Dame-aux-Nonnains, Troyes; Cistercian nunneries, Archives départementales de l'Aube" in a careful cursive hand. Ted's deep knowledge of these archives and my naive conviction that there *must* be something more to say about religious women led me to the hundreds of charters that lie behind this book. Ted has read multiple versions of the manuscript, from its initial form as a dissertation to its final incarnation. He is perhaps the only person who knows the men and women of Champagne by name, and I have benefited from his wisdom in countless ways. I hope it is suitable thanks.

A number of institutions provided financial assistance over the years: funding from the History Department at Princeton University, the Center for the Study of Religion, and the Graduate School supported me and allowed me to travel to the archives in France several times as a student. Princeton shaped my thinking as a historian, and I am grateful for the guidance and conversation with many there, especially Peter Brown, Molly Green, and Gyan Prakash, as well as the environment of the Davis Center. Support from the History Department at the George Washington University facilitated my first return to the archives as the project grew into a book. An Andrew Mellon postdoctoral fellowship at the Medieval Institute at the University of Notre Dame was instrumental in the book's reshaping, and I thank Tom Noble, Remi Constable, and John Van Engen for their support. While there, Caroline Bruzelius, Barbara Newman, and especially Martha

Newman offered extremely useful comments on an earlier version. One lunchtime conversation with John Van Engen in particular made me see the landscape of this book and its comparative framework in a new way, and I remain immensely grateful for his comments and confidence in this project. Likewise, an offhand comment from Paul Cobb about the crusader families of Champagne provided the genesis for chapter 5. Funding from the University of Colorado, the Center for the Humanities and the Arts, as well as summer grants for junior faculty from the Council on Research and Creative Work, an Implementation of Multicultural Perspectives and Approaches in Research and Teaching (IMPART) Award, and a Eugene M. Kayden Research Grant all allowed me to return to France at critical points. The Inter-Library Loan staff at the University of Colorado also helped me acquire printed materials with remarkable efficiency. And a Eugene M. Kayden Book Subvention Award from the University of Colorado generously supported the production of this book and the accompanying images.

One of the most delightful parts of writing a book about France is learning and living in its archives. A Chateaubriand Fellowship supported my first year there, and I am grateful to Jean-Claude Schmitt and Nicole Bériou for their generosity and guidance while in Paris. The staff at the Institut de recherché et d'histoire des textes in Paris, and especially the expertise of Annie Dufour, made the Salle diplomatique a welcoming place. I am deeply indebted to the wonderful staff at the Archives départementales of the Marne, Haute-Marne, Yonne, and especially the Aube, who were always warm and generous in helping me find the documents I needed.

I owe a special debt to Caroline Goodson, a remarkable friend and colleague, for preparing the map. Thanks also to Terryl Kinder, who graciously photographed L'Amour-Dieu for me during one of her many trips between Belgium and Pontigny. I owe Peter Potter at Cornell University Press great thanks for his interest and patience in seeing me through this process. Thank you also to Candace Akins and the Press staff for bringing the book to print. Finally, an earlier version of chapter 5 previously appeared in the *Journal of Medieval History* (2009).

Several people have read parts of this book, including Barbara Engel, Paul Hammer, Martha Hanna, Susan Kent, and Maryanne Kowaleski, and I am grateful for their feedback at critical points. In addition to Bill Jordan and Ted Evergates, Mark Gregory Pegg read the manuscript in full, and his incisive comments, queries, and attention to the art of writing history have made me think differently about what we do and how. I also thank the anonymous reader from Cornell University Press and Sharon Farmer for their comments, which have greatly improved the book and its argument. Thanks also to Kevin Lord and Brianna Gustafson for their labors proofreading.

Finally, the patience and generosity of many friends and colleagues nurtured this book and my questions over many years. Their confidence in me and in the project has been more important than I can say. My interest in the past was fostered early on by two remarkable teachers, Dorothy Strang and Earl Bell. Through their prompting I was introduced to the delights of difficult questions and to the depths of Regenstein Library at a precocious age and never wanted to leave. Indeed, the penultimate version of this book was completed in its quietude. Further inspiration came from Amy Remensyder's dazzling teaching, Joseph Pucci's gifts for close reading, and Sheila Bonde's and Clark Maines's on-site schooling. Their confidence is something I remain eternally grateful for. Many other friends shared conversations, comments, and questions over the years about history, hockey, fashion, academia, writing, Champagne cocktails, and so much else. Their generosity sustains me and I thank them here: Lisa Bailey, Lucy Chester, Meri Clark, Paul Cobb, Giles Constable, James Cunningham, M. Cecilia Gaposchkin, Guy Geltner, Jason Glenn, Caroline Goodson, Geoffroy Grassin, Mark Huey, Peter Low, Christopher McEvitt, Maureen Miller, R. I. Moore, Molly Polk, Janneke Raaijmakers, Lauren Redniss, Suman Seth, Edith Sheffer, Mindy Smith, Susannah Strang, and Carol Symes.

My family, Eric and Audrey, Lucy and George, Bill, Bob and Matt, have borne with this project for a long time, and their curiosity and encouragement (and heroic summers of babysitting) allowed me to bring it to completion. I am profoundly grateful to be in this whole endeavor with my husband, Scott, who has patiently helped me to see what is good in this book, to fix what is faulty, and live with all the rest. There simply are not words to express my thanks or my love. And to Mira, my marvel, I owe a delight and inspiration I never imagined; and to Vivienne, who arrived just in time. This book is for you three.

A.E.L.
Istria, HPK

❧ On Currencies, Names, and Transcriptions

In Champagne, as in most of Europe during the medieval period, money was reckoned in pounds (*l.*, French *livres*, Latin *libri*), shillings (*s.*, French *sous*, Latin *solidi*), and pence or pennies (*d.*, French *deniers*, Latin *denarii*), with 12 pence = 1 shilling, and 20 shillings = 1 pound. The currency was based on a silver standard. Although Italian merchants occasionally employed gold coins at the Champagne fairs, the majority of economic transactions in Champagne were paid in the Champagne currency of *provinois* or French *tournois*. Most small payments were paid out in pence, one pound being equal to 240 pennies. Half pennies also existed (Latin *obolus*), and many customary payments and rents were rendered in this denomination. Because of the dominance of the Champagne fairs during the High Middle Ages, money *provinois*, minted in the comital capital of Provins, circulated more widely than any other northern French coin. Although the money *provinois* initially held a high silver content, around 1224 it was debased to conform to the value of money *tournois*. After the county was incorporated into the royal domain in 1284, money *tournois* was minted in Champagne in place of money *provinois*. Cistercian nuns received payments in all of these currencies, but for ease of narrative I have employed the following abbreviations for coinage when mentioned in the text: *l., s.,* and *d.*

Whenever possible I have employed modern English naming patterns, favoring Stephen over Étienne, Alice over Aalydis. Where a French equivalent has come into common usage, however, I have used that form, as is the case with Jacques de Vitry and Jean de Joinville. With respect to Latin citations from original archival sources, in most cases I have silently expanded abbreviated words according to classical norms and followed modern principles of punctuation. When citations are taken from printed sources I have followed the convention of the edition employed. This study is built around a core collection of archival material, much of which has never been transcribed before. Although I have endeavored to keep the notes as unencumbered as possible, at times fuller quotations from the documents are included for those unable to consult the archival collections or the more obscure printed editions that reference them.

Abbreviations and Short Titles

AASS	*Acta Sanctorum*. 70 vols. Ed. Jean Bollandus et al. Paris: Victorem Palme, 1863.
AD	Archives départementales (Aube, Haute-Marne, Marne, Yonne)
AN	Archives nationales, Paris
Annales ESC	*Annales: Economies, sociétés, civilisations*
BEC	*Bibliothèque de l'école des chartes*
BM	Bibliothèque municipale
BNF	Bibliothèque nationale de France, Paris
DHGE	*Dictionnaire d'histoire et de géographie ecclésiastiques*. Paris, 1912–present.
GC	*Gallia christiana in provincias ecclesiasticas distributa*. 16 vols. Paris, 1715–1865.
Layettes	*Layettes du trésor des chartes*. 5 vols. Ed. A. Teulet et al. Paris, 1863–1909.
MAT	Médiathèques de l'Agglomération Troyenne
MGH SS	*Monumenta Germaniae Historica inde ab anno christi quingentesimo usque ad annum millesimum et quingentisimum. Scriptores in folio*. 32 vols. Hannover and Leipzig, 1826–1934.
MSA	*Mémoires de la Société academique d'agriculture des sciences, arts et belles-lettres du département de l'Aube*
MSM	*Mémoires de la Société d'agriculture, commerce, sciences et arts du département de la Marne*
MSP	*Mémoires de la Société de l'historie de Paris et de l'Ile de France*
Olim	*Les Olim, ou Registres des ârrets rendus par la cour du roi*. 3 vols. in 4 parts. Ed. Arthur Beugnot. Paris, 1839–48.
PL	*Patrologiae cursus completus, Series Latina*. 221 vols. Ed. J.-P. Migne. Paris, 1844–64.
RHGF	*Recueil des historiens des Gaules et de la France*. 24 vols. Ed. Martin Bouquet et al. Paris, 1738–1904.

VArnf	Goswin of Bossut, *Vita Arnulfi* in *AASS*, June, 7:606–31. Trans. Martius Cawley as "The Life of Arnulf, Lay Brother of Villers," in *Send Me God*, 125–208. All references are to book and paragraph number.
VAS	*Vita Aleydis de Scarembecanea* [Alice of Schaarbeek], in Chrysostomos Henriquez, *Quinque prudentes virgines* (Antwerp, 1630), 168–98; and *Vita Alsydis*, in *AASS*, 11 June, 24:471–77. Trans. Martinus Cawley as *Alice the Leper: Life of St. Alice of Schaerbeek* (Lafayette, OR, 2000). All references are by paragraph number.
VBJ	Hugh of Floreffe, *Vita beatae Juettae* [Yvette of Huy], in *AASS*, 13 January, 2:145–69. Trans. Jo Ann McNamara as *The Life of Yvette of Huy by Hugh of Floreffe* (Toronto, 2000). All references are by chapter and paragraph number.
VIN	Goswin of Bossut, *Vita Idea Nivellensis,* in Chrysostomos Henriquez, *Quinque prudentes virgines* (Antwerp, 1630), 199–297. Trans. Martinus Cawley as *The Life of Ida the Compassionate of Nivelles,* in *Send Me God,* 27–120. All references are by paragraph number.
VJC	*Vita Iulianae Corneliensis* [Juliana of Cornillon], in *AASS*, 7 April, 10:435–75; trans. and ed. Jean-Pierre Delville as *Vita Julianae*, in *Fête-Dieu (1246–1996) II:Vie de Sainte Julienne de Cornillon* (Louvian-la-Neuve, 1999). Trans. Barbara Newman as *The Life of Juliana of Mont-Cornillon* (Toronto, 1991; reprint, 2002). All references are by book and chapter number.
VJM	*Vita de B. Joanne de Monte Mirabili*, in *AASS*, September, 8:186–255.
VMO	Jacques de Vitry, *Vita Mariae Oigniacensis,* in *AASS*, 23 June, 25:547–72. Trans. Margot H. King as *The Life of Mary of Oignies by James of Vitry,* in *Mary of Oignies.* All references are by chapter and paragraph number.
VMO-S	Thomas of Cantimpré, *Vita Mariae Oigniacensis, Supplementum,* in *AASS*, 23 June, 25:572–81. Trans. Hugh Feiss, OSB, as "The Supplement to James of Vitry's Life of Mary of Oignies by Thomas of Camtimpré," in *Mary of Oignies.* All references are by chapter and paragraph number.
VMY	Thomas of Cantimpré, *Vita Margarete de Ypres,* ed. G. Meersmann, in "Les frères prêcheurs et le mouvement dévot en Flandres au XIIIe siècle," *Archivum Fratrum Praedicatorum* 18 (1948): 106–30. Trans. Margot H. King as *The Life of Margaret of Ypres by Thomas de Camtimpré* (Toronto, 1990).

CREATING CISTERCIAN NUNS

Introduction
Written Fragments and Living Parts

In October of 1224 Beatrix, the widow of Thomas of St.-Rémy, came before an official of the bishop's court in Reims and drew up a donation charter for the nuns of Clairmarais, the new Cistercian nunnery taking shape just beyond the city's walls (fig. 2). She gave the women, among whom was her daughter Sara, an annual rent of 60 s. collected from two houses in different parts of the city. The charter records Beatrix's gift but goes on to indulge her concerns about the viability of the new nunnery. Beatrix offered her donation contingent upon certain conditions: "If it should happen that the nuns were dispersed and the house of Clairmarais came to nothing and her daughter Sara should transfer to another house of the Cistercian order, the aforementioned rents were to transfer with her and belong to that house."[1] Clairmarais was a novel institution, something unknown and untried in Reims. Beatrix continued: "If it should happen that after her daughter's death the house of Clairmarais should be annulled and dispossessed, the [Cistercian] abbots of Igny and Val Regis ought to give the

---

1. "si contingat predictas moniales dispergi et domum de Claromarisco ad nichilum devenire filia sua Sarra que ibidem monialis est adhuc superstire et ad aliam domum cisterciensis ordinis transeunte redditus antedictus ad eamdem domum cum ea transferbit et illius domus erit." AD Aube, 3 H 3784 (October 1224).

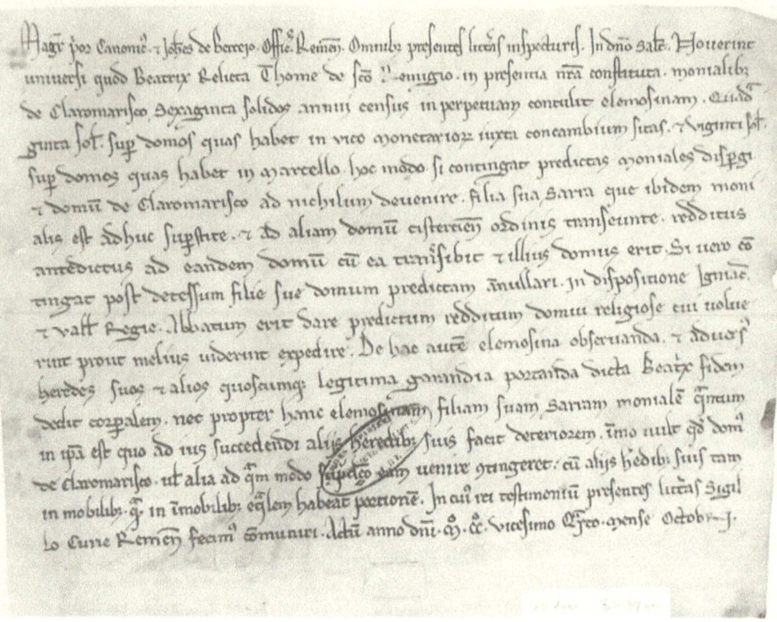

FIGURE 2. Donation charter from Beatrix of St.-Rémy for the nuns of Clairmarais. AD Aube 3 H 3764 (October 1224). Photo by the author.

rents to a religious house that they deem most worthy."[2] Beatrix's charter is in many respects a routine and unremarkable document, but her careful planning for contingencies exposes the impermanence and informality of the new female community on the outskirts of Reims. Her concerns, inflected by a mother's caution, evoke a process of institutionalization that was taking place throughout Europe during the first decades of the thirteenth century: the reform of protean and dynamic religious movements into monastic orders. Beatrix played a role in this process in its distinctive form in Champagne where communities of religious women adopted Cistercian customs and became Cistercian nuns. Yet it was not at all clear that this reform would succeed or what it meant to become a Cistercian nun. Indeed, in Beatrix's mind, even Clairmarais's status as part of the *ordo Cisterciensis* did not guarantee its success or longevity beyond her daughter's lifetime.

---

2. "Si vero contingat post decessum filie sue domum predictam annullari in dispositione Igniacis et Vallis Regie abbatum erit dare predictam redditum domui religiose cui voluerunt prout melius viderint expedire." AD Aube, 3 H 3784 (October 1224).

We know little about Beatrix or Sara except that Sara was part of the first community of women who populated the nunnery of Clairmarais. Only two years earlier, in 1222, a local goldsmith had given these women a tract of land and probably a small building near Reims (*juxta Remensis*), which they used as a church and convent.[3] In 1229 three of Sara's sisters joined her and professed at Clairmarais, at which time Beatrix added seven measures of land and another house to her initial gift.[4] Neither Beatrix nor her daughters have titles or occupational markers appended to their names. Given the relative modesty and location of her donations, Beatrix and her deceased husband, Thomas, were most likely members of the growing burgher class of Reims and would have been involved in credit networks tied to the archiepiscopal court or in the trade and manufacturing of cloth.[5] We are left to wonder what compelled the daughters of burghers to take up a life of religion, to live communally outside their city, and to create a life outside the social world their mother still inhabited.

Through their early association with the women of Clairmarais, Sara and her sisters may have understood themselves to be part of a broader religious movement present in Champagne—part of a group of like-minded women who had adopted a new orientation toward the religious life, specifically the ideals of the *vita apostolica,* which valorized an embrace of poverty, charity, and penitential piety. The term "religious movement"—let alone a women's religious movement—is challenging to define with precision. This movement as it was manifest in Champagne did not have an identifiable leader—a Saint Francis or Saint Clare—nor did it have explicitly recorded aims that articulated an agenda for social or religious change, such as a written critique, a proposal for a new monastic rule, or new customs. Yet such goals are visible in the actions of the women: in the fact of their communal existence independent of hierarchical sanction, and in the notice they attracted—both praise and critique—from those around them who described their prayers, habits of dress, and practices of caring for the poor and sick.

More clearly discernable in the texts is a collective identity shared by many religious women in Champagne in the first decades of the thirteenth century. Those women who came together in communities like Clairmarais, which predated any kind of institutional formalism or juridical definition and affiliation with a monastic order, did so because they shared common interests, experiences, and solidarities informed by gender, class, and perceptions of the

---

3. AD Aube, 3 H 3766 (May 1222); and *GC* 9, instr. 61.
4. AD Aube, 3 H 3784 (March 1229).
5. See Pierre Desportes, *Reims et les rémois aux XIIIe et XIVe siècles* (Paris, 1979).

social community around them, focused through the apostolic ideals circulating in contemporary preaching and pastoral care.[6] It was during the first decades of the thirteenth century, particularly between the 1220s and 1240s, that women began to assert their collective identity in public life. A desire for greater participation in the religious life and a heightened commitment to the practice of charity and penance defined the unwritten goals of a discernable women's religious movement. Throughout Champagne—as will be shown here—women were consistent in their actions and commitments to these shared ideals. It did not take the production of a religious tract or a hagiographical model to articulate this desire; rather women's actions resonate clearly in the documents of practice like the one Beatrix produced.

The movement in Champagne shares much in common with analogous movements in the southern Low Countries (involving beguines), in Germany (involving canonesses), and in northern Italy (involving penitent sisters and Poor Clares). In this way it is possible, as Herbert Grundmann and other scholars have done, to talk about a women's religious movement that took place on a broad scale. Yet the special value of the case of Champagne and the communities that formed there lies in the fact that the exceptional or extraordinary—the Mary of Oignies, Elizabeth of Hungary, or Clare of Assisi—does not eclipse the broader lived experience of religious ideals and reform at work on the ground. Indeed, it is striking that no significant corpus of hagiographical texts detailing the lives of religious women or Cistercian nuns was produced in Champagne as we find, for instance, in the diocese of Liège or the urban centers of northern Italy. The reasons for this remain unclear. Perhaps male confessors and authors were concerned with other tasks, or the urgency of proving the orthodoxy of the region's religious commitments was less pressing, or those men of literary talent—one thinks of Jacques de Vitry, who hailed from Champagne—left the region to pursue vocations elsewhere. The texts that proliferate in Champagne are of a more day-to-day type: charters, petitions, bequests, sales, and donations that expose the women's religious movement as it was reformed and its communities made into Cistercian convents. These texts demand that we recast our view of the women's religious movement for they shed light on what could be called the collective sociological process of institutionalizing a religious movement in all of its minute and detailed articulations. This is not to say

---

6. See the definitions used in Leila J. Rupp and Verta Taylor, "Forging Feminist Identity in an International Movement: A Collective Identity Approach to Twentieth-Century Feminism," *Signs* 24 (1999): 363–86, esp. 365–66; and Charles Tilly, "From Interactions to Outcomes in Social Movements," in *How Social Movements Matter*, ed. Marco Giugni, Doug McAdam, and Charles Tilly (Minneapolis, 1999), 253–70, although I disagree with Tilly that there were no discernable social movements before 1800.

that tropes and ideals present in the female *vitae* produced in Liège did not inform and resonate with women in Champagne. They certainly did. But Champagne's texts—largely documents of practice—complement and complicate our previous understanding of religious women, reform, and the role of monastic orders in the thirteenth century. Most important, the Champagne texts were not written to glorify or reaffirm the established church but rather to record what men and women esteemed and hoped to foster as ideals of the religious life. When we encounter bishops, legates, and clerics in these texts, they are often responding—tellingly—to the women and lay patrons taking part in this religious movement. The case of Champagne thus offers a new perspective on the dynamics of religious reform and the monastic life in the decades after the Fourth Lateran Council of 1215.

The chief aim of this book is to understand the shape of this movement in its earliest forms and to analyze how it was transformed into an institutional framework: to trace the creation of Cistercian nuns. For historians, who depend on written texts, it is impossible to find social movements or collective identity apart from language, that is, without records of women and men coming together either to identify as groups (as articulated, for example, in monastic customs or rules) or to be categorized in descriptive texts as different and distinct (as in the case of inquisitors' records). Moreover, language and institutions are self-generating, and the examples from the Cistercian convents of Champagne make this very clear.[7] In Champagne, we cannot see the women's religious movement at work until bishops, clerics, and patrons begin to name these women—typically calling them *mulieres religiosae, Filles-Dieu,* or *mulierculae*—and to describe their behavior. These first references appear in charters like that drawn up by Beatrix, and in the earliest records of Cistercian convents that began to proliferate in the 1220s and 1230s.

It is clear that many of the new Cistercian nunneries sprang from an intense spiritual fervor on the part of local, often urban bourgeois women rather than a larger monastic effort for expansion or an aristocratic patron's wish to found a new nunnery. Beatrix and her contemporaries understood far more than we do about how collective identities and movements of the thirteenth century might coalesce as institutions and the significant contingencies involved. The ephemeral nature of the earliest women's religious communities is clear from her words: should the nuns disperse, or should the house fail or come to nothing (*ad nichilum devenire*), other plans had to be made for her daughters,

---

7. See the conceptual arguments in John R. Searle, *The Construction of Social Reality* (New York, 1995), and more forcefully articulated in idem, *Making the Social World: The Structure of Human Civilization* (Oxford, 2010).

her donations, and for the care of her own soul. Beatrix's pragmatism reveals the challenges of transforming lived religion into a sanctioned institution that took on the onerous yet necessary obligations of property ownership, administration, and disciplined oversight. Yet it was precisely this process of transformation, which harnessed a living religious ideal and gave it an approved institutional form, that occurred in dynamic ways across northern France and Champagne during the thirteenth century. Moreover, as women understood, institutionalization—although fraught with its own compromises—promised a kind of permanence, at least for a time. It also made women part of the institutional church and offered the possibility of changing, critiquing, and reforming the church in turn.

Between the turn of the thirteenth century and 1244, roughly forty Cistercian convents were founded in northern France, half of which fell within the region of Champagne. The impetus for their foundation came initially from women in the laity. One of the effects of this growth was to bring a new class of women into the existing church, for many of these new convents had townswomen, like Beatrix and Sara, as their first nuns and patrons. In some cases new nunneries formed from groups of repentant women known as *Filles-Dieu,* who may have lived in poverty and prostitution before taking up a religious life. In other cases, convents grew out of groups of women serving the poor, sick, and leprous in small hospices known as *domus-Dei.* Often Cistercian nunneries integrated several different classes of women together, suggesting that the ideals of the *vita apostolica* at least initially addressed fundamental issues of poverty and equality.

The second goal of the book is to analyze why and how, in the context of Champagne, the women's religious movement was reformed as part the Cistercian order. This analysis relies on a close reading and contextualization of the legislative texts the order generated as it deliberated and ultimately compromised about the role of women under its jurisdiction and following its customs. Indeed, by reading the Cistercian statutes through the lens of the archival documents from Champagne, one can see the order, the papacy, and local bishops responding to the actions of local women and creating a definition of Cistercian nuns for the first time. In turn, the surprising flexibility of the Cistercian order comes to light, particularly during the first half of the thirteenth century as the very concept of a religious order took shape in a new language of juridical precision. By accepting women's communities within their order, the Cistercians changed the ways they were seen and defined as a force for religious reform.

Finally, *Creating Cistercian Nuns* aims to contextualize the reform of religious women in Champagne within the broader world of lay spirituality and the ideals of charity, penitential piety, and crusading that shaped religious culture and practices of devotion during the thirteenth century. In doing so, the book makes it clear that religious women became Cistercian nuns in large part because the women's practices in many respects accorded well with the ideals of the order, which esteemed manual labor and charity. Moreover, even as Cistercian nuns the women were allowed and at times encouraged and required to continue to serve the sick and poor as they had before adopting the order's customs. Cistercian affiliation also accorded well with the laity's support for crusading and an expanding understanding of crusade spirituality, which associated suffering in the East with Christ's suffering. Cistercian nuns benefited from these connections because their own devotions were seen as a kind of *imitatio Christi* within the cloister, and their prayers were constructed as especially efficacious when channeled in support of crusading and its commemoration. Perhaps more than any other order of the early thirteenth century, the Cistercians were tightly bound to a crusade ideology, and this association informed the articulation of a unique Cistercian female spirituality. Surprisingly, despite all of these connections, there has never been a study tracing the history of women, reform, and the Cistercian order.

Historiographical Frame

The history of women in the Cistercian order has proved to be particularly contentious. Founded in 1098, the Cistercians were one of several new monastic orders that emerged at the turn of the twelfth century out of the climate of the Gregorian Reform, which sought to impose a rigorous separation of the sexes and the cultivation of a chaste male clergy. Moreover the Cistercians began as a male monastic order, and from the order's inception its members had an ambivalent relationship with religious women. On the one hand they attempted to avoid contact with women institutionally and juridically by eschewing formal legal oversight of communities of nuns, while on the other hand individual abbots and monks cultivated relationships of spiritual advice and guidance with religious women and occasionally with female monastic communities. As Constance Berman and others have shown, some Cistercian nunneries were founded during the twelfth century, but nuns do not appear in the official documents of the order or in the annual statutes until the very last decade of the century. When nuns are mentioned, it is in legislation that is often restrictive. From 1218 onward many of the statutes attempt to limit the participation and incorporation of women in the order, and much of the rhetoric about women, both legal and theological, has a discernable misogynistic tone. In 1225 and again in 1228 the order passed statutes that—as it is commonly interpreted—effectively banned the creation and association of new female houses in the order; there were to be, according to their legislation, no new female convents.[8]

Yet by the beginning of the thirteenth century the Cistercian order had become the center of religious authority: the monks were lauded for their spirituality and Eucharistic piety, they were petitioned for the efficaciousness of their prayers, and Cistercian abbots rose to prominent positions as bishops, crusade preachers, and papal legates.[9] In 1215 at the Fourth Lateran Council, Pope Innocent III hailed the Cistercians as the model monastic order and used the Cistercian administrative organization as a template for all other monastic orders in Christendom.[10] Despite Cistercian rhetoric, it seemed clear to the pope and to his successors and cardinals that the customs of the order, known as the Cistercian *Institutes,* would function well as a set of guidelines for reforming many of the religious groups that still stood outside the formal institutional church, particularly groups of religious women.

Reconciling the Cistercian order's legislation banning new female convents with the archival evidence that speaks of the clear proliferation of new Cistercian nunneries during the 1230s and 1240s has been one of the great challenges within the historiography on the order. This is in part because few scholars separate out the actors involved in this process. A history of religious orders as self-generating institutions has dominated the intellectual paradigm of religious history, which means that scholars have not seen the new Cistercian nunneries of the thirteenth century within the broader context of reform and regularization, but rather have assumed that women wanted to be formally associated with the order, to live according to the Cistercian *Institutes,* and to "enjoy" the rigors of claustration and monastic visitation. Moreover, the idea that in northern France the women's religious movement was reformed under Cistercian customs during the 1230s stands in confrontation with the dominant historiographical narrative first suggested

---

8. See, for example, Sally Thompson, "The Problem of Cistercian Nuns in the Twelfth and Early Thirteenth Centuries," in *Medieval Women,* ed. Derek Baker (Oxford, 1978), 227–53; and Brigitte Degler-Spengler, "The Incorporation of Cistercian Nuns into the Order in the Twelfth and Thirteenth Century," in *Hidden Springs: Cistercian Monastic Women,* 2 vols., ed. John A. Nichols and Lillian Thomas Shank (Kalamazoo, MI, 1995), 1:85–134. Constance Berman takes up this issue in "Were There Twelfth-Century Cistercian Nuns?" *Church History* 68 (1999): 824–64; and idem, *The Cistercian Evolution: The Invention of a Religious Order in Twelfth-Century Europe* (Philadelphia, 2000).

9. See Jean-Berthold Mahn, *L'ordre cistercien et son gouvernement: Des origines au milieu du XIIIe siècle (1098–1265)* (Paris, 1982); and Martha G. Newman, *The Boundaries of Charity: Cistercian Culture and Ecclesiastical Reform, 1098–1180* (Stanford, 1996).

10. Innocent's admiration for the Cistercian order is reflected in canon 12 of the Fourth Lateran Council. See *Decrees of the Ecumenical Councils,* ed. Norman P. Tanner, 2 vols. (Washington, DC, 1990), 1:241; and chap. 3, n. 47, below.

by Joseph Greven and Herbert Grundmann.[11] Writing in 1912 and 1935, respectively, both historians posited that after 1228, when the Cistercian General Chapter passed a statute decreeing that "no more nunneries would be constructed or associated with the order," the Cistercians had effectively closed their doors to women.[12] As a consequence both men argued that religious women turned elsewhere for spiritual care, typically to Franciscan and Dominican friars, under whose auspices they formed new female communities, which would eventually become new orders, while other women remained quasi- or semi-religious women living as beguines or *pinzochere*, that is, living independently—often in small urban houses—as penitent and pious women.

Despite a growing body of scholarship devoted to Cistercian nuns, this narrative has dominated modern historiography.[13] In part this is because it makes a good story, foregrounding the emergence of new religious orders and progressing in an appealing narrative arc: the first decades of the thirteenth century saw the founding of the friars, so it should be that the spiritual care of religious women would pass from the Cistercians to the friars as the century progressed. More important, however, this thesis also formed part of Grundmann's monumental book-length synthesis of the religious movements animating Christendom at the turn of the thirteenth century. His argument centered on the dichotomy whereby "all religious movements of the Middle Ages achieved realization either in religious orders or in

---

11. See Joseph Greven, *Die Anfänge der Beginen* (Münster, 1912); idem, "Der Ursprung des Beginenwesens," *Historisches Jahrbuch* 35 (1914): 26–58; and Herbert Grundmann, *Religious Movements in the Middle Ages: The Historical Links between Heresy, the Mendicant Orders, and the Women's Religious Movement in the Twelfth and Thirteenth Century with the Historical Foundations of German Mysticism*, trans. Steven Rowan (Notre Dame, IN, 1995). See also the remarks in John B. Freed, "Urban Development and the 'Cura Monialium' in Thirteenth-Century Germany," *Viator* 3 (1972): 311–27.

12. This narrative is also clearly articulated in Richard W. Southern, *Western Society and the Church in the Middle Ages* (New York, 1970), 312–19. Remarkably this discussion appears in the chapter titled "Fringe Orders and Anti-Orders."

13. Even recent synthetic studies of the development and reform of the women's religious movement adhere in their outlines to this general presentation. See, for example, Kaspar Elm, "Die Stellung der Frau in Ordenswesen, Semireligiosentum und Häresie zur Zeit der heiligen Elisabeth," in *Sankt Elisabeth: Fürstin Dienerin Heilige* (Sigmaringen, 1981), 7–28; Brigitte Degler-Spengler, "'Zahlreich wie die Sterne des Himmels': Zisterzienser, Dominikaner und Franziskaner vor dem Problem der Inkorporation von Frauenklöstern," *Rottenburger Jahrbuch für Kirchengeschichte* 4 (1985): 37–50; Gert Melville, "'Diversa sunt monasteria et diversas habent institutiones.' Aspetti delle molteplici forme organizzative dei religiosi nel Medioevo," in *Chiesa e società in Sicilia. I secoli XII–XVI*, ed. G. Zito (Turin, 1995), 323–45; and Martina Wehrli-Johns, "Voraussetzungen und Perspektiven mittelalterlicher Laienfrömmigkeit seit Innozenz III. Eine Auseinandersetzung mit Herbert Grundmanns 'Religiösen Bewegungen,'" *Mitteilungen des Instituts für Österreichische Geschichtsforschung* 104 (1996): 286–309.

heretical sects."[14] It was Pope Innocent III, he remarked, who first understood the need to "bridge the gap" between the evangelical life, voluntary poverty, and apostolic preaching and the realities of the hierarchical church. In turn, according to Grundmann, Innocent's policies offered a choice between the church and heresy.[15] This led to the "formation of a series of associations, congregations, and orders in which the movement for religious poverty found orthodox forms, recognized by the Church.... [Thus] the formless fermentation of the religious movement would bring forth great new orders and rules."[16] Grundmann's book, *Religious Movements in the Middle Ages,* first published in 1935 and again in a revised edition in 1961, largely set the research agenda for more than two generations of scholars, who either delved into the subversively compelling world of heretical sects or followed the careful creation of new orders built upon the charisma of their founders and the juridical acumen of university men who legislated their permanence in the religious landscape.[17]

What Grundmann did not address was how religious movements were *re-formed* along existing institutional lines—for example, how and why the women's religious movement was incorporated into *existing* religious orders. The why was relatively simple: after canon 13 of the Fourth Lateran Council forbade the creation of new religious orders, women were left to find institutional definition within those orders already approved by the church.[18] How this occurred was more complex. Indeed, Grundmann devotes only one and a half pages to the Cistercian order, though his notes betray what he does not take on: the fact that "the relationship of the Cistercian order to women's houses [has] never been fully clarified" and that "women's houses joined [the Cistercian order] as a result of the conditions of the time, not in response to legislation."[19] Yet despite these asides buried in his notes, Grundmann took the Cistercian legislation of 1228 as a defining pronouncement and concluded that "the opportunity of reaching the goals of reform and regulation

---

14. Grundmann, *Religious Movements,* 1.
15. Ibid., 5, 31–32.
16. Ibid., 32.
17. See John Van Engen, "The Christian Middle Ages as an Historiographical Problem," *American Historical Review* 91 (1986): 519–52. A call to bridge the gap between the two and consider the complexities of religious life is addressed in idem, "The Future of Medieval Church History," *Church History* 71 (2002): 492–522. On Grundmann's influence and the impact of his conclusions, see Anneke B. Mulder-Bakker, "General Introduction," in *Mary of Oignies: Mother of Salvation,* ed. Anneke B. Mulder-Bakker (Turnhout, 2006), 18–24.
18. Grundmann, *Religious Movements,* 90, makes clear why this occurred.
19. Ibid., 78, 91–92, 309nn5–6.

presented itself [most effectively] at this very moment through the aid of the orders of Dominic and Francis."[20]

In crafting this synthesis, Grundmann and many others who have followed him articulated a compelling historical progression that charted the spiritual care of religious women as their oversight passed successively from the Premonstratensian canons to the Cistercians to the friars. Thus following Grundmann most scholarship concerning religious women by 1250 has focused on the integration of women into the "new orders" as Poor Clares, Dominican penitents, or beguines and tertiary lay sisters.[21] When scholars characterize Cistercian female convents in the thirteenth century, they typically construe the communities as examples of decadence, which highlight the ways in which "realities," like the profit economy, proximity to urban centers, poverty, and taxation, degraded the ideals of the once great male monastic order.[22]

This narrative is very much at odds with the archival evidence. Life in its living is never so simple. While the order itself, as many scholars have described, displayed in its legislation an ambivalent attitude toward religious women, the role of bishops and of the women themselves in this process of institutionalization and incorporation has largely been overlooked. Indeed, many of the convents connected to the order during the 1230s were reformed communities of penitential women, who privileged an ideal of poverty and mobility, so the possibility presents itself that these women did not want to live as strict Cistercian nuns but rather preferred to "emulate" the customs of the order, guided in religious matters by a local priest or chaplain and content with more flexible interactions with the order's monks, *conversi,* grange managers, and porters. To be sure, such a religious life was not in accordance with the ideals of the hierarchical church, but it may offer another explanation for the contentious and conflicted relationship between the Cistercians and religious women. It also shows that there were many more similarities among the women of northern France and the early

---

20. Ibid., 92.
21. In the past decade there has been a remarkable amount of scholarship dedicated to thirteenth-century religious women, but most of it pertains to women in the "new" orders. See, for example, Walter Simons, *Cities of Ladies: Beguine Communities in the Medieval Low Countries, 1200–1565* (Philadelphia, 2001); Mulder-Bakker, *Mary of Oignies: Mother of Salvation;* Sean Field, *Isabelle of France: Capetian Sanctity and Franciscan Identity in the Thirteenth Century* (Notre Dame, IN, 2006); Lezlie Knox, *Creating Clare of Assisi: Female Franciscan Identities in Later Medieval Italy* (Leiden, 2008); and Maiju Lehmijoki-Gardner, *Worldly Saints: Social Interaction of Dominican Penitent Women in Italy, 1200–1500* (Helsinki, 1999).
22. The classic example of this characterization is Louis Lekai, *The Cistercians: Ideals and Reality* (Kent, OH, 1977).

Clarissan (that is, female Franciscan) and Dominican female communities of northern Italy than often noted.

Documents from Champagne suggest a new narrative. In this context, the Cistercian order continued to play a role in the reform of the women's religious movement, even alongside the activities of the friars. Thus, it is more productive to think of the institutionalization of the broader women's religious movement as part of a series of regionally distinct micro-reforms carried out during the first half of the thirteenth century.[23] In Italy, as a result of the proximity of the papacy, the friars, and the tireless energies of Cardinal Hugolino of Ostia (future Pope Gregory IX), many informal penitential communities of women became Poor Clares, cloistered under a set of regulations written for Francis's friend and companion Clare of Assisi and her community at San Damiano and inflected by the ideals of the papacy.[24] In cities like Orvieto, Siena, Venice, and towns of southern Germany, by contrast, Dominican friars oversaw female penitential communities, whose regulations, as Maiju Lehmijoki-Gardner has shown, evolved over the course of the thirteenth, fourteenth, and fifteenth centuries.[25] In like manner, the micro-reform of the women's religious movement in the region of Champagne was tied to the Cistercian order. Here the context was different from that in Italy and Germany: the proximity of the first Cistercian monasteries of Cîteaux and Clairvaux; the reforming impulses of northern French bishops, many of whom were educated in Paris and in a milieu that esteemed Cistercian organization; and the appeal of Cistercian spirituality, which emphasized manual labor and practical charity, all contributed to the adoption of the Cistercian order as the model of reform.

Plan of the Book

The book opens in the 1230s with the religious women themselves. It traces the origins of the Cistercian nunneries to groups of semi-religious women,

---

23. Here I borrow from Peter Brown's notion of "micro-Christendoms" that emerged in the West during the seventh century. See Peter Brown, *The Rise of Western Christendom: Triumph and Diversity, 200–1000* (Oxford, 1996), 218.

24. See Maria Pia Alberzoni, *Clare of Assisi and the Poor Sisters in the Thirteenth Century* (Saint Bonaventure, NY, 2004), esp. 15–16; Clara Gennaro, "Clare, Agnes, and Their Earliest Followers: From the Poor Ladies of San Damiano to the Poor Clares," in *Women and Religion in Medieval and Renaissance Italy*, ed. Daniel Bornstein and Roberto Rusconi, trans. Margaret J. Schneider (Chicago, 1996), 39–55; and Anna Benvenuti Papi, "Mendicant Friars and Female Pinzochere in Tuscany: From Social Marginality to Models of Sanctity," in Bornstein and Rusconi, *Women and Religion*, 84–103.

25. See Freed, "Urban Development and the 'Cura Monialium'"; and Maiju Lehmijoki-Gardner, "Writing Religious Rules as an Interactive Process: Dominican Penitent Women and the Making of Their *Regula*," *Speculum* 79 (2004): 660–87.

some called *Filles-Dieu* and others who had gathered in small hospitals and hospices to care for lepers and the sick, and situates these women within the broader currents of spirituality and reform animating the thirteenth century. The second chapter analyzes the social world from which the new female communities grew and gained support. The Champagne fair towns of Troyes, Provins, Bar-sur-Aube, and Lagny, which lay at the heart of the county, provided a continuous annual market and drew merchants, travelers, credit, and profits to the heart of northern France. The first supporters of the religious women came largely from the urban bourgeoisie but also included local secular canons and women, many of whom were widowed or acting of their own accord. Chapter 3 addresses how these communities were reformed as Cistercian convents and sets this process within the broader context of the formation of new monastic orders founded during the thirteenth century. For Popes Innocent III and Gregory IX, the Cistercian order was a model of administration that offered a compelling framework for regulation, possessing as it did a uniform customary that was already widely circulated and adopted throughout its many houses. A flurry of legislation generated within the order between 1200 and 1228 articulated what affiliation entailed for women and how Cistercian nuns were defined. Yet in many cases communities of Cistercian nuns continued to practice a life in accordance with the *vita apostolica,* living in small convents and committed to poverty and charity to an extent that was often at odds with the administrative rigors of the order. Chapters 4 and 5 set the reform of Cistercian convents in the wider context of thirteenth-century spirituality. Examining how and why Cistercian nuns continued to care for the poor, sick, and leprous even after they joined the order, chapter 4 argues that women who cared for such "miserable persons" took on a specific type of penitential piety and suffering that brought them closer to the model of the suffering Christ, which in turn made them exemplars of pious behavior that resonated with their patrons, local preachers, and Cistercian monks. Chapter 5 analyzes the social and religious connections fostered between Cistercian nunneries and crusader families dependant in part on a shared understanding of the *imitatio Christi* as a lived devotional ideal. Finally, chapter 6 addresses the administration of the Cistercian convents, particularly their role in the financial and social networks of the later thirteenth century. By the end of the thirteenth century Cistercian convents were buying and selling small plots of suburban land outside the fair towns and in effect creating, with their patrons, spaces of charity where the nuns administered their holdings, including hospitals and leper houses, in the pursuit of penitential ends. The book closes with an epilogue evoking the effects of fiscal crisis, famine, and the Hundred Years' War, compounded exigencies that precipitated the collapse of many of the Cistercian convents in Champagne. Beginning in 1399 the Cistercian order formally legislated the suppression of the smaller convents, which were transformed and subsumed—along with their archives—into male priories of the order. The study of the Cistercian convents of Champagne demonstrates the importance of women in the broader context of religious reform and the role of the Cistercian order in this process. It is my hope that this book gives life to the written fragments it draws upon and evokes the living parts of this process.

 CHAPTER 1

Concerning Certain Women
The Women's Religious Movement in Champagne

On a spring day in 1230, a group of religious women gathered to sing the psalms. Their voices resonated across the parish of St.-André, which lay just beyond the town walls of Troyes in a suburb known as Chichéry. The singing carried over the patchwork of farm plots and back gardens and was audible to the nearby monks of Montier-la-Celle. We know almost nothing about these women: nothing of who they were, when they first gathered outside of Troyes, or under whose impetus or direction they took up praying the Psalter together. By 1230 it is clear that this group of "certain women" (*quedam mulieres*), as they were called, formed a religious community in a farmhouse in Chichéry that belonged to Stephen of Champguyon, a prominent citizen of Troyes, and their evident patron (see fig. 3). They used one of the farm buildings as a chapel, where they sang and prayed together and where they celebrated the divine office under the guidance of a local priest. Though not formally professed as nuns or incorporated into a monastic order, the women at Chichéry wore white habits and endeavored to live according to their own religious ideals as upright converted women. Their white garments symbolized their commitment to a life of penance and studied piety. In their comportment and demeanor and their disinterest in an organized religious affiliation, they were part of a movement of religious renewal taking hold in Champagne and throughout Europe that saw similar groups of women adopt a life of penance and religious conversion.

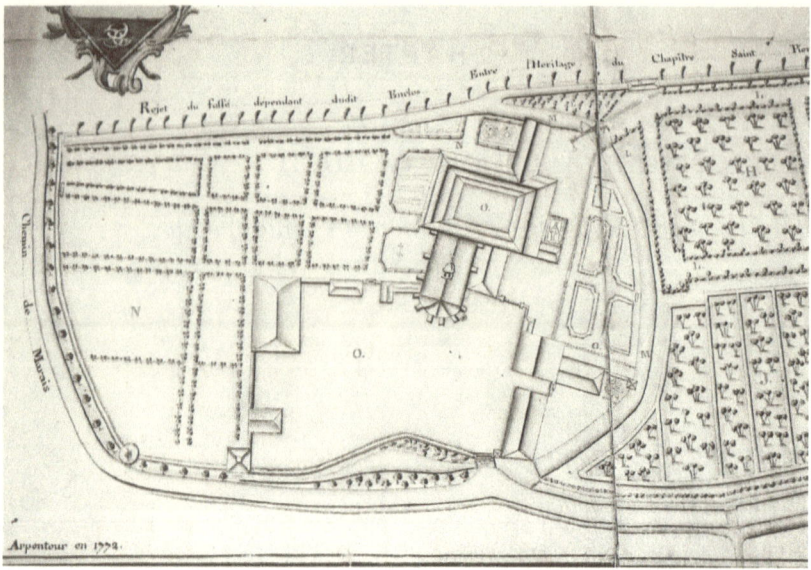

FIGURE 3. Detail, plan of Notre-Dame-des-Prés, Troyes. 1772. Drawn and measured by Marrey at the request of Abbess Marie Arnoul de Rouchegude. AD Aube, 23 H 353. Photo by the author.

The women at Chichéry never described their religious commitments or behavior in their own words. Rather they first appear in the historical record in a *libellus,* a formal legal complaint, which the monks of neighboring Montier-la-Celle submitted to Pope Gregory IX in the same year.[1] The *libellus* brought a suit against Stephen of Champguyon for disregarding the monks' parochial claims. Here the monks first described the grange-chapel of Chichéry and bemoaned the presence of "certain women" living there. Over the course of the next five years, this relatively minor dispute with a townsman over parish rights expanded into a full papal investigation. In 1231, responding to the monks' initial *libellus,* Gregory IX asked the abbot of St.-Jacques in Provins and the prior of Chalautre-la-Petite in the diocese of Sens to investigate Stephen and the women living on the outskirts of Troyes. Little progress was made on the case, and by 1234 the matter was passed on to Cardinal Sinibaldo Fieschi, titular priest of San Lorenzo in Lucina and the pope's judge-delegate on the matter.[2] By this time the women had acquired

---

1. Lucien Auvray, *Les registres de Grégoire IX: Recueil des bulles de ce pape publiées ou analysées d'après les manuscrits originaux du Vatican,* 3 vols. (Paris, 1896–1910), 1:1281–83, nos. 2479–80. The *libellus* was copied into the pope's initial response to the monks dated 3 July 1230, Auvray, no. 2479.

2. The case was referred to Cardinal Sinibaldo Fieschi, the future Pope Innocent IV (1243–54), sometime before 16 March 1234. Ibid., 1:1281, no. 2478.

formal legal representation from one Jacob, a priest of Colaverdey, just south of Troyes.[3]

As the monks' complaint passed through the papal bureaucracy, a dossier of texts accrued detailing the activities and perceptions of the women at Chichéry.[4] In reply to the monks' initial letter, Pope Gregory IX explained that the women were commonly called *Filles-Dieu* (daughters of God).[5] The papacy was consistent on this point, and throughout the correspondence the women were referred to as *mulieres, quedam mulieres,* and *quibusdam religiosis mulieribus,* that is, certain women or certain religious women.[6] By the time Cardinal Sinibaldo became involved, in 1234, the monks had sharpened their tone and expanded their initial accusations: they denounced the women with force, stating that they had taken up monastic habits and had installed themselves in the grange by their own authority (*auctoritate propria*). Moreover, although they professed to be part of the Cistercian order, they did not observe the customs of Cîteaux. And, the monks noted, neither had they been incorporated into the order nor did they keep to the confines of a cloister. Indeed, the women were known to wander about (*per diversa loca vagentur*), which the men observed could only bring grave scandal and ill repute to the monks themselves, who lived so nearby.[7] In the monks' rhetoric, they remained certain, suspect, women, not nuns. Only with Cardinal Sinibaldo's final decision, which granted to the women sanctioned status in the parish, were they called nuns (*moniales*).[8]

The monks' *libellus* is a carefully crafted text, designed to present the women at Chichéry in a negative light. As such, it tells us a great deal about

---

3. There may be a connection between this priest of Colaverdey and Isabelle of Colaverdey, the first abbess of the Cistercian nunnery of La Piété near Ramerupt. See Alphonse Roserot, *Dictionnaire historique de la Champagne méridonale (Aube) des origines à 1790,* 3 vols. (Langres, 1942–48; reprinted, Marseilles, 1983), 1:340–43.

4. See Auvray, *Les registres de Grégoire IX,* 1:1038–39, no. 1900, and 1:1280–84, nos. 2477–80. See also *GC* 12:289–91, instr. 60.

5. "qua quedam mulieres, que Filie Dei vulgariter appellantur"; Auvray, *Les registres de Grégoire IX,* 1:1282, no. 2479.

6. On this terminology, see Elizabeth Makowski, *"A Pernicious Sort of Woman," Quasi-Religious Women and Canon Lawyers in the Later Middle Ages* (Washington, DC, 2005), 3–22; and idem, "*Mulieres Religiosae,* Strictly Speaking: Some Fourteenth-Century Canonical Opinions," *Catholic Historical Review* 85 (1999): 1–14.

7. "quod quedam mulieres, in monachali habitu auctoritate propria intruse ibidem...mulieres sint posite antedicte, que verbo Cisterciensem ordinem profitentur, sed facto non observant eundem, cum nec incorporate sint ei, nec in claustro continuam residentiam faciant, qui[n] potius frequenter per diversa loca vagentur, per quarum vicinitatem eorum monasterium, quod fuit hactenus magne fame, plurimum diffamatur, et timendum est ne, occasione vicinitatis hujusmodi, que presumptionem malam inducit, penitus destruatur." Auvray, *Les registres de Grégoire IX,* 1:1038, no. 1900.

8. Ibid., 1:1280, no. 2477.

the fears monks harbored concerning communities of religious women unencumbered and undefined by a formal religious rule or strict enclosure. Yet, for all its vitriol, the *libellus* presents a picture of the women's religious movement in Champagne as it came into its own. In their communal association, suburban setting, penitential dress, and absence of formal regulation, the women at Chichéry shared much in common with other iterations of the women's religious movement animating Europe during the decades on either side of 1200. Like similar texts in Cistercian convent archives that give shape to women's lives before their incorporation into the order, the *libellus* described a group of religious women who had adopted a life of piety and devotion independent of the church hierarchy and of their own initiative. They found support from a well-connected and wealthy citizen of Troyes, a burgher, who offered them the use of his suburban farm building, which was large enough to accommodate twenty women and a space for prayer.[9] The *libellus* describes religious women already engaged in a specific devotional life, integrated into a network of patronage and in association with a priest who supported their endeavors years before they found institutional affiliation with the Cistercian order. The fact that the monks of La Celle noted an association with the Cistercian order may indicate that the women had connections to Cistercian monks serving as priests or preachers in Troyes, or that they had developed a spiritual friendship with a priest who favored the Cistercian way of life.

The women at Chichéry were not unusual. Independent groups of women practicing a religious life lay behind the vast majority of Cistercian convents founded and reformed in thirteenth-century Champagne. Yet most religious women appear only fleetingly in the documents of practice, mainly in charters and disputes that predate official incorporation into the order. Existing records often resist the endeavor of resuscitating such women for they generally document the process of institutionalization: the creation of convents from groups of women who were already there as part of the religious landscape at the center of their own lives and offering inspiration to others. The challenges of identifying these earlier noninstitutionalized female communities are particularly acute, for "this is a history we are all trained not to write," as Jo Ann McNamara observed, "a history in confrontation with our sources rather than in conformity with them."[10] When confronted, the

---

9. On Stephen of Champguyon, see chap. 2, 57–61.

10. Jo Ann McNamara, "*De Quibusdam Mulieribus:* Reading Women's History from Hostile Sources," in *Medieval Women and the Sources of Medieval History,* ed. Joel T. Rosenthal (Athens, GA, 1990), 237–58, at 239.

libellus and many of the earliest documents from the Cistercian convents of Champagne reveal the ambitions and ideals of the women who were responsible for the staggering proliferation of nunneries that marked the thirteenth century as unique in the history of religious revival and reform.

With rare exception, nearly all of the Cistercian convents founded in the county of Champagne between 1226 and 1239 trace their beginnings to earlier communities of unaffiliated religious women. Throughout northern France significant numbers of women left the comforts of families, the sociability of kin, households, towns, and rural estates to live in granges, small chapels, hospices, hospitals, and leper communities on the margins of urban centers or alongside the major trade routes that connected the Seine and Marne valleys. Many of these women were penitents, known by the familiar names: *mulieres religiosae, quedem mulieres,* or *Filles-Dieu*. It would be precocious to think of them as beguines, for in Champagne they did not take that title and would not do so until the classifications of canon law demanded it in the fourteenth century. Other women, also with a penitential mindset, cared for the sick and poor, laboring within or near small *domus-Dei,* hospices, and leprosaria, where they put into practice the ideals of poverty and charity that animated the *vita apostolica,* the life in imitation of the Apostles.[11]

The number of new women's houses created from such humble origins speaks to the power and appeal of this movement (see map). By 1240, in Champagne nearly all of these communities had been incorporated into the Cistercian order as new Cistercian convents. One could not have traveled the county without encountering the new nunneries. To move northwest along the river Aube from Bar-sur-Aube to Troyes and on to Paris would have entailed passing the small chapel and cluster of buildings just outside of Bar-sur-Aube that housed the Cistercian nuns of Val-des-Vignes, and then the grange once known as Chichéry that in 1235 took the name Notre-Dame-des-Prés near Troyes. Heading north, it was no more than twenty kilometers to Ramerupt and the nuns of La Piété. Between that stronghold of the counts of Brienne and the walls of Paris one would find the convents of Jardin-lès-Pleurs, La Grâce, and Belleau, each housing at least twenty women, as well as servants, lay sisters, and any number of indigent and needy sick and poor.

---

11. See the appendix. Also see Constance Berman, "Fashions in Monastic Patronage: The Popularity of Supporting Cistercian Abbeys for Women in Thirteenth-Century Northern France," *Proceedings of the Annual Meeting of the Western Society for French History* 17 (1990): 36–45, at 40–41; and Anne Bondeelle-Souchier, "Les moniales cisterciennes et leurs livres manuscrits dans la France d'ancien régime," *Cîteaux* 45 (1994): 193–337.

MAP 1. Sites in Champagne and the neighboring provinces, ca. 1250, which are discussed in this volume. The map includes thirty-one Cistercian convents. Prepared by Caroline Goodson.

These were, for the most part, small and humble communities strikingly different from the royal foundations of Maubuisson or Le Lys closer to Paris. If one traveled from the north, encounters with religious women would be similar. Descending from Reims to Troyes, along the familiar route connecting the county of Flanders to that of Champagne, a merchant or papal legate would have passed the women of Ormont installed in the hospital of Courlandon and the community of Clairmarais outside of Reims. From there, traveling south, it was not far to L'Amour-Dieu, where nuns lived in the small *domus-Dei* of Troissy. To the west lay Pont-aux-Dames, founded by the counts of Châtillon in an abandoned hospice, and to the east one could see on the hilltop Countess Blanche of Navarre's (d. 1229) foundation of Argensolles, the only lavishly endowed Cistercian nunnery founded in Champagne. Argensolles was exceptional, though it would eventually find its match in Count Thibaut IV's (d. 1253) Franciscan convent, known as St. Catherine's, built in 1248 on a hillside over-looking Provins. Finally, to journey north from Sens to Paris—perhaps the most well traveled of all the routes in the county—one would pass the convents of La Joie-lès-Nemours and La Cour Notre-Dame-de-Michery. Farther north sat Mont-Notre-Dame, outside of Provins, and finally St.-Antoine-des-Champs at the southeastern gate of Paris. In 1244 near the same route, Queen Blanche of Castile (d. 1252) broke ground for her new convent, Le Lys, which still towers in its gothic splendor as a powerful witness to the integration of the women's religious movement into the Cistercian order and into the prodigious network of royal support.[12]

By the mid-thirteenth century, communities of Cistercian nuns could be found outside of all the major urban centers of the county and along its trade routes. The convents were built upon the humble foundation of unaffiliated women that formed the core of the women's religious movement and whose distribution throughout the county defined the movement's spread. Although not all religious women in Champagne adopted the customs of Cîteaux—some became canonesses or hospital sisters under the *Rule of Augustine* and a rare few remained in the world as holy women, some of whom on notable occasions were persecuted as heretics for this choice—the vast majority became Cistercian nuns. In doing so, however, they held onto many of their original ideals and commitments to penance and charity that defined their participation in the women's religious movement more broadly.

The Women's Religious Movement in the Thirteenth Century

As many scholars have recognized, the women's religious movement grew out of currents of religious change that had roots in the Gregorian Reform of the late eleventh century and the monastic reforms of the twelfth. By 1200 the pious pursuits of laywomen were one manifestation of a more complex interlocking dynamic of religious enthusiasms reflected in a new embrace of the ideals of the *vita apostolica,* the crusade movement, and a growing trend

---

12. Anselme Dimier, *Saint Louis et Cîteaux* (Paris, 1954).

within the institutional church to discern the truly religious from the malignantly heretical.[13] A disavowal of worldly ambitions in favor of the communal pursuit of the religious life, that is, a life of conversion directed at spiritual goals, came to characterize the women's religious movement. At times this would result in formal profession in a monastic house, but more often during much of the early thirteenth century the movement engaged laywomen who remained in the world as part of their initial conversion. This was of course not conversion to another faith but, as medieval people more commonly understood the term, a conversion that entailed setting aside family and friends, letting go of their sense for "social striving" and worldly ambition to adopt a more dedicated spiritual life generally manifest in a deep and daily commitment to prayer, chastity, poverty, and public charity.[14] As John Van Engen stated, "converts sought to realize a 'perfect' life, implicitly calling into question the adequacy of ordinary religious practice."[15] They became extraordinary in their devotion, dedication, and capacity to transform religious ideals and institutions. The proficient converts were those women who had "forgotten" their bonds to "their community and kin—their people—and the home of their father, preferring," as Jacques de Vitry remarked of the holy women of Liège, "to endure distress and poverty than to abound in riches."[16] To take part in such a religious life was to pursue a radical reorientation of the self and one's place in the world. It was to imagine a broader Christian community that did not distinguish among family, kin, or class but sought to create a new kind of social body. This reorientation took hold of several thousand women in Flanders, the southern Low Countries, northern France, Germany, Italy, and in other parts of Europe to varying degrees. Their turn toward religion provoked the admiration and anxiety of abbots, chroniclers, bishops, and popes.[17] Their conversions were individual, but the collective expression of such personal transformations created the women's religious movement.

---

13. On Herbert Grundmann and the term "women's religious movement," see the introduction, 7–12.

14. Herbert Grundmann, *Religious Movements in the Middle Ages: The Historical Links between Heresy, the Mendicant Orders, and the Women's Religious Movement in the Twelfth and Thirteenth Century with the Historical Foundations of German Mysticism*, trans. Steven Rowan (Notre Dame, IN, 1995), 137.

15. John Van Engen, *Sisters and Brothers of the Common Life: The Devotio Moderna and the World of the Later Middle Ages* (Philadelphia, 2008), 14.

16. "Ipsae tamen obliviscentes populum suum et domum patris sui, malebant angustias et paupertatem sustinere, quam male acquisitis divitiis abundare, vel inter pomposos seculares cum periculo remanere." *VMO*, prologue, para. 3.

17. For such numbers, see Margot King, "The Desert Mothers Revisited: The Mothers of the Diocese of Liège," *Vox Benedictina* 5, no. 4 (1988): 325–54, at n. 7.

Their pious actions coupled with a deeper spiritual striving often focused on a mystical unity with Christ distinguished women in the movement from their cloistered sisters in Augustinian and Benedictine convents. Their focus on the meaning of the apostolic life, a commitment to poverty and spiritual work, and the relationship between the active imitation of Christ and the search for deeper understanding and unity with the divine, often paralleled that of the male mendicant orders.[18] Some of the earliest examples of these female converts were from the Low Countries, most prominently from the diocese of Liège, where they would later be called beguines.[19] From the 1180s, if not earlier, chroniclers, abbots, and priests noted small groups of pious laywomen who convened in houses at the margins of their towns to care for lepers and the sick, incorporating manual labor into an understanding of the studied imitation of Christ.[20] Mary of Oignies began her religious life laboring among the lepers of Willambroux near Nivelles.[21] Her reputation for sanctity brought other like-minded women to the informal community she founded to follow her example. In 1207 Mary moved to Oignies to live as a recluse among a group of religious women already in residence near the local priory church.[22] Jacques de Vitry, who cultivated a special friendship with Mary and who eventually wrote her first *vita,* described this community, which came to be known as the first example of the beguine way of life. Mary was not unique. A decade before she underwent her conversion, Yvette of Huy, a widowed mother of three, against the will of her friends and father, renounced everything she had—her house, her inheritance, and her children—and moved outside the walls of Huy to live among lepers in a dilapidated leprosarium with one old chapel and deteriorating buildings.[23]

---

18. See Caroline Walker Bynum, "Women Mystics in the Thirteenth Century: The Case of the Nuns of Helfta," in her *Jesus as Mother: Studies in the Spirituality of the High Middle Ages* (Berkeley, 1982), 170–262.

19. See Walter Simons, *Cities of Ladies: Beguine Communities in the Medieval Low Countries, 1200–1500* (Philadelphia, 2001).

20. On the astounding hagiographical outpouring associated with the diocese of Liège, see Simone Roisin, *L'hagiographie cistercienne dans le diocèse de Liège au XIIIe siècle* (Louvain, 1947); and idem, "L'efflorescence cistercienne et le courant feminine de piété au XIIIe siècle," *Revue d'histoire écclésiastique* 39 (1943): 342–78.

21. *VMO,* 1, 14. See Anneke B. Mulder-Bakker, ed., *Mary of Oignies: Mother of Salvation,* trans. Margot King and Hugh Feiss (Turnhout, 2006), for a bibliography on Mary of Oignies.

22. This group of women appears to have already been in place before Mary joined them. See *VMO,* 2, 54; *VMO-S,* 10. Edouard Poncelet, "Chartes du Prieuré d'Oignies de l'ordre de Saint Augustin," *Annales de la Société Archéologique de Namur* 31 (1913): 1–104, at nos. lx–lxi. See also Brenda Bolton, "Mary of Oignies: A Friend to the Saints," in Mulder-Bakker, *Mary of Oignies,* 199–220, at 200–201.

23. "Fuit in eo loco ecclesiola quaedam vetus, et prae nimia vetustate sui pene casum minitans, in qua interdum Missarum agebantur sacramenta infirmis, licet raro. Nam quia pauper erat locus,

There on the margins Yvette embraced a new life of humility and active service among the sick and miserable, which according to her hagiographer led her into deeper contemplation and fulfillment in her knowledge of God. Here too Yvette gained a holy reputation and attracted other women to her community who wished to follow her example.

Many women in the German Empire likewise took part in this movement, and communities of penitent women and recluses emerged in Strasbourg, Cologne, and throughout the towns of the Rhine valley, which later became institutionalized as Cistercian nunneries or Dominican tertiary houses and béguinages.[24] The German lands had their own female saints as well who conformed to the general pattern articulated in Mary of Oignies's *vita*. Elizabeth of Thuringia or Hungary (d. 1231), as she was also known, became a scion of female sanctity.[25] After the death of her husband, the marquis of Thuringia, she began a regime of punishing asceticism and self-mortification under the direction of her confessor, Conrad of Marburg, in order to transform herself from a royal widow into a handmaid of Christ and a living example of the ideals of the *vita apostolica*. Elizabeth severed her connections to the world and used her inheritance to found a hospice for lepers in Marburg, where she spent the final four years of her life caring for the sick.[26] As a laywoman who had been married and lived in the world but adopted a religious life after marriage and motherhood, Elizabeth inspired many emulators and supporters not only among the German nobility, but also at the French royal court and within the central European dynasties.[27]

---

et nulli Ecclesiae redditus, vix inveniebatur qui Missam in loco celebrare vellet, aut bis in hebdomada, nisi religiosi quique Sacerdotes, quos interdum devotio eo trahebat, aut caritas invitabat." *VBJ*, chap. 10, para. 33.

24. John B. Freed, "Urban Development and the *Cura Monialium* in Thirteenth-Century Germany," *Viator* 3 (1972): 311–27; Jean-Claude Schmitt, *Mort d'une hérésie: L'Église et les clercs face aux béguines et aux béghards du Rhin supérieurs du XIVe au XVe siècle* (Paris, 1978); and Makowski, "*Pernicious Sort of Woman*," 3–67.

25. On the sources for Elizabeth's life, see Albert Huyskens, ed., *Quellenstudien zur Geschichte de hl. Elisabeth, Landgräfin von Thüringen* (Marburg, 1908). The most recent edition of Caesarius of Heisterbach's *Vita Sancte Elyzabeth* is in *Das Leben der heiligen Elisabeth und andere Zeugnisse*, ed. Ewald Könsgen (Marburg, 2007). See also Dietrich von Apolda, *Vita S. Elysabeth*, in *Das Leben der heiligen Elisabeth*, ed. Monika Rener (Marburg, 2007); and Dyan Elliott, *Proving Woman: Female Spirituality and Inquisitional Culture in the Later Middle Ages* (Princeton, 2004), 85–116.

26. "parentibus et pueris et proprie voluntati et omnibus pompis mundi et hiis que salvator mundi in e[v]angelio consulit relinquenda renuntiavit." Huyskens, *Quellenstudien zur Geschichte*, 157.

27. See Anna Petrakopoulos, "Sanctity and Motherhood: Elizabeth of Thuringia," in *Sanctity and Motherhood: Holy Mothers in the Middle Ages*, ed. Anneke B. Mulder-Bakker (New York, 1995), 259–96; and Gábor Klaniczay, *Holy Rulers and Blessed Princesses: Dynastic Cults in Medieval Central Europe*, trans. Éva Pálmai (Cambridge, 2000), 195–294.

A similar ambition to live out a holy life animated groups of women in other parts of Europe. When we put aside the heretical imaginings of Cistercian monks and Dominican friars, the actions, clothes, diet, and religious bearing of the "good women" who lived between the Rhône and Garonne, known to their inquisitors as "the heretics," resonated with their female counterparts to the north and south. Many of the attributes that provoked suspicions of heresy in such good women (and men) found parallels among the women of Liège, Assisi, and even Champagne: "a noble wearing undyed cloth, a young girl in a loose shirt tied with a leather cord, an old matron in coarse woolen hose, were all modest variations on mundane attire that, by disguising the human, enriched the sacred."[28] All such religious men and women understood the power of this kind of renunciation and self-mastery; all were striving after a kind of religious perfection; and all donned a version of penitential dress to do so. Disciplining the flesh had been the backbone of traditional monasticism since the option of martyrdom receded from the grasp of the Christian witness. Athletic training of the mind and body—asceticism—became the new way to bear witness to the triumph of Christianity. By the thirteenth century, living like the apostles, modeling a renunciation of the self like that Christ endured, became the way of communicating intense devotion that set its practitioner apart as a *bona femna* (in Provençal), a *mulier sancta*, a *Fille-Dieu*, or *pinzochere*, that is, a certain kind of woman worthy of notice and emulation precisely because she attempted to escape the bonds of social status.

In Italy too this commitment to conversion flourished. Many women who would eventually come under the guidance of Franciscan or Dominican confessors began their commitments independently outside of formal connections to monastic houses or friars. Clare of Assisi initially lived as a penitent with a small group of women in her own domestic space, her parent's home, an arrangement that looked very much like the communities of women found in Liège or even in the mountain towns near Montauban.[29] Only later was her community transferred to the newly rebuilt church at San Damiano, reformed under papal auspices, and given a formal rule.[30] Although

---

28. Mark Gregory Pegg, *A Most Holy War: The Albigensian Crusade and the Battle for Christendom* (Oxford, 2008), 38.
29. See Jörg Feuchter, *Ketzer, Konsuln und Büßer: Die städtischen Eliten von Montauban vor dem Inquisitor Petrus Cellani (1236–1241)* (Tübingen, 2007).
30. See *Legenda sanctae Clarae*, in *AASS*, 12 August, 2:739–68. Also Ingrid Petersen, "Like a Beguine: Clare before 1212," in *Clare of Assisi: Investigations* (Saint Bonaventure, NY, 1993), 7:47–67; and Clara Gennaro, "Clare, Agnes, and Their Earliest Followers: From the Poor Ladies of San Damiano to the Poor Clares," in *Women and Religion in Medieval and Renaissance Italy*, ed. Daniel Bornstein and Roberto Rusconi, trans. Margery J. Schneider (Chicago, 1996), 39–55.

the Poor Clares were not successful in their ambition to live only according to the precepts of Saint Francis, to possess nothing, and to live the spirit of poverty, their initial impulse paralleled the founding goals of the broader women's religious movement.[31]

Indeed, similar penitential women, known in the Italian vernacular as *pinzochere* and *bizoke,* living alone and in small groups in their parents' homes or in the houses of female relatives and pious widows, transformed the spiritual geography of Milan, Florence, Padua, Cortona, and Rome, while pursuing their own interpretations of the religious life.[32] The lives of the converts (*conversi*) and penitents (*penitenti*) of the Italian communes followed a dedicated rhythm of prayers, fasts, feasts, confessions, masses, and charitable work.[33] Many impressed the clerical elite, who composed their *vitae* as examples of penitential piety in the world. Margaret of Cortona (d. 1297) became one of the more widely venerated *pinzochere* of the later thirteenth century. Margaret came from a peasant household outside of Montepulciano. At the age of fifteen she fell in love with a merchant's son whose family forbid their marriage, but they persevered and she lived for nine years as his concubine and bore him a son. When her child was still an infant, her lover was killed by robbers, his body left in a ditch. Upon finding his corpse, Margaret fled the city with her illegitimate son, was turned away by her natal family, and found shelter with holy women in Cortona. She soon converted and began to live as a penitent, eventually turning her full attention to caring for the poor and sick of Cortona, working as a midwife, and practicing harsh asceticism but remaining a laywoman.[34] For Margaret her life as a penitent redeemed her earlier sins. As proof of her resolve and devotion, while at mass one day Christ spoke to her, saying "Daughter, I will place you with the seraphim where the virgins aflame with love are found." Stunned by the revelation, she asked "how is this possible if I was so great a sinner?" He responded: "Your many punishments will purify your soul of every impurity... your contrition will restore your virginal

---

31. See Brenda M. Bolton, "Mulieres sanctae," in *Sanctity and Secularity,* 88–89; and Maria Pia Alberzoni, *Clare of Assisi and the Poor Sisters in the Thirteenth Century* (Saint Bonaventure, NY, 2004).

32. See Brenda M. Bolton, "Daughters of Rome: All One in Christ Jesus!" reprinted in idem, *Innocent III: Studies on Papal Authority and Pastoral Care* (Aldershot, 1995), 101–15; Luigi Pellegrini, "Female Religious Experience and Society in Thirteenth-Century Italy," in *Monks and Nuns, Saints and Outcasts,* ed. Sharon Farmer and Barbara H. Rosenwein (Ithaca, 2000), 97–122; and Antonia Rigon, "A Community of Female Penitents in Thirteenth-Century Padua," in Bornstein and Rusconi, *Women and Religion,* 28–38.

33. See Augustine Thompson, *Cities of God: The Religion of the Italian Communes, 1125–1325* (University Park, PA, 2005), 69–102.

34. Friar Giunta Bevegnati, Margaret's confessor, completed her *vita* in 1308. See Giunta Bevegnati, *Legenda de vita et miraculis Beatae Margaritae de Cortona,* ed. Fortunato Iozzelli (Grottaferrata, 1997), which now supersedes *AASS,* February, 3:304–462.

purity."[35] Margaret embodied the transformative power of a personal religious commitment, which could remake the self but also affect the social world in which women lived, worked, and prayed; therein lay its appeal.[36]

There was much to be said for this kind of "freelance" spirituality.[37] It was individually chosen and to a degree personally modified and thus different from joining a monastic community regulated by the regiments of daily corporate prayer and routine. Over the course of the thirteenth century, religious women who remained outside of a specific order, unencumbered by the boundaries of a cloister, acquired an accepted—albeit continually negotiated—status as beguines in the north, canonesses in Germany, and *humiliatae, conversae,* and *pinzochere* in Italy. All of these groups shared a commitment to live in a state of conversion, in imitation of the apostles, and to retain a connection to the world. These commitments and their reinterpretation outside the cloister were, in part, what defined female converts and penitents as part of a movement, a way of life that was dynamic, changing, and deliberately not fully institutionalized.

Stories of holy laywomen traveled widely throughout Europe, offering inspiration and eliciting imitators. And thirteenth-century people would have known of the holy men and women living in their midst or near towns and cities like Liège, Cologne, Cortona, and Assisi. These holy people brought renown and a spiritual caché to their hometowns. Many of the men, often local priests, canons, and later friars, who composed the *vitae* of these holy women, also preached with passion about the living saints they had known, in turn spreading the religious ideals such women practiced. Evocative vignettes from the same *vitae* often found their way into sermons and exempla collections, which compiled short edifying stories to be reused and deployed when preachers saw fit. Physical texts—bound manuscript booklets, sermon copies, and spiritual guides—traveled as well, spreading the ideas behind the women's religious movement, and the same texts could be excerpted and glossed as the situation demanded. Cistercian monks and lay brothers, papal legates and friars often carried the stories of these women with them to inspire others to holy imitation.[38] Letters too conveyed the ideals and practices of holy women.

---

35. Bevegnati, *Legenda de vita et miraculis Beatae Margharitae,* 231–32.
36. See Bernard Schlager, "Foundresses of the Franciscan Life: Umiliana Cerchi and Margaret of Cortona," *Viator* 29 (1998): 141–66; and Katherine L. Jansen, "Mary Magdalen as Model for Uncloistered Religious Women of Late Medieval Italy," in *Donne tra Medioevo ed Età Moderna in Italia. Ricerche,* ed. Giovanna Casagrande (Perugia, 2004), 103–52.
37. For the term, see Thompson, *Cities of God,* 87, passim.
38. On the dissemination and copying of the *Life of Mary of Oignies,* see Suzan Folkerts, "The Manuscript Transmission of the *Vita Mariae Oigniacensis* in the Later Middle Ages," in Mulder-Bakker, *Mary of Oignies,* 221–41.

In a letter penned in 1216, Jacques de Vitry described groups of Italian *humiliatae,* who renounced their possessions and lived from the labor of their own hands while remaining outside the confines of a monastic rule, and noted the striking parallels to the religious women he knew at home in his diocese of Liège, who did the same.[39] Their similarities in devotion and studied penitence characterized the primary features of the European-wide women's religious movement that would be reconstructed centuries later by historians.

Finally, the importance of women's networks must not be overlooked: webs of kin, spiritual friendship and guidance, and pious caregiving that found women opening their houses to other women in need, like Margaret of Cortona, all fostered the transmission of these practices and ideas. Trade routes, like those connecting Montepulciano and Cortona, or Troyes, Provins, and Paris, facilitated the transmission of stories and the movement of people, practices, and devotion. Geographically—at the heart of this holy circulation—sat the county of Champagne. Merchants, creditors, legates, pilgrims, and crusaders all crossed through the county, stayed in its taverns and inns, met in its market places, and talked about the living saints and penitents they knew or had encountered in reality or rumor. Certainly those women who took up new religious lives as converts and penitents between the Meuse and the Aube were part of this interconnected world, inspired by the examples of women in Italy, southern France, and Liège.

Spiritual Networks and the Foundation of Argensolles

In 1220 the saintly lay brother Arnulf of Villers (d. 1228) had "a wondrous vision," in which he saw "a hen, bright white and with chicks of the same color all following her as a mother who afforded them the warmth of her wings."[40] This image came in response to the request for spiritual guidance and aid solicited by Blanche of Navarre, countess of Champagne. Blanche had sent her friend Gerard, a monk of the Cistercian abbey of Larrivour not far from Troyes (see map), to Arnulf in the hopes that the holy man could help her bring peace to the county, which had been bitterly divided by civil war. Initially puzzled by the vision, Arnulf asked God to reveal its meaning. The hen and her chicks, heavenly revelation informed him, represented an

---

39. Jacques de Vitry, *Lettres de Jacques de Vitry (1160/70–1240),* ed. R. B. C. Huygens (Leiden, 1960), Letter 1, lines 49–61, pp. 72–73. He also made comparisons in his *ad status* sermons. See Carolyn Muessig, *The Faces of Women in the Sermons of Jacques de Vitry* (Toronto, 1999).

40. *VArnf,* 2, paras. 30–32. This may also be an allusion to Matthew 23:37, in which Jesus invokes the same metaphor.

abbess and her nuns. Arnulf then advised Gerard, "Return in peace, dear friend, to the lady countess who sent you; greet her in my name and explain to her that, if she would found a monastery for Cistercian nuns," from the moment she conceives of the foundation, peace will return to the county and "concord will ensue."[41]

The vision narrative, embedded in the *vita* of Arnulf of Villers, is one version of the foundation story for Argensolles, the first Cistercian nunnery founded in Champagne during the thirteenth century.[42] The anecdote was most likely honed at Argensolles, and told and retold to those within the community and among the Cistercian monks in the houses nearby who provided spiritual care and administrative services to the nuns. It also situates Countess Blanche's foundation within the broader context of Cistercian spirituality, monastic travel between Flanders and Champagne, and the circulation of ideas and people who fostered the women's religious movement. As Arnulf and Gerard make clear, Cistercian monks and lay brothers played a significant role in this transmission. Although Cistercian legislation forbid monks from having contact with women in their own cloisters, hagiographical accounts and chronicles describe the intense friendships that developed among Cistercian nuns, monks, and religious women in the decades around 1200.[43] Many monks from Clairvaux and the great male abbeys of Villers in Flanders, and Heisterbach, Eberbach, and Schönau in Germany, formed spiritual relationships with religious women, offering them advice, guidance, and prayers, and occasionally hearing confession and performing the mass. Incidental remarks in exempla collections, like those of Caesarius of Heisterbach and Thomas of Cantimpré, as well as the manuscript collections of abbeys that contain books of spiritual guidance for women, point to the pervasiveness of such contacts between religious women and monks.[44] These were connections of mutual benefit, for monks often found such women good to think and to pray with. This was heightened, as Caroline Walker Bynum has noted, by the intellectual

---

41. *VArnf,* 2, para. 31.

42. See N. Donnet, "La fondation de l'Abbaye d'Argensolles," *Cîteaux* 10 (1959): 212–18; and A. Kwanten, "L'Abbaye Notre-Dame d'Argensolles," *MSM* 84 (1969): 75–85.

43. Josephus-Mia Canivez, *Statuta Capitulorum Generalium Ordinis Cisterciensis ab anno 1116 ad annum 1786,* 8 vols. (Louvain, 1933–41), 1:(1198)4 and (1204)8; Bernard Lucet, *La codification cistercienne de 1202 et son évolution ultérieure* (Rome, 1964), Distinction [abbreviated Dist. hereafter] 10:28, 29, 30; and Dist. 14:30. See also Brian Patrick McGuire, "The Cistercians and the Transformation of Monastic Friendships," *Analecta Cisterciensia* 37 (1981): 1–63, reprinted in idem, *Friendship and Faith: Cistercian Men, Women, and Their Stories, 1100–1250* (Aldershot, 2002), at 11–12.

44. McGuire, "Cistercians and the Transformation of Monastic Friendships"; and Martha G. Newman, "Crucified by the Virtues: Monks, Lay Brothers, and Women in Thirteenth-Century Cistercian Saints' Lives," in *Gender and Difference in the Middle Ages,* ed. Sharon Farmer and Carol Braun Pasternack (Minneapolis, 2003), 182–209.

association with women and the body, and specifically with bodily asceticism. Pious women and nuns could achieve an imitation of Christ's physical suffering that was not open in the same degree to monks in positions of religious power and authority.[45] Advising women and offering them council and guidance was a way for monks to have a share in female piety. Spiritual friendships became spiritual networks through which the ideals, practices, and virtues of the women's religious movement came into Champagne.[46]

Argensolles, located several kilometers outside of Epernay in the diocese of Soissons, was the first Cistercian nunnery that had a direct connection to the new ideals of the women's religious movement that had taken shape in Flanders.[47] When Argensolles's buildings were finally completed, Blanche of Navarre turned again to the diocese of Liège and "assembled a community of virgins" from there and elsewhere, "all to be trained as regulated by the Cistercian order."[48] The nunnery was initially populated by thirty-five nuns under the leadership of the saintly abbess Ida from the nunnery of Val-Notre-Dame near Huy in the diocese of Liège.[49] As a child, Ida was given to the nunnery of St.-Leonard, where she grew up working in a hospital overseen by the abbey. Ida cared for the sick, and—according to her hagiographer—even suffered from leprosy as a child. Like other holy women of Liège, she cultivated an intimate relationship with God through her chastity and humility and was granted divine knowledge of the final damnation or salvation of those around her.[50] Ida embodied the ideals and practices of the women's religious movement as it took shape in Liège, and as abbess she imported this spirituality into the county. Val-Notre-Dame, where Ida had been prioress before coming to Argensolles, had been founded only a decade earlier by the count of Moha.[51] In 1220 Thibaut IV of Champagne confirmed

---

45. Bynum, *Jesus as Mother*, 110–69; and idem, "The Female Body and Religious Practice in the Later Middle Ages," in her *Fragmentation and Redemption: Essays on Gender and the Human Body in Medieval Religion* (New York, 1991), 181–238.

46. In addition to Gerard of Larrivour, Adam of Perseigne (d. 1221), the Cistercian abbot and crusade preacher, was a friend and correspondent of Blanche of Navarre. See John F. Benton, "The Court of Champagne as a Literary Center," *Speculum* 36 (1961): 551–91, at 582–84.

47. Argensolles lay between Vertus and Epernay along the eastern edge of the county. A seventeenth-century cartulary survives in AD Marne, series 70 H, but no buildings remain. See Theodore Evergates, *The Aristocracy in the County of Champagne, 1100–1300* (Philadelphia, 2007), 42–43.

48. *VArnf*, 2, para. 32.

49. Ida died in 1226. Thomas of Cantimpré mentions her in his *Bonum universale de apibus*, bk. 2, chaps. 46 and 72. Philip de La Charmoye composed her *vita* but the Latin text is now lost: E. Brouette, "Philip de La Charmoye," in *Dictionnaire des auteurs cisterciens* (Rochefort, 1975), 557. A French version is Epernay, BM, MS 55, edited by E. Héron de Villefosse, "Vie manuscrite de la bienheureuse Ide, première abbesse du monastère d'Argensoles (Marne)," *Revue de Champagne*, 2nd ser., 1 (1889): 481–98.

50. Villefosse, "Vie manuscrite de la bienheureuse Ide."

51. GC 3:1035–36.

Val-Notre-Dame's foundation while he performed homage to Hugh, bishop of Liège, for the county of Moha, which he acquired by marriage following the end of the civil war.[52] Thus the spiritual cross-pollination that saw nuns move from the diocese of Liège to Champagne further fortified the peace agreement that the countess had brokered. Moreover, the importation of nuns from the diocese of Liège meant that Argensolles served as a conduit for the spread of Cistercian spiritual ideals and practices from the Low Countries to northern France. In this sense, Argensolles's foundation drew from currents of female spirituality that flourished to the north and that drew inspiration from the active piety of women like Mary of Oignies and Yvette of Huy.

The earliest charters for Argensolles support the hagiographical narrative strikingly well. Beginning in 1213 Champagne was in political crisis. In that year Erard of Brienne, an ambitious baron who controlled the lordship of Ramerupt, had departed for the Holy Land to marry Philippa, the youngest daughter of Count Henry II (r. 1181–1197), Thibaut III's elder brother who had died in the East. After his marriage, Erard claimed Champagne and Brie as Philippa's inheritance and was able to enlist considerable support from a faction of barons in the northeast of the county. A succession crisis ensued. Blanche had ruled the county as a regent from the spring of 1201, when her husband, Thibaut III, died before departing on crusade, until 1222, when her son came of age. In response to the challenge to her rule, Blanche of Navarre negotiated a series of agreements with the king of France, Philip Augustus (r. 1180–1223), and Pope Innocent III (r. 1198–1216) and managed through astute politics to thwart Erard's claims.

In 1217 Erard renewed his rebellion against the countess. Open conflict was confined to the eastern borders of the county and involved only Erard's closest allies and relatives. At the close of 1218, Blanche resorted to force and, according to local chroniclers, took up arms herself at the head of an army, marched on Nancy, and burned the town. The duke of Lorraine and the rebel barons supporting Erard of Brienne surrendered in humiliation, and each made their own peace with the countess.[53] Blanche then negotiated the marriage of her son, the future Count Thibaut IV, to Gertrude of Dagsburg, the sixteen-year-old widow of the duke of Lorraine, thereby further cementing peace between their households and territorially connecting Champagne and the northern provinces.[54] It was following his marriage that Thibaut acted as a witness to Val-Notre-Dame's foundation near Huy.

---

52. Donnet, "La fondation de l'Abbaye d'Argensolles," 215–18.
53. On the events of the crisis, see Evergates, *Aristocracy*, 39–49.
54. Ibid., 39–42.

In 1221—when peace returned to the county—Blanche purchased a grange known as Argensolles with its surrounding woodlands and pastures from the monks of Hautvillers.[55] Over the next two years the countess used her dower income to acquire vast tracts of woodland in various locations, supplemented by income from tithes, annual rents of rye and oats, meadowlands and their rents, a patchwork of vineyards, annual money rents from the Champagne fairs, the proceeds of a mill between Dandon and Sézanne, and several smaller fiefs from local knights, all of which she gave as an endowment to her new abbey.[56] In 1223 Thibaut IV affirmed his mother's donations and augmented them with his own gifts.[57] A year later, with the initial buildings in place, and "with the consent of William [of Joinville], archbishop of Reims, and Jacques, bishop of Soissons, [Blanche] gave [Argensolles] as a perpetual gift to Lady Ida, abbess, and to the nuns serving God there... for the salvation of [her] soul and the soul of [her] dearest son Thibaut [IV], [and] for the good memory of [her] husband Thibaut [III, d. 1201] and [her] ancestors."[58]

As its founder, Blanche not only secured the nunnery's economic well-being but was instrumental in its official incorporation within the Cistercian order. In 1224, during the meeting of the General Chapter, the abbots of Cîteaux, La Ferté, Pontigny, Clairvaux, and Morimond recognized the abbey and gave license for the community to expand to up to ninety nuns, ten lay converts, and twenty clerics and laymen.[59] Such an agreement made Argensolles a tremendously significant foundation that would only find rivals among the nunneries founded by the royal families of France and Castile and the countesses of Flanders.[60] The Cistercian abbots further stipulated that the convent was "to be fully part of our order with the right to wear the prescribed habit, and that the abbot of Clairvaux will be the father of the house, as he is of monasteries of monks."[61]

---

55. AD Marne, 70 H 12 (August 1221); GC 9:130–31, instr. 49.

56. AD Marne, 70 H 12 (1224); GC 9:132–33, instr. 53. Much of the charter was copied into Honorius III's confirmation of the foundation in 1225: GC 9:134–35, instr. 56.

57. AD Marne, 70 H 12 (1223) and 70 H 12 (20 October 1223). Concerning Thibaut's future donations, see Evergates, *Aristocracy*, 78n137.

58. AD Marne, 70 H 12 (1224); GC 9:132–33, instr. 53; translated in Theodore Evergates, ed. and trans., *Feudal Society in Medieval France: Documents from the County of Champagne* (Philadelphia, 1993), 137–39, no. 104.

59. GC 9:133, instr. 54.

60. Argensolles may have been intended from its inception as the head of a filiation of female houses. On this, see chap. 3, 112–113.

61. "plenariter incorporatae ordini nostro et unitae, habentes integrum habitum secundum formam ordinis,... quae praescriptum ferunt habitum, unico pellitio utantur, non mantellis, et abbas Claraevallensis sit ejusdem domus pater, sicut est abbatiarum monachorum." GC 9:133, instr. 54.

In the same year, 1224, Countess Blanche retired to Argensolles. She slowly extracted herself from political life, turning the county over to her son. She carried into the cloister, however, a copy of all the charters, peace accords, letters patent, and correspondence generated during her twenty-one-year rule and on occasion came out of retirement to consult on political matters until her death in 1229.[62] Argensolles's foundation, intertwined as it was with political turmoil and spiritual consolation, underlines the connections between the women's religious movement in the southern Low Countries, religious ideas in Champagne, and the networks the Cistercian order fostered between the two. The key ecclesiastical figures to aid in the peace negotiations following the 1218 rebellion were the Cistercian abbots of Cîteaux, Clairvaux, Quincy, and Pontigny, three of the same abbots present at Argensolles's incorporation.[63] Blanche's decision to turn again to Liège to populate her new nunnery is also indicative of the transmission of ideas between the two regions.

Filles-Dieu and the Piety of Penance

Within a decade of Argensolles's foundation, numerous smaller Cistercian nunneries began to appear throughout the county. Though not so explicitly connected to the spiritual currents of Liège as Countess Blanche's foundation, the new Cistercian convents shared characteristics with the women's religious movement that were fundamental to its definition and attraction. An aspect of this was the importance of penance as a practice and a state of mind. Living as a penitent could expiate one's personal sins but was also a renunciation of one's past with the ambition of remaking the self, guided by a commitment to apostolic ideals. The idea of remaking the self held particular appeal for those women who had lived in the world, been married and borne children, perhaps even outside of marriage. Moreover, the kind of penitential piety that women like Mary of Oignies, Yvette of Huy, Elizabeth of Hungary, and Margaret of Cortona practiced—when pursued rigorously enough—had the potential to restore women to their prior state of chastity, and thus potential holiness, and it was part of the very process of conversion described earlier.

A penitent, strictly speaking, was someone on whom the church had imposed a public penance for a particularly significant sin. Yet by the twelfth century the term took on a wider meaning, applying also to a layperson who

---

62. BNF, Lat. 5993; Theodore Evergates, ed., *The Cartulary of Countess Blanche of Champagne* (Toronto, 2010).

63. Evergates, *Cartulary of Blanche,* nos. 103 and 116.

had personally and often spontaneously taken on or "converted" to a life of asceticism. The penitent's life brought together a consuming and rigorous devotion expressed through regular attendance at mass, participation in processions, vigils, daily prayer, and fasts, and the performance of penance, which often included charitable work, caring for the sick, housing the poor, and an unflagging bodily discipline that bore the promise of purging one's own sins and even the sins of one's community in the hopes of redemption.[64] Such practiced piety was meant to combat many sins: lechery, sloth, envy, and avarice—specifically the dangers and moral ills associated with economic gain as pursued in the growing towns and cities of Europe. In almost all of the *vitae* that describe thirteenth-century women's piety, some aspect of penance is related to their association, either through familial or spousal connections, with profit and an attempt to expiate the sins that accrued from its pursuit.[65]

In a general way all of the women in the new Cistercian nunneries in northern France pursued a penitential ideal, yet in some cases it was a specific desire for penance that determined the spiritual life that took shape in these communities, for they grew out of groups of penitent women who had come together on their own, independent of formal oversight. In this regard, names are very telling. *Filles-Dieu* was the most common colloquial appellation given to these women. This was how Gregory IX referred to the women of Chichéry outside of Troyes in his correspondence of 1234; and it is a designation that surfaces in many descriptions of religious women during the early 1230s. Although terms like *Filles-Dieu* and *mulieres religiosae* seem ambiguous, they were more often than not specifically chosen to convey a particular set of associations and meanings.[66] These were converts, laywomen, and devout, but not nuns.

By the middle of the thirteenth century many female communities in northern France were known as *Filles-Dieu*. In many cases these were foundations specifically created to shelter repentant prostitutes. Although some twelfth-century charismatic preachers, such as Robert of Arbrissel (ca. 1050–1116), founder of the nunnery of Fontevraud, had accepted penitent prostitutes among their followers, by the thirteenth century the redemption of prostitutes—and their desire to be "redeemed"—became part of an

---

64. Thompson, *Cities of God.*
65. See Jo Ann McNamara, "The Need to Give: Suffering and Female Sanctity in the Middle Ages," in *Images of Sainthood in Medieval Europe,* ed. Renate Blumenfeld-Kosinski and Timea Szell (Ithaca, 1991), 199–221.
66. See Makowski, *"Mulieres Religiosae,"* 2–3.

overarching effort to reform the religious life of the laity.[67] Upon becoming pope in 1198, Innocent III emerged as a great advocate for this form of lay renewal. He called on laymen to come to the aid of such women, offering remission of sins to those who would marry them or provide them with dowries.[68] In the same year, Fulk of Neuilly, who had been a student with Innocent III at the University of Paris and was an influential preacher in his own right, founded the convent of St.-Antoine-des-Champs outside the walls of Paris initially to shelter prostitutes who converted to a life in religion.

Whether as reformed prostitutes or penitent women, many of the Cistercian nunneries in Champagne began as communities of *Filles-Dieu*. The women at Chichéry were referred to as *Filles-Dieu* before they became the convent of Notre-Dame-des-Prés. Only a year earlier, in 1229, a pious knight named Philip of Mécringes had supported thirteen young women who went by the name of *Filles-Dieu* and began the process of founding the Cistercian convent of La Piété-Dieu near Ramerupt, along the road that connected Troyes to Vitry-le-François to the north.[69] Like St.-Antoine and Notre-Dame-des-Prés, it was also transformed to some extent after its incorporation within the order. As a catalyst to the process of incorporation, two Cistercian convents founded nearby, La Grâce and Le Jardin, sent pairs of nuns to populate La Piété. The movement of nuns between newly founded Cistercian convents, like the importation of women from Val-Notre-Dame to Argensolles, speaks to the fluidity of the women's religious movement and the ways in which examples of piety, practice, and customs were transmitted. If the thirteen *Filles-Dieu* whom Philip of Mécringes assembled outside of Ramerupt had been illiterate and unable to sing the liturgy from texts or unfamiliar with the Cistercian customs, the guidance of women with a personal experience of the regulated life would have been necessary.

By the 1230s *Filles-Dieu* had become a common term for religious women in the county, but it still had considerable flexibility. Giving alms in 1231 to "nuns of the house of the mother of the Savior which is called the house

---

67. On Robert of Arbrissel, see Jacques L. Dalarun, *Robert of Arbrissel: Sex, Sin, and Salvation in the Middle Ages,* trans. Bruce L. Venarde (Washington, DC, 2006). Also Gábor Klaniczay, "Religious Movements and Christian Culture: A Pattern of Centripetal and Centrifugal Orientations," in idem, *The Uses of Supernatural Power: The Transformation of Popular Religion in Medieval and Early-Modern Europe,* ed. Karen Margolis and trans. Susan Singerman (Princeton, 1990), 28–50, at 42.
68. *PL,* 214, col. 102; and André Simon, *L'ordre des pénitents de Ste Marie-Madeleine en Allemagne au XIIIeme siècle* (Fribourg, 1918), 2.
69. "Beatae Mariae de Pietate-Dei Parthenon juxta Ramerucum, medio itinere Victoriacum Francicum inter et Treces, septem leucis ab urbe distans, utraque, suam debet originem Philippo militi domino *de Meeringes,* qui anno 1229 coactis tredecim puellis, quas nuncupavit *Filias-Dei,* locumque Pietatem B. Mariae, ab episcopo habitum religiosum colore album donari curavit." *GC* 12:609–10.

of the *Filles-Dieu* next to Bar," seemed to cover all possibilities for Erard de Porta and his wife, burghers of Bar-sur-Aube, who were the first supporters of the community that would become the convent of Val-des-Vignes.[70] These women had come together to serve God in the hamlet of Ailleville, less than two kilometers outside of Bar-sur-Aube and not far from the monastery of Clairvaux. They took up residence in a building complex close to the old Roman road that linked Langres and Reims, near one of the leprosaria of Bar.[71] Their patrons and the local priest who drew up the charter used the terms nuns (*monialia*) and *Filles-Dieu* interchangeably, encompassing both kinds of religious women by creating a slippage between the two. The women's earliest house was dedicated to "the mother of the Savior," a title that alludes to Mary's compassionate role as a co-suffering and co-redeeming mother rather than her image as an uncorrupted virgin. Identifying with the suffering of Mary complemented the role the women may also have played in caring for the community of lepers nearby. Early donations from the 1230s and 1240s alternately refer to the community as the "nuns of the Mother of the Savior" or the "*Filles-Dieu* next to the house of the lepers of Bar" or simply "the nuns of Bretonval."[72] References to the *Filles-Dieu* at Bar-sur-Aube suggest a penitential identity linked to suffering and caregiving very much in line with the ideals of the women's religious movement.

Similarly the Cistercian convent of Mont-Notre-Dame founded in 1236 just outside of Provins also began as a group of *Filles-Dieu*, though the archival record for this community offers virtually no details about their way of life.[73] *Filles-Dieu* also appeared along the borders of the county. In 1234, Louis IX gave the *Filles-Dieu* of Orléans, to the west of Champagne, several acres of vineyard near the chapel of St.-Aignan. By the end of the same year a second donation referred to the women of Orléans as wearing white habits. Within a decade the community moved to the small church of St.-Loup and was incorporated into the Cistercian order.[74]

---

70. "Erardus de Porta...dedit et concessit in perpetuam elemonsinam pro anniversario suo et uxoris sue faciendo monialibus de domo matris salvatoris que d[i]ctus domus filiarum Dei juctus barrum." AD Aube, 3 H 4079 (1231).

71. See Jean Mercier, "L'Abbaye du Val-des-Vignes à Ailleville," *MSA* 115 (1990): 135–52.

72. The charters that refer to the nunnery as *Beate Marie de Matris Salvatoris* date mainly from the first ten years of the community's history. See AD Aube, 3 H 4079 (1231); 3 H 4003 (1231); 3 H 4037 (1232 and 1235); 3 H 4076 (1232); 3 H 4077 (1232); 3 H 4082 (1236); 3 H 4123 (*vidimus* 1235); 3 H 4071 (1237). They are also described as "filiabus Dei que sita iuxta domum leprosarum Barri super albam"; AD Aube, 3 H 4037 (1232). Two charters refer to the community as "monialibus de Bretonval"; AD Aube, 3 H 4011 (1242 and 1246).

73. *GC* 12:70, instr. 92.

74. See André Laurenceau, *Essai historique sur l'Abbaye royale de Saint-Loup-lez-Orléans* (Orléans, 1974).

In the early thirteenth century the institutional life of houses of *Filles-Dieu* was not precisely defined. Rather such communities shared affinities with Penitent Sisters in Italy, where women lived together, wore a religious habit, and followed an agreed-upon rule, but were not cloistered as nuns. These distinctions and various processes of monastic affiliation played out over the course of the thirteenth century. For example, in 1204, St.-Antoine, the house founded by Fulk of Neuilly, was reformed under the Cistercian customs; in 1206 it was incorporated into the Cistercian order and gained the support of noble and bourgeois families whose daughters joined the convent throughout the thirteenth century. As a consequence, St.-Antoine no longer took in repentant prostitutes.[75] To fill this need, in 1225, William of Auvergne, master of theology at the university and later bishop of Paris, founded a second community to accommodate *repenties*, which was known simply as the *Filles-Dieu* of Paris. Located just outside of the city near the leper hospital of St. Lazar, the house of *Filles-Dieu* was designated specifically "for poor women, who were newly converted."[76] The *Filles-Dieu* benefited from the patronage of King Louis IX, who gave them 400 *l.* a year. "The hostel housed," so Joinville recalled in his biography of the king, "a large number of women who through poverty had abandoned themselves to the sins of the flesh."[77]

By the middle of the thirteenth century the *Filles-Dieu* became an order of their own. The Cistercian chronicler Aubry of Trois Fontaines, writing in the early 1240s, stated that after William of Auvergne founded the house of *Filles-Dieu*, "this order began to spread into other cities."[78] What Aubry meant exactly by "order" is not clear. Most likely, the women lived according

---

75. See Sharon A. Farmer, *Surviving Poverty in Medieval Paris: Gender, Ideology, and the Daily Lives of the Poor* (Ithaca, 2002), 147; and Constance Berman, "Cistercian Nuns and the Development of the Order: The Abbey of Saint-Antoine-des-Champs outside Paris," in *The Joy of Learning and the Love of God: Studies in Honor of Jean Leclercq*, ed. E. Rozanne Elder (Kalamazoo, MI, 1995), 121–56.

76. "hospitale ad opus pauperum mulierum de novo conversarum"; Léon Le Grand, "Les maisons-Dieu et léproseries du diocèse de Paris au milieu du XIVe, d'après le register de visites du délégué de l'évêque (1351–1369)," *Mémoires de la Société de l'Histoire de Paris et de l'Île de France* 24 (1897): 61–365, at 250; for the *Filles-Dieu* generally, see 250–68. See also Farmer, *Surviving Poverty*, 129–32, 147–49. Concerning William of Auvergne, see Peter Biller, *The Measure of the Multitude: Population in Medieval Thought* (Oxford, 2000), 74–76.

77. Jean de Joinville, *Vie de Saint Louis*, ed. J. Monfrin (Paris, 1995), para. 725. Although Joinville credits Louis IX with the foundation of the *Filles-Dieu*, it is more likely that Louis gave funds to rebuild the house after his return from crusade in 1254. In 1265 he bequeathed to them water rights from the font at St. Lazar. Following his death, the *Filles-Dieu* also came to possess a finger relic of St. Louis. See the comments in William Chester Jordan, *Louis IX and the Challenge of the Crusade* (Princeton, 1979), 188–89, specifically n. 50.

78. "in aliis civitatibus cepit hic ordo dilatari"; Aubry de Trois-Fontaines, "Chronicon," *MGH SS*, 23:917.

to common practices and routines of prayer and penance adhered to by all houses of *Filles-Dieu*. As André Simon showed, houses for repentant prostitutes in Germany, known as the Order of the Penitent Sisters of Blessed Mary Magdalene, also spread rapidly.[79] "Order" in this sense connoted the members' converted status as penitent sisters and their reform under a designated set of monastic customs.[80] *Filles-Dieu* and penitent sisters were thus related by virtue of their conversion and commitment to repentance. By the middle of the thirteenth century, communities of *Filles-Dieu* were listed as recipients of gifts in local charters and wills from Reims and Sens. From at least 1240 there was a house of *Filles-Dieu* in Rouen, which may have begun simply as a group of charitable women informally associated with a *domus-Dei* in the city, though recent research suggests that they too began as a community of repentant prostitutes similar to William of Auvergne's foundation in Paris, who perhaps took on care of the sick as a penitential act.[81]

It is unclear whether all women designated as *Filles-Dieu* came to the religious life through the channel of prostitution and penance. If it is possible to generalize, in all likelihood these were women who had lived in the world, perhaps as wives and mothers, or as servants or single women, who had chosen to take up a new spiritual life conditioned on penance as a conversion to a new religious identity.[82] While some may have been poor women led to prostitution out of necessity, that does not seem to have always been the case. Some *Filles-Dieu* were no doubt simply converts to the penitential life, like Mary of Oignies or Yvette of Huy, who had chosen their new lives purposefully. The sense that they were still part of, or at least marked out by, their previous experiences in the world was part of the significance behind the term. Unlike nuns, *Filles-Dieu* were not consecrated or bound by a monastic vow, but rather were "daughters of God," transformed through a personal commitment and aided by the grace of God in the cultivation of a new religious life that hinged upon repentance.[83] By cultivating a new

---

79. Simon, *L'ordre des penitents*.

80. See ibid., 21–65. For penitent sisters in Italy, see Thompson, *Cities of God*, 74–82. In most cases these customs were initially those of the Cistercians. See chap. 3, 87–92.

81. Fabienne Chaube, "Les *Filles-Dieu* de Rouen aux XIIIe–XVe siècle: Étude du process de regularization d'une communauté religieuse," *Revue Mabillon*, n.s. 1 (1990): 179–211, at 186.

82. During the twelfth century, perhaps 30 percent of female communities housed formerly married women. See Bruce Venarde, *Women's Monasticism and Medieval Society: Nunneries in France and England, 800–1215* (Ithaca, 1997), 95–103. For the aristocracy in Champagne, see Evergates, *Aristocracy*, 147–48. See chap. 2, 69–77.

83. Contrition, confession, and repentance were all integral components in the reform of the laity central to the efforts of the Fourth Lateran Council of 1215. On this transformation generally, see Paul B. Pixton, *The German Episcopacy and the Implementation of the Decrees of the Fourth Lateran*

religious consciousness and taking up a life of penance and prayer outside of formal institutions, the *Filles-Dieu* of Champagne were part of the women's religious movement, echoing its fervor to the north and south.

Domus-Dei, Leper Houses, and the Work of Mercy

Penance and charity were always closely linked. Penitential piety was often expressed through acts of mercy, including feeding the hungry, clothing the naked, providing hospitality, caring for the sick, visiting those in prison, and tending to the dead. These actions were apostolic injunctions. As Christ stated in the Gospel of Matthew (25:35): "Whoever therefore through these works shows charity to his neighbor applies that charity to God." Caring for the sick was likened to caring for Christ himself. Moreover, taking up a life devoted to those who had been rejected from society, such as lepers, strangers, and the poor, was a way to renounce vividly and publicly any social ambitions in the secular world. Women seemed to have been particularly drawn to acts of caregiving, and vignettes of self-sacrificing care feature prominently in the *vitae* of many religious women. Mary of Oignies, Yvette of Huy, and Elizabeth of Hungary, as well as Saint Francis and Saint Louis, all cared for the sick and leprous, and doing so often came at pivotal moments in their spiritual conversions.[84]

During the twelfth century, as the numbers of hospitals began to expand across Europe, many devout laymen and women worked in these new foundations as *donats* and *conversae,* or helped to fund such institutions on their own estates and in their own houses.[85] Several families in Troyes, for example, gave houses or parts of their estates to the leprosarium of Les Deux-Eaux on the southern outskirts of the town to support daughters and wives, who joined the community as *conversae*.[86] Married couples also joined hospital communities together so they could live out the remainder of their lives serving the sick and the poor. In 1250, Thierry le Lorgnes and his wife, Christina, both citizens of Troyes, "willingly gave themselves to God and to the leper

---

Council, 1216–1245 (Leiden, 1994); Mary Mansfield, *The Humiliation of Sinners: Public Penance in Thirteenth-Century France* (Ithaca, 1995); and Thompson, *Cities of God,* 273–308.

84. For a more detailed discussion of these hagiographical tropes, see chap. 4, 139–143.

85. Charles de Miramon, *Les donnés au Moyen Âge: Une forme de vie religieuse laïque (v. 1180–v. 1500)* (Paris, 1999), 337–86; and François-Olivier Touati, "Les groups de laics dans les hôpitaux et les léproseries au Moyen Âge," in *Les mouvances laïques des ordres religieux,* ed. Pierrette Paravy and Nicole Bouter (Saint-Étienne, 1996), 137–62.

86. M. Harmond, "Notice historique sur la léproserie de la ville de Troyes," *MSA* 7–8 (1847–48): 429–669, esp. 537 (1197) and 557–58 (1235).

house of Les Deux-Eaux" and put on a religious habit to care for the lepers.[87] Offering charity to the sick was a way for laymen and women to take part in the new religious consciousness and ideals of the *vita apostolica* while remaining in the world, outside of a monastic profession. Although couples engaged in such acts together, caregiving with its active and penitential qualities became a defining aspect of the women's religious movement, particularly as it was manifest in Champagne.[88]

Over half of the female communities in Champagne that became Cistercian nunneries during the 1230s began as groups of women connected to hospices (*domus-Dei*) or leper houses (leprosaria).[89] Most hospices and leper houses were small, independent sites of local charity and care, quite different from more formal hospitals like Les Deux-Eaux. Smaller *domus-Dei* relied almost exclusively on alms and charity for their existence. In Champagne, in the absence of more vivid testimonies like those preserved in hagiography, the proliferation of these small charities is its own witness to the appeal of the converted life. Caring for the poor, the outcast, the illegitimate, and the sick, many of whom may have rather indiscriminately fallen under the umbrella term of "lepers," was a critical part of late twelfth-century religion and its social commitments. In many cases caring for the sick and poor in a local hospice was the first stage of a religious vocation, the beginning of a conversion process.

By the end of the twelfth century, not more than two kilometers outside of the new town of Villeneuve-l'Archévêque, just east of the city of Sens, a community of lepers was founded in the hamlet of Viluis. In 1191 a group of women—living in a grange up the road—were given a crusader's alms for caring for the lepers.[90] In 1225, the archbishop of Sens formally recognized the community of women and in the following year they were incorporated into the Cistercian order as La Cour Notre-Dame-de-Michery.[91] Similar connections

---

87. "Terricus, dictus li Lorgnes, et Cristiana, uxor ejus, cives trecenses, cupientes, ut asserunt, sub regulari habitu vitam ducere temporalem, recognoverunt coram nobis, ex certa scientia dedicasse se et sua Deo et domui leprosorum de Duabus Aquis juxta Trecas." Ibid., 572–73 (1250).

88. See Sharon Farmer, "The Leper in the Master Bedroom: Thinking through a Thirteenth-Century Exemplum," in *Framing the Family: Narrative and Representation in the Medieval and Early Modern Periods*, ed. Roalynn Voaden and Diane Wolfthal (Tempe, AZ, 2005), 79–100, at 93. Even when couples joined together, women typically predominated as caregivers for the afflicted.

89. See the appendix; and Bondeelle-Souchier, "Les moniales cisterciennes," 210n73 and passim.

90. Maximillien Quantin, ed., *Cartulaire général de l'Yonne*, 2 vols. (Auxerre, 1854–60), 2:436 (no. 182).

91. Maximillien Quantin, ed. *Recueil de pièces pour faire suite au cartulaire général de l'Yonne (XIIIe siècle)* (Paris, 1873), 144–45 (nos. 328–29). For the basic chronology of events at La Cour, see William Chester Jordan, "The Cistercian Nunnery of La Cour Notre-Dame de Michery: A House That Failed," *Revue bénédictine* 95 (1985): 311–20.

to houses of lepers lay behind the foundation of Val-des-Vignes discussed earlier. The women of Val-des-Vignes, although referred to in their earliest documents as *Filles-Dieu*, also lived in a building complex close to a leper house outside of Bar-sur-Aube. It is likely that, as part of their religious commitment to penance, the women cared for the lepers nearby. The leprosarium and Val-des-Vignes were less than two kilometers outside of Bar, just off the main roadway. Donations offered to the nuns over the course of the thirteenth century make reference to the proximity of the two houses and associate the communities in a common locale.[92] These early foundations were fluid and independent, the product of local impulses toward social charity rather than episcopal reform, housing the sick and the women who cared for them.

While proximity created affiliations with lepers for practical and pious reasons, other nunneries were founded within preexisting hospitals and *domus-Dei*. The groups of women already serving in these institutions thus became nuns when their communities were given a formal rule and defined cloister. In 1226 Hugh of Châtillon founded the nunnery of Pont-aux-Dames in the *domus-Dei* on the bridge in the parish of Couilly near Meaux, from the community of women serving in the same hospital.[93] Several years later in 1232, Hugh of Châtillon and the knight Philip of Mécringes founded L'Amour-Dieu in the *domus-Dei* of Troissy near Châtillon.[94] The women in this community were, as mentioned previously, initially referred to as *Filles-Dieu*. Strikingly, the women's obligations to the poor who convalesced in the *domus-Dei* continued even after the house acquired formal affiliation with the Cistercians. L'Amour-Dieu's foundation charter explains that the *domus-Dei* "was, should be and always will be a hospital for the poor."[95]

Similar Cistercian foundations grew out of *domus-Dei* and hospices throughout the county. In 1233 Count Thibaut IV formed the nunnery of St.-Jacques de Vitry from a small *domus-Dei* near Vitry.[96] Blanche of Navarre, Thibaut IV's mother and the founder of Argensolles, also oversaw the

---

92. See n. 72, above; and Anne E. Lester, "Cares beyond the Walls: Cistercian Nuns and the Care of Lepers in Twelfth- and Thirteenth-Century Northern France," in *Religious and Laity in Western Europe, 1000–1400: Interaction, Negotiation, and Power*, ed. Emilia Jamroziak and Janet Burton (Turnhout, 2006), 197–224, at 211–12.

93. GC 8:1723–28, instr. 12, col. 558; Claude-Hyacinthe Berthault, *L'Abbaye de Pont-aux-Dames, ordre de Cîteaux* (Meaux, 1878); and Robert Martin, "Aux sources de l'Abbaye de Pont-aux-Dames," *Bulletin de la Société Littéraire et Historique de la Brie* 40 (1984): 17–36.

94. GC 9:135, instrs. 58–60; and Albert Noël, "L'Abbaye de l'Amour-Dieu de l'ordre de Cîteaux (1232–1802)," *Revue de Champagne et de Brie* 1 (1876): 144–53.

95. "in domo illa quae dicitur *Amor-Dei*, quae quidem domus hospitale pauperum quondam fuit, fiat et fit in perpetuum abbatia monialium Cisterciensis ordinis"; GC 9:137, instr. 63.

96. AD Marne, 71 H 4 (February 1233); and A. Kwanten, "L'Abbaye Saint-Jacques de Vitry-en-Perthois," *MSM* 81 (1966): 93–109.

foundation of a community of women to care for the poor in her comital residence at Château-Thierry. Although initially founded in 1213 as a *domus-Dei* for the poor, the community was given over to Cécile d'Arcy and incorporated into the Cistercian order in 1240 as the nunnery of La Barre.[97] In other cases care for the poor may have been less formalized. A group of women, simply described as "serving the poor of Christ" and "leading a religious life," became the first nuns of Willencourt, founded by the count of Ponthieu in 1199.[98] And such examples could be multiplied (see the appendix).

Profession by Their Own Hands

Evidence for the women's religious movement in Champagne not only reveals a new interest in the religious life, but it also shows women pursuing this interest on their own initiative, interpreting a life of devotion and penitence outside the direction or guidance of the ecclesiastical hierarchy. Whether the religious women of Champagne sought to live a life of penance and charity independent of a monastic rule or formal profession remains a difficult question to answer. Some of the earliest charters for these communities, however, often mention a telling detail: in many cases, before the women were recognized as nuns or incorporated into the Cistercian order, they took to wearing white habits.[99] Donning this type of dress may simply have served as a visual marker of the penitential life. Yet it may have also provided a way for communities of religious women to associate themselves with the Cistercian order in a more informal manner. Yvette of Huy adopted a white habit in imitation of Cistercian nuns during the last years of her life, though she never actually took vows and professed as a nun. It is possible that all that the women of Champagne hoped for was just this type of association: to garner the spiritual esteem of an order so highly praised and regarded in the region, but nonetheless to live out their own ideals and interpretations of

---

97. C. Nusse, "Charte de fondation d'un Hôtel-Dieu à la Barre," *Annales de la Société historique et archéologique de Château-Thierry* (1874): 191–92; and A. E. Poquet, "L'Abbaye de Barre et son recueil de chartes," *Mémoires de la Société historique et archéologique de Château-Thierry* (1884): 117–77. See chap. 2, 65.

98. *GC* 10:334–35, instrs. 59–60: "Ego Willermus comes Pontivi pro anima patris mei et redemptione animae meae concessi in eleemosynam Deo servientibus pauperibus Christi, et futuris earum successoribus habitantibus in loco prope Alteiam." And instr. 60: "priorissae et monialibus in loco qui dicitur Insula-Senardi, religiosam vitam ducentibus," implying that they had been living a religious life before they were officially founded as a nunnery.

99. For example, several years before they became Cistercian nuns, the women at Chichéry were described as "quaedam moniales habitum album"; AD Aube, G 3101 (August 1231).

the apostolic life, with a commitment to care-giving and poverty that formal juridical incorporation within the order may not have permitted them.

And yet, if this was the ideal, it rapidly proved to be untenable. The women of Champagne pursued a religious life without formal profession just as the church hierarchy was itself reevaluating the meaning and practices of monastic profession. By the middle of the twelfth century the church and the papacy in particular had to face increasingly complex questions of canon law regarding profession during oblation and the desires of some men and women to renounce their previous commitments and return to the secular world. Gratian (fl. 1140s) was one of the first canonists to take up the question of monastic profession and consent. By the start of the thirteenth century consent emerged as a defining principle of monastic profession, which involved not simply putting on a monastic habit but making a public vow before a bishop and submitting oneself to ecclesiastical authority.[100] In this context, however, the importance of wearing the monastic habit could not be overlooked as a sign of intention. At the same time Hostiensis, the cardinal-bishop of Ostia and great legal compiler and commentator, allowed that even in the absence of an explicit profession or vow anyone who chose to wear a monastic habit for a year and a day should be considered professed. Wearing a habit for so long a time could only be the product of careful consideration and deliberate intention. Indeed the individual had in effect submitted to a new lifestyle, even if it was done outside of the official channels of the church.[101] The habit made the lay penitent just as it made the nun.[102] For those women of Champagne found to be wearing white habits, a change of garment was the way they marked out their consent and commitment to a new religious life, freely chosen independent of the sanction of a bishop or abbot.

When the monks of La Celle complained that the women of Chichéry had taken habits "by their own hands," they meant this remark as an indictment accusing the women of usurping an episcopal prerogative. Yet it is also possible to read in this detail the initiative of the women themselves who took on their own form of profession. To be sure, the unmediated agency of such women was certainly controversial, as the monks' *libellus* makes clear. These were women who made claims to the religious life that were not defined for them, but that they came to define through their own actions, devotions, and social connections. Moreover, the spiritual authority that was

---

100. See John Van Engen, "Professing Religion: From Liturgy to Law," *Viator* 29 (1998): 323–43.
101. Ibid., 340–41.
102. Thompson, *Cities of God,* 82.

associated with religious women because of their commitment to a life of penance and prayer was clearly threatening to religious groups on the outside of the movement, especially to monks like those of La Celle or the canons of St.-Pierre in Troyes. In their own way the religious women of Champagne defined not only the women's religious movement but also how patrons, the ecclesiastical hierarchy, and the Cistercian order would respond to them in the decades to come.

The earliest documents for the Cistercian convents of Champagne expose the shape and impulses of a women's religious movement at work within the region decades before these women became Cistercian nuns. Throughout the county—along its trade routes and waterways, at Vitry, Château-Thierry, outside of Meaux, between Sézanne and Montmirail, and along the margins of three of the four major fair towns, at Bar-sur-Aube, Troyes and Provins—communities of religious women assembled as penitents and *Filles-Dieu* in service to the poor and sick. Some were perhaps reformed prostitutes, laboring under the weight of worldly sins, of *luxuria* and pride, who forged a new religious identity. Others offered care to the sick and poor. The *Filles-Dieu* and religious women of northern France and Champagne were part of a broader religious impulse to engage in a spiritual life initially outside of institutional definitions, customs, and limitations. The appeal of this type of spirituality was significant, particularly to members of the urban bourgeoisie, to lesser knights, and to secular canons, who became the first patrons of many of these communities.

 CHAPTER 2

Cities of Refuge
The Social World of Religious Women

Toward the end of his universal chronicle, the Cistercian monk Aubry of Trois-Fontaines commented dryly that in the year 1231 "the count of Champagne created communes of townsmen and peasants, whom he trusted more than his knights."[1] Aubry's text, the only local history of Champagne composed in the thirteenth century, follows the descent of aristocratic families, enumerates their genealogies, describes crusades and their recruits, and faithfully notes the passing of abbots and the founding of new religious houses. His terse remark on a matter of social class is provocative for it alludes obliquely to the series of urban franchises that Count Thibaut IV granted between 1230 and 1232 to six of the major towns within the county. Although the count and his predecessors had bestowed franchises to communities in the past, the scale of the grants made in the 1230s to Troyes, Provins, and Bar-sur-Aube—the three most prominent fair towns—as well as the castle towns of St.-Florentin, Villemaur, and Bar-sur-Seine was unprecedented.[2] For the attentive Aubry it signaled a significant

---

1. "Comes Campanie communias burgensium et rusticorum fecit, in quibus magis confidebat, quam in militibus suis." Aubry of Trois-Fontaines, "Chronicon," ed. Paul Scheffer-Boichorst, in *MGH SS* (Hannover, 1874), 23:621–950, at 929; also Mireille Schmidt-Chazan, "Aubri de Trois-Fontaines, historien entre la France et l'Empire," *Annales de l'Est* 36 (1984): 163–92.

2. See Theodore Evergates, *Feudal Society in the Bailliage of Troyes under the Counts of Champagne, 1152–1284* (Baltimore, 1975), 41–57.

social change. It heralded the rising burgher or bourgeois class's eclipse of the traditional nobility, a change that would have a tremendous impact on urban spirituality, social networks, and Cistercian patronage.

Urban franchise was liberation. Two main effects followed for those city dwellers given comital charters in the 1230s: the arbitrary tax levied by the count (the *taille*) and the personal taxes and inheritance restrictions (often called *mainmorte*) over the count's men and women were converted into a standard-rate tax on wealth.[3] This annual payment granted unrestricted movement and economic freedom within the urban community. In addition, the count's charters instituted a *jurée* of twelve townsmen (comparable to the groups of *échevins* and *scabini* of other northern French towns) and a mayor to oversee tax collection, facilitate municipal affairs, and render judgments in legal cases involving townsmen. Thus the major towns in the county came to enjoy a measure of self-government. Once created, such institutions fostered a mentality of independence that persisted and shaped the bourgeois class.[4] Self-government became a necessity after 1234, when Count Thibaut IV inherited the kingdom of Navarre from his uncle and the towns of Champagne were forced to function in his absence. Theodore Evergates concludes that ultimately the "new tax system and municipal self-administration separated those" free residents of the comital towns "from all other rural and urban tenants under private lords and still subject to the old obligations and restrictions." By sealing and confirming the charters of franchise in 1230–31, "the count had effectively created a new social category."[5]

The charters of franchise fostered four new groups that were closely tied to urban society and whose members shaped Champagne's religious and economic trajectory in significant ways. First, under the direct lordship of the count, a new category of non-noble, non-knighted, small landholders (known as *armigeri* or *escuiers*, rather than *milites* or *domini*) began to play a more prominent role in politics and society. At the same time, women, who had always had access to property through the practice of partible inheritance customary in Champagne, also began to exercise a greater degree of control over the disposal of land and wealth. Added to this was the appearance of

---

3. The tax was proportional to wealth and assessed at "a rate of 2 *d.* per pound of real estate and 6 *d.* per pound value of movables, excluding clothes and household furniture, but including gold and silver utensils, especially wine cups." Evergates, *Feudal Society,* 49. The charter for Troyes was a model for the subsequent grants. See Dominique Coq, ed., *Chartes en langue française antérieures à 1271 conservées dans les départements de l'Aube, de la Seine-et-Marne, et de l'Yonne* (Paris, 1988), 3–6, no. 1, translated in Theodore Evergates, ed. and trans., *Feudal Society in Medieval France: Documents from the County of Champagne* (Philadelphia, 1993), 23–26, no. 18.

4. See Elizabeth Chapin, *Les villes de foires de Champagne: Des origines au début du XIVe siècle* (Paris, 1937), 163–224.

5. Evergates, *Feudal Society,* 55.

a new group of secular canons, who were instrumental in the revolution of document production that facilitated the administration of the county. Finally, a growing burgher-merchant class (whose status was described variously as bourgeois, *civis,* or simply by profession) populated the franchised towns of Champagne and initiated new patterns of economic activity, labor mobility, and landholding practices.

It is not coincidental that these four social groups (a non-knighted aristocracy, women, secular canons, and a bourgeoisie) emerged at the same moment that the women's religious movement took shape in Champagne and began to coalesce as Cistercian nunneries. These two events—one sociological in nature and the other religious—were intimately bound. Although the daughters and sisters of townsmen formed the initial groups of *mulieres religiosae* who would be re-formed as nuns, within a generation the Cistercian nunneries received rents, houses, and income that entangled them in this same changing economic and social world. In turn, as nuns the women prayed and labored for the redemption of these new social groups. Moreover, the patronage of Cistercian nunneries enhanced the social capital and reinforced networks of the same townsmen and women just as bonds of kinship and shared social space tied the nuns to the urban milieu and the ideals of the *vita apostolica*. What is even more striking, however, is that patronage of the new Cistercian nunneries had the effect of uniting these new social groups with the traditional knightly and baronial aristocracy, who had deep ties to the Cistercian order, creating a community of patrons allied in their combined support for the nuns. Common networks of patronage also reflected the social origins of those within the convents. Among those creating communities we find daughters and sisters of burghers, canons and artisans, aristocratic widows, and repentant women, all of whom came together to serve the poor and lepers for a time or to take up a life of pious prayer and spiritual contemplation. This social mix, certainly not without its challenges, reflected the ideals of the first apostolic communities, which offered refuge from the world, joining men and women in charity to lead lives of service and devotion.[6]

Class, Consumption, and Mobility

The county of Champagne stretched across the fertile and chalky plains that unfolded between the Rhine River and the French royal domain. There were

---

6. This was an ideal among lay religious communities that persisted through the Middle Ages. See John Van Engen, *Sisters and Brothers of the Common Life: The Devotio Moderna and the World of the Later Middle Ages* (Philadelphia, 2008), 89, 123–25.

few topographical features to distinguish the county's political limits from the neighboring lordships, though over the course of the twelfth century the counts began to define their authority over a delineated principality.[7] By 1200 the formal borders of the county roughly followed the banks of the Meuse River to the east, skirting the forest of the Ardennes along the linguistic border that separated the French-speaking Champenois from their German neighbors. To the south ran the border of the diocese of Langres, from whose limestone hills sprang the source of the Seine, Aube, and Marne rivers, the principle waterways that cut through the county and facilitated the profit making and exchange of the Champagne fairs. At the southwest corner ran the Yonne River and its tributary the Armançon, which cleaved Champagne from the region of the Sénonais to the south. The bishops of Sens and the counts of Auxerre, Tonnerre, and Nevers were formidable neighbors and often present in the county. Following the curve of the Yonne the fiefs of Champagne continued northward to the border of the Île-de-France and the royal domain, encompassing the territories of Brie and the county of Meaux, which the counts secured through homage to the king of France. The county continued northward still, past the town of Lagny nestled in the Marne valley to the juncture of the Aisne and Oise rivers in the heart of the diocese of Soissons.[8]

It was a gentle landscape that facilitated movement. Merchants, townsmen, freed peasants, and pilgrims traversed its roads and waterways with relative ease. The central plateau of Champagne, supporting the more prominent towns of Troyes, Provins, Lagny, Épernay, Vitry, Chaumont, and Bar-sur-Aube, enjoyed softly undulating fields and pastures cut by small hills and valleys, whose slopes accommodated grape cultivation surprisingly well given its northerly latitude. During the twelfth century there were still dense forested regions to the northeast, particularly the forests of the Ardennes, the Othe, and the Der, as well as the smaller woods of Argonne, Beaumont, Boissicant, and Clairvaux, all of which attracted recluses and monks seeking spiritual retreat. The thirteenth century saw much of this woodland cleared, put to the plow, or transformed

---

7. Henri d'Arbois de Jubainville, *Histoire des ducs et des comtes de Champagne*, 7 vols. (Paris, 1859–69), is unsurpassed in its detailed discussion of the formation of the county and its administration. See also Theodore Evergates, *The Aristocracy in the County of Champagne, 1100–1300* (Philadelphia, 2007), 5–31; and Michel Bur, *La Champagne médiévale: Recueil d'articles* (Langres, 2005), esp. 141–218.

8. In 1270 the Parlement of Paris ordered stone markers (*bourne*) to be placed along the border dividing the royal domain from the county. See Auguste Longnon, ed., *Documents relatifs au comté de Champagne and Brie (1172–1361)* 3 vols. (Paris, 1901–14), 1:507–9; and Jean Humbert, "La frontière occidentale du comté de Champagne du XIe au XIIIe siècle," in *Recueil de travaux offert à M. Clovis Brunel,* 2 vols. (Paris, 1955), 2:11–30.

into new towns—*villeneuves*—that facilitated traffic along increasingly busy trade routes.⁹

This geographic outline does not convey the complexity of personal relationships forged through mutual aid, protection, dominance, and subordination, which crossed topographical divisions and tied men and women to plots of land, known as fiefs. The counts bestowed fiefs to their vassals and prebends to their canons, but they also held larger swaths of territory in fief from other lords, including the bishops of Langres, Auxerre, and Reims as well as the duke of Burgundy, the abbot of St.-Denis, and the king of France.[10] At its height, the lands of the county fell within the ecclesiastical provinces of Reims, Soissons, Châlons, Toul, Sens, Meaux, Troyes, and Langres, and the bishops of these sees—and their officials and rural deans—drew up many of the charters that reconfigured power and social class within the county. Yet in the first decades of the thirteenth century most men and women held fiefs from the count or from local knights and nobles. Over time, these parcels of land grew fragmented through the effects of partible inheritance and the pressures of aristocratic debt that forced familial estates to be mortgaged or sold off piece by piece. The older bonds and social order characterized by the shared "culture of the fief" were giving way to a world guided by the economic realities of profits and credit, arbitrated through contracts rather than personal promises and the intimate embrace of hands that had traditionally concluded a peaceful agreement.[11]

Indicative of these changes was the stratification of the Champenois aristocracy. Between 1178 and 1250 the social distinctions separating a lord (*dominus*) from a knight (*miles*) began to collapse. At the same time, men who had been part of knightly families descended in status to live as non-knighted squires (*armigeri*). Changes in titles reflected economic realities. By the mid-thirteenth century most men and women in the county held only modest fiefs valued at 20 to 25 *l.* a year, and many fiefs were worth far less, compared with the 40 to 60 *l.* paid as prebends, or stipends, to the count's secular canons at St.-Étienne or St.-Quiriace. The makeup of fiefs changed

---

9. See *Dictionnaire topographique du département de l'Aube,* ed. Théophile Boutiot and Émile Socard (Paris, 1874), i–xxiii. On forests, see Richard Keyser, "The Transformation of Traditional Woodland Management: Commercial Sylviculture in Medieval Champagne," *French Historical Studies* 32 (2009): 352–84. For *villeneuves* and rural-urban migration, see Evergates, *Feudal Society,* 41–47; and William Chester Jordan, *From Servitude to Freedom: Manumission in the Sénonais in the Thirteenth Century* (Philadelphia, 1986), 37–58.

10. Jean Dunbabin, *France in the Making, 843–1180,* 2nd ed. (Oxford, 2000), 190–96 and 310–18; Evergates, *Feudal Society,* 1 and 136–53; and idem, *Aristocracy,* 8–21.

11. See Evergates, *Aristocracy,* 63; and the essays in Pierre Bonnassie, ed., *Fiefs et féodalité dans l'Europe méridonale: Italie, France du Midi, Péninsule Hispanique du Xe au XIIe siècle* (Toulouse, 2002).

as well. Far fewer knights held lands in return for castle guard or military service as they once did. Rather, with the exception of the landed-fiefs and castellanies along the border with Burgundy and the Empire, most fiefs had become money-fiefs—grants of revenues from tolls (*péages*), taxes (*tailles*), and stalls in the fairs or rents from other urban centers of the county. The changes in social status and the nature of fiefs brought the squires and *damoiselles* (*domicellae*) into closer contact with their bourgeois neighbors. Moreover, the increased reliance on money in the form of fixed rents and payments for service and credit embedded the lesser aristocracy in the economic rhythms of urban society.

During the first decades of the thirteenth century women appear in far greater numbers than ever before as fief-holders and heads of households in control of portions of familial estates.[12] Landed property and fiefs came to women through inheritance, dowry, as well as the designation of a dower at the time of marriage.[13] The custom of partible inheritance, which saw familial estates divided among all heirs regardless of sex, meant that all women inherited and had access to property of one kind or another. Thus, from the mid-twelfth century, women in Champagne held castles, estates, houses, rents, and urban properties in their own names and could use, inhabit, and dispose of those properties as they chose. Women also appear frequently in the chancery records and feudal registers as legal actors when their husbands were absent on pilgrimage or crusade. Because so many of the Champenois barons and knights took the cross during the twelfth and thirteenth centuries, it became commonplace for women to assume the guardianship of minor children, to negotiate marriage contracts, to confirm documents and land transactions, to arbitrate disputes, and to manage the seigneurial and economic affairs of their estates.[14] As a marker of their new authority and public role, from the 1160s aristocratic women also began to possess and use their own personal seals to confirm transactions.[15]

---

12. See Theodore Evergates, "The Aristocracy of Champagne in the Mid-Thirteenth Century: A Quantitative Description," *Journal of Interdisciplinary History* 5 (1974): 1–18; and the essays in idem, ed., *Aristocratic Women in Medieval France* (Philadelphia, 1999).

13. See Evergates, *Aristocracy*, 101–18 (on dowry, dower, and marriage practices) and 119–39 (on inheritance practices).

14. In his extensive study of the feudal records of the county Evergates found that when men went on crusade, "in no case did a married man designate someone other than his wife to govern his land or to be guardian of their children in his absence." See ibid., 96.

15. Ibid., 94–99, observes that the sealing practices of women proliferated after the Second Crusade. See also Brigitte Bedos-Rezak, "Women, Seals, and Power in Medieval France, 1150–1350," in *Women and Power in the Middle Ages*, ed. Mary Erler and Maryanne Kowaleski (Athens, GA, 1988), 61–82.

Non-aristocratic or bourgeois women enjoyed similar control over the property and income they held through inheritance and dower. Municipal law required the consent of townswomen, who were accorded the status of citizens (*cives*), for property transfers such as gifts and sales undertaken by their husbands. Thus, couples regularly appear together in urban records. Women with their own seals and widows acting as the heads of households drew up documents of their own initiative just as men did, while married women and widows of lesser status often went before the officials of the episcopal courts or before local canons in the employ of the count's chancery to create documents recording their wishes in their own names.[16] Why women began to enjoy greater rights, responsibilities, and freedoms over the control of property and wealth by the thirteenth century is difficult to explain. Changes in tenurial practices, the demilitarization of fiefs, the effects of the crusades upon familial estates, and the prominent role of the regent-countesses undoubtedly had an effect. The prominence and economic freedoms women enjoyed also meant that when women embraced the *vita apostolica* through conversion or charity, they often controlled wealth and had the legal capacity to bestow it as they saw fit.

The growing prominence of squires and women was linked to the rise of another new social category: clerics and educated men whom the counts and barons promoted within their administration.[17] These men were part of an expanding cadre of secular canons, schooled in episcopal centers like Paris and Reims. Many gained prominence as masters and university students, eventually finding employment in princely or episcopal bureaucracies.[18] In the mid-twelfth century, when Count Henry I (r. 1152–1181) began to transform Champagne into a comital state, he designated Troyes and Provins as the capitals of the county and constructed a comital residence in each town, adding another to the southeast in Bar-sur-Aube. In total, he founded six communities of secular canons, the most important of which, St.-Étienne in Troyes (founded in 1157), St.-Quiriace in Provins (refounded in 1157),

---

16. On the legal status of townswomen in northern France, see Martha C. Howell, *The Marriage Exchange: Property, Social Place and Gender in Cities of the Low Countries, 1300–1550* (Chicago, 1998); and idem, "The Gender of Europe's Commercial Economy," *Gender and History* 20 (2008): 519–38. For Champagne, see chap. 6, 180–92.

17. See Patrick Corbet, "Les collégiales comtales de Champagne (v. 1150–v.1230)," *Annales de l'Est* 29 (1971): 195–241; and Ad Putter, "Knights and Clerics at the Court of Champagne: Chrétien de Troyes's Romances in Context," in *Medieval Knighthood V: Papers from the Sixth Strawberry Hill Conference 1994*, ed. Stephen Church and Ruth Harvey (Woodbridge, 1995), 243–66.

18. Putter, "Knights and Clerics"; and Pierre Haidu, *The Subject Medieval/Modern: Text and Governance in the Middle Ages* (Stanford, 2004).

and St.-Maclou in Bar-sur-Aube (1159), sat adjacent to the count's palace complexes.[19]

While Henry remained a prodigious supporter of the many reformed monastic communities in the county, his new houses of canons formed the backbone of the principality's bureaucracy.[20] This was a trend shared by his princely neighbors. In 1172 the duke of Burgundy founded a house of canons to supply his chancery.[21] The counts of Flanders had, likewise, informally relied on the canons and clerics of St.-Donatian of Bruges to staff their chancery, and eventually the royal bureaucracy would do the same with the canons of St.-Martin of Tours.[22] Secular canons did not follow a specific rule or adhere to monastic vows, nor were they required to live communally in a cloister. Like the canons in cathedral communities, they assumed the public tasks of preaching, teaching, and creating official written records.[23]

With these foundations Count Henry brought to prominence a new class of trained men who served as professional administrators, drafting hundreds of documents and crafting a language and a technology of the comital state.[24] As a result, wherever the count was in residence, in any of his towns, he had a chancery at his disposal. As bureaucratic culture became integral to the princely state, the reliance on trained secular clerics grew. Between 1188 and 1218 Count Henry II (r. 1187–1190), Countess Marie (regent 1190–1198), Countess Blanche (regent 1201–1221), and Count Thibaut IV

---

19. Henry I's first foundation was the modest community (initially only three canons) of St.-Nicholas de Pougy established following his return from the Second Crusade (1154). This was soon followed by St.-Quiriace, St.-Étienne, St.-Maclou, St.-Nicholas in Sézanne (1176), and the chapel of Notre-Dame in the comital palace of Provins (1179). See Corbet, "Les collégiales," 195–207; and Jean Mesqui, "Le palais des comtes de Champagne à Provins (XIIe–XIIIe siècles)," *Bulletin Monumental* 151 (1993): 321–55.

20. For Henry I's patronage, which earned him the appellation "the Liberal," see the lists compiled by Arbois de Jubainville, *Histoire des ducs et des comtes de Champagne*, 3:170–83; and John F. Benton, Michel Bur, and Dominique Devaux, eds. *Recueil des actes d'Henri le Libéral, comte de Champagne, 1152–1181*, vol. 1 (Paris, 2009).

21. Corbet, "Les collégiales," 196. On the foundation of Chapelle-le-Duc in Dijon, see Jean Richard, *Les ducs de Bourgogne et la formation du duché du XIe et XIVe siècle* (Paris, 1954), 398–99.

22. Henri Pirenne, "La chancellerie et les notaires des comtes de Flandre avant le XIIIe siècle," in *Mélanges Julien Havet* (Paris, 1895), 733–48; Quentin Griffiths, "The Capetian Kings and St. Martin of Tours," *Studies in Medieval and Renaissance History* 9 (1987): 83–133; and idem, "Les collégiales royales et leurs clercs sous le gouvernement capétien," *Francia* 18 (1991): 93–110.

23. On the duties of secular canons as deans, clerks, and counselors, see John Baldwin, *The Government of Philip Augustus: Foundations of French Royal Power in the Middle Ages* (Berkeley, 1986), 115–25; Fernando Picó, "Membership in the Cathedral Chapter of Laon, 1217–1238," *Catholic Historical Review* 61 (1975): 1–30; and Quentin Griffiths, "Les collégiales royales."

24. See Putter, "Knights and Clerics," 250–54; and Theodore Evergates, "The Chancery Archives of the Counts of Champagne," *Viator* 16 (1985): 159–79.

(r. 1221–1253) each founded additional houses of canons.[25] The utility of such canons was clear to Henry's vassals and neighboring barons, who followed the count's example by creating their own houses of canons on a more modest scale. Throughout the second half of the twelfth century, Anseau II de Traînel, Geoffroy de Joinville, Milon de Bray, and Hugh de Plancy endowed smaller houses on their local estates and within their castles with between five to ten prebends each. Manasses II de Rethel and the count's brother, William aux Blanches-Mains, founded houses of canons in Pleurs, Ramerupt, and Mézières.[26] Like the count, the lesser barons employed their canons to draw up their charters and letters patent, in effect creating small personal chanceries in imitation of the count.

The counts used the judicious patronage of prebends as another means of consolidating their political power and social capital.[27] A prebend typically consisted of a small residence near the chapter's church and a fixed income or rent, the fruits of which a canon enjoyed throughout his life. In contrast to professed religious, secular canons held personal property and collected revenues that they freely alienated at the end of their lives in testaments and charters, often giving generously to the female communities outside the towns.[28] Moreover, secular canons were only required to be in residence six months out of the year, which allowed them to be employed in other ways. The comital foundations were endowed with 196 prebends, which the counts bestowed as they saw fit on the sons of local aristocrats, foreign émigrés, and "new men" from the local burgher-artisan class.[29] The counts drew from an increasingly broad social network in choosing canons, some of whom were promoted to the upper echelons of the comital administration, serving as chancellors or treasurers, and even later rising to episcopal sees. Many of these literate men pursued their own interests in vernacular culture and composed verses, romances, sermons, and chansons, or copied volumes of

---

25. These were small communities with between 3 and 34 prebends each. Henry II was associated with the foundation of St.-Jean of Vertus (1188). Countess Marie founded Notre-Dame du Val in the lower town of Provins (before 1198). Countess Blanche founded Notre-Dame de Vitry in her castle there (1212) (which was subsequently re-founded as the Cistercian nunnery of St.-Jacques de Vitry). Finally Thibaut IV became the patron of St.-Georges of Bar-sur-Seine in 1218. See Corbet, "Les collégiales," 208–11.

26. Ibid., 207–8.

27. Ibid., 229–31.

28. See the cartularies of St.-Maclou (Paris, BNF, lat. nouv. acq. 110) and St.-Étienne (Paris, BNF, lat. 17098). For a detailed example of a canon's gifts to Cistercian nunneries, see AD Aube, 3 H 336 (November 1286).

29. Evergates, "Chancery Archives"; and Arbois de Jubainville, *Histoire des ducs et des comtes de Champagne,* 4.2:530–44.

these works at the behest of their patrons.[30] The canons were a new class of men who were learned, took part in the market economy, and were mobile in a way that the count's serfs (*homme et femme de corps*) were not.

Yet, more than any other factor, the economic success of the fair towns had the greatest impact on the social and religious life of the county. Today Troyes, Provins, and Bar-sur-Aube are quaint provincial *villes,* with Bar-sur-Aube little more than a hamlet with one tabac and one café. While these places were never large cities during the Middle Ages, they were defined by their curtain walls and, at their height around 1230–50, would have boasted upward of 10,000 people or more when the fairs were in session.[31] During the reign of Henry I (r. 1152–1181) the fair towns began to eclipse Reims and Châlons as regional centers of trade and production. Although merchants from Flanders, Picardy, Hainaut, and Ponthieu frequented the fairs of Champagne in the 1140s, mostly to market cloth, by the 1170s Italian merchants from Siena and Genoa came regularly to trade and to sell spices, silks, and cotton. Other merchants and bankers profited from changing currencies and the creation of official letters of credit and bills of sale. By the thirteenth century the yearly cycle of fairs fostered not only a reliance on the dynamics of the profit economy but facilitated the rise of an influential burgher class that developed long-distance social and economic networks, connecting the aristocracy of the county with the world beyond.[32] By the thirteenth century the fair towns had become the center of a vast network of international trade and the pound *provinois* was one of the strongest and most widely used currencies in Europe.

Count Henry administered the fairs as a unity, initiating a regular cycle of six fairs that created a virtually continuous market within the county. Thus merchants and creditors, local purveyors, producers and comital officials traveled constantly from town to town, circulating throughout the county. The

---

30. Chrétien de Troyes and Bertrand of Bar-sur-Aube both held comital prebends. See Putter, "Knights and Clerics," 253–55; John Benton, "The Court of Champagne as a Literary Center," *Speculum* 36 (1961): 551–91, reprinted in his *Culture, Power and Personality in Medieval France,* ed. Thomas N. Bisson (London, 1991), 3–43; and Quentin Griffiths, "Royal Counselors and Trouvères in the Houses of Nesle and Soissons," *Medieval Prosopography* 18 (1997): 123–37.

31. Chapin, *Les villes de foires,* 37–52.

32. Ibid., 105–34; and the articles reprinted in Robert-Henri Bautier, *Sur l'histoire économique de la France médiévale: La route, le fleuve, la foire,* ed. Olivier Guyotjeannin (London, 1991). See also R. D. Face, "Techniques of Business in the Trade between the Fairs of Champagne and the South of Europe in the Twelfth and Thirteenth Centuries," *Economic History Review* 10 (1958): 427–38; idem, "The *Vectuarii* in the Overland Commerce between Champagne and Southern Europe," *Economic History Review* 12 (1959): 239–46; and Rosalind Kent Berlow, "The Development of Business Techniques at the Fairs of Champagne from the End of the Twelfth Century to the Middle of the Thirteenth Century," *Studies in Medieval and Renaissance History* 8 (1971): 3–31.

effect was to foster an entire economic region, not a single urban center like Paris or Arras. The Champagne fairs functioned as a zone of commerce, larger than a city and its hinterland. Moreover, most economic transactions were linked to the fairs' annual cycle. Debts and payments were carried from one fair to the next or paid out incrementally over a series of fairs. A debt contracted at the May Fair in Provins could be repaid in installments at the following fairs, half at the St.-Jean fair in Troyes the following August and half again at the St.-Rémy fair in November. Fief-rents and tolls were likewise paid out in similar biannual or quarterly installments, as were crusader debts contracted in the East with Italian merchants, which were repaid to their representatives in Champagne.[33] Payments were finalized at the end of each fair, signaled in Bar-sur-Aube, for example, by the singing of the psalm *Oculi Mei* in the parish churches, a sound familiar to all in attendance.[34] The habits of mind that grew within a market economy pervaded the county, blurring the lines between rural and urban, center and margin, for all roadways and routes were part of this larger network of commerce.

The rise of the fairs promoted not only the circulation of goods and currency, but also of people. Italian, German, Flemish, and English merchants began to establish permanent ties in the region, marrying into local families and settling in the towns as members of a wealthy immigrant class. A robust rental market in stalls, houses, and hostels emerged, whose rents became valuable sources of income that were frequently donated to monastic houses to fund anniversary masses or in support of kin who had joined. Larger domestic spaces inside the towns were divided and let out as single rooms, often to widows, merchants, and canons.[35] It was in just such a "hostel," across from St.-Ayoul in Provins, that in the early thirteenth century the scribe Giout copied (and autographed) Chrétien de Troyes's *Yvain*.[36] As foreign trade increased, whole neighborhoods (*vici*) took shape inhabited by

---

33. Mario Chiaudano, "Il libro delle fiere di Champagne della compagnia degli Ugolini mercati senesi nella seconda metà del secolo XIII," in idem, ed. *Studi e documenti per la storia del diritto commerciale italiano nel sec. XIII* (Torino, 1930), 143–208; John F. Benton, "The Accounts of Cepperello da Prato for the Tax on *Nouveaux Acquêts* in the Bailliage of Troyes," reprinted in his *Culture, Power and Personality*, 255–74; and Wesley J. Hoffmann, "The Commerce of the German Alpine Passes during the Early Middle Ages," *Journal of Political Economy* 31 (1923): 826–39, at 835–37.

34. See Chapin, *Les villes de foires*, pièces justificatives, 313–14, no. 17. This was Psalm 122. See also Jacques Le Goff, "Merchant's Time and Church's Time in the Middle Ages," reprinted in his *Time, Work, and Culture in the Middle Ages,* trans. Arthur Goldhammer (Chicago, 1990), 29–42.

35. Chapin, *Les villes de foires,* 105–34.

36. "Cil qui l'escrit Guioz a nom / devant Nostre Dame del Val / est ses ostex tot a estal." Chrétien de Troyes, *Les romans de Chrétien de Troyes: IV Le Chevalier au Lion (Yvain),* edited from the copy of Guiot (BNF fr. 794), ed. Mario Roques (Paris, 1982), 207.

Germans, Flemings, and Parisians, providing a cosmopolitan composition to once-provincial capitals such as Troyes and Provins.

Concomitant with foreign immigration was the movement of newly freed serfs into the fair towns, and more often into the new towns (*villeneuves*) of Champagne.[37] From the middle decades of the twelfth century new towns were created throughout the county through detailed agreements (*pariages*) regularly contracted between secular lords and monastic houses looking to profit from the new settlement.[38] Both parties would agree upon a parcel of land or a nascent village and designate a number of serfs who would be granted franchise in return for a fixed monetary payment. Franchises, or freedom from the burdens of customary payments that were indicative of servile status, were offered to future inhabitants as an incentive for relocation and in return for the toil and moil of land clearance and building.[39] The lordly parties retained rights to and revenues from justice, banal ovens, mills, and presses as well as taxes and tolls, which could later be alienated as fiefs or gifts. New towns proliferated during the thirteenth century and were one of the main factors contributing to demographic growth and the rise of a free and mobile labor force, which would later immigrate to larger towns and cities like Troyes, Provins, Sens, Reims, and Paris.[40]

The movement of people and goods generated revenue as well. Immense profits accrued from changing money, from the tolls assessed at town gates, and from taxes collected on goods bought and sold at the fairs. Revenue from tolls on specific goods marketed at specific fairs was carefully calculated and became a common source of income for funding new fief-rents, prebends, and pious gifts and alms. It is not surprising that in this social world—so like that of northern Italy and the southern Low Countries—the ideals of the *vita apostolica* took hold at the turn of the thirteenth century. The poverty movement and the women's religious movement were a powerful critique of the norms of behavior linked to profit making and social ambition that proliferated in these regions. It is also no surprise that the women who first converted to a penitential life and joined the communities that would become

---

37. See Henri Sée, "Étude sur les classes serviles en Champagne du XIe au XIVe siècle," *Revue Historique* 56 (1894): 225–52 and 57 (1895): 1–21; and Jordan, *Servitude to Freedom*.

38. See the discussion in Evergates, *Feudal Society*, 41–47.

39. On the role of *villeneuves* in the lives of freed and unfree tenants, see Chapin, *Les villes de foires*, 9–10; and Jordan, *Servitude to Freedom*, 40–41.

40. See Jordan, *Servitude to Freedom*, 37–58. By the end of the thirteenth century, immigration contributed to the intensifying economic pressures. See Sharon Farmer, *Surviving Poverty in Medieval Paris: Gender, Ideology, and the Daily Lives of the Poor* (Ithaca, 2002), 11–38; and Esther Cohen, "Patterns of Crime in Fourteenth-Century Paris," *French Historical Studies* 11 (1980): 307–27.

Cistercian convents came from those classes most closely immersed in the urban world of Champagne's bustling fair towns.

The Social Networks of Cistercian Nuns

Marriages, economic agreements, service to the count, bureaucratic ties, and monastic patronage linked the new social groups of Champagne with one another and with the older baronial and knightly families of the county. The fortunes of Stephen of Champguyon and his family are emblematic of the social changes under way during the thirteenth century and offer a useful case study. Stephen had given his suburban farmhouse outside of Troyes to the religious women at Chichéry, which later became the Cistercian nunnery of Notre-Dame-des-Prés. He was a citizen of Troyes, probably one of many who gained his freedom in the franchise of 1230.[41] He was part of the rising burgher-artisan class, which would form the heart of the patrician elite who would effectively run Troyes in the count's absence. In addition to his grange in Chichéry, he also had a house in Troyes near the parish church of St.-Jean, next to the goldsmiths, and it is possible that Stephen practiced this lucrative trade himself.[42] This would go some way toward explaining the lands and rights he had amassed outside the town in the parishes of St.-Savine and St.-André.[43] When he gave his grange to the women of Notre-Dame-des-Prés he was a man of mature years, for several of his children were grown and married with children of their own. By 1248 he and his wife, Andrea, had died, and patronage of the new community of nuns was taken up by the next generation.[44]

While Stephen did quite well for himself, his children benefited even more profoundly from the intricate process of upward mobility open to a family such as the Champguyons. He and his wife had two sons and three daughters. His eldest son, John of Champguyon, became a prominent businessman with good connections and was known as John "le Grand." He also possessed a house in Troyes on the rue des Lorgnes as well as smaller

---

41. AD Aube, 23 H 5, fol. 2r (February 1236); AD Aube, 23 H 268 (4 May 1239); and Chapin, *Les villes de foires,* 121n71.

42. Chapin, *Les villes de foires,* 82–83n125.

43. In 1239 Stephen and his wife, Andrea, gave all their arable land, fields, vines, houses, all other possessions, and his part of the wood called Beton in the two parishes to the nuns of Notre-Dame-des-Prés: AD Aube, 23 H 268 (4 May 1239). In 1248 their daughter Alice and her husband, Peter, disputed the rights to one-quarter of these possessions, presumably what would have been Alice's inheritance had they not been given to the nuns: AD Aube, 23 H 268 (September 1248).

44. AD Aube, 23 H 268 (September 1248).

properties, ovens, and rents scattered throughout the town and its suburbs.[45] In 1236 John and his wife, Félise, donated half of an oven and several vineyards to the nuns of Notre-Dame-des-Prés.[46] Stephen's other son, Guy, had taken up a life in the church and become a canon at St.-Étienne in Troyes. Guy's vocation speaks to the prestige, reputation, and social connections the Champguyons enjoyed, for his appointment at St.-Étienne implies a closeness to the count and his chancery.[47]

Stephen's daughters all married well, forging ties that were indicative of the family's rise. Alice, the eldest, married a citizen and burgher of Troyes, Peter le "Concierge" and probably traveled in the same circles as her brother John "le Grand."[48] By contrast, Isabelle, Stephen's second daughter, married into the lower aristocracy, wedding the knight Luc de Waudes, the brother of William, knight and lord of Lézinnes. Luc and William were grandsons of Geoffrey of Villehardouin, the marshal of Champagne (1185–1204), who chronicled the Fourth Crusade of 1204 and settled in the Peloponnese as a lord of the Frankish Morea. William of Lézinnes was part of the Villehardouin line that remained in Champagne. Like his father and grandfather, he served as marshal of the county from 1231 to 1246. In short, Isabelle married into a cadet line of the Villehardouin family.[49] As a couple they supported the nuns of Notre-Dame-des-Prés and gave them rights and lands in St.-Savine just beyond the gate of Troyes. In 1246, however, after Isabelle was widowed, she and her two daughters, Katherine and Agnes, gave all of their possessions in dower and inheritance to the nuns and joined the community themselves.[50] Finally, Stephen's third daughter, Marguerite, married Bernard de Montcuq, a merchant and financier from Cahor in Gascony, who had come to Troyes in the first years of the thirteenth century.[51] Bernard was a close associate of the count, and in 1222 Thibaut IV granted him and his wife full franchise status in Troyes in return for an annual payment

---

45. Chapin, *Les villes de foires,* 92n162, and 121.

46. "medietatem furni vinearum siti ultra pontem ecclesie Beate Marie Magdalene cum quadam platea juxta predictum furnum, que durat usque ad fossata ville." AD Aube, 23 H 334 (June 1236). John had acquired this land in 1226 from Milo de Bar, a canon in the cathedral of Troyes: AD Aube, 23 H 334 (May 1226).

47. AD Aube, G 3101 (July 1251).

48. AD Aube, 23 H 268 (September 1248).

49. William, lord of Lézinnes, renounced all rights he had over any of the lands of his brother Luc. In return the nuns agreed to celebrate an anniversary mass for him as was agreed by the General Chapter: AD Aube, 23 H 300 (1240). For the Villehardouin and Lézinnes, see Evergates, *Aristocracy,* 135, 187, and 263.

50. AD Aube, 23 H 268 (November 1246).

51. Chapin, *Les villes de foires,* 120–22.

of 40 s.[52] Bernard acquired extensive properties inside Troyes and beyond the city walls. In 1230 he served as the count's chamberlain, and in 1236, 1237, and 1239 he was the mayor of Troyes.[53] When the town's franchises were revoked in 1241, Bernard de Montcuq and his brother-in-law John "le Grand" of Champguyon were two of the six leading citizens charged with reorganizing the finances of the town to repay its crushing debts.[54] He may have been perceived as particularly devout or well connected in matters of religion and spirituality, for in 1259 Bernard served as Thibaut V's procurer when the count founded a lavish house for the Franciscan friars in Troyes.[55] The wealth and influence of this couple were unmatched among townsmen in the capital, and in the decades after Stephen's death Marguerite and Bernard de Montcuq would have been a powerful connection for the nuns of Notre-Dame-des-Prés.[56]

Why Stephen and his family took such a keen interest in the religious women they sheltered in the grange at Chichéry is hard to know. Perhaps one or more of those women were relatives of Stephen or his wife, Andrea. One daughter and two granddaughters eventually joined the community. It may be that Stephen was a particularly devout and wealthy townsman, or a man taken to contemplating his position and its meaning for his place in the hereafter. The reputation and social position of his children define the networks of patronage that cut across the social world of Champagne, connecting local townsmen with the count and his canons, with local knightly families and crusaders, and with influential yet pious immigrants. Although the Champguyon were of higher social standing than many in the towns, their connections and patronage were indicative of new social bonds forming throughout Champagne, and in many ways they are representative of the kinds of families that lay behind the Cistercian convents taking shape throughout the county.

The convents, like the families that patronized them, were involved in overlapping relationships that embedded them in the pious needs and ambitions of the lesser nobility, the bourgeoisie, canons, and women. These new social groups dominate the convents' surviving documents. Occasionally a

---

52. Ibid., 121n72. Also noted by Arbois de Jubainville, *Histoire des ducs et des comtes de Champagne*, catalogue, n. 1520.
53. Chapin, *Les villes de foires*, 121–22. In his capacity as mayor, Bernard oversaw Bartholomew de Villa Basot's sale of three arpents of arable land and fields to the nuns in 1237: AD Aube, 23 H 153 (December 1237).
54. See *Layettes*, 2:447–48, no. 2910; and Chapin, *Les villes de foires*, 168–69.
55. Chapin, *Les villes de foires*, 94n171, 121.
56. As a testament to their wealth, in 1255 the couple sold the Templars 2,500 arpents of woods in the forest of the Der. See *Layettes*, 3:256–57, no. 4193.

major baronial lord can be found donating land or rents. By the second half of the thirteenth century the count, and later the king of France, would give money in alms or oversee the sale of a fief to the nuns. Yet for the most part the Cistercian convents were overwhelmingly bourgeois and lesser aristocratic foundations. Support for the loosely defined groups of *mulieres religiosae* and *Filles-Dieu* came initially from the new social groups of the county. Moreover, founding and sustaining female communities was different and often entirely separate from incorporating these houses as formal monastic institutions within the Cistercian order, as we shall see in chapter 3. What is clear is that these houses grew from urban social roots, from the financial resources and spiritual anxieties of men and women deeply entrenched in the networks and needs of the urban economy. Likewise, the women who joined these convents came from the same social world and critiqued its values and mitigated its ill effects by embracing the ascetic life.

Members of the urban bourgeoisie—typically men identified as citizens or burghers practicing a particular profession—with their wives were the most consistent supporters of the new communities of nuns. Donations of houses or smaller plots of land provided a community with a fixed place to take root and expand. In the case of Notre-Dame-des-Prés near Troyes, Stephen of Champguyon's grange outside the urban enceinte provided just such a refuge. In 1236, after the nuns acquired more extensive domains and were officially incorporated into the Cistercian order, Stephen and his wife stood in front of the cathedral of Troyes and in a public act formally bequeathed to the nuns not only the grange of Chichéry and all that belonged to it, but also "all of their property in the parishes of St.-Savine and St.-André in lands, fields, vines and rents."[57] Such public pronouncements were not unusual by that time. Nearly a decade earlier, in May 1222, Briard, a citizen of Reims and a goldsmith (*aurifaber*), with his wife, Agnes, gave the nuns of Clairmarais eleven perches of land in the fields to the northwest of the city on the condition that the nuns move to that location and build a house and church there.[58] While Briard and his wife are never explicitly called founders, their gift provided the initial endowment around which the nuns amassed a patrimony and became established in the landscape. Similarly,

---

57. "locum ipsum in quo abbatia sita est cum toto proprisio suo, qui locus antiquitus Chicherius dicebatur et totam hereditatem suam quam ipsi habebant in parrochia Sancte Savine et in parrochia Sancte Andree, in terris, pratis, vineis et in censivis et in omnibus aliis modis et in commodis." AD Aube, 25 H 5, fol. 2r (February 1236). This charter was officiated by the abbots of Larrivour and Boulancourt and a canon of the cathedral of St.-Pierre of Troyes. Note that he gave allodial lands (*hereditatem*), not fiefs.

58. AD Aube, 3 H 3766 (May 1222); and *GC* 9:58, instr. 61.

when the Cistercian nuns of Le Sauvoir outside of Laon transferred from their original residence at Bricom, it was a citizen of Laon, one Soibert, who bequeathed to the women his suburban property at La Ramée just below the city.[59]

Gifts from bourgeois donors not only provided for the foundation of such communities, but also formed a significant proportion of the endowment that supported the nuns. Couples like Stephen and Andrea of Champguyon and Briard and Agnes of Reims periodically reaffirmed and augmented their donations throughout their lives. At some point before 1261, Briard and Agnes drew up their testaments which stipulated that an additional 50 *s.* in annual rents from houses in Reims as well as an additional lump sum of 100 *l.* should pass to the nuns of Clairmarais to construct a chapel in their church.[60] Heirs often confirmed and perpetuated their parents' donations, occasionally augmenting them with gifts from their inheritance. Stephen's daughters, for example, gave the nuns of Notre-Dame-des-Prés additional lands near their parents' gifts that they had held as dowries, thus creating a familial tradition of benefaction.[61]

Cistercian nunneries founded outside the walls of urban centers with significant populations of burghers and artisans sustained ties with these groups. Nearly half of the surviving records for Notre-Dame-des-Prés outside of Troyes, Clairmarais near Reims, Le Sauvoir outside of Laon, and Val-des-Vignes near Bar-sur-Aube record gifts and sales from the bourgeoisie, men and women alike. Many patrons were artisans and tradesmen, like Briard and Stephen, who were both goldsmiths or connected to the trade.[62] Leather workers, like Peter and his wife, Marguerite, who contracted an annuity in 1245 with the nuns of Notre-Dame-des-Prés on two houses that they possessed in the tannery of Troyes, made good livings and forged sustaining ties

---

59. Anselme Dimier, "L'Abbaye du Sauvoir-sous-Laon," *MSM* 86 (1971): 121–31, at 122.

60. "Quinquaginta solidos parisis [annuatis] super census pro quadraginta et sex libris parisis que restabant solvende de summa centum librarum dicte ecclesia legatam adictis Briardo et Agnete quondam civis uxore ad emendos redditis pro quadam capellania in dicta ecclesia de Claro Marisco construenda." AD Aube, 3 H 3769 (May 1261). Matthew of Marly and his wife, Mabilie, also funded the construction of a familial chapel at Port-Royal: *Cartulaire de l'Abbaye de Porrois,* 2 vols., ed. A. de Dion (Paris, 1903), 1:79–80, no. 61.

61. "dicta Ysabellis ratione dotis et dicte ejus filie ratione juris hereditarii." AD Aube, 23 H 268 (November 1246). Two years later, following a dispute, Stephen's daughter Alice agreed to give up her claims to the same lands which she held "per alium ratione hereditatis, propinquitatis, successionis, dotalicii sive quacumque alia ratione"; AD Aube, 23 H 268 (September 1248).

62. One of the major bourgeois patrons to Port-Royal was also a goldsmith, John of Lagny, "aurifaber, burgensis Parisiensis." See *Cartularie de l'Abbaye de Porrois,* 1:299–303, nos. 305–6.

with the convents.⁶³ Several years later Peter's son, a cleric named Simon, gave all the rights he had over properties in the town to the nuns.⁶⁴ Other professions of lesser status appear among the nuns' patrons as well. In 1268 Renard of Bar, a baker, gave the nuns of Val-des-Vignes a vineyard near Bar along with all of his moveable goods so that his sister and his daughter could become nuns there. In the same transaction he created a lifetime annuity with the nuns so that he too could join the community and live as a *conversus* at the nunnery.⁶⁵

Men and women identified simply as citizens or burghers of a specific town or city commonly contracted gifts and sales with the nuns as well. Transactions involving citizens of Reims dominate the first forty years of Clairmarais's history. In April 1234, Henry, the son of Richard Le Jardiner, and his wife, Hevida, citizens (*cives*) of Reims, sold several houses to Droard Le Berbisi and his wife, Sibille, also citizens, which they eventually donated to the nuns.⁶⁶ Likewise, in the same year, Bertran Berrangier, a butcher, and his wife, Amelie, both citizens of Reims, sold an annual rent of 40 *s*. on a house in the city to the nuns for 12 *l*.⁶⁷ By the end of the thirteenth century Clairmarais possessed so many urban residences and rents that the community drew up a rental list (*censive*) enumerating over seventy separate urban properties.⁶⁸ Even in the smaller comital towns, citizens were prominent donors to the nuns. The earliest gifts to Val-des-Vignes outside of Bar-sur-Aube came from Erard de Porta, a prominent townsman, whose family held the mayorship of the town for several generations.⁶⁹

Foreign immigrants who settled in Champagne also gave to the nuns. In 1237 Ralph Anglicus and his wife, Mathilda, gave a house in the neighborhood (*banno*) of St.-Timothy of Reims and two gardens to the nuns of Clairmarais.⁷⁰ It may be that they had come from England and settled there, for in

---

63. AD Aube, 23 H 316 (December 1245). Peter is alternatively called *de Maccereria* (of the tannery) or *cordubanarius* (one who works with leather in the Cordoban style).

64. AD Aube, 23 H 75 (*vidimus* dated March 1257).

65. AD Aube, 3 H 4074 (September 1268).

66. AD Aube, 3 H 3785 (April 1234).

67. AD Aube, 3 H 3785 (March 1234). This may have been a portion of Amelie's dower as a clause specified that the rent could not be reclaimed by reason of dower or inheritance. Their children and spouses also agreed to the sale.

68. AD Aube, 3 H 3782 (undated, but probably from the late thirteenth century). Pierre Desportes, *Reims and les rémois aux XIIIe et XIVe siècles* (Paris, 1979), 305, underestimates the number of urban holdings controlled by Clairmarais. He may have only looked at the cartulary, which would not have included a rental list like this.

69. AD Aube, 3 H 4079 (1231).

70. AD Aube, 3 H 3745 (June 1225) details their purchase of the house; (July 1237) details the first gift in alms to the nuns, which was reconfirmed in 1240. Concerning similar gifts from

the three charters that bear their names Ralph is dubbed *Anglicus* and the two are never identified as citizens of Reims.[71] Likewise, in 1297, Adam Bourdon and his wife, Agnes, "citizens of Paris," gave the house they purchased in the drapery of Troyes to the nuns of Notre-Dame-des-Prés to establish an anniversary mass for themselves after their deaths.[72] It is not a stretch to imagine that Adam and Agnes were cloth merchants who had invested in real estate in Troyes for use perhaps during the fairs. They would have made contacts in the town and could have known the families of the nuns at Notre-Dame-des-Prés. Bourgeois benefaction of this sort was not unique to Champagne. In Paris, burghers, citizens, and clerics associated with the university stand out as early patrons of the Cistercian nuns of St.-Antoine-des-Champs outside of Paris.[73] The community of Port-Royal, which lay to the west of the royal capital, also benefited from the patronage of the burgher and merchant class of the city.[74] Shortly after Louis IX endowed the béguinage of Paris, its first and most consistent supporters were burghers, *cives*, and canons.[75] Even the nunnery of L'Abbaye-aux-Bois, founded on a relatively isolated estate belonging to Jean I of Nesle in the woods near Compiègne, received donations from local burghers (*burgenses*) connected to the nearby towns of Roye, Nesle, Péronne, and St.-Quentin.[76]

Like their aristocratic counterparts, bourgeois donors gave and sold suburban or rural allodial lands, that is, lands free of obligation and restriction, often gardens and fields beyond the city walls. More ubiquitous, however, were gifts of urban assets, such as market stalls, rented rooms, houses, and the income such spaces generated, as well as rents and tolls. Donors often appointed the latter types of gifts and sales themselves, whereas the accu-

---

foreigners, see Constance Berman, "Dowries, Private Income, and Anniversary Masses: The Nuns of Saint-Antoine-des-Champs (Paris)," *Proceedings of the Western Society for French History* 20 (1993): 3–12, at 6–7.

71. The area around the parish of St.-Timothy, where the nuns of Clairmarais held several properties, lay in a part of the city that was less developed, where land values were considerably lower. See Desportes, *Reims et les rémois,* 457–85.

72. AD Aube, 23 H 313 (March 1297).

73. Constance Berman, "Cistercian Nuns and the Development of the Order: The Abbey at Saint-Antoine-des-Champs Outside Paris," in *The Joy of Learning and the Love of God: Studies in Honor of Jean Leclercq,* ed. E. Rozanne Elder (Kalamazoo, MI, 1995), 121–56, at 124 and passim; and idem, "Dowries, Private Income and Anniversary Masses," 3–12.

74. In December 1220, for example, Pétronille of Auvergne gave the nuns an annual rent of 10 *s.* from her shop on the Grand-Pont in Paris: *Cartulaire de l'Abbaye de Porrois,* 1:71, no. 51.

75. Tanya Stabler Miller, "Now She Is Martha, Now She Is Mary: Beguine Communities in Medieval Paris (1250–1470)," (Ph.D. dissertation, University of California at Santa Barbara, 2007), 68–114.

76. Brigitte Pipon, *Le chartrier de l'Abbaye-aux-Bois (1202–1341): Étude et édition* (Paris, 1996), 54–56, and nos. 91, 105, 164, 301.

mulation of the former—landed property—betrays a convent's institutional interests in deliberately amassing suburban holdings or consolidating fields near their houses.[77] Townsmen and women frequently contracted leases and annuities from urban properties, which produced rents and were well suited to this practice. They remained in the house, receiving payment during their lifetime, and upon their deaths the property would revert to the nuns.[78] The nuns in turn rented the urban real estate they acquired to generations of burghers and merchants, creating a relatively stable but profitable investment.

By the thirteenth century, bourgeois benefaction had become an important part of the income and domains of male and female monastic communities alike, Cistercian or otherwise. The support of burghers, canons, and middle-class men and women was critical for the growth of friars as well as lay confraternities. As with the friars and houses of canons, bourgeois patronage tied the Cistercian nunneries to the fortunes of the profit economy and injected the dynamics of trade and markets into the economic lives of the nuns. Yet, unlike male and female monasteries founded before the thirteenth century, the new Cistercian communities were not—with rare exceptions—endowed with vast rural estates that produced goods for market or consumption. Indeed, there is no evidence that female Cistercian communities in Champagne produced goods for sale in the many available markets, like monks of their order. Rather, their livelihood was tied to the profits of trade, the collection of urban tolls, and to the rental markets of the region. As the fairs flourished, money came in to support the nuns and their charitable works. Yet when the fairs began to decline and rental values stagnated at the close of the thirteenth century, the nuns suffered the effects acutely.

The networks of sociability and kin that grew up in urban centers like Troyes and Provins—rarely if ever recorded in chronicles or charters—often remain opaque. Yet family connections were certainly crucial to social mobility, as was the cultivation of reputation, contacts, civic service, and preferment. The Champguyon family was not unusual in having one son in clerical orders and a daughter who professed later in life. Secular canons and clerics were often related to townsmen and were frequently avid patrons of

---

77. This was a common Cistercian economic practice. See Mireille Mousnier, *L'Abbaye cistercienne de Grandselve et sa place dans l'économie et la société méridionales (XIIe–XIVe siècles)* (Toulouse, 2006); and Constance Berman, "Abbeys for Cistercian Nuns in the Ecclesiastical Province of Sens: Foundation, Endowment and Economic Activities of the Earlier Foundations," *Revue Mabillon* 69 (1997): 83–113, at 93–110.

78. On annuities, see William Chester Jordan, *Women and Credit in Pre-Industrial and Developing Societies* (Philadelphia, 1993); Robert Génestal, *Rôle des monastères comme établissements de crédit étudié en Normandie du XIe à la fin du XIIIe siècle* (Paris, 1901); and chap. 6, 191–92.

the new communities of religious women, in several instances taking a prominent role in the creation of new Cistercian convents. In 1235, or perhaps earlier, Peter Quercus, a canon, and Fursy Botte, a burgher of Péronne, joined together to support a group of religious women giving them an estate known as Biache, along with all of the buildings and rights there, to be used for the construction of a proper monastery.[79] This would become the nunnery of La Biache-lès-Péronne in the diocese of Noyon to the west of the county. While such men did not have the resources of the landed aristocracy, their simple gifts of a house or several arpents of land or tithes were often enough to initiate the process of foundation, which could later attract more powerful and wealthy donors. Moreover, the piety of secular canons and clerics, living in the urban world of Champagne, was often closely aligned with that of the women's religious movement, attuned to the significance of caregiving, private prayer and contemplation, and the needs of the poor.

Supporting religious women may have been yet another step in a life of conversion for men who had served as canons and clerics. In 1211 Guy de la Barre, a canon at the chapel of St.-Thibaut in the comital castle of Château-Thierry, donated to God his house and grange and all that pertained to it between the castle and the leper house of Château-Thierry to serve as a *domus-Dei* for the poor. Because the house of La Barre fell within the comital domain, Countess Blanche oversaw Guy's gift, renounced her rights over the house, and facilitated a similar acquittal from all the men and women who had rights or tithes in the donated properties. The countess's role effectively rendered Guy's lands allodial property to be converted freely into a religious house.[80] In 1235, after La Barre had served as a hospital for the poor for twenty-four years, Thibaut IV gave it to Cécile d'Arcy, who, with the community of women already in residence, converted it into the Cistercian nunnery of La Barre, which continued to maintain the original *domus-Dei*.[81]

In some cases, local canons worked in concert with reform-minded bishops to found new Cistercian convents. So it was in 1219 when Gérard Baleine, a canon of Notre-Dame-de-la-Cité in Auxerre, gave a place called Celle near the city, along with accompanying lands, tithes, a vineyard, and revenues, to establish a house of Cistercian nuns, which took the name Les Isles. Gérard

---

79. *GC* 9:1138; and *GC* 10:382, instr. 24 (founded 1235).
80. C. Nusse, "Charte de fondation d'un Hôtel-Dieu à Barre," *Annales de la Société historique et archéologique de Château-Thierry* 48 (1874): 191–92. On La Barre, see Alexandre-Eusèbe Poquet, "L'Abbaye de Barre et son recueil des chartes," *Annales de la Société historique et archéologique de Château-Thierry* 58 (1884): 117–77, this and related donations at 132–37; and *GC* 9:130, instr. 48.
81. Poquet, "L'Abbaye de Barre," 138, 141–42.

did so with the support of Guillaume of Seignelay, bishop of Auxerre, who gave Gérard a rent of 20 *l.* from a house in the market of Auxerre, which would revert to the nuns after the canon's death.[82] It was a full decade later that the nunnery would come to the attention of Mathilda of Courtenay, countess of Auxerre, and her husband, Guy, who endowed the nuns with lands farther up the river Yonne in a place more suitable for a monastic enclosure.[83] Similarly in 1236, John Bouvier, a cleric in Provins, had the support of Gautier Cornut, archbishop of Sens, when he gave all that he had inherited in land, vineyards, gardens, taxes, and tithes to found the Cistercian nunnery of Mont-Notre-Dame-lès-Provins, just beyond the town walls.[84]

Clerics and canons continued to give or sell to Cistercian nuns properties and incomes they had access to within the towns or along its suburban fringe, linking the nunneries to the places where they themselves professed and held prebends. The bonds between clerics and nuns would persist over generations, strengthened by the sale of urban houses, rents, and tolls, as well as small gardens and vines or sums of money bequeathed upon a canon's death. In 1256, for example, long after Val-des-Vignes had become a well-established Cistercian convent outside Bar-sur-Aube, Radulfo de Priugeio, a canon of St.-Maclou, gave in alms to the nuns half a piece of arable land just outside the nunnery's gate, which had belonged to his mother, Margaret de Pont, and passed to him after her death.[85] Canons appear as patrons even among relatively isolated nunneries like Argensolles, which was several kilometers outside of Épernay. In 1243, Master Peter of Épernay, a local canon, with the consent of his sister and her husband, sold the nuns several houses and rents in the town for 300 *l.*[86] In other instances clerics and priests were the recipients of lifetime leases on urban houses in the nuns' possession.[87] The use of these houses may simply signal the creation of an annuity on the part of the clerics, but such transactions may also have functioned as a form of payment

---

82. AD Yonne, H 1749 (1220); and *GC* 12:480–82. See also René Courtet, "Histoire de l'abbaye des îles, anciennement de Celles," *Bulletin de la Société des sciences historiques et naturelles de l'Yonne* 120 (1988): 47–69; and Marie-Élisabeth Henneau, "Les Isles," in *Les cisterciens dans l'Yonne,* ed. Terryl N. Kinder (Pontigny, 1999), 163–71.

83. AD Yonne, H 1749 (1229); and Henneau, "Les Isles."

84. *GC* 12:129 and instr. 92, col. 70.

85. AD Aube, 3 H 4037 (July 1256). The de Porta family, founders of Val-des-Vignes in Bar-sur-Aube, supplied a steady stream of sons to St.-Maclou, who in turn gave to the nuns from their familial properties or consented to gifts and sales made by family members. See AD Aube, 3 H 4077 (May 1250), 3 H 4079 (September 1256).

86. AD Marne, 70 H 5 (August 1243) and 70 H 6 (August 1243).

87. See AD Aube, 23 H 301 (December 1249); AD Aube, 3 H 4071 (January 1263); and AD Marne, 70 H 10 (October 1234).

in return for spiritual care (*cura monialium*) performed for the nuns.[88] For although Cistercian in regulation, in many cases, even after nunneries were incorporated into the order, secular canons still heard the confessions and officiated at mass for these female communities.[89]

The growth of the fair towns not only promoted certain new classes—new men and women of the burgher elite and their kin in positions as secular canons, clerics, and bureaucrats—it also brought lesser knights, squires, and household men into this social world. These were families who had received townhouses and rents from the counts as fiefs, not great castles, and who had to borrow money or sell property to fund their crusading exploits. Like Luc de Waudes, they married the local bourgeoisie and integrated into the patrician class of the burgeoning towns. It is not surprising then that the growing ranks of the lesser aristocracy, the *armigeri* and *damoiselles,* were also early supporters of religious women. In later decades, these same individuals, townsmen, and lesser knights would share a common culture of devotion, reading the same treatises, commissioning similar personal Psalters, and endowing private family chapels. In the 1230s these men and women also founded small communities of religious women that would in time be incorporated into the Cistercian order. They did so not in the cities or suburbs, as canons and burghers had, but rather within their lesser estates and local houses in the smaller towns along the roadways of the county. Yet to imagine these nunneries as parallels to the isolated rural Cistercian monasteries founded in the early twelfth century, which saw Cistercian monks creating houses in the "deserts" of Burgundy and Champagne, would be wrong. Rather, these were small nunneries that grew out of castle chapels and aristocratic granges, easily accessible from the roads connecting the fairs and the major episcopal centers, in locales that saw considerable traffic.[90] And such concourse was necessary, for many of these communities subsisted in part from alms. Moreover, many of these nunneries, much like La Barre in Château-Thierry, administered hospices and *domus-Dei* that brought religious women in constant contact with the traveling poor, the sick, and pilgrims.

---

88. For example, Garsius, provost of St.-Quiriace in Provins, received a mill as a lifetime possession from the nuns of Argensolles for his counsel and help in acquiring the property. See AD Marne, 70 H 10 (October 1234). On payments to secular canons, see Penelope D. Johnson, *Equal in Monastic Profession: Religious Women in Medieval France* (Chicago, 1991), 180–91.

89. See chap. 3, 95–96, 113–14.

90. The majority of such houses were founded along the main trade route that connected Troyes with Soissons, and then farther north to Flanders, as well as Paris with Reims. See Desportes, *Reims et les rémois,* 104–16.

One of the challenges presented by these foundations is that in many cases the role of lordly patrons often obscures the earlier dynamics of foundation that involved men and women of lower status. For example, lesser knights and *armigeri* needed to receive permission from their lords before alienating property that was once part of a fief. Barons then appear in the records "giving" property to their knights, when such grants merely constituted consent for the pious undertaking. Thus, while many new Cistercian convents in Champagne did have lordly patrons or acquired them before incorporation into the order, a significant number of these houses drew initial support from aristocratic families of lesser means who shared the devotional proclivities of the bourgeoisie.

Networks of knightly and familial piety are discernable behind the foundations of several nunneries established between 1223 and 1242 in the heart of the county between the Marne and Aube rivers. In 1223, shortly after Countess Blanche of Navarre founded the convent of Argensolles, two brothers, Barthélemy and Colard, lords of Bergères and fief-holders of the counts, offered the earliest donations to the nunnery of La Grâce Notre-Dame between Montmirail and Sézanne.[91] While La Grâce went on to attract the interest and support of local lords, such as Matthew of Montmirail, Jean of Chartres, Engerrand of Coucy, and Agnes of Noyers, the impetus behind its foundation lay with families of lesser status. The lords of Bergères were part of a group of knights in the radius of Montmirail who expressed their piety through the support of Cistercian convents.[92] The patronage of the knight Philip of Mécringes offers the clearest example of this type of foundation. While Philip held the title of *miles* in his charters, he never attained a castle lordship of significance to warrant any greater title. He appears in the feudal registers holdings fiefs from the lords of Montmirail but is not listed as a liege vassal of the count. Philip married Agathe of Bergères, the mother of the lords who founded La Grâce.[93] In 1229 Philip founded the nunnery of La Piété near Ramerupt, providing for the group of *Filles-Dieu* who had been living there connected to the *domus-Dei*.[94] Three years later, in 1232 he founded the nunnery of L'Amour-Dieu in the *domus-Dei* of Troissy, which his lord and friend Hugh V of Châtillon had given to him.[95] Several years later, in 1239, Philip and his wife donated lands to the nuns of La Barre

---

91. *GC* 12: 506, 534; and M. R. Mathieu, *Montmirail en Brie: Sa seigneurie et son canton* (Paris, 1975), 88.
92. Mathieu, *Montmirail en Brie*, 88–89; and *VJM*, commentary, paras. 23–58.
93. Mathieu, *Montmirail en Brie*, 89.
94. See chap. 1, n. 69; and chap. 5.
95. *GC* 9: 135–36, instrs. 58–60.

from their holdings at Fontenelle and half a measure of winter wheat from Montmirail.⁹⁶ Philip's gifts were modest and often required the consent of his lord. In this way he supported the nuns but also provided a stimulus to further noble and knightly support. As a knight who held lands in fief from different lords, he was a linchpin in the broader religious networks the nuns cultivated. In several cases greater barons in Champagne did found and patronize Cistercian nunneries, as we shall see in chapter 5, yet even in these cases they often took their cues from lesser knights with reputations for great piety. For these men, like Philip of Mécringes, the devotions of the *Filles-Dieu* were extremely compelling, and they promoted these women throughout the county.

Patrons, whether knights, clerics, or burghers, rarely if every explain what compelled them to give their houses, chapels, or granges over to a group of devout women. Many were moved by piety or divine love, some through charity. Unfulfilled vows, be they personal vows of penance or crusader vows left incomplete, motivated some barons, knights, and their families to found convents. In other cases, female relatives who had themselves taken up a life of religion may have motivated their families to offer them support. Preachers frequently related stories of pious wives and mothers who opened their houses to the traveling poor and sick, and thereby often provided sufficiently persuasive examples of practiced charity to motivate their husbands to support them or follow them into a converted state. Some time between 1227 and 1240 Jacques de Vitry recorded the story of a noblewoman from northern France, married to a knight, whose compassionate care for lepers eventually led her through a miraculous encounter with Christ to convert her husband. It is not surprising that women were another powerful group founding and supporting new Cistercian convents. Scholars have long recognized that women from the upper aristocracy played a significant role in the foundation of Cistercian convents throughout northern France.⁹⁷ Countess Blanche of Navarre's foundation of Argensolles in 1222 was an early example, but it was not exceptional by midcentury. Queen Blanche of Castile founded two nunneries of the order, Maubuisson and Le Lys, and the countesses of Chartres, Auxerre, and Flanders were also influential founders and patrons of Cistercian convents on their domains.⁹⁸

---

96. Poquet, "L'Abbaye de Barre," 139.
97. Blanche of Castile's role has dominated this discussion. See Anselme Dimier, *Saint Louis et Cîteaux* (Paris, 1954). More recently Constance Berman has noted the role of other female lords; see Berman, "Abbeys for Cistercian Nuns," 88–93.
98. See Berman, "Abbeys for Cistercian Nuns"; Terryl Kinder, "Blanche of Castile and the Cistercians: An Architectural Re-evaluation of Maubuisson Abbey," *Cîteaux* 27 (1976): 161–88; Erin

Women of the upper aristocracy often endowed their foundations from lands and revenues that were part of their dower or their inheritance, that is, with properties over which they had exclusive control.[99] In some cases such women were responsible for the final decision to found a female Cistercian house, even if the donation came partly from their husband's lands. In 1202, Geoffrey IV, count of Perche, died before he could fulfill his crusade vow. Before his death he instructed his wife, Mathilda of Brunswick, to create a religious house to redeem what he could not. She founded the Cistercian nunnery of Les Clairets to the west of Chartres.[100] Similarly, in 1220, after her husband's death, Amice, lady of Breteuil, used the endowment they had initially set aside to create a house for Dominican friars to found instead a convent for Cistercian nuns at Villiers. A shift in patronage like this was significant. It took six years for her to receive permission to do so from the archbishop of Sens and the Dominican prior.[101]

Although women of the aristocracy often appeared with their husbands and male relatives in charters recording donations and sales, as the use of personal seals became more common among women they authorized their own donations. In 1241 Isabelle, countess of Chartres and lady of Montmirail, augmented her husband's donations with her own sealed charter gifting rents and lands that she held in dower to the nuns of L'Amour-Dieu.[102] Many of the earliest donors to Notre-Dame-des-Prés outside of Troyes were women with disposable or surplus wealth. In 1233, for example, Maria of St.-Mards gave the nuns half a measure of grain, which she had from two different mills. Her gift in alms was part of a fief that she held from Jacques, viscount of Joigny, who appears prominently in the document consenting to the alienation of the fief.[103] Maria was part of the growing category of women fief-holders

---

Jordan, "Patronage, Prayers and Polders: Assessing Cistercian Foundations in Thirteenth-Century Flanders and Hainaut," *Cîteaux* 53 (2002): 99–125; and idem, *Women, Power, and Religious Patronage in the Middle Ages* (Houndmills, 2006).

99. Maubuisson and Le Lys were founded with Blanche of Castile's dower money and properties. See Berman, "Abbeys for Cistercian Nuns," 92. The large endowment that Countess Blanche of Navarre amassed for Argensolles in 1224 was mostly purchased using her dower revenues. See Evergates, *Documents*, 137–39, no. 104, and concerning dower rights generally, idem, *Aristocracy*, 110–15.

100. GC 8:1324; and instrs. 78–79, cols. 349–50; Vicomte de Souancé, ed., *Abbaye royale de Notre-Dame des Clairets: Histoire et Cartulaire, 1202–1790* (Nogent-le-Rotrou, 1894), esp. 1–2 and nos. 3–5; and Constance Berman, "Fashions in Monastic Patronage: The Popularity of Supporting Cistercian Abbeys for Women in Thirteenth-Century Northern France," *Proceedings of Western Society for French History* 17 (1990): 36–45, at 39.

101. GC 12:242–43; instr. 84, col. 65. Basile Fleureau, "Histoire de l'Abbaye de Villiers au diocèse de Sens," *Annales de la Société historique et archéologique du Gatinais* 11 (1893): 6–11.

102. AD Marne, 69 H 21 (April 1241).

103. AD Aube, 23 H 150 (May 1233).

who appear in the *Rôles des fief* with regularity during the second half of the thirteenth century.[104] A year later in 1234, the knight Hugh of St.-Maurice and his wife gave a quarter of all of their property with additional rents specifically to sustain the nuns so that they could become viable candidates for incorporation into the Cistercian order. Among the rents in kind, paid in measures of oats and rye, was a portion allotted specifically from Margaret's dowry, which required her additional consent.[105] Women who became widows often took over the management of familial properties and estates, particularly if their children were still young. In this capacity they also appear in the nuns' archives following up donations made earlier before their spouses' death or contracting sales with the consent of their children.[106]

Townswomen and women of lesser status were frequent patrons of the convents of Champagne as well. Municipal law required their approval and consent, as wives and mothers, for gifts and sales contracted with their husbands and children. As widows and single women, however, they could act alone in disposing of their possessions, creating annuities, or simply paying rent to the nuns for small garden plots or urban residences.[107] One of the earliest gifts made to the nuns of Clairmarais came in 1221 from Agnes, the widow of Eudes de Marehello and a *conversa* at the hospital for the poor in Reims. Agnes gave the women 2 s. of annual rent from a house in the city.[108] It was a small sum, reflective of her status as a convert and a widow with little means, but significant nonetheless for what it says about her commitments and the spiritual networks that may have connected the hospital and the Cistercian nuns. In 1243 Ameline of Metz-Robert, a widow, gave the nuns of Notre-Dame-des-Prés a field, which she held at Souligny, to fund an anniversary mass for herself and her husband. The scribe recording the

---

104. Similar small fiefs of only a few measures of grain, which women held by dower or inheritance from vassals of the count, fill the pages of the *Rôles des Fiefs* compiled between 1249 and 1252.

105. "legaverunt itaque eidem ecclesie decimam suam de Brion et totam partem suam heredum Bernierrensium et unum modium avene mensuram Autissiodorensem annuatim percipiendum in terris et coustumis de Fossagilet, item duos modios baldi, medietatem siliginis et medietatem avene ad mensuram Roureti, percipiendos in decima et molendino suo de Sancto Audeolo, qui de capite dicte domine Margarete movere dicuntur." AD Aube, 23 H 9 (June 1234). On the importance of gifts from the knightly class for incorporation into the order, see chap. 3, 102–7.

106. In January 1262, Maria, widow of the knight Peter de Maseillio, carried out a bequest to the nuns of Val-des-Vignes initiated by her husband that funded an anniversary mass in his honor: AD Aube, 3 H 4069 (January 1262). For similar transactions, see AD Aube, 3 H 4086 (March 1274) involving Margaret of Chaumont and her children; and AD Aube, 3 H 4111 (July 1274), with Agnes, lady of Jaucourt.

107. See chap. 6, 189–91.

108. AD Aube, 3 H 3784 (March 1221).

transaction took pains to make clear that it was Ameline's property.[109] Likewise, Agnes the widow of Thomas de Mareio, with the consent of her heirs, sold the nuns of Val-des-Vignes an urban back garden (*varranna*) for 20 *l*. As a security for the sale, she assigned to the nuns the third part of a grange that she held as part of her dower.[110] Because of the increased role of women as donors and sellers of property, rights, and rents, it is possible to trace what could be called "female properties" as they moved into the nunneries' control. For example, in many cases the land that men donated often came from lands that were originally part of the dower properties their wives brought with them upon marriage, which they promised not to reclaim "either by right of dower or by any other reason."[111] In other instances, lands passed to nunneries that had moved from mother to daughter, generation to generation, through the female line.[112] Thus even behind some male actors, women were crucial and necessary supporters of the first Cistercian convents and the women's religious movement as it took institutional form.

Seeking Refuge

The intensity of social relationships that developed during periods of rapid economic growth must have been overwhelming at times. Pressures to marry well, to make connections, to find the appropriate use for newly accumulated wealth—wealth without precedent—may have led women and men to seek another way, a life outside this environment. The Cistercian convents, certainly in their initial stages, were a space of refuge for women, separate and distinct from the urban merchant world but nonetheless close enough to share its social ties but without the same struggles. The patronage of women often bridged this gap, for women could go one step farther in their relationship with a convent by giving themselves to the community and living

---

109. "quamdam hoschiam suam quam habebat, ut dicitur, dicta Amelina"; AD Aube, 23 H 302 (January 1243).

110. "Que grangia cum varranna supradicta ab Agnete et Thoma marito suo fuerunt acquiste durante matrimonio inter ipsos." AD Aube, 3 H 4073 (April 1243).

111. See the discussion in Evergates, *Aristocracy*, 110. For examples, see AD Aube, 3 H 3785 (May 1237); AD Aube, 3 H 3786 (January 1242); and AD Aube, 3 H 3765 (September 1244).

112. In April 1257 Milo, the provost of Chacenay, and Maria, his wife, gave the nuns of Val-des-Vignes land that had belonged to Margaret de Pontibus, Maria's mother: "quadam pecia terre arabilis quo fuit quondam defuncte Margarete de Pontibus matris Marie uxoris Milonis supradicti"; AD Aube, 3 H 4037 (April 1257). Similarly, when Jacques de Méry and his wife, Adine, arranged to give 100 *s*. in annual rent to the nuns of Notre-Dame-des-Prés in Troyes, the rent came from a house in the Drapery that belonged to Adine's father, which she had inherited: AD Aube, 23 H 313 (September 1245).

out their lives as *conversae* or professed nuns, while maintaining connections to kin and friends in the world through patronage and prayer. Who these women were is harder to account. Champagne has no extant visitation records, no lists of nuns from the Cistercian convents, no registers naming the professed, such as one can find in fourteenth-century England or in Germany and the Low Countries by the fifteenth century.[113] The names of nuns only surface in charters drawn up when women professed or in charters and testaments that mention specific women in Cistercian houses.

During the thirteenth century most nuns were from the bourgeois class of local urban landowners and artisans and from families of local knights. Alice and Alix, both daughters of townsmen and local landholders, joined the community of Notre-Dame-des-Prés during its first decades.[114] Similarly Isabelle, the daughter of Stephen of Champguyon, and her two daughters may also have professed there as nuns in 1246.[115] In 1275, Renard de Bordis, a canon of St.-Étienne, gave the nuns half a stall in the butcher's hall at the time his niece Katherine professed.[116] Nuns in other Cistercian convents confirm the connection to the burgher class. In 1229, Beatrix, widow of Thomas de St.-Rémy and a townswoman of Reims, donated to the nuns of Clairmarais to provide for her four daughters who professed there as nuns.[117]

Ambitious townsmen could shower great favor on humble convents. In 1263 Notre-Dame-des-Prés received a gift of 100 marks of silver for anniversary masses to commemorate the widow of a local shoemaker.[118] The gift came from Jacques de Panteleon in honor of his mother. Born in Troyes, Jacques grew up in a house above his father's shop in the center of the town. He became a cathedral canon in Troyes, before he was promoted to Laon and continued to rise through the ecclesiastical hierarchy until 1261, when he was elected pope, and took the name Urban IV. After his father's death, Jacques's mother may have professed at Notre-Dame-des-Prés, not long after

---

113. Compare with the kinds of prosopographical registers compiled by Marilyn Oliva, *The Convent and the Community in Late Medieval England: Female Monasteries in the Diocese of Norwich, 1350–1540* (Woodbridge, 1998), appendix 4; and Eva Schlotheuber, *Klostereintritt und Bildung: Die Lebenswelt der Nonnen im späten Mittelalter. Mit einer Edition des 'Konventstagebuche' einer Zisterzienserin von Heilig-Kreuz bei Braunschweig (1484–1507)* (Tübingen, 2004); or the election list for Notre-Dame-aux-Nonnains in Troyes, see Charles Lalore, "Documents sur l'Abbaye de Notre-Dame-aux-Nonnains de Troyes," *MSA* 38 (1874): 5–236, at 116–17, no. 187 (29 and 30 May 1262).
114. AD Aube, 23 H 75 (1243) and (1252).
115. See above, n. 50.
116. AD Aube, 23 H 336 (January 1276).
117. AD Aube, 3 H 3784 (March 1229).
118. Lalore, "Nonnains," no. 191 (9 September 1263).

the community was founded, and it was among the Cistercian nuns that she elected to have her tomb. As a canon in Laon, Jacques had preached to the Cistercian nuns of La Sauvoir, and he clearly esteemed the spirituality of the new Cistercian convents.[119] Despite his meteoric rise to power, he and his mother were still part of the local urban artisan class of Troyes and identified that way. In recognition of his humble origins Pope Urban IV purchased his family house and built a small but opulent foundation of canons, St.-Urbain, in the center of Troyes. Yet his support of Notre-Dame-des-Prés fits within the general pattern of a canon's support for his female kin. Tired of the kind of ambition her son embraced, Jacques's mother may have craved a retirement in the quiet calm of the Cistercian cloister.

Joining the townswomen were the daughters and relatives of knights, like Tecelina and Contessa, who professed at Ormont and lived alongside the daughters of Héluiz, widow of the knight Gerbert of Vassy.[120] There were also notable exceptions to the trend of bourgeois and knightly family professions. In 1233 Beatrix of Dampierre, the daughter of the prominent Dampierre family, professed as a nun at the new convent La Piété.[121] Thirty-six years later, in 1269, Sybille of Brienne, daughter of Erard of Brienne, lord of Ramerupt, joined the same house, which clearly attracted women from the upper aristocracy of the county.[122] Indeed, by 1278, when Marie de Esternay drew up her will, she left 4 *l*. to the four Chappes sisters at La Piété, the Chappes being one of the oldest lordly lineages in the county.[123]

Patterns of profession in the Cistercian nunneries confirm the connections these communities formed with the new social classes of Champagne, yet they also conformed to older models of religious behavior that bound families to monastic houses as a way of securing familial and often specifically female bonds.[124] Many nuns appear to have chosen their vocation as young women, often with one or both parents deceased. In some instances, younger women entered a convent with a sister, as was the case with Tecelina and Contessa, and Sara and her three sisters. Mothers and daughters also professed together. And mothers and sisters often supported their female kin

---

119. See Jacques Foviaux, "Les sermons donnés à Laon, en 1242 par le chanoine Jacques de Troyes, futur Urban IV," *Recherches Augustiniennes* 20 (1985): 203–56.

120. AD Aube, 3 H 9 (1229).

121. GC 12:610.

122. GC 12:610.

123. "Cartulaire de l'Abbaye du Paraclet," in *Collection des principaux cartularies du diocèse de Troyes*, 7 vols., ed. Charles Lalore (Paris, 1875–90), 2:259–60, no. 294; translation in Evergates, *Documents*, 72–73, no. 54. On the Chappes family, see Evergates, *Feudal Society*, 168–69.

124. See Johnson, *Equal in Monastic Profession*, 13–34; and Theodore Evergates, "Aristocratic Women in the County of Champagne," in *Aristocratic Women in Medieval France*, ed. Evergates, 104–9.

when they joined Cistercian communities. In 1230 Emeline de Bazouches gave 40 s. to her daughter Isabelle, a nun at La Cour Notre-Dame.[125] Likewise, Marguerite de Villuis gave a perpetual rent of 40 s. to the same nunnery for her daughter Isabelle, who was also a nun there.[126] And in 1340, when the *damoiselle* Gillette de Galende became a nun at La Cour, her sister Marie assigned her an annual rent of 100 s., "out of love and great affection" (sa très grande affection d'amour).[127] In one very unusual case, a father took the habit of a *conversus* and joined his daughter among the nuns of Val-des-Vignes.[128]

Widows also joined Cistercian convents, taking on a "second career" within the cloister, where they could bring to bear their knowledge and experience in the secular world as landholders or managers of estates or businesses.[129] Certainly some of the first communities to become Cistercian convents also had women of lesser status who were penitents or even repentant prostitutes, women who had lived in the world and who were mothers or single women before taking up a new life of religion. The nunnery of La Cour was formed in part from a group of nuns sent from St.-Antoine-des-Champs in Paris. St.-Antoine began as a community of reformed prostitutes, and some of the women coming to La Cour may have belonged to that social group as well.

The concatenation of social classes in the convents is striking and may have been a goal within the communities, part of a real intent to remake oneself, to shed one's social status and connections and simply live together in religion. Because most of the Cistercian nunneries in Champagne remained small foundations with between twenty and forty sisters, these would have been tightly knit communities defined by familial bonds and well entrenched in local networks. In cases where women of lesser status lived among women of the aristocracy, these relationships need not have been close. Social distinctions (urban/rural; knightly/bourgeois/poor) certainly persisted, but at times—particularly during initial conversions to the religious life—the inversion of such differences was transformative. This inversion and elision lay behind the very ideal of *voluntary* poverty and caring for the sick and leprous. The socially and economically mixed houses of Champagne parallel other communities of women committed to the *vita apostolica*. The groups

---

125. AD Yonne, H 787 (1230).
126. AD Yonne, H 805 (1292).
127. AD Yonne, H 787, fol. 56v (1340). See Andrée Mignardot and Maurice Mignardot, *Histoire d'un village du nord-Sénonais, Michery* (Sens, 1996), 60.
128. AD Aube, 3 H 4074 (September 1268).
129. Evergates, *Aristocracy*, 146–48.

of women surrounding Mary of Oignies, Yvette of Huy, and Clare of Assisi were part of extended families and kin networks that often united women across classes.[130] Later communities of Devout Sisters who became beguines and tertiaries in the Low Countries "took pride in their poor" and in the variety of classes living together in their houses.[131]

Although charters rarely mention religious motivations for profession, saints' lives often take notice of the desire to retreat from the world, particularly from urban society burdened by credit obligations and class-consciousness. By the second and third decades of the thirteenth century it would have been nearly impossible to escape the culture of the Champagne fairs. Even if one did not live in or near a fair town, almost all business transactions—whether changing money, paying debts, collecting fief-rents, or drawing up charters—revolved around the rhythms of the fairs. That this fostered a mental outlook tinged with anxiety about money and profit or, worse, a fear of financial loss or falling into poverty, is not surprising. Escape from the burdens of family and business transactions pervades the conversion narratives of many holy women. Patronage of the nuns may have been seen as a potential remedy for the spiritual contaminants of commercial life. This explains, at least a little, why so many initial patrons hailed from the artisan-burgher class. In two cases the founders of Cistercian nunneries were goldsmiths, men who had made money from luxury goods and who dealt in items of great value and religious prestige.[132] In the face of such changes, the early communities of penitential women that became Cistercian convents offered refuge and even the possibility of redemption.

The women of Champagne sought something similar to what later groups of lay religious would desire, generally speaking: "shelter from the public life of medieval towns, from burgher and marital and merchant expectations, from the dangers that came with being a woman in the world. They sought peace with independence, and they sought it in religion"—initially—"without the hindrance of taking vows, while also thinking of themselves as 'religious'."[133] The social world in which these new nunneries

---

130. Brenda Bolton, "Mary of Oignies: A Friend to the Saints," in *Mary of Oignies: Mother of Salvation,* ed. Anneke B. Mulder-Bakker (Turnhout, 2006), 199–206; and Ingrid Peterson, "Like a Beguine: Clare before 1212," in *Clare of Assisi: Investigations,* ed. Mary Francis Hone (Saint Bonaventure, NY, 1993), 47–57.

131. Van Engen, *Sisters and Brothers,* 127.

132. See n. 57 and n. 58, above. The initial supporters of Mary of Oignies's community were a family of goldsmiths. See Jean-Baptiste Lefèvre, "Le cadre religieux," in *Autour de Hugo d'Oignies,* ed. Robert Didier and Jacques Toussaint (Namur, 2003), 21–36.

133. Van Engen, *Sisters and Brothers,* 125.

took shape was much like that which fostered the friars and Poor Clares, the beguines and penitents. The Cistercian convents were a manifestation of the same spiritual impulses coming from an analogous social milieu. How these bourgeois and knightly female communities should exist in the world and in relation to the church hierarchy and monastic regulations remained a question of growing concern.

CHAPTER 3

Under the Religious Life
Reform and the Cistercian Order

Early in the winter of 1234 officials in the county of Champagne seized a widowed townswoman of Provins named Gila. Suspected of heresy, she was imprisoned in the count's jail and her house and possessions confiscated.[1] Gila was one of many people who the Dominican friar Robert le Bougre accused of heresy in the diocese of Sens between 1234 and 1239. Pope Gregory IX himself had appointed Robert in 1233 to investigate rumors of heresy in northern France and Burgundy.[2] Philip, the chancellor of the University of Paris, an intellectual and inquisitor in his own right, had worked with Robert and had observed that widows and women of ill repute were often the objects of the Dominican's investigations.[3] In 1236, Robert "burned heretics throughout Gaul and a great apostolic council

---

1. See Charles Homer Haskins, "The Inquisition in Northern France," in his *Studies in Medieval Culture* (New York, 1929; reprint, 1965), 193–244, at 215–17; and Michel Veissière, *Une communauté canoniale au Moyen Âge: Saint-Quiriace de Provins (XIe–XIIIe siècles)* (Provins, 1961), 323, no. 114A, and 325, no. 117.

2. On Robert, see Haskins, "Inquisition in Northern France"; Jules Frederichs, *Robert le Bougre, premier inquisiteur général en France* (Ghent, 1892); and Yves Dossat, "L'hérésie en Champagne aux XIIe et XIIIe siècles," reprinted in his *Église et hérésie en France au XIIIe siècle* (London, 1982), 57–63.

3. See David A. Traill, "Philip the Chancellor and the Heresy Inquisition in Northern France, 1235–1236," *Viator* 37 (2006): 241–54, at 248. On male inquisitors and female religious, see Dyan Elliott, *Proving Woman: Female Spirituality and Inquisitional Culture in the Later Middle Ages* (Princeton, 2004).

found many lowly women—*mulierculae*—to be part of the Manichean sect." These heretics, a contemporary chronicler stated, were exposed "not only through their words, but also through their actions."[4] What sorts of words or actions, we may wonder. Shunning wealth and family in favor of a life of piety? Adopting a penitential habit and living as if the body and the self had no consequence in this world? Caring for the leprous and the poor? Begging alms and giving away any sign of personal gain? In short, the very same actions that characterized the life of conversion taken up by *Filles-Dieu* and religious women across Champagne.

In May 1239 Robert's career of questioning culminated in a grand extirpation of heresy. Condemning 180 men and women from the diocese of Sens, the Dominican oversaw a great burning of heretics at the comital stronghold of Mont-Aimé in the center of Champagne. Count Thibaut IV and many of the barons were present, joined by the major prelates of the region, including the archbishop of Reims and bishops of Soissons, Tournai, Arras, Cambrai, Thérouanne, Noyon, Laon, Senlis, Beauvais, Châlons-sur-Marne, Orléans, Troyes, Meaux, Verdun, and Langres, among many other abbots, priors, and deans.[5] The burning at Mont-Aimé coincided with Thibaut IV's preparations to depart on crusade. Such a display, presided over by the count, was an act of purification that declared Champagne free of heresy and therefore a fully— indeed zealously—Christian territory.[6] The ecclesiastical hierarchy was complicit with the papacy's efforts to organize and institutionalize the religious ambitions of the laity.

Yet Gila was initially spared. She agreed—under what pressure or circumstances we cannot know—to tell Robert and the bishops in attendance about "heretics" who were still at large. In the few charters that allude to these

---

4. "Frater Robertus, qui hoc tempore haereticos per Galliam comburebat, cum esset vir magne religionis apparens et non existens, circa tempus magni concilii apostaviti, secutusque mulierculam manichaeam Mediolanum abiit, et factus est de secta illa pessima per annos viginti, ita quod inter eos fuit perfectissimus. Qui de novo resipiscens ad mandatum pape multos hereticos denudavit: per solam loquelam et per solos gestus, quos habent heretici, deprehendebat eos." Aubry of Trois-Fontaines, "Chronicon," ed. P. Scheffer-Boichorst, in *MGH SS,* 23:940.

5. Several chroniclers describe this event: Aubry of Trois-Fontaines, "Chronicon," 944–45; Philip Mouskes, *Chronique rime de Philippe Mouskes,* 2 vols., ed. Frédéric de Reiffenberg (Brussels, 1836–38), 2:608–9; *Extràits de la chronique attribuée à Baudoin d'Avesnes,* in *RHGF,* 21:166; and *Anecdotes historiques, légends et apologues, tirés du recueil inédit d'Étienne de Bourbon, Dominicain du XIIIe siècle,* ed. A. Lecoy de la Marche (Paris, 1877), 150 and 415. The different contemporary accounts agree to a striking degree on the numbers burned at Mont-Aimé: Aubry gives 183, Mousket 187, and Stephen of Bourbon says "about 180" and later "more than 80."

6. See Michael Lower, "The Burning at Mont-Aimé: Thibaut of Champagne's Preparations for the Barons' Crusade of 1239," *Journal of Medieval History* 29 (2003): 95–108; and idem, *The Barons' Crusade: A Call to Arms and Its Consequences* (Philadelphia, 2005), 1–36, 93–115.

events—one in Robert's own hand—and in almost all the chronicle accounts, Gila is called "the abbess."[7] While not a consecrated abbess in the formal sense, among laymen and women in Provins she was a woman of standing and clearly possessed a measure of local authority and religious prestige. Perhaps she was known for her pious dress, ascetic bearing, and devotion to charity; there was something about her that evoked a religious seriousness beyond any formal institutional definition. Gila was, moreover, part of a group of like-minded women condemned for heresy. These other women, Aubry of Trois-Fontaines observed, had cleverly adopted false names in the course of their questioning: "one woman was called *sancta Maria,* another *sancta Ecclesia* or *Lex Romana,* another *sancta Baptisma* or *Matrimonium* or *sancta Communio,* so that when they were asked if they believed in the holy Church or Roman Law, they could say yes, but truly mean that they believed in the woman who had taken that name."[8]

Suspicion bore down heavily on women in this period. Legislation, chronicles, treatises, and letters expressed an acute concern for "lesser women" or "little women"—*mulierculae* is their term—who, in the words of the apostle Paul, lacked discernment and were easily lead astray by false piety and counterfeit prophets.[9] Philip the Chancellor referred to beguines as *mulierculae,* noting that such religious women met in "conclaves" under the guise of religion.[10] Thomas Aquinas and Gilbert of Tournai wrote of *mulierculae* when characterizing the semi-religious women in Flanders and northern France.[11] And in 1231

---

7. "Fuit etiam ibi vetula magne fame de Pruino, Gisla nomine, que dicebatur abbatissa, cuius mors dilata est, eo quod promiserit fratri Roberto, quod adhuc alios in quantitate magna manifestabit." Aubry of Trois-Fontaines, "Chronicon," 945. For Robert's charter, see Haskins, "Inquisition in Northern France," 215n3.

8. Aubry of Trois-Fontaines, "Chronicon," 945. For similar naming patterns, see Barbara Newman, "The Heretic Saint: Guglielma of Bohemia, Milan, and Brunate," *Church History* 74 (2005): 1–38.

9. 2 Timothy 3:4–6; Robert E. Lerner, "Vagabonds and Little Women: The Medieval Netherlandish Dramatic Fragment *De Truwanten,*" *Modern Philology* 65 (1968): 304.

10. Philip used this term in several of his sermons, as noted in Lerner, "Vagabonds and Little Women," 305n31. For example, *In Psalterium Davidicum CCXXX sermones* (Paris, 1523), I, fol. 296v (cited in Lerner): "Unde periculosa est quorundam religio qui in conclavi cum mulierculis conveniunt et colloquuntur: sicut dicuntur facere Beghuini et bagardi: [sic] de quibus Apostolus ii Thimo. iii. Habentes speciem quidem pietatis, virtutem autem eius abnegantes. Ex his sunt qui penetrant domos et captivas ducunt mulierculas oneratas peccatis etc." A similar quotation appears in an unpublished thirteenth-century sermon in the Troyes collection: "Quantum ad personas quibus consueverunt predicare scilicet mulierculis et simplicibus." MAT, MS 1100, fol. 226r. It is possible that this sermon collection was available to the monks of Clairvaux. See also Traill, "Philip the Chancellor."

11. See Lerner, "Vagabonds and Little Women," 304n26, citing Thomas Aquinas, *Commentary on the Epistles, In omnes S. Pauli Apostoli Epistolas commetaria,* 5th ed. (Turin, 1917), 2:248. Gilbert of Tournai writes of *mulierculae* in his *Collection of the Scandals of the Church* prepared for the Council of Lyons in 1274. See Gilbert of Tournai, *Collectio de scandalis ecclesiae,* in P. Autbertus Stroick, "Collectio de scandalis ecclesiae. Nova editio," *Archivum Franciscanum Historicum* 24 (1931): 33–62, at 62.

the Cistercian General Chapter forbade its abbots, monks, porters, and grange wardens to meet with or shelter any *mulierculae* who came to their door.[12]

After her final inquisition in 1239, Gila disappears from the historical record. Following his success at Mont-Aimé, Robert le Bougre retired under a cloud of suspicion about his own conduct. Gila, as a popular "abbess," and Robert, as the hand of institutional orthodoxy, mark two extremes in the religious transformation affecting Champagne and northern France at this time. Popular piety and the pressure toward greater juridical precision created a deep tension with respect to the institutional church and its acceptance of religious movements involving women. In Champagne this was worked out in the relationship between women and the Cistercian order. It was no coincidence that in northern France the papal initiatives against heresy occurred at precisely the same time that the pope and local bishops vigorously encouraged the incorporation of women into the Cistercian order and the writing of new rules to regulate female religious. In 1235, the year after Gila's imprisonment, a local cleric in Provins with the aid of the archbishop of Sens founded the nunnery of Mont-Notre-Dame-lès-Provins. It was associated with the Cistercian order within the year.[13] Robert's investigation and the founding of Mont-Notre-Dame are not explicitly related, but the Dominican's arrests gave a clarity and urgency to the reality that religious women—whether *mulierculae, Filles-Dieu,* or *mulieres sanctae*—had to be regulated within an existing religious order and reformed within the church.

This chapter examines the expansion of Cistercian convents in Champagne and the relationship between women and the order within the broader context of religious reform during the thirteenth century. Scholarship on this issue has largely been a history written from within the order, confined to conclusions generated almost exclusively from the Cistercian annual statutes, which after 1191 frequently mention new nunneries and their incorporation.[14] Yet the relationship between women and the Cistercian order was

---

For the wider context, see Barbara Newman, "Possessed by the Spirit: Devout Women, Demoniacs, and the Apostolic Life in the Thirteenth Century," *Speculum* 73 (1998): 733–70; and Nancy Caciola, *Discerning Spirits: Divine and Demonic Possession in the Middle Ages* (Ithaca, 2003), 3–5, 31–78.

12. "Provideant cellerarii et portarii Ordinis, ac magistri et hospitalarii grangiarum, ut mulierculae notam ferentes prostitutionis a portis domorum Ordinis, quanto longius fieri poterit repellantur, alioquin ipsi graviter puniantur." Josephus-Mia Canivez, *Statuta Capitulorum Generalium Ordinis Cisterciensis ab anno 1116 ad annum 1786* (Louvain, 1933–41), 2:(1231)5; also Bernard Lucet, *Les codifications cisterciennes de 1237 et de 1257* (Paris, 1977), Dist. 10: 23 (1237); and Dist. 10: 21(1257).

13. Canivez, *Statuta,* 2:(1235)40; and *GC* 12:70, instr. 92.

14. On the statutes as a source for incorporation, see Simone Roisin, "L'efflorescense cistercienne et le courant feminine de piété au XIII siècle," *Revue d'histoire ecclésiastique* 39 (1943): 342–78; and Brigitte Degler-Spengler, "The Incorporation of Cistercian Nuns into the Order in the Twelfth and

far more complicated than the legislation alone conveys. Incorporation was continually negotiated and modified, and different strategies for providing the *cura monialium*—the spiritual care of nuns—were attempted and implemented in various ways.[15] To look for a uniform body of juridical practices for incorporation is to miss the fact that each community enjoyed a specific set of relationships that in turn informed its association with the order. The growth of the order and the way it functioned as an institution are revealed in this nuance and in the careful decision-making that went into evaluating each community. Ultimately, while the incorporation or association of women with the Cistercians vastly extended the order, it changed it as well. Indeed, what is most striking about the Cistercians is their willingness in practice—despite the rhetoric of the statutes—to incorporate the spirituality of new groups of women during the first half of the thirteenth century. And while it is clear that unaffiliated women had much to gain from their incorporation into the Cistercian order, the benefits were not without cost.

Twelfth-Century Precedents and the *Cura Monialium*

From their inception, the Cistercians cultivated close relationships with women.[16] Detailed local studies have shown that women were associated with the foundations of Cîteaux and Clairvaux, and formal female communities following the Cistercian customs quickly took root. Founded between 1113 and 1115, Jully-les-Nonnains accommodated women interested in Cistercian ideals, both those living at the fringes of male communities and those female relatives of the men who had joined Cîteaux and Clairvaux. Jully became a priory of Molesme, the male community that precipitated the Cistercian reform. About ten years later, between 1120 and 1125, the

---

Thirteenth Century," in *Hidden Springs: Cistercian Monastic Women,* ed. John A. Nichols and Lillian Thomas Shank (Kalamazoo, MI, 1995), 1:171–200.

15. For England, see Sally Thompson, "The Problem of Cistercian Nuns in the Twelfth and Thirteenth Centuries," in *Medieval Women,* ed. Derek Baker (Oxford, 1978), 227–53; and Coburn V. Graves, "English Cistercian Nuns in Lincolnshire," *Speculum* 54 (1979): 492–99. For Belgium, see Roger De Ganck, "The Integration of Nuns in the Cistercian Order Particularly in Belgium," *Cîteaux* 35 (1984): 235–47; and Roisin, "L'efflorescense cistercienne." See Degler-Spengler, "Incorporation," for Switzerland. For German Cistercian nunneries, see John B. Freed, "Urban Development and the *Cura Monialium* in Thirteenth-Century Germany," *Viator* 3 (1972): 311–27; Marne Kuhn-Rehfus, "Cistercian Nuns in Germany in the Thirteenth Century: Upper-Swabian Cistercian Abbeys under the Paternity of Salem," in Nichols and Shank, *Hidden Springs,* 1:135–58; and Anja Ostrowitzki, *Die Ausbreitung der Zisterzienserinnen im Erzbistum Köln* (Cologne, 1993).

16. See Constance Berman, "Were There Twelfth-Century Cistercian Nuns?" *Church History* 68 (1999): 824–64; and Bernadette Barrière and Marie-Elizabeth Henneau, eds., *Cîteaux et les femmes* (Paris, 2001).

nunnery of La Tart was founded and associated with Cîteaux, following the customs of the Cistercians and adopting an institutional structure that paralleled Cistercian male houses.[17] Over the course of the twelfth century, female communities emerged in the surrounding northern French dioceses and were drawn into the administrative orbit of La Tart. Montreuil-les-Dames, founded in 1136, and its "daughter house" Fervaques, founded in 1140, are well-known examples.[18] In some instances male Cistercian houses founded female daughter houses. As Benoît Chauvin has shown, this was the case with the male house of Morimond and the nunnery of Belfay.[19] Although other female communities would be incorporated into the Cistercian order during the twelfth century, the earliest nunneries took root near the first male houses along the borders of Champagne.[20]

Cistercian nunneries did not generate their own monastic customs but adopted the *Rule of Benedict* and the "institutes of the brothers of Cîteaux," a set of texts originally compiled for male houses in the order.[21] These customs reflected the synthesis of several generations of Cistercian texts. Constitutional documents describing the founding of the order, namely, the *Exordium parvum* and its later and longer version, the *Exordium magnum*, joined administrative, liturgical, and disciplinary legislation whose regulations affected all abbeys of the order. The latter included the *Carta caritatis*, which defined the structure of the order and outlined the practice of visitation and the annual General Chapter meetings; the *Instituta generalis capituli*, the customary proper, containing legislation pertaining to the church offices and other concerns of the monastery; the *Ecclesiastica officia*, detailing the liturgy; and a

---

17. Berman, "Were There Twelfth-Century Cistercian Nuns?" 824–33; and Laurent Veyssière, "Cîteaux et Tart, foundations parallèles," in Barrière and Hennau, *Cîteaux et les femmes,* 179–90.

18. For a general overview of such foundations, see Armelle Bonis and Monique Wabont, "Cisterciens et cisterciennes en France du nord-ouest: Typologie des fondations, typologie des sites," and Benoît Chauvin, "L'intégration des femmes à l'Ordre de Cîteaux au XIIe siècle, entre hauts de Meuse et rives du Léman," both in Barrière and Hennau, *Cîteaux et les femmes,* 151–75 and 193–211, respectively.

19. Benoît Chauvin, "Morimond et la *conversio* des femmes au XIIe siècle: Belfays, abbaye cisterciennes feminine dans l'orbite de Morimond (vers 1130?–1393)," *Les Cahiers Haut-Marnais* 196–99 (1994): 55–106.

20. See Bernadette Barrière, "The Cistercian Monastery of Coyroux in the Province of Limousin in Southern France, in the Twelfth and Thirteenth Centuries," *Gesta* 31 (1992): 76–82; and Francis R. Swietek and Terrence M. Deneen, "The Roman Curia and the Merger of Savigny with Cîteaux: The Import of the Papal Documents," *Revue bénédictine* 112 (2002): 323–55.

21. The most common phrase used to define the regulation of Cistercian nunneries was "ordo monasticus qui secundum Deum et Beati Benedicti regulam atque institutionem Cisterciensium fratrum"; AD Aube, 23 H 11 (1246). On this formula, see J. Dubois, "Les orders religieux au XIIe siècle selon la curie romaine," *Revue bénédictine* 78 (1968): 283–309. There could be great variation, however; see below, 91–96.

separate set of texts governing the practices of the order's lay brothers.[22] In addition, the annual statutes, that is, decisions agreed upon at the yearly meeting of Cistercian abbots, supplemented and modified these customs, updating Cistercian practices, augmenting liturgical commemorations, and responding to pressing issues of the day. Over time a formal customary circulated among houses of Cistercian women, just as it did in male houses.[23]

The uniform adoption of the Cistercian *Institutes* among male and female monasteries in the order was unusual during the twelfth century.[24] The decision may have been a deliberate acknowledgment that men and women *could* and perhaps *should* follow the same customs or that monastic legislation could have the effect of suppressing the distinctions of gender within the religious life. Certainly, the application of the Cistercian customs to men *and* women represents another answer to Heloise's observation about the *Rule of Benedict:* women could follow rules and customs designed for men and sometimes excelled at this.[25] To interpret the universal application of one monastic regime to male and female houses as the product of misogyny, as some scholars have done, is to miss the larger ideal of the Cistercian order as it extended its sway over men and women.[26] What was esteemed about Cistercian communities was the continuity of practice among monks and nuns, particularly liturgical practices and spiritual ideals. The women who followed Cistercian customs in effect became part of the Cistercian order.[27]

---

22. See Chrysogonus Waddell, ed. and trans., *Narrative and Legislative Texts from Early Cîteaux* (Cîteaux, 1999); and Jean A. Lefèvre and Bernard Lucet, "Les codifications cisterciennes au XIIe et XIIIe siècles d'après les traditions manuscrites," *Analecta Sacri Ordinis Cisterciensis* 15 (1959): 3–22.

23. The women's text was translated into Old French and mirrors the Latin customary used in male houses, with the exception that the pronouns were changed from masculine to feminine. See the edition in Philippe Guignard, *Les monuments primitifs de la règle Cistercienne* (Dijon, 1878), lxxiv–lxxxviii, and 407–642.

24. It stands in contrast to the customs produced specifically for female communities, like the *Institutes* of the Paraclete and the instructions drawn up by Robert of Arbrissel for the women of Fontevraud. See Fiona J. Griffiths, "The Cross and the *Cura monialium:* Robert of Arbrissel, John the Evangelist, and the Pastoral Care of Women in the Age of Reform," *Speculum* 83 (2008): 303–30; Constant J. Mews, "Negotiating the Boundaries of Gender in Religious Life: Robert of Arbrissel and Hersende, Abelard and Heloise," *Viator* 37 (2006): 113–48; and Jacques Dalarun, "*Capitula regularia magistri Roberti:* De Fontevraud au Paraclet," *Comptes-Rendus des séances de l'académie des inscriptions et belles-lettres* 147 (2003): 1601–36.

25. See Peter Abelard, "The Letter of Heloise on Religious Life and Abelard's First Reply," ed. J. T. Muckle, *Mediaeval Studies* 17 (1955): 240–81; and idem, "Abelard's Rule for Religious Women," ed. T. P. McLaughlin, *Mediaeval Studies* 18 (1956): 241–92. See also Linda Georgianna, "Any Corner of Heaven: Heloise's Critique of Monasticism," *Mediaeval Studies* 49 (1987): 221–53, updated and reprinted in Bonnie Wheeler, ed., *Listening to Heloise: The Voice of a Twelfth-Century Woman* (New York, 2000), 187–216.

26. For such an interpretation, see Constance Berman, *The Cistercian Evolution: The Invention of a Religious Order in Twelfth-Century Europe* (Philadelphia, 2000), 42.

27. Although there are real problems with several aspects of her argument, particularly relating to the dating of certain key Cistercian texts and legislation, the general outlines of this process are traced in Berman, *Cistercian Evolution*.

For many historians this type of affiliation based on imitation is frustratingly vague.[28] We must remember, however, that the juridical formalism of religious orders as they were understood at the time of Fourth Lateran in 1215 and in the decades that followed was not yet in place. It is no surprise that debates over monastic habits, the definition of poverty, collection of taxes, and the like occurred only in the decades following the council. To look for juridical descriptions of a monastic order or for legal agreements about incorporation during the twelfth century would be misplaced, even premature. Rather, as Martha Newman has argued, a "conception of the order depended instead on a shared culture shaped by common customs, a common interpretation of texts, and a common appreciation of oral tales about illustrious Cistercians and the special favors bestowed on them by God."[29] In theory, women as much as men could and did participate in this shared culture, thereby becoming Cistercians.

Networks of friendship, kin, and spiritual like-mindedness facilitated this shared culture, but these relationships almost never appear in the legal texts produced by the order. Yet, during the last quarter of the twelfth century, Cistercian monks and lay brothers played a significant role in the spiritual care of nuns. Although the statutes from either side of the year 1200 uniformly forbid Cistercian monks to have contact with women in their monasteries, at their gates, or on their granges, they were not prohibited from leaving their monasteries to converse with women with their abbot's permission.[30] In all likelihood it was through casual contact, familial networks, conversation, and spiritual guidance offered during times of travel and in the spirit of hospitality that the new opening to women within the order began.[31] Indeed, such conversation lay behind Blanche of Navarre's request for spiritual advice from a monk of Larrivour, who received permission from his abbot to travel north to Villers to seek direction from the holy lay-brother Arnulf on behalf of the countess.[32]

Cistercian monks, particularly those within the orbit of Clairvaux—including the great male abbeys of Villers in Flanders, and Heisterbach,

---

28. See Ernst Günther Krenig, "Mittelalterliche Frauenklöster nach den Konstitutionem von Cîteaux," *Annalecta Sacri Ordinis Cisterciensis* 10 (1954): 1–105; and Sally Thompson, "The Problem of Cistercian Nuns." Although these are older interpretations they have enjoyed considerable longevity.

29. Martha G. Newman, "Real Men and Imaginary Women: Engelhard of Langheim Considers a Woman in Disguise," *Speculum* 78 (2003): 1184–1213.

30. See, for example, Canivez, *Statuta,* 1:(1198)4 and (1204)8, which makes reference to the *Libellus diffinitionum* first compiled in 1202. See Bernard Lucet, *La codification cistercienne de 1202 et son évolution ultérieure* (Rome, 1964), Dist. 10: 28, 29, 30; and Dist. 14: 30.

31. Brian Patrick McGuire, "The Cistercians and the Transformation of Monastic Friendships," *Analecta Cisterciensia* 37 (1981): 1–63, reprinted in his *Friendship and Faith: Cistercian Men, Women, and Their Stories, 1100–1250* (Aldershot, 2002), esp. 11–12.

32. See *VArnf,* bk. 2, chap. 10.

Eberbach, and Schönau in Germany—were not only compelled to form spiritual relationships with female religious, but found such relationships spiritually beneficial.[33] It was widely believed that pious women and nuns shared a corporeal understanding of Christ's suffering and a capacity for compassion that was not as easily attainable for monks in positions of religious power and authority.[34] From such friendships monks engaged in the more mundane obligations of spiritual guidance and care in exchange for proximity to this kind of the divine favor. The dynamics of these relationships are reflected in the incidental remarks of exempla collections, but also in the manuscript collections of male abbeys. Clairvaux, for example, possessed numerous treatises on spiritual direction for women, including a copy of the letters of Abelard and Heloise, the only copy of the anonymous *Epistolae duorum amantium,* and numerous copies of the *Speculum virginum,* the most widely circulated text of female spiritual direction in the late twelfth century.[35] The presence of these texts betrays the fact that the Cistercians were as involved in the spiritual care of women as the other new reform orders.[36]

What distinguished the Cistercian order, however, was the juridical and legislative framework it possessed that had the potential to structure these friendships within an institution that maintained the separation of men and women in distinct communities. That is, unlike Fontevraud, the Paraclete, and houses of Premonstratensian and Augustinian canonesses, the Cistercians forbade men and women from living together, even for the purposes of spiritual care. It was this latter aspect that made the order and its customs so attractive to thirteenth-century reformers as a framework for institutionalization readily applicable to new female communities. As we shall see, what must have been shocking to some within the order, however, was that its customs were applied at the direction of bishops and the pope to communities of women who were not within the monks' own circles of friendship and kin. Unlike Argensolles, founded through Blanche of Navarre's networks,

---

33. See John Coakley, "Gender and the Authority of Friars: The Significance of Holy Women for Thirteenth-Century Franciscans and Dominicans," *Church History* 60 (1991): 445–60.

34. See Caroline Walker Bynum, "The Female Body and Religious Practice in the Later Middle Ages," in her *Fragmentation and Redemption: Essays on Gender and the Human Body in Medieval Religion* (New York, 1991), 181–238.

35. See *Epistolae duorum amantium: Briefe Abaelards und Heloises?* ed. Ewald Könsgen (Leiden, 1974); also the manuscript list in *Speculum virginum,* ed. Jutta Seyfarth, *Corpus Christianorum. Continuatio Mediaevalis,* 5 (Turnhout, 1990), 56–123; and Julia Barrow, Charles Burnett, and David Luscombe, "A Checklist of the Manuscripts containing the Writings of Peter Abelard and Heloise and Other Works Closely Associated with Abelard and His School," *Revue d'Histoire des Textes* 14–15 (1984–85): 183–302.

36. See Constant J. Mews, ed., *Listen, Daughter: The "Speculum virginum" and the Formation of Religious Women in the Middle Ages* (New York, 2001).

the order began to include—by virtue of its common customs—repentant women, converts, and *Filles-Dieu,* women who had determined their own religious lives and commitments but, because of their social and economic status, were outside the traditional affiliations of Cistercian monks.

The Papacy and the Reform of Religious Women

At the turn of the thirteenth century, the relationship between women and the Cistercian order began to change in significant ways. A process for incorporating female houses into the order became formalized, defining with far greater specificity what it meant for women to be Cistercian nuns. Incorporation drew upon precedents laid down during the twelfth century but was ultimately shaped by two trends distinctive to the thirteenth century: the institutional ideal of religious reform that emphasized above all else female claustration under a formal rule, and the evolving norms of canon law that demanded a heightened level of juridical formalism.[37] Always present—forcing this issue—was a nagging fear of heresy and suspicion of the religious life outside of institutional oversight and regulation, of *religio* without *regulae.* As a consequence, reform and incorporation emerge in sharper relief because they had become juridically necessary to make the process explicit and codified either in charters or in the statutes of the order, or some combination of the two. In short, over the course of the first three decades of the thirteenth century, the Cistercians wrote about their relationships with women differently, indeed, more explicitly, extending a degree of legal status to women in the order that had previously been unnecessary. The convents associated with the order in northern France between 1200 and 1242 offer exceptional insight into the process and negotiations that incorporation entailed.

By the thirteenth century, religious reform had become a complex ideal. During the twelfth century, reform was essentially a project that sought to distinguish as clearly as possible the clergy from the laity. By 1200 the goals of reform grew more varied and intertwined, as many more laymen and women sought to emulate the clergy by taking on preaching, teaching, and a semi-monastic status of their own accord. Reform in its thirteenth-century

---

37. For these trends as they affected religious women, see Maria Pia Alberzoni, *Clare of Assisi and the Poor Sisters in the Thirteenth Century* (Saint Bonaventure, NY, 2004), 155–207; and Degler-Spengler, "Incorporation," 94–99. See also John Van Engen, "From Canons to Preachers: A Revolution in Medieval Governance," in *Domenico di Caleruega e la Nascita dell'ordine dei Frati Predicatori* (Spoleto, 2005), 261–95.

iteration had either to condemn such behavior or to find ways to acculturate it within the church and expand the sphere of accepted practice to sanction the spiritual striving of the laity. Within this new climate, regulating the lives of religious women became an abiding concern for the papacy and for reform-minded bishops, many of whom were schooled in Paris and guided in their thinking by their knowledge of moral theology. These men, however, were not only concerned with the ideals of regulation but also with the records that codified its administration. The Cistercian nunneries founded in northern France in the early thirteenth century were the product of this context, which brought together broader papal ideals with the needs of local bishops, the Cistercian order, and the women themselves.

The pontificate of Innocent III (1198–1216) brought new vigor, design, and a programmatic coherence to the reform of the church directed both at the clergy, secular and monastic, and at the laity. His campaigns against heresy in the south of France and his renewed calls for crusade pressed the urgency of his vision, which was worked out over a decade and a half, culminating in the seventy-one canons of the Fourth Lateran Council of 1215.[38] Although the canons touched a vast array of topics, from the Latinity of the clergy, to usury, marriage, confession, crusade, and transubstantiation, strikingly a general reform of religious women did not appear among them. Nevertheless, the reform of religious women was a major part of Innocent's vision both within Rome—his own episcopal see—and throughout Christendom. The regulation of religious women and nuns appeared as a topic in all the local councils leading up to Fourth Lateran.[39] And Innocent's ideas shaped a general policy of claustration and regulation for new female communities that consumed the efforts of many churchmen around him, in his chancery, among his legates and those who followed him on the papal throne.[40]

Innocent began in Rome. There he found a wide variety of religious women—nuns, *bizoke, zoccoli, conversae,* and other penitent women, most of whom lived outside of regular monastic vows. In 1204 he set in motion a plan for creating one great monastery for women (*universale cenobium monialium*) that would unite all religious women—nuns and penitents alike—in one convent

---

38. On his reform vision, see Michele Maccarrone, *Studi su Innocenzo III* (Padua, 1972); Brenda Bolton, *Innocent III: Studies on Papal Authority and Pastoral Care* (Aldershot, 1995); and Andrea Sommerlechner, ed., *Innocenzo III: Urbs et Orbis. Atti del Congresso Internazionale Roma, 9–15 settembre 1998,* 2 vols. (Rome, 2003).

39. See chap. 4, 125–26.

40. Certainly many of legates under Innocent III shared his goals, as did many of the local bishops in France who had trained with him in Paris. See Galland Bruno, "Les hommes de culture dans la diplomatie pontificale au XIIIe siècle," *Mélanges de l'école française de Rome* 108 (1996): 615–43.

under one rule.[41] The hope was to eschew diversity in favor of uniformity, even conformity, among monastic houses, an ideal referenced later in canon 13 of the Fourth Lateran Council that prohibited the creation of new religious orders after 1215.[42] San Sisto, the new nunnery, was still under construction at the time of Innocent's death, and the project fell to his successors, Honorius III (1216–1227) and Gregory IX (1227–1241), to complete. Initially Innocent III had approached the English canons of Sempringham with an invitation to oversee the spiritual care of the nuns in Rome. When they declined shortly before his death, Pope Honorius turned to Saint Dominic, whose friars were already associated with the house of women at Prouille in southern France. In 1218 Dominic consented and sent a small group of Dominican friars to oversee the women of San Sisto.[43] Although San Sisto became a convent affiliated with the Dominicans, it remained one convent among many in the city; Innocent's vision for *one* universal female institution in Rome never saw fruition. Nonetheless his overarching ideal—to cloister and regulate unaffiliated religious women—became the guiding principle for papal reform as it dealt with the women's religious movement in Italy and beyond.

As Honorius turned to Dominic and the *Rule of Augustine* in completing San Sisto, his successor, Gregory IX, turned to the *Rule of Benedict* and the customs of the Cistercians and Franciscans. In 1218–19, Hugolino (future Pope Gregory IX), in his capacity as cardinal-bishop of Ostia, began to regulate groups of women who had come to live in imitation of Saint Clare and her community at San Damiano.[44] Hugolino unified these houses into the Order of the Poor Ladies of the Spoleto Valley or Tuscany (*Ordo pauperum dominarum de valle Spoleti sive Tuscia*). In 1219, he composed a short rule for them based on the *Rule of Benedict* and appointed a Cistercian as the visitor to their houses. Because they adhered to a traditional rule and were overseen by a Cistercian, they were not considered a wholly new order in the church. When Hugolino became pope in 1227, he joined these houses (approximately twenty-three convents in all) to Clare's foundation and gave them a new designation as the Order of San Damiano (*Ordo San Damiani*). Although they continued to follow the constitutions he had drawn up in 1219,

---

41. Vladimir J. Koudelka, "Le 'Monasterium Tempuli' et la fondation dominicaine de San Sisto," *Archivum Fratrum Praedicatorum* 31 (1961): 5–81; and Brenda Bolton, "Daughters of Rome: All One in Christ Jesus!" in Bolton, *Innocent III: Studies*, 101–15.

42. *Decrees of the Ecumenical Councils*, ed. Norman P. Tanner, 2 vols. (Washington, DC, 1990), 1:242; and Alberzoni, *Clare of Assisi*, 159–61.

43. See Julie Ann Smith, "Prouille, Madrid, Rome: The Evolution of the Earliest Dominican *Instituta* for Nuns," *Journal of Medieval History* 35 (2009): 340–52.

44. Alberzoni, *Clare of Assisi,* passim; and Joan Mueller, *The Privilege of Poverty: Clare of Assisi, Agnes of Prague, and the Struggle for a Franciscan Rule for Women* (University Park, PA, 2006).

the pope transferred their oversight to the Franciscan Minister General and began the process of linking the convents—the Order of San Damiano—to houses of Franciscan friars who could oversee the nuns. The struggle for uniformity among these female houses would continue for decades. Clare was certainly not pleased with these interventions, and in 1228, after nearly ten years of frustration and petitioning, she received from Gregory IX the famed "Privilege of Poverty" protecting her association with Francis and her rejection of property, yet only in the case of San Damiano.[45]

For our purposes, what is most striking is that the Cistercian customs offered a crucial precedent informing these new regulations. Scholars who have studied the early rules for Prouille and the *Ordo San Damiani* have noted the similarities between these texts and the *Institutes* used to govern Cistercian women's houses. Maria Alberzoni has suggested that Hugolino and Honorius III explicitly modeled their new female foundations in Italy on the example of Cistercian monasticism.[46] A close examination of these texts is outside the scope of this study, but it is clear that from the turn of the thirteenth century the practices of the Cistercian order had a profound influence on the popes, from Innocent III onward. Innocent certainly saw the Cistercians as the model of monastic administration and recognized that the *Institutes* provided a system for the oversight and regulation of female convents that could be readily adopted and replicated.[47]

The embrace of Cistercian customs as a model for the reform of women religious was not confined to Italy. In 1227, the same year Gregory IX initiated the Order of San Damiano in Tuscany, he also placed the Penitent Sisters of Mary Magdalene in Germany under the *Rule of Benedict* and the *Institutes* of the Cistercian brothers, reforming these German religious women in the same way he had reformed penitent communities in Italy.[48] Five years later,

---

45. See Sean Field, *Isabelle of France: Capetian Sanctity and Franciscan Identity in the Thirteenth Century* (Notre Dame, 2006), 66–84.

46. Alberzoni, *Clare of Assisi*, 164–70. As Alberzoni points out, two of the men responsible, with Saint Dominic, for reforming the women of San Sisto were Cistercian cardinals: Stefano of Fossanova and Niccolò of Tuscolo; citing G. Cariboni, "Comunità religiose femminili legate ai Cistercensi a Piacenza e in Lombardia tra I pontificati di Innocenzo III e Alessandre IV" (Ph.D. dissertation, Università Cattolica del Sacro Cuore, Milan, 1997). In 1216, Hugolino himself petitioned to have "a certain house" in Italy incorporated into the order. See Canivez, *Statuta*, 1:(1216)70.

47. Innocent's respect for the organization of the Cistercian order is reflected in canon 12 of the Fourth Lateran Council. See Alberzoni, *Clare of Assisi*, 158–60; and Gert Melville, "Ordensstatuten und Allgemeines Kirchenrecht: Eine Skizze zum 12/13 Jahrhundert," in *Proceedings of the Ninth International Congress of Medieval Canon Law*, ed. P. Landau and J. Mueller (Vatican City, 1997), 691–712.

48. André Simon, *L'ordre des pénitentes de Ste Marie-Madeleine en Allemagne au XIIIeme siècle* (Fribourg, 1918), 24–28 and 183, nos. 4–6.

in 1232, he revised this initial decision and replaced the Cistercian *Institutes* with the *Rule of Augustine* and the *Institutes* of San Sisto in Rome, perhaps because they were more suitable to penitent sisters, who were active in the world and in need of more porous claustral regulation, as was the case with many hospital sisters.[49] That Gregory IX would embrace the Cistercian *Institutes* in the case of France throughout the 1230s is not surprising. Not only were the Cistercian texts readily available, but they had been the backbone of other rules and constitutions, which he himself composed and approved. Moreover, in the case of northern France, Cistercian male houses proliferated, facilitating visitation and spiritual care. Finally, Cistercian oversight was the model Innocent III had set in place over a decade earlier in France, as his successors were well aware.

Between 1203 and 1210, at the time that Innocent began the project of San Sisto in Rome, he also played a role in the creation of new Cistercian nunneries to the north. The climate of moral reform and crusade propaganda motivated the creation of a number of new nunneries in the region around Paris. Innocent took an interest in these new convents and authored a series of bulls identifying them as Cistercian houses at a time when the General Chapter did not view it as necessary to record the creation or incorporation of female houses in their annual statutes as they would in the 1230s. There is no evidence that these houses had different degrees of affiliation with the order; they were Cistercian convents. Yet what is clear is that the legal language of incorporation had not yet been formalized. The meaning of oversight, visitation, and regulation was still being worked out. The process itself unfolds in the language of the papal texts.

Innocent addressed the first bull of this type to the prioress and sisters of Les Clairets in the diocese of Chartres. It took the form of *Prudentibus virginibus*, the standard formula expressing papal protection directed toward nuns.[50] Innocent not only extended apostolic protection over the temporal goods of Les Clairets but put into legal language the women's connection with the Cistercians: they were "to live according to God and the *Rule of Benedict* and to observe the *Institutes* of the brothers of Cîteaux."[51] In 1210 he sent another

---

49. Ibid., 29–46, and 202, no. 44; and Smith, "Prouille, Madrid, Rome," 347–52.

50. Vicomte Hector de Souancé, *Abbaye royale de Notre-Dame des Clairets: Histoire et cartulaire, 1202–1790* (Nogent-le-Rotrou, 1894), 67–70, no. 3 (26 January 1203). For the use of the bull *Prudentibus virginibus*, see Edwin Hall and James Ross Sweeney, "An Unpublished Privilege of Innocent III in Favor of Montivilliers: New Documentation for a Great Norman Nunnery," *Speculum* 44 (1974): 662–73.

51. "in primis si quidem statuentes ut ordo monasticus, qui secundum Deum et beati Benedicti regularm, atque institutionem Cisterciensium fratrum in eodem monasterio institutus esse digno-

near identical bull to the women of Parc-aux-Dames, which the countess of St.-Quentin had founded five years earlier in the diocese of Senlis. It also stipulated that the nuns follow the *Rule of Benedict* and the *Institutes* of the brothers of Cîteaux.[52] In both cases Innocent's bull was the first text to define these communities as Cistercian convents, but there was still no juridical formula or standard language in existence for identification as a Cistercian female house. For example, two other bulls for newly founded convents at Port-Royal (from 1209) and L'Abbaye-aux-Bois (1206) were simply confirmations addressed to "the nuns of Porrais of the Cistercian order" and "the abbess and nuns of the new monastery next to *Belle-Locus* of the Cistercian order."[53] To follow the *Institutes* of the brothers of Cîteaux was the same thing as being nuns of the Cistercian order.[54] In all of these cases, it was Innocent's words that conferred on the nuns their formal status as Cistercian convents. No mention of these houses appears in the statues, no vote by the abbots of the order seems to have taken place on this issue. Indeed, Innocent did not address how the nunneries were connected to male houses in the order nor how that administrative relationship was to function. These details—crucial and contentious as they would prove to be—he left to local bishops and abbots and ultimately to the women and the General Chapter to work out.

The General Chapter and Cistercian Nuns

Over the course of the first two decades of the thirteenth century the order responded to the papal and episcopal recognition of Cistercian nuns by defining what was expected of women under its care. It was during this time that a language and a process for incorporation began to take shape.[55] The story of this process is disappointingly fragmented, reported only in the one-sided legislation of the annual statutes. Juridical pronouncements relating specifically to nuns began to appear in the first quarter of the thirteenth century.

---

scitur perpetuis ibidem temporibus inviolabiliter observetur." Souancé, *Abbaye royale de Notre-Dame des Clairets*, 67.

52. Although this bull does not use the phrase "prudentibus virginibus," the opening of the bull is identical to that given to Les Clairets, as is the formula associating the nuns with the Cistercian *Institutes*. See GC 10, instr. 43.

53. "filiabus monialibus Porrasii Cisterciensis ordinis"; *Cartulaire de l'abbaye de Porrois aux diocèse de Paris plus connue sous son nom mystique Port-Royal*, ed. A. de Dion (Paris, 1903), 39, no. 15 (9 November 1209). "abbatisse et monialibus novi monasterii juxta Bellum Locum, Cisterciensis ordinis"; Brigitte Pipon, *Le chartrier de l'Abbaye-aux-Bois (1202–1341): Étude et édition* (Paris, 1996), 105, no. 12 (1 December 1206).

54. This process, using different language, had precedent in the second half of the twelfth century. See Berman, *Cistercian Evolution*, 222–25.

55. For an overview of this process, see Degler-Spengler, "Incorporation."

Occasionally petitions from bishops or laymen requesting the incorporation of female houses surface, but this was not a regular practice until the late 1220s. The statutes report only what the General Chapter decided and decreed, revealing none of the debates, pressures, or anxieties behind each decision.

The first official juridical pronouncement acknowledging women in the order appeared in 1206.[56] The General Chapter convened in September under Arnaud Amaury, the abbot of Cîteaux, who had just returned from Montpellier and its diseased hinterland, infected with "heresy" that the tonic of monastic preaching seemed unable to cure.[57] With the ills of heresy on his mind, the abbot turned to regulating nuns and to the discipline of his own order.[58] Amaury was a keen administrator. Four years earlier, in 1202, he had ordered the first formal compilation of the order's legislation, which by the thirteenth century had burgeoned into an unwieldy mass of material. The fruit of this labor was *Libellus diffinitionum,* the book of definitions, which would be revised three more times over the course of the century.[59] This slim text, easily copied and disseminated, supplemented and clarified the *Institutes* and defined with greater precision the Cistercian religious life. The 1206 statute regulating nuns was, however, a modest reform. Other than recognizing in formal juridical language that there *were* nuns in the order, the statute merely prohibited the education of children in women's monasteries.

Seven years elapsed before nuns appeared in the statutes again, by which time Arnaud Amaury had preached himself hoarse, overseen the massacre of men and women at Béziers during the Albigensian Crusade, and exchanged his abbatial staff for the powers of the *cathedra* of Narbonne.[60] The 1213 statute was more elaborate: "All nuns incorporated in the order, by the authority of the General Chapter, must not leave their cloisters except with the permission of their father-abbot. Moreover, any houses incorporated in the future will be admitted only on the condition that total enclosure is maintained."[61] Enclosure became the common theme of all subsequent legislation pertaining to nuns.

---

56. Canivez, *Statuta,* 1:(1206)5.

57. Peter of les Vaux-de-Cernay, *The History of the Albigensian Crusade: Peter of les Vaux-de-Cernay's Historia Albigensis,* trans. W. A. Sibly and M. D. Sibly (Woodbridge, 1998), 16–18.

58. See Berman, *Cistercian Evolution,* 230–31.

59. Lucet, *Codification 1202;* idem, *Codifications 1237 et 1257;* and J. Lefèvre and B. Lucet, "L'ère des grandes codifications cisterciennes (1202–1350)," in *Études d'histoire du droit canonique dédiées à G. Le Bras* (Paris, 1965), 249–62.

60. Mark Pegg, *A Most Holy War: The Albigensian Crusade and the Battle for Christendom* (Oxford, 2008), 69–79.

61. "Item constituitur auctoritate Capituli generalis ut moniales quae iam etiam incorporatae sunt Ordini, non habeant liberum egressum, nisi de licentia abbatis sub cuius cura consistunt, quia omnino non expedit animabus earum. Si quae vero fuerint incorporandae de cetero, non aliter admittantur ad Ordinis unitatem, nisi penitus includendae." Canivez, *Statuta,* 1:(1213)3.

In 1218 its necessity was reiterated as a defining aspect for association with the order. Nuns were to be fully enclosed, they were to possess nothing of their own, and permission to leave the cloister could be granted only to the abbess and two other nuns, but even then only rarely and when unavoidable.[62] Statutes issued in 1219, 1220, and 1225 all echoed this decision.[63] In 1220 the General Chapter also advocated restraining the incorporation of female houses. Behind this ruling seems to have been the challenge of achieving the ideal of complete enclosure, for the same statute acknowledged that there were nuns who did not want to live under full enclosure and if that were the case, those women should be removed from the custody of the order.[64] Only a statute from 1222 tacitly recognized the administrative challenges behind the ideal of full enclosure, for this decision established that no monks or *conversi* were allowed to live in houses of nuns as was the custom in other orders charged with the *cura monialium*.[65] The celebration of the mass, the lifting of excommunication, and the veiling of nuns, as well as all administrative matters, were left in the hands of local monks and abbots. Cistercian nuns were to confess—through windows dressed with iron grillwork—to father-abbots or priests who visited the female communities under their care.[66] A carefully prescribed dynamic governing the relationship of women within the order was forming, all against the backdrop of lived experience, the realities of which are almost wholly unrecoverable from the statutes.

As monks and nuns began to live with an emerging juridical definition of Cistercian nuns and the reality of enclosure, the process of incorporation was made more explicit. In 1225 the abbots decreed that new communities of women would not be incorporated until their buildings were completed and they were sufficiently endowed and enriched, conditions meant to ensure that they could exist as fully enclosed and economically independent nunneries, for "it is not proper for them to beg."[67] The following year, in 1226, the General Chapter recognized the petitions of the bishop of Chartres

---

62. Ibid., 1:(1218)84.

63. Ibid., 1:(1219)12, (1220)4; 2:(1225)7.

64. Ibid., 1:(1219)4.

65. "Supplicandum Domino Papae, ne compellat nos ad mittendos monachos nostros et conversos ad cohabitandum cum monialibus, et in temporalibus eisdem providendis; vergit enim res ista ad praeiudicium Ordinis et periculum animarum." Ibid., 2:(1222)30. This contrasts with female communities in northern Italy under Franciscan and Dominican care where small groups of friars lived with or near the nuns. See Brigitte Degler-Spengler, "'Zahlreich wie die Sterne des Himmels': Zisterzienser, Dominikaner und Franziskaner vor dem Problem der Inkorporation von Frauenklöstern," *Rottenburger Jahrbuch für Kirchengeschichte* 4 (1985): 37–50.

66. Canivez, *Statuta*, 2:(1225)7, much of which is reiterated in (1228)16.

67. "nec ullae de cetero incorporentur Ordini, aut incorporatae ad novas mittantur abbatias, donec peractis competenter aedificiis, et ita possessionibus et rebus necessariis sufficienter dotatae fuerint et ditatae, quod possint includi penitus, et inclusae sustentari de suo, ita quod eas non oporteat

and the archbishop of Sens to incorporate the new nunneries of L'Eau-les-Chartres and La Cour Notre-Dame-de-Michery, respectively. In both cases local abbots were assigned to investigate whether the nuns had what was sufficient to sustain themselves so that they could be cloistered according to the requirements outlined by the General Chapter.[68] This would become the common practice as sufficiency became the defining aspect of incorporation in the decades to come. As a concept, sufficiency was intended to counter the challenges of true institutional poverty and to allay the need or desire for public mendicancy, which brought nuns outside their cloisters and into positions of vulnerability and scandal, making them appear more like *mulierculae* than *moniales*. Yet the General Chapter's legislation could not counteract the religious meaning and spiritual power of mendicancy and its corollary, charity. To beg was to walk in the way of the Lord, to think nothing of the morrow, to humble oneself, to perfect oneself. The statutes could not silence the cacophony of thirteenth-century preaching that vaunted this ideal.[69]

At some point after 1225, annual legislation modifying the order's relationship toward women became a tiresome exercise for its abbots. A new solution was found in 1228 when the General Chapter stipulated that the order would no longer accept nuns under its jurisdiction, though it would not prohibit the association or construction of houses of nuns that wanted to emulate (*aemulari*) the Cistercian *Institutes*. The statute also prohibited monks of the order from offering spiritual care or visiting such nunneries (*sed curam animarum earum non recipiemus, nec visitationis officium eis impendemus*).[70] Behind this new ordinance was the sense that many monks had been drawn away from their own abbeys to care for women, which weakened the order as a whole.[71] Yet, for all of the forceful rhetoric behind the 1228 statute, it did not stop the incorporation of new female houses into the order. Indeed, the decade that followed (1231–41) saw the greatest number of petitions for the incorporation of women's houses than at any other time.[72] What was different after 1228 was that there were now juridical procedures in place for admittance into the order. Patrons, bishops, and the pope submitted formal petitions to

---

mendicare. Illae autem quae a quatuor annis incorporatae sunt, sicut statutum est, includantur, aut ab Ordinis corpore abscindantur." Ibid., 2:(1225)7.

68. Ibid., 2:(1226)29; and in the case of La Cour (1226), 33.

69. Concerning mendicancy, charity, and the theology of almsgiving, see James William Brodman, *Charity and Religion in Medieval Europe* (Washington, DC, 2009).

70. Canivez, *Statuta*, 2:(1228)16.

71. Walter of Utrecht, abbot of Villers (1214–1221), turned over several nunneries to the oversight of Cîteaux for this reason. See Edmond Martène and Ursin Durand, *Thesaurus novus anecdotorum*, 3 vols. (1717; reprint, New York, 1968), 3:1277; and Roisin, "L'efflorescense cistercienne," 355–56.

72. See Roisin, "L'efflorescence cistercienne," 351–61; and Degler-Spengler, "Incorporation."

the General Chapter, and abbots were routinely sent to evaluate new communities and to assess the material sufficiency of each proposed house. After 1228, religious zeal had to contend with the administrative realities of building fabric, gifts, endowments, rents, taxes, and all the matters of daily life that ensured stability, regulation, and claustration.

Finding Sufficiency: Incorporation after 1228

The steady number of new Cistercian convents incorporated into the order after 1228 makes it clear that the statute was not prohibitive. Nonetheless, it had an effect on the new Cistercian nunneries and the institutionalization of the women's religious movement. From that point on, the majority of female houses admitted to the order were communities that had existed for some time in an informal capacity but were now reformed and regulated under the Cistercian *Institutes*. In this sense they were part of the much broader reform intent on regulating and enclosing religious women. The statutes of 1225 and 1228 functioned, especially in northern France, as guidelines for the process of transforming a religious movement and bringing it in line with an established order. Indeed, these houses—particularly the nunneries founded in Champagne during the 1230s—offer an example of how a religious movement was successfully regularized and incorporated into the institutional church. The foundation of Cistercian convents in Champagne parallels the emergence of Franciscan and Dominican convents for men and women. All three endeavors harnessed existing religious impulses and practices, brought them under the direction of a rule within specific locales and buildings, and bound them through administration and oversight, thereby tethering the holy to the mundane practicalities of the Christian life. Bishops, patrons, and Cistercian abbots looked for the willingness and ability of women to secure permanent buildings that could become cloisters, to cultivate patrons to provide for their needs, to adopt an appropriate habit or mode of dress that marked them out as regularized religious, and to submit to episcopal and abbatial oversight. These were precisely the requirements outlined in the statutes of 1225 and 1228, which came to define a monastic order in the thirteenth century: permanence, obedience, dress as a marker of profession, and a cultivated connection to the laity who supported the same women.

Buildings

Stability defined the regulated life. Buildings in turn were crucial to the process of becoming Cistercian nuns. In most cases, communities of women joining the order after 1228 already resided in a set of buildings sufficient for their religious needs, with a chapel, living quarters, storage and perhaps a hospice nearby. It was often bishops and lay patrons who provided suitable sites for women to take up the service of God. In 1234, after a group of religious women had petitioned him for a small place to live (*habitaculum*), Jacques de Bazoches, the bishop of Soissons, settled them in the leper house of Berneuil.[73] By Jacques's own admission the buildings at Berneuil were dilapidated and in need of restoration, both spiritual and physical.[74] The women, who were also reformed as Cistercian nuns, provided both. Within a month, Pope Gregory IX brought the women under papal protection as the "monastery of Notre-Dame La Joie of the Cistercian order." Six years later the General Chapter formally incorporated La Joie at the request of Blanche of Castile.[75] Settling the women into a fixed set of buildings, even a humble structure formally inhabited by lepers, was a crucial step in the process of incorporation and institutionalization.

Many of the initial communities of religious women that became Cistercian nunneries inhabited leper houses, hospital buildings, *domus-Dei,* or granges, that is, simple farm buildings. In the diocese of Soissons, the same Jacques de Bazoches oversaw the creation of Cistercian convents in *domus-Dei* and leper houses at La Barre in Chateau-Thierry and L'Amour-Dieu in Troissy (fig. 4). The nunnery of St.-Jacques de Vitry was founded in Count Thibaut IV's comital hospice, while the women of La Piété-Dieu in the diocese of Troyes were initially given a *domus-Dei* at Ramerupt as their first permanent residence.[76] Equally amenable for the settlement of new nunneries were grange buildings, many of which lay just outside the major towns of Champagne in the suburban margin. So it was with Stephen of Champguyon's grange outside of Troyes, which he gave to be used as an ad-hoc chapel and convent for the nuns of Notre-Dame-des-Prés. Likewise, the nuns of La Cour Notre-Dame-de-Michery, who first lived in the leper house of Viluis, later moved into a grange nearby, which they converted into a permanent convent and chapel (fig. 5).[77]

Only rarely were nunneries founded and built anew. Even Blanche of Navarre's foundation at Argensolles was constructed by expanding a grange the

---

73. Louis Carolus-Barré, "L'abbaye de La Joie-Notre-Dame à Berneuil-sur-Aisne (1234–1430)," in *Mélange à la mémoire du Père Anselme Dimier,* ed. Benoît Chauvin, 3 vols. in 6 (Arbois, 1982–87), 2:487–504, at 499.

74. Ibid., 499.

75. Ibid., 500, no. 2; and Canivez, *Statuta,* 2:(1240)51.

76. See chap. 1, 41.

77. AD Yonne, H 563 (1240); also chap 1, 40–41.

FIGURE 4. L'Amour-Dieu, exterior of the abbey church, east end of the nave. Photo by Terryl Kinder, with permission.

countess purchased from the monks of Hautvillers.[78] By contrast, Blanche of Castile's lavish patronage of new Cistercian convents was exceptional. When the queen founded the richly endowed convent of Le Lys in 1248, for example, the charter made clear that she was "founding and building" a house for Cistercian nuns, which included a "cloister, dormitory, refectory,

---

78. For this foundation, see chap. 1. 28–33.

FIGURE 5. La Cour Notre-Dame-de-Michery, exterior of the abbey church, east end of the nave. Photo by the author.

cellar and all of the individual buildings and walls that would be needed."[79] In Champagne, only St.-Dizier, founded and patronized by William of Dampierre and his wife, Countess Margaret of Flanders, appears to have been constructed from the ground up. Gifts in 1228 from Gosbert, lord of Aspermont, refer to the convent as "newly built."[80] The considerable income of the countess of Flanders probably made the building of St.-Dizier possible.

The settlement of religious women in preexisting buildings, specifically those suffering from neglect, had practical and spiritual significance. In the most practical terms, these modest structures offered habitation that obviated the cost of new construction. Religious women could gather with episcopal sanction and begin the process of establishing a more permanent religious life in a fixed settlement, which would lead to enclosure and the adoption of a monastic rule. Such arrangements also occurred in direct dialogue with the new Cistercian statutes that required a permanent dwelling before religious women would be recognized by the order. This was in essence a way for bishops and patrons to cope with a requirement set by the order. Rather than wait for wealthy patrons to fund the construction of a new cloister, which could take months or years to complete, abandoned granges and *domus-Dei* proved a practical expedient.

---

79. *GC* 12, instr. 96.

80. "noviter edificare que nominata S[anct]i Desidium in qua etiam sunt institute moniales Cisterciensis ordinis." AD Marne, 71 H 6 (July 1228). It is also possible Le Paraclet in the diocese of Amiens may have been newly built as well, see n. 111 below.

Founding convents in old buildings was an act of restoration as well that doubled as a visible sign of spiritual reform and renewal. By the early decades of the thirteenth century, architectural restoration had become a metaphor for the reform of the church more generally. In 1228, when Thomas of Celano completed the *Vita prima* of Saint Francis, he gave a prominent place in his narrative to the holy man's experiences rebuilding the churches of San Damiano, San Pietro, and Portiuncula outside of Assisi.[81] As Thomas explained, in each case "[Francis] did not build a wholly new church, [but] rather restored an old one. He did not tear down the old foundation, but built upon it, observing, though he was unaware of it, the prerogative always reserved to Christ: For another foundation no one may lay, but that which has been laid, which is Jesus Christ."[82] San Damiano was the building complex given to Clare and her followers, who in turn reconstructed the building further to suit their community.[83] It was in similar neglected structures that Cistercian nuns took up residence. The renewal of these buildings corresponded to the new life adopted by the women who settled in them and who in turn came closer to meeting the guidelines for incorporation within the order. For the bishops and patrons who sponsored such associations, the reform of religious women corresponded to the remaking of the local religious landscape.[84]

Rebuilding grange buildings and *domus-Dei* became necessary as communities of nuns expanded. Yet renovation did not mean a change in religious ideals. Even as these convents added chapels and augmented their churches they remained small communities that embraced their humble origins. By 1247 the bishop of Troyes granted the nuns of Val-des-Vignes a special license to collect alms for work on their church.[85] The nuns had begun as a small group of *Filles-Dieu* in a building across from a leper house outside of Bar-sur-Aube. Twenty years after their foundation, as their numbers grew, they sought to enlarge and embellish their church, yet still it was alms from the faithful that propelled this expansion, not aristocratic patronage.

---

81. See Edward Peters, "Restoring the Church and Restoring Churches: Event and Image in Franciscan Biography," *Franziskanische Studien* 68 (1986): 213–36.

82. "domum construit Deo, illamque non de novo facere tentat, sed veterem reparat, vetustam resarcit; non fundamentum evellit, sed super illud aedificat, praerogativam, licet ignorans, semper reservans Christo: *Fundamentum enim aliud nemo potest ponere, praeter id quod positum est, quod est Christus Iesus.*" Thomas of Celano, *Vita Prima*, in *Analecta Franciscana*, 10, fascs. 1–3 (Quarrachi, 1926–48), I Celano, bk. 1, chap. 8.

83. See Lezlie Knox, *Creating Clare of Assisi: Female Franciscan Identities in Later Medieval Italy* (Leiden, 2008), 19–55.

84. See Anne E. Lester, "Making the Margins in the Thirteenth Century: Suburban Space and Religious Reform between the Low Countries and the County of Champagne," *Parergon* 27 (2010): 59–87.

85. AD Aube 3 H 4010 (July 1247).

Similarly, the nuns of La Cour Notre-Dame to the north of Sens began to rebuild their sanctuary at some point before 1260. They too solicited alms to accomplish this, but between caring for the community of lepers from which they grew and maintaining their own needs the burdens of rebuilding proved too great. By the 1280s the nuns turned to public mendicancy to pay off the costs of their modest renovations, consisting chiefly of the addition of a glazed window at the east end of their simple church (see fig. 5).[86] In other cases, patrons encouraged and financed rebuilding. Over the course of the thirteenth century, some commissioned private chapels in monastic churches. In these new spaces, opening out from the east end, nuns offered prayers for the dead following the instructions benefactors often detailed in their wills. In 1261 the nuns of Clairmarais received 46 *l.* from the will of their major patron, Briard, a goldsmith and citizen of Reims. This sum rounded out his previous gifts to a total of 100 *l.* intended for the construction of a chapel in the nuns' church.[87] Restoration in this sense did not entail a lavish building campaign; gifts of alms and testamentary funds were not enough to provide for building on a royal scale. Sufficiency remained the guiding principle.

Although the presence of new communities of nuns contributed to the restoration of forgotten buildings on the margins of towns, they did not transform such buildings into lavish monastic sites. Most of the Cistercian convents retained their contours as grange buildings and hospices, often returning to their original purpose by the fifteenth century, when the nunneries were suppressed or converted into male priories or granges of the order.[88] The modest origins of the convents may in fact offer a practical explanation for the architectural feature of flat-ended apses favored in Cistercian convents during a period of Gothic building obsessed with radiating chapels.[89] The majority of the Cistercian convents of Champagne were places where one went to be humbled, to renounce one's former status in the world, and to

---

86. AD Yonne H 787, fols. 21–23; and William Chester Jordan, "The Cistercian Nunnery of La Cour Notre-Dame de Michery: A House That Failed," *Revue bénédictine* 95 (1985): 311–20.

87. "pro quadam capellania in dicta ecclesia de Claro marisco construenda"; AD Aube, 3 H 3788 (April 1261).

88. See epilogue, 206–8. Also Constance H. Berman, "Buildings in Wood, Brick, Stone, Tiles: Vestiges of the Architecture for Cistercian Nuns in Southern France," in *Cistercian Nuns and Their World*, vol. 6 of *Studies in Cistercian Art and Architecture*, ed. Meredith Parsons Lillich (Kalamazoo, MI, 2005), 23–59; and Berman, *Cistercian Evolution*, 123–42, 221–36.

89. See Marcel Aubert, *L'architecture cistercienne en France*, 2 vols. (Paris, 1953), 2:173–204; Anselme Dimier, "L'architecture des églises de moniales cisterciennes," *Cîteaux* 25 (1974): 8–23; and Michel Desmarchelier, "L'architecture des églises de moniales cisterciennes, essai de classement des différents types de plans (en guise de suite)," in Chauvin, *Mélanges à la mémoire du père Anselme Dimier*, 3:79–121.

be transformed.⁹⁰ It was in the physical fabric of the Cistercian convents that the apostolic ideal of poverty persisted in its studied simplicity. The small buildings and chapels, which often accommodated no more than twenty professed nuns, were not meant to be places that glorified God in a precious opulence but rather were deliberately left as places where one might encounter Christ. They retained their quality as mangers, granges, and hospices for the poor and sick, embellished perhaps by the occasional lancet window and flash of color, hard won from the alms of the faithful.

To Endow and Enrich

The transformation of unaffiliated religious women into Cistercian nuns entailed integrating these new institutions into the social hierarchies of lay society and thereby creating bonds that would be mutually dependent. From the perspective of the Cistercian order, this meant cultivating patrons who would endow and enrich the new nunneries, ensuring the women's long-term sufficiency. For many of the Cistercian convents in Champagne this occasioned a significant reorientation. The initial support for the new communities had come from members of the bourgeoisie and lesser aristocracy, men and women like Stephen of Champguyon and Beatrix of St.-Rémy, who prospered in the new economy of the thirteenth century.⁹¹ Yet, as the abbots of the order and local bishops understood, small bourgeois gifts were not enough to ensure the success of an institution. The social capital and powerful wealth of the nobility, even the lesser nobility, was instrumental for creating the conditions of sufficiency necessary for the survival and acceptance of the new Cistercian convents.

The early history of the patronage of Notre-Dame-des-Prés outside of Troyes bears out this dynamic explicitly. Although Stephen of Champguyon was the first to shelter the women of Notre-Dame-des-Prés, offering them his grange building for use as a chapel and supporting them in their earliest impulses toward the religious life, his patronage was not what led to their admittance into the order. When the women came to the attention of Nicholas of Brie, the bishop of Troyes, in 1234, he approached Hugh of St.-Maurice, a local knight, and his wife, Margaret. Hugh had close ties to the comital family and held numerous landed fiefs along the southern boundary of

---

90. On the spiritual significance of poor buildings, see Barrière, "Cistercian Monastery of Coyroux"; Berman, "Buildings in Wood, Brick, Stone, Tiles," 36–37; and Roberta Gilchrist, *Gender and Material Culture: The Archaeology of Religious Women* (London, 1994), 1–21.

91. See chap. 2, 57–64.

the county.⁹² Together Hugh and Margaret endowed Notre-Dame-des-Prés with a quarter of all their possessions, including arable lands, fields, vineyards, woods, water rights, and rights to justice, and to ensure sufficiency of the new foundation they also assigned to the nuns annual rents in kind.⁹³ The nuns in turn agreed to recognize Hugh and his wife as the "patrons and founders" of their community.⁹⁴ Hugh and Margaret were called upon as patrons in a formalized act of foundation that was tied to their status as members of the aristocracy and to their ability to endow the community with lands and— perhaps more importantly—rents, which provided long-term stability for the nunnery.⁹⁵ The ecclesiastical hierarchy and the Cistercian order considered aristocratic patronage to be a necessary component of sufficiency, which tied new female communities to the local landed elite in ways that ensured their prosperity as institutions. By contrast, Stephen of Champguyon and his family were never referred to in Notre-Dame-des-Prés's documents as patrons or founders. Although they continued to donate to the nuns throughout the thirteenth century and perhaps had the resources to endow the community at a sufficient level, they lacked the social capital intrinsic to the aristocracy, which bound the higher class to the count through marriage, council, and crusading. In 1235, the year after Hugh and Margaret became formal patrons

---

92. In 1198 Hugh of St.-Maurice-aux-Riches-Hommes was one of eleven barons listed among Count Thibaut III's closest men when the count paid homage to Philip Augustus. See Theodore Evergates, ed., *Littere Baronum: The Earliest Cartulary of the Counts of Champagne* (Toronto, 2003), appendix. 1, no. 122. In 1205 he pledged surety of 100 *l*. for a sale contracted by Jean of Brienne: *Littere Baronum*, no. 22. An entry in the *Rôles des fiefs*, compiled during 1249–52, lists the fiefs that Margaret, the widow of Hugh of St.-Maurice, held in dower, which included lands, mills, water rights, men, rents, and woods, which the scribe estimated at a value of 35 *l.t.* (*libertus terre*). See *Rôles des fiefs du comté de Champagne sous le règne de Thibaud le Chansonnier (1249–52)*, ed. Auguste Longnon (Paris, 1877), 126, no. 584. Margaret's dower reflects only a fraction of the total fiefs and possessions that Hugh of St.-Maurice controlled.

93. "ad fundationem ipsius loci et sustentationem sanctimonialium ibidem degentium sub regula Beati Benedicti, et, quia ad fundationem loci predicti donatio rerum predictarum non sufficeret, quasdam elemosinas bladi quas idem Hugo et ejus uxor predicta diversis locis fecerant…ad fundationem predicti loci et sustentationem sanctimonialium ampliandam totum predictum baldum annui redditus eisdem monialibus assignarunt." AD Aube, 23 H 9 (June 1234).

94. "coram nobis recognoverunt ipsos Hugonem et eius uxorem esse patronos et fundatores dicti loci, promittentes eisdem quod ipsos semper et in omnibus pro dominis et patronis habebunt eosque honorifice recipient in loco predicto quandocumque eisdem militi et eius uxori placuerit, et si forte quod absit, ad inopiam devenirent, ipsis tamquam veris patronis et fundatorbius suis pro modulo sub possibilitatis de bonis propriis domus sue necessaria ministravent." AD Aube, 23 H 9 (June 1234).

95. There were clear spiritual and social benefits accrued by identifying oneself as a founder and patron of a new Cistercian nunnery. The social capital of such a title was not lost on Hugh, who seems to have been at pains to make known and ensure his role as founder, for in 1237–38 Guiard, dean of Christianity of Bar-sur-Aube, and Robert, master of the Hôtel-Dieu of St.-Nicholas in Bar, drew up an official copy of Hugh's charter, which was deposited with the documents of the treasury of the crown of France. See *Layettes,* 2, no. 2287.

of the nuns, Robert of Thourotte, bishop of Langres, petitioned the General Chapter to receive Notre-Dame-des-Prés into the order as a daughter house of Clairvaux.[96] The following year, the abbots of Clairvaux, Boulancourt, and Larrivour inspected the house and oversaw the nunnery's incorporation.[97] Tellingly, Hugh and Margaret seem to have been founders primarily in name, for their endowment in 1234 marks their only appearance in the nunnery's archival record. Hugh and his wife did not cultivate the kind of sustained connection to the nuns of Notre-Dame-des-Prés that the Champguyon family maintained or that other lesser aristocratic families fostered.

Aristocratic patronage was part of a mutually beneficial dynamic. Just as female communities needed the endowments of such patrons as part of the process of incorporation, patronage of new Cistercian nunneries reinforced the aristocratic identity of families new to this class. Indeed, the formal foundation and incorporation of Val-des-Vignes coincided with the emergence of the Jaucourt family within the ranks of the baronial aristocracy.[98] Val-des-Vignes grew out of a group of women who had gathered outside of Bar-sur-Aube in the hamlet of Ailleville in a small building across from one of the town's leper houses. Between 1231 and 1232 the women attracted the modest patronage of local townsmen and widows, who gave in alms what they could manage—small strips of land and rents—but nothing that would qualify as a sufficient endowment in the eyes of the Cistercian order.[99] Such endowments only came in 1236, when Peter of Jaucourt and his wife, Alice, gave the nuns a portion of the tithes they collected in Chaumont.[100] Several years later Alice donated 200 measures of wine and oats paid from additional local tithes.[101] In 1237, Peter's brother, Thomas of Jaucourt, added his own endowment of 10 s. in annual rent from a house in Bar-sur-Aube.[102] In the same year, 1237, Peter personally petitioned the General Chapter for

---

96. Canivez, *Statuta*, 2:(1235)24. Robert of Thourotte was a great promoter of religious women, and Cistercian nuns specifically. In 1240 he was elected to the see of Liège where he was a supporter of Juliana of Mont-Cornillon and helped promote the feast of Corpus Christi. See Anneke B. Mulder-Bakker, *Lives of the Anchoresses: The Rise of the Urban Recluse in Medieval Europe*, trans. Myra Heerspink Scholz (Philadelphia, 2005), 78–117.

97. AD Aube, G 3101 (April 1236).

98. For the Jaucourt family, see Theodore Evergates, *The Aristocracy in the County of Champagne, 1100–1300* (Philadelphia, 2007), 188–89; and Alphonse Roserot, *Dictionnaire historique de la Champagne méridonale (Aube) des origines à 1790*, 3 vols. (Langres, 1942–48; reprint, Marseilles, 1983), 1:143–45, and genealogical table 7.

99. See chap. 2, 57–64, 71–72. AD Aude, 3 H 4079 (1231), 3 H 4077 (October 1232), and 3 H 4037 (1232).

100. AD Aube, 3 H 4082 (August 1236).

101. AD Aube, 3 H 4011 (December 1242).

102. AD Aube, 3 H 4071 (October 1237).

the association of Val-des-Vignes in the order, and the abbots of Fontenay, Quincy, and Auberive were charged with inspecting the house and its possessions, setting in motion the judicial procedures for incorporation.[103] The Jaucourt family patronized the nuns for two more generations, and Val-des-Vignes became the familial necropolis.[104] Peter's role as the major patron of the nunnery also reinforced his identity as a member of the aristocracy, just as it ensured the nuns' sufficiency and juridical association with the order.

The exact nature of sufficiency that the General Chapter had in mind is difficult to determine and was never explicitly delineated. Abbots were sent to inspect potential new communities primarily to view their buildings and calculate incomes to see that a new house would be able to live according to the form of life prescribed by the order. That there was an acceptable point of sufficiency is clear from the cases that did not meet this standard. In 1230 Philip of Nemours, a knight and intimate of Louis IX, endeavored to found an abbey for nuns of the order. No mention is made of existing buildings, or the composition of the community, but Philip gave the women ten arpents of his fief unencumbered by rents or service, which he held from King Louis.[105] Yet within two years it was clear that such a modest property was not enough to sustain the new community. With the counsel of "good men," including Gautier Cornut, archbishop of Sens, and certain brothers of the Order of Preachers (that is, Dominican friars), and with the consent of his wife, Aglentine, Philip added an additional two arpents of land to augment his endowment because it had not been "sufficient to found an abbey."[106] Four years later, after a petition from Queen Blanche of Castile, the abbots of Preuilly, Barbeaux, and Vaux-de-Cernay inspected the new community and found that the house, its rents, and its buildings were finally suitable.[107] Only then did the General Chapter agree to associate La Joie-lès-Nemours with the order. In turn, Philip and his wife received all the benefits of the order, presumably including prayers for the dead and burial in the abbey church or cloister.[108] Aristocratic patrons were thinking carefully and explicitly about what constituted sufficiency for incorporation. In the case of La Joie-lès-Nemours, the advocacy of Louis IX and Blanche of Castile

---

103. Canivez, *Statuta,* 2:(1237)67.
104. See chap. 5, 160.
105. *GC* 12, instr. 87.
106. "Ad augmentationem itaque dicti loci, qui ad fundandam abbatiam minime sufficiens videbatur, quasi duo arpenta terrae quae juxta dictum locum diversi homines possidebant, acquisivimus ab eisdem." *GC* 12, instr. 89.
107. Canivez, *Statuta,* 2:(1236)63.
108. *CG* 12, instr. 90.

certainly helped ease the process. Yet there may also have been an interest on Philip's part to preserve an ideal of apostolic poverty and thus to endow the house with only what was necessary. The king and queen mother, although they advocated for La Joie-lès-Nemours, did not contribute significant donations to the new nunnery, only their social capital and permission for the alienation of Philip's fief. This form of royal support was common to many new nunneries of the order. But royal advocacy must be distinguished from patronage. The assumption that all houses with royal charters accumulated the kind of wealth that the king's or queen's personal foundations enjoyed was simply not the case.[109]

By the early thirteenth century, in defiance of the early Cistercian prohibitions on collecting tithes and rents, sufficiency for many female communities was yoked to the possession of annual rents in kind and cash.[110] Many of these houses, founded on small plots of land within modest buildings, depended on income that could sustain a community of women, who would ideally have no cause to leave their enclosure. Collecting rents—paid in cash or measures of grain, wine, wood—would ensure that the women could maintain themselves without the distractions of earning income from their own labor or from marketing goods. It was precisely the sustaining gifts of rents in kind that the aristocracy could provide, for this was the very backbone of landed wealth. Before departing on the Fifth Crusade in 1219, Enguerrand, lord of Boves, took elaborate measures "to found and build" the Cistercian nunnery of Le Paraclet on his lands in the diocese of Amiens. He gave the new community twelve journals of land, but it was not the land itself that was important so much as the annual income it produced, valued at 40 *l.* a year.[111] If such an income was not sufficient, Enguerrand explained, it could be supplemented by additional rents owed to him from other lands near Boves. He gave the nuns rents in kind as well: wheat from his mill; oats rendered after the August harvest; the use of wood from his forests; a mill to be built near their house with water rights; and access to the wealth of fish and eels harvested from the adjacent mill pond, on top of which he donated 100 eels annually from the 1,000 his own mill in Boves produced.[112]

---

109. For the wealth of such royal foundations, see Anselme Dimier, *Saint Louis et Cîteaux* (Paris, 1954). For the difference between advocacy and patronage, see Anne E. Lester and William Chester Jordan, "La Cour Notre-Dame de Michery: A Response to Constance Berman," *Journal of Medieval History* 27 (2001): 47–48. On the amortization of fiefs, see chap. 6, 192–99.

110. See Jean-Berthold Mahn, *L'ordre cistercien et son gouvernement: Des origines au milieu du XIIIe siècle (1098–1265),* 2nd ed. (Paris, 1982), 102–18; and Constance Berman, "Cistercian Women and Tithes," *Cîteaux* 49 (1998): 95–127.

111. *GC* 10, instr. 65.

112. *GC* 10, instr. 65.

Enguerrand offered his endowment to the bishop of Amiens and to William the abbot of Valloires, who the General Chapter had designated to oversee the nunnery's incorporation.[113]

The Cistercian legislative requirement of sufficiency in endowment, like the necessity of a building, was yet another component that transformed the impulses of the women's religious movement into formal institutions. Sufficiency for women in the thirteenth century privileged the possession of rents in kind and in cash rather than land itself. The aristocratic patronage that endowed and enriched the new nunneries also anchored the communities within legitimizing social networks. These donations united the nuns with patrons and advocates who were fief-holders of the count and the king. In turn, they brought to the nunneries and to the Cistercian order a considerable degree of social prestige that augmented their endowments. This also linked the new nunneries to the social world and religious needs of the landed aristocracy. The piety of these women, many of whom came to the religious life through ministering to the sick or who were themselves penitents and extraordinary ascetics, appealed to this class, but the cultivation of such patronage typically came after the initial communities were assembled; it came as a consequence of institutionalization.[114]

Habits and Dress

Institutional affiliation and Cistercian identity were also signaled visibly, announced by the monastic habit. For new female communities, permission to wear the distinctive white or undyed Cistercian garb was granted as a privilege. In 1224, when the abbots of Cîteaux, La Ferté, Pontigny, and Clairvaux approved the incorporation of Argensolles, Countess Blanche of Navarre's foundation, they specifically extended to the new convent "the right to wear the prescribed habit, that is, scapulars and monastic cowls without hoods."[115] The monastic habit, like the penitent's garb, became a clear marker of one's commitment to a particular religious order, to a quality of religious devotion.[116] Regulations of the monastic habit paralleled a growing concern with outward appearance and the meaning of clothing as a social signifier. Dress

---

113. GC 10: 1335 and instr. 65.
114. See chap. 5, 167–70.
115. AD Marne, 70 H 12 (1224); GC 9, instr. 54; English translation in Theodore Evergates, ed. and trans., *Feudal Society in Medieval France: Documents from the County of Champagne* (Philadelphia, 1993), 139, no. 104(B).
116. See Cordelia Warr, "*De Indumentis:* The Importance of Religious Dress during the Papacy of Innocent III," in Sommerlechner, *Innocenzo III: Urbs et Orbis,* 489–502.

and its modifications distinguished rich from poor, Jew from Christian, penitent from sinner, pilgrim from local.[117] For monks and nuns, ascetic dress conveyed a voluntary commitment to humility and the renunciation of the world, differentiating them from laymen by making their vows visible.[118] The long black cowl that Benedictine monks and nuns traditionally wore symbolized the death shroud that they donned—metaphorically—upon entry into the monastic life, when they became dead to the world. In contrast, reformed orders like the Cistercians and the nuns of the Paraclete wore white or undyed wool habits signifying poverty and humility and their commitment to live by the letter of the *Rule of Benedict*.[119] Preachers and the public took notice of these differences. Three of the most influential preachers of the century—Jacques de Vitry, Humbert of Romans, and Gilbert of Tournai—composed separate sermons for nuns who wore black habits and those who wore white or gray.[120] The color of the habit underscored distinctions in piety that lay at the heart of changing interpretations of monastic spirituality.

By the mid-thirteenth century Cistercian nuns began to wear a distinctive habit, making visible their sanctioned association with the order. Although prescriptions about the Cistercian habit are rarely mentioned in foundation charters, in 1235—in the midst of the new wave of female incorporations—the General Chapter decreed that all nuns were to wear a uniform habit consisting of an undyed cowl or mantle, a scapular (similar to an apron), and a veil. The cowl should be worn at all times and the scapular for times of labor. The veil must always be black (see cover image).[121] Clothed in these habits, Cistercian nuns expressed their commitment to poverty, humility, and active

---

117. Canons 16 and 68 of the Fourth Lateran Council prescribed specific clothing and markers for the clergy and for Jews; crusaders were marked with a cross as a sign of their vow. *Decrees of the Ecumenical Councils,* 1:243 and 266. See also Ruth Mellinkoff, *Outcasts: Signs of Otherness in Northern European Art of the Late Middle Ages,* 2 vols. (Berkeley, 1993).

118. See Stewart Gordon, ed., *Robes and Honor: The Medieval World of Investiture* (New York, 2001).

119. See Giles Constable, "The Ceremonies and Symbolism of Entering Religious Life and Taking the Monastic Habit, from the Fourth to the Twelfth Centuries," in *Segni e riti nella chiesa altomedievale occidentales, Spoleto, 11–17 aprile 1985* (Spoleto, 1987), 771–834, reprinted in Constable, *Culture and Spirituality in Medieval Europe* (Aldershot, 1996); and Cistercian *Institutes,* 4: "De vestuti: Vestitus simplex et vilis absque pelliciis carnisiis staminiis qualem denique regula"; as quoted in Waddell, *Narrative and Legislative Texts,* 459.

120. Humbert of Romans, *De eruditione religiosorum praedicatorum,* bk. 2, tractatus 1, in *Maxima bibliotheca veterum patrum et antiquorum scriptorum ecclesiasticorum,* ed. Marguerin de la Bignes (Lyon, 1677), 25:456–506; Jean Longère, "Quatre sermons ad religiosas de Jacques de Vitry," in *Les religieuses en France au XIIIe siècle,* ed. Michel Parisse (Nancy, 1985), 215–300; and Nicole Bériou, "La prédication au béguinage de Paris pendant l'année liturgique, 1272–1273," *Recherches Augustiniennes* 13 (1978): 105–229.

121. Canivez, *Statuta,* 2:(1235)3.

service or manual labor. They presented a visible contrast to older aristocratic houses of nuns, such as Notre-Dame-aux-Nonnains in Troyes, whose sisters wore black habits and veils, or the nuns in the order of Fontevraud, whose regulations allowed them fur coats and long tight-fitted sleeves over their tunics and wimples if worn discreetly under their linen veils, as well as open tunics with fringe, though gloves were forbidden.[122] Only the nuns of the Paraclete, Heloise's house, which was strongly influenced by Cistercian ideals, wore simple undyed habits "made not of precious cloth, but of whatever can be made or procured cheaply."[123] Sharing this esteem for simplicity and sufficiency, Cistercian nuns were also given a scapular to wear while they labored. The implication that Cistercian nuns should engage in manual labor as part of their monastic vocation set them apart from all other orders.[124] Indeed, an element of Cistercian female spirituality was articulated through their habits, through the uniformity of their black veils and the sanctioned appearance of the scapular during times of labor.

For the Cistercians, dress became a means of regulation and recognition, marking out those within the order. In 1235 Cistercian abbots performing monastic visitations were expressly charged to oversee the uniformity of nuns' habits. This legislation was reissued in 1237 and again in 1257 as part of the revisions to the *Libellus diffinitionum*.[125] Regulation and uniformity became increasingly important at a time when many unregulated female communities adopted the penitential dress or white habits for themselves by choice. A simple white or undyed tunic of cheap cloth was the traditional dress of the penitent.[126] Many *Filles-Dieu* wore white habits before they were incorporated into the Cistercian order. Some women, like Yvette of Huy, who lived a semi-religious life caring for lepers in the diocese of Liège, took to wearing the Cistercian habit at the end of her life, though she remained outside of a monastic community and was never bound by a formal vow.[127] Whether such women were expressing their own desires to be part of the

---

122. *Regulae sanctimonialium Fontis Ebraldi, PL* 162, col. 1079B–C.

123. *Institutiones nostrae, PL*, 178, cols. 313–14: "De habitu: Habitus noster vilis est et simplex. In agninis pellibus, in lineis et laneis vestibus. In [h]iis emendis vel faciendis non eleguntur preciosa, sed quod vilius comparari vel haberi potest." Chrysogonous Waddell, ed., *The Paraclete Statutes Institutiones Nostrae: Troyes, Bibliothèque Municipale, MS 802, ff. 89r–90v* (Trappist, KY, 1987), 9–10.

124. Labor in this case was most often charity and caring for the poor and sick. See chap. 4, 143–46.

125. Lucet, *Codifications 1237 et 1257*, Dist. 15: 6(1237), Dist. 15: 8(1257). Both editions essentially repeat, with variations in grammar, the statute of 1235.

126. See the descriptions throughout Mary C. Mansfield, *The Humiliation of Sinners: Public Penance in Thirteenth-Century France* (Ithaca, 1995).

127. *VBJ*, chap. 13, paras. 39–41. On beguines who wore the Cistercian habit, see Ernst W. McDonnell, *The Beguines and Beghards in Medieval Culture: With Special Emphasis on the Belgian Scene* (New Brunswick, NJ, 1954), 184.

order or were simply penitents imitating the order's customs is unclear, but the elision is important. The adaptability of a distinct form of dress—the white habit—and the order's flurry of legislation and insistence on uniformity coincide in a critical way. The prescribed monastic habit became a way of recognizing and overseeing certain women who had been formally incorporated into the order. In this sense it was also a way of disciplining the religious body.[128]

Obedience and Oversight

It is a great irony that despite an increase in legislative references to nunneries after 1228, very few texts shed light on the juridical connections between male and female Cistercian houses. The documents that survive from northern French Cistercian nunneries offer virtually no trace of the administrative relationships outlined in the *Carta caritatis*.[129] Only on rare occasions do records of visitation survive. Other than during the process of incorporation, abbots, monks, or other male visitors almost never appear in the documents of female houses during the thirteenth century. By contrast male *conversi* appear more frequently.[130] Yet the first four decades of the thirteenth century was a period when these relationships were worked out in a climate of urgency and administrative expediency as many new nunneries gained incorporation.

Throughout the twelfth and early thirteenth centuries most nunneries were founded or incorporated under the care of a specific male abbey in close proximity to the new convent and thus able to provide administrative and spiritual care with ease.[131] Villers and Aulne in Flanders cultivated a network of local female houses initially incorporated under the guidance of their monks.[132] Port-Royal outside of Paris maintained a similar connection

---

128. On this development during the thirteenth century, see Cordelia Warr, "Religious Habits and Visual Propaganda: The Vision of the Blessed Reginald of Orléans," *Journal of Medieval History* 28 (2002): 43–72.

129. See the remarks in Pipon, *Chartrier*, 44.

130. See Anne E. Lester, "Cleaning House in 1399: Disobedience and the Demise of Cistercian Convents in Northern France at the End of the Middle Ages," in *Oboedientia. Zu Formen und Grenzen von Macht und Unterordnung im mittelalterlichen Religiosentum,* ed. Sébastien Barret and Gert Melville (Münster, 2005), 423–44; and Jörg Oberste, *Die Dokumente der Klösterlichen Visitationen* (Turnhout, 1999).

131. See Chauvin, "L'intégration des femmes."

132. See Simone Roisin, *L'hagiographie cistercienne dans le diocèse de Liège au XIIIe siècle* (Louvain, 1947), 23–76; and Goswin of Bossut, *Send Me God: The Lives of Ida the Compassionate of Nivelles, Nun of La Ramée, Arnulf, Lay Brother of Villers, and Abundus, Monk of Villers,* trans. Martinus Cawley (Turnhout, 2003; reprint, University Park, PA, 2006), 1–18.

with the abbot and monks of Vaux-de-Cernay.[133] Networks of filiation in these cases frequently grew out of previous spiritual friendships.[134] By the mid-1220s, however, as Cistercian abbots began to legislate their relationship with women in the order, they set in place more precise lines of filiation. No statute was passed detailing the new dynamic, but it is clear that female convents newly admitted into the order after the 1220s were typically affiliated directly with Cîteaux or Clairvaux.[135]

The order also experimented with female lines of filiation, that is, with convents that were intended to serve as motherhouses.[136] Writing in 1204, when St.-Antoine-des-Champs was officially incorporated into the Cistercian order, Eudes of Sully, the bishop of Paris, described the nunnery as a "special daughter of Cîteaux," ensuring that the abbess had full authority and the nunnery enjoyed all of the immunities of the Cistercian order.[137] Four years later, the father-abbots extended to St.-Antoine "and all the abbey's daughter houses" the privileges of full incorporation.[138] What this reference meant in 1208 is unclear, but, as Constance Berman has suggested, by the 1240s St.-Antoine became the motherhouse for its own filiation of communities of Cistercian nuns in the archdiocese of Sens.[139] In 1219, nuns from St.-Antoine

---

133. "apud Porrois fiat abbatia mulierium Cisterciensis ordinis, que abbatie Vallium Sarnaii sit subjecta, salva tamen in omnibus jure episcopi ecclesie Parisiensisi, nec non et salvis privilegiis et libertatibus a Sede Apostolica ordini Cisterciensis concessis." *Cartulaire de l'abbaye de Porrois,* 46, no. 22 (March 1214–15). Ten years later the abbess agreed to admit two monks, one from Savigny and one from Vaux-de-Cernay, to be the spiritual directors for the nuns; see 97–98, no. 82 (1225). This close relationship was severed in 1257 when Port-Royal passed into the care of Cîteaux. See Lucet, *Codifications 1237 et 1257,* Dist. 15: 1.

134. McGuire, "Cistercians and the Transformation of Monastic Friendships," 17–63; and Newman, "Real Men and Imaginary Women."

135. Although it is incomplete, see J.-M. Canivez's list of houses affiliated with Cîteaux in *DHGE,* 12: 860–62; also, Bonis and Wabont, "Cisterciens et cisterciennes en France du nord-ouest"; and Degler-Spengler, "Incorporation," 95.

136. This was distinct from the administrative system governing female communities within the filiation of Tart and Las Huelgas in Castile. See Degler-Spengler, "Incorporation," 87–95.

137. "facta sit domus Cistercii filia specialis, et etiam ibidem abbatissa sit auctore Domino instituta; eidem domui benigne concessimus et concedimus immunitates illas quibus gaudent caeterae Cisterciensis ordinis abbatiae." Hippolyte Bonnardot, *L'abbaye royale de Saint-Antoine-des-Champs de l'ordre de Cîteaux étude topographique et historique* (Paris, 1882), pièces justificatives, 87, no. 1 (1204).

138. "concessimus abbatissae et conventui [S]ancti Anton[ii] Parisiensis, et omnibus filiabus suis, quod sint plenarie incorporatae ordini nostro ut ante concessimus." Ibid., 88, no. 3 (1208). The abbots of Cîteaux, La Ferté, Pontigny, Clairvaux, and Morimond authorized this charter. They also granted lay brothers from nuns' houses full admission to the church, chapter, dormitory, and refectory of other male abbeys. A freedom of movement among *conversi* implied that this was one way of regulating female houses in the order.

139. Constance Berman, "Abbeys for Cistercian Nuns in the Ecclesiastical Province of Sens: Foundation, Endowment and Economic Activities of the Earlier Foundations," *Revue Mabillon* 69 (1997): 83–113, at 89.

were sent to populate the new female house of La Celle near Auxerre. When La Cour Notre-Dame-de-Michery was incorporated in 1226, the community professed to the "use and customs of the Cistercian order according to the monastery of St.-Antoine in Paris."[140] In the 1230s Blanche of Castile requested nuns from St.-Antoine to populate her new foundation of Maubuisson. From there the women were sent to Le Lys in the 1240s. Among these communities there was certainly an affiliation through shared customs, liturgical texts, observations and prayers, transmitted orally by the nuns themselves and perhaps also in written form.[141] Whether the abbess of St.-Antoine was charged with visiting these new nunneries or whether such disciplinary tasks fell to the abbot of Cîteaux as her immediate father-abbot is never noted.

St.-Antoine was not the only nunnery granted the status of a motherhouse. The countess of Champagne's foundation, Argensolles, also oversaw daughter houses. Incorporated into the order in 1224, Argensolles was granted extensive administrative privileges. The lay brothers of Argensolles were allowed to wear the same habits as *conversi* of the order and could move among Cistercian houses. The abbots allowed Argensolles to accommodate ninety nuns, with ten lay converts and twenty clerics and laymen attached to the house. And they formally recognized the community as a daughter house of Clairvaux.[142] The size of Argensolles and the privilege of movement granted to the community's *conversi* mirror the privileges extended to St.-Antoine and its *conversi* two decades earlier.[143] In 1225, the abbots gathered at Cîteaux for the General Chapter meeting conceded to Argensolles all of the powers customary of a mother house over all of the daughter houses it might found, with the disclaimer that the abbess could not appoint or remove other abbesses.[144] While virtually no sources survive listing the nunneries under Argensolles, in 1232, as Hugh, count of St.-Pol, and Philip of Mécringes transformed the *domus-Dei* of Troissy into the nunnery of L'Amour-Dieu, the bishop of Soissons accorded the new foundation the same status as that of Argensolles. The nuns made their profession to the bishop and lived under episcopal jurisdiction just like the nuns of Argensolles.[145] In this way Argensolles pro-

---

140. "abbatiam ad usus et consuetudines cisterciensis ordinibus prout monasterium Sancti Anthonii Parisiensis eiusdem ordinis." AD Yonne H 787, fol. 12v; Maximilien Quantin, ed. *Recueil de pièces pour faire suite au cartulaire général de l'Yonne (XIIIe siècle)* (Auxerre, 1873), no. 329.

141. See Berman, "Abbeys for Cistercian Nuns."

142. See Canivez, *Statuta*, 2:(1221)48, concerning inspection and approval of the abbey; (1224)20, on the habit and movement of *conversi*. See also *GC* 9, instr. 53; translated by Evergates, *Feudal Society*, 139, no. 104 (B).

143. See n. 138.

144. Canivez, *Statuta*, 2:(1225)8. Only Brigitte Degler-Spengler has noted Argensolles's role in this regard ("Incorporation," 95).

145. AD Marne, 69 H 24 (August 1232); *GC* 9, instr. 59.

vided a juridical model for foundations in the same region. It may be that in this area of northern France Argensolles was intended to act as the head of a female branch of the order, encompassing those houses overseen by the abbot of Clairvaux, just as St.-Antoine acted as a motherhouse to nunneries overseen by Cîteaux. The lines of filiation connecting L'Amour-Dieu through Argensolles to Clairvaux were extremely important to its founders. Indeed, in 1239 Philip of Mécringes made it absolutely clear that his foundation was to be incorporated into the Cistercian order as a daughter of Clairvaux.[146]

By 1240 the abbots of the order had streamlined the administration of nunneries under their care. Female houses fell either under the paternal oversight of Cîteaux or Clairvaux. While in theory this was a clear and simplified solution to the growth of the order's female houses, in practice it must have been extremely difficult for two male abbeys to oversee so many convents successfully or comprehensively. Moreover, as Brigitte Degler-Spengler has argued, "the abbot of Clairvaux directed the convents linked to his authority in a less centralized manner than did the abbot of Cîteaux; they were not combined into a comprehensive association."[147] Visitations did occur, though not as regularly as the legislation would have us imagine. Stephen of Lexington, abbot of Savigny and father-abbot over the Cistercian nunneries in the region of Normandy, left a revealing record of his visitations during the 1230s.[148] He appears initially to have maintained his interest in female administration after he became the abbot of Clairvaux in 1242. In that same year he sent visitors to the nunnery of Parc-aux-Dames, where they met fierce resistance from the abbess and her nuns, who—maintaining their vow of silence—expressed their displeasure with the abbot's admonitions by standing up and walking out of the chapter room while the visiting abbot spoke.[149] This may reflect the fact that such visitations were not typical or routine but depended on the personality and reforming zeal of a particular abbot.

In many cases, however, it was bishops who claimed and maintained jurisdiction over new Cistercian convents, freeing the order's monks from such burdens. Indeed, it was the local bishop who had the power to consecrate nuns and who was instrumental in approving the creation of new convents in

---

146. AD Marne, 69 H 21 (April 1239).
147. Degler-Spengler, "Incorporation," 95.
148. Lexington became abbot of Savigny in 1229 and in 1242 was elected abbot of Clairvaux. See P. B. Griesser, ed. "Registrum Epistolarum Stephani de Lexinton abbatis de Stanlegia et de Savigniaco," *Analecta Sacri Ordinis Cisterciensis* 2 (1946): 1–118; also Griesser, "Stephan Lexington, Abt von Savigny, als Visitator der ihm unterstehendem Frauenklöster," *Cistercienserchronik* 67 (1960): 14–34.
149. See Canivez, *Statuta,* 2:(1242)15–18, (1243)6–8, 61–68, and (1244)8. After Stephen's promotion, nuns appear with much greater frequency in the statutes.

his diocese.[150] The register of Archbishop Eudes Rigaud is replete with notes from his visitations of Cistercian convents and suggests that bishops filled in for the order in overseeing its nuns.[151] Moreover, after 1228, as the Cistercian order absolved itself from spiritual care for new convents, it fell to the secular clergy and parish priests to serve as chaplains and perform the mass in the smaller nunneries of northern France. For those convents founded in leper houses or *domus-Dei,* a connection with the diocesan clergy was often already in place.[152] These relationships did not have the juridical clarity that the Cistercians were known for and were only occasionally committed to parchment, but they remained absolutely crucial for the spiritual life of the nuns. In some sense then, after 1228 a kind of benign neglect ensued between the Cistercian order and its female houses. Only in times of acute financial pressure on the order as whole did the abbots manifest a keen interest in these convents.[153]

The Losses of Incorporation

Traditional historiography has portrayed the entry of women into the Cistercian order during the thirteenth century in seismic terms. Richard Southern characterized this process as an act of submission whereby "the legislators had to bow before the force of feminine liberty." Likewise, Louis Lekai described the inclusion of women as a kind of violation, noting that "some time between 1190 and 1210 the gates of the order had been forced open for the admission of nuns."[154] This perception was founded in part on a deeply ingrained understanding—inflected by the rhetoric of popes like Innocent III and Gregory IX—that true religion was ordered religion, guided by a rule and tethered by obedience. This narrative also takes the Cistercian legislation at face value, without sufficiently contextualizing it in the broader religious changes of the thirteenth century.

---

150. This relationship was spelled out in many of the nunneries' foundation charters. See, for example, Notre-Dame-des-Prés, AD Aube, G 3101 (April 1236); L'Amour-Dieu, GC 9, instr. 62–63, col. 137; and for L'Abbaye-aux-Bois, Pipon, *Chartrier,* no. 47, annex II, nos. 3–4 and 45–46.

151. See Odo Rigaldus, *The Register of Eudes of Rouen,* trans. Sydney M. Brown (New York, 1964); and Penelope Johnson, *Equal in Monastic Profession: Religious Women in Medieval France* (Chicago, 1991).

152. See chap. 4, 129–34; and Pipon, *Chartrier,* 47–48, which states that in some cases local abbots could have performed *cura monialium* even if an abbey was subject to Clairvaux specifically.

153. See epilogue, 203–8, and Pipon, *Chartrier,* 50.

154. See, for example, Richard Southern, *Western Society and the Church in the Middle Ages* (New York, 1970; reprint, 1979), 317; and Louis Lekai, *The Cistercians: Ideals and Reality* (Kent, OH, 1977), 349.

Rarely if ever is an argument offered to explain why women may have wanted to join the Cistercian order in the early decades of the thirteenth century. It is presumed that the benefits of incorporation, specifically freedom from episcopal oversight and tithe exemption, compelled women in great numbers. Or likewise, that the profound influence of Bernard of Clairvaux, Cistercian spirituality, and Cistercian preaching had a powerful appeal for women. Although the latter explanation may hold, the former cannot. First, most of the Cistercian convents founded in the thirteenth century submitted to episcopal jurisdiction. Second, while some female houses were exempt from paying tithes on lands they cultivated, much of the income nunneries received came from rents or the proceeds of tithes. Fundamentally, there is little evidence that suggests that women themselves ardently sought admission into the order.

Rather, pressure on the order came most profoundly from the papacy, secular patrons, and reform-minded bishops seeking to regulate the apostolic movements animating their dioceses. Reform was often initiated in an atmosphere of urgency, galvanized by fears of heresy and anxiety about the legitimate role of *mulierculae* in the church. In the 1220s and 1230s the Cistercian order offered a clear and well-defined set of regulations that could be applied to new communities of women reformed as nuns. Thus it was not so much, as Herbert Grundmann once argued, that the Cistercians were "the most accommodating tool of the curia in opposing the religious movement," but that the order proved the most accommodating in its ability to extend its legislation to unaffiliated religious women.[155]

By turning the question of Cistercian affiliation on its head and asking what was lost for these women rather than what was gained, the effects of incorporation grow more transparent. The most profound loss was a freedom of movement that resulted from the Cistercian regulations about claustration.[156] No longer could women move with the same impunity among family, friends, and neighbors, offering prayers, advice, and charity. Second was the abandonment of the practice of avowed poverty. The legislation governing sufficiency was intended to ensure that nuns would not immiserate their communities. Freedom of movement and poverty were at the heart of the lived apostolic ideal. Moreover, they made the virtuous pursuit of mendicancy possible. Movement and poverty facilitated holy begging, which brought

---

155. Herbert Grundmann, *Religious Movements in the Middle Ages: The Historical Links between Heresy, the Mendicant Orders, and the Women's Religious Movement in the Twelfth and Thirteenth Century*, trans. Steven Rowan (Notre Dame, IN, 1995), 77.

156. Lucet, *Codifications 1237 et 1257*, Dist. 15: 5(1237), Dist. 15: 7(1257).

humility and salvation to both the alms-giver and receiver by allowing each to imitate Christ as the holy poor and the holy savior.

The tenacity with which religious women clung to these practices even after their incorporation shows how central they were to the devotional life of the movement. Indeed, many of the houses incorporated during the 1230s subsisted at the level of poverty, even as they were endowed with land and rental incomes in cash and kind. The nuns in these convents chose to live consistently close to the bone, aided in this by the hospices and leper communities they maintained. To be sure, this was not the case with all female Cistercian foundations. Some, like Argensolles and Parc-aux-Dames or the royal houses of Le Lys and Maubuisson and the nunneries of St.-Antoine-des-Champs and Port-Royal, flourished economically. Yet because such economic success was possible, it makes clear that in some cases it was all the more deliberately eschewed in favor of charity fostered through the commitment to poverty.

Many of the smaller Cistercian convents in Champagne practiced a particular kind of charity that channeled the nunneries' incomes to the poor, the traveling sick, the leprous and needy—the *minores et miseratos, infirmos et pauperes Christi*—leaving the nuns themselves with the bare minimum necessary for institutional survival. As a consequence of real poverty many communities sent nuns out to beg alms. Indeed, by the second half of the thirteenth century charges of mendicancy were the most frequent abuse to appear in the official records of the order.[157] Such accusations reveal less about the financial inabilities of nuns or poor endowments (something the order attempted to correct for among houses it incorporated), than they do about the tenacious appeal of cultivated poverty.[158] This ideal persisted from the practices of the early communities of religious women that were incorporated into the order. Unlike some of their Cistercian contemporaries, these nuns were not focused on the profits of grange agriculture or amassing vast monastic endowments, but were intent on expanding the boundaries of charity. The fact that nuns did so even at the risk of disobedience to the order articulates the power and persuasiveness of the *vita apostolica* and these women's continued implementation of its ideals.

---

157. See Jordan, "Cistercian Nunnery of La Cour," 318–19; Lester, "Cleaning House in 1399," 431–36; and Henri d'Arbois de Jubainville, *Histoire des ducs et des comtes de Champagne* (Paris, 1859–69), 4.2: 613, and 5, register no. 3301.

158. See Katherine Gill, "*Scandala*: Controversies concerning *Clausura* and Women's Religious Communities in Late Medieval Italy," in *Christendom and Its Discontents: Exclusion, Persecution, and Rebellion, 1000–1500*, ed. Scott L. Waugh and Peter D. Diehl (Cambridge, 1996), 177–203, esp. 178, 187, 195, and 201.

CHAPTER 4

The Bonds of Charity
The Special Cares of Cistercian Nuns

Around 1225, Yvette of Huy, a recluse living in the southern Low Countries, took on a final penitential act of conversion to the religious life: she began to wear the rough Cistercian habit under her clothes, a commitment she kept until her death several years later. Yvette's adult life encompassed a series of personal religious conversions that were indicative of the kinds of transformations many women of northern France experienced as they entered the religious life. Yvette had been a wife and mother of three. After the death of her husband, when she was eighteen, she lived for five years as a widow, in a semi-religious status of mourning and devotion to Christ, offering hospitality to the sick and alms to the poor from her urban home.[1] At twenty-three, a more radical orientation took hold.[2] She gave away all of her possessions—furniture, clothes, jewelry, everything—encouraged her older son to join the Cistercian order, left the younger in the care of her father, and began to live among lepers in an old and neglected

---

1. *VBJ*, chap. 6, para. 16; chap. 9, para. 32. She chose publically to be a "bride of Christ" (*illa se Christum elegisse in sponsum*). On this as a legal status which women understood, see Sarah McNamer, *Affective Meditation and the Invention of Medieval Compassion* (Philadelphia, 2010), 25–57.
2. *VBJ*, chap. 9, para. 32. At this point, more mature in years, she began to consider her whole life (*coepit totius vitae suae statum*) and desired to live apart, in solitude, where she could redeem her life by serving Christ, for whom to serve is to reign (*coepit concupiscere aliquem solitudis locum, ubi reliquum vitae suae tempus redimeret, astricta magis eius servitio, cui servire regnare est*).

117

leprosarium across the river Meuse beyond the city walls of Huy.³ There she tended the sick, "ate and drank among them and washed herself in their bath water and even mixed her blood with theirs," and prayed to become a leper herself.⁴ Her commitment and dedication inspired many men and women to join her in a life of service to God and care of the sick. After living like this for eleven years, at thirty-four, she took on a new vow and had herself enclosed in a cell connected to the lepers' chapel.⁵ There she lived out the next thirty years of her life as a *mediatrix* for her community, connecting her social world with the divine.⁶ It was here, in the last years of her life, that she took the final step of acquiring the Cistercian habit, a private act for she did not live with other women in a Cistercian nunnery. The Cistercian habit was the last marker of her commitment to a life of penance, charity, and prayer, a visible sign of her private vow. Yvette died in 1228, the same year the Cistercian order passed its most definitive statute concerning the acceptance of new Cistercian nunneries. She died in the order's tunic, one of many like-minded and similarly clothed religious women whose habits conveyed their religious ideals and sense of regular, rigorous devotion.

Yvette's closeness with lepers—first caring for them and then living in a chapel connected to their community—is often depicted as unusual and exemplary, and that is perhaps what her hagiographer, a canon of the Premonstratensian community of Floreffe, wanted his readers to believe. Yet Yvette's choices were more common than often imagined. In the context of Champagne her behavior and her final acceptance of the Cistercian habit would not have been atypical at all. As discussed previously, many convents were founded in leper houses or small local hospices and *domus-Dei*, only later to become formal institutions following the Cistercian customs. In

---

3. *VBJ*, chap. 1, para. 13; chap. 9, para. 25; and chap. 10, para. 34. Eventually her father became a Cistercian monk at Villers and her older son a Cistercian monk at Orval. Later, her younger son joined Trois-Fontaines. Her mother had also professed the religious life, but Hugh never states where or in what capacity. Her youngest child died as an infant. See Jennifer Carpenter, "Juette of Huy, Recluse and Mother (1158–1228): Children and Mothering in the Saintly Life," in *Power of the Weak: Studies on Medieval Women*, ed. Jennifer Carpenter and Sally-Beth MacLean (Urbana, IL, 1995), 57–93.

4. "manducabat et bibebat cum leprosis, lauabatque se de aqua balnei ipsorum: minuebat quoque eis ipsamet sanguinem, ut sanguine eorum inficeretur, ut sordes attraherent sordes, et lepra efficeret lepram." *VBJ*, chap. 11, para. 36.

5. *VBJ*, chap. 14, para. 42. On Yvette's role as a recluse, see Anneke B. Mulder-Bakker, *Lives of the Anchoresses: The Rise of the Urban Recluse in Medieval Europe*, trans. Myra Heerspink Scholz (Philadelphia, 2005), 51–77.

6. "ut internis caelestium secretorum consiliis tam frequenter admissa, mediatrix quodammodo haberetur ad correctionem multorum, inter caelestia et terrestria, visibilia et invisibilia, inter Deum et homines." *VBJ*, chap. 41, para. 107.

many instances, however, communities sustained these connections long after their nunneries were officially incorporated into the order. The administration of hospices and *domus-Dei* and the care of the sick and poor were ways that Cistercian nuns retained a connection to the ideals of the *vita apostolica*.[7] Moreover, as was the case with Yvette, caring for the sick was often part of the religious transformation of devout women into Cistercian nuns. In offering such care, nuns extended the Cistercian ideal of charity (*caritas*) outside the monastic context and melded it with the practices of penitential piety so fundamental to thirteenth-century spirituality.[8]

This chapter traces how and why Cistercian nunneries assumed these administrative duties and what it meant for the nuns to care for the poor and sick. This institutional affiliation had its roots in the goals of the Third (1179) and Fourth (1215) Lateran Councils, which sought to reform informal hospital communities, whose numbers had burgeoned at a staggering pace in the previous century. When bishops and patrons founded Cistercian nunneries within older leper houses, or gifted hospitals and *domus-Dei* to the nunneries, they did so with the double aim of reforming these institutions along monastic lines and institutionalizing the ideal of apostolic charity as outlined in the conciliar degrees. This practical connection had a deep spiritual significance based on the complex and often competing religious meanings attendant with poverty and leprosy. Providing for and living with the poor, leprous, and suffering marked a pivotal moment of progress within the religious life. By the mid-thirteenth century active charity, manual labor, and service for those who suffered in this world became fundamental components of a distinctive kind of Cistercian female spirituality.

A Revolution in Charity

Charity, *caritas,* had defined Cistercian concepts of religious affiliation for nearly a century. Yet institutionalized *caritas* that encompassed the larger social body outside the monastic cloister presented itself as an issue for the order only at the turn of the thirteenth century and specifically through the development of the order's nunneries. Although hospitality was a common part of the monastic life and other religious orders provided for their sick in

---

7. See Augustine Thompson, *Cities of God: The Religion of the Italian Communes, 1125–1325* (University Park, PA, 2005), 87–88, 188–200; and Anna Benvenuti Papi, "Pubblica assistenza e marginalità femminile," in her *"In Castro poenitentiae": Santità e società femminile nell'Italia medievale* (Rome, 1991), 656–58.
8. See Martha Newman, *The Boundaries of Charity: Cistercian Culture and Ecclesiastical Reform, 1098–1180* (Stanford, 1996), 17–19, 117–21, and chaps. 5–9 more generally.

an infirmary, the care Cistercian nuns bestowed differed from that of traditional monastic houses for it extended to those beyond their own communities and embraced the care of marginal populations.[9] Charity responded to need. The staggering economic and social changes of the twelfth century that fostered thriving new urban centers across Europe also heightened the divisions between rich and poor, local and foreigner, the well-connected and the marginalized. The destitute and miserable—those outside the expanding economy, without social connections or kin—became both more visible and increasingly anonymous. Whether directed by bishops and local clergy or growing from a common understanding of social need, men and women responded to these transformations by embracing a return to the Gospels. Apostolic charity provided a model for social care, just as a new devotion to the humanity of Christ valorized the spiritual power of poverty. Moreover, the idea that the poor and sick had a special relationship with Christ in that they shared in His suffering and in turn enjoyed a privileged role as intercessors with God became a common theme of sermons and exempla collections and contributed to a realignment in thinking about the care of such miserable persons. The shift in mentality and behavior during the decades on either side of 1200 constituted a veritable "revolution in charity" reflecting the changed social conditions of the thirteenth century.[10]

Charitable institutions, large and small, formal and informal, expanded rapidly during the twelfth century apace with unprecedented population growth. In France not only did major cities like Paris, Rouen, Montpellier, and Orléans experience profound demographic change, but smaller towns and parishes, particularly in the archdioceses of Sens and Reims, expanded rapidly as well.[11] Over the course of the thirteenth century Paris

---

9. See, for example, David N. Bell, "The Cistercians and the Practice of Medicine," *Cîteaux* 40 (1989): 139–73. Moreover, by the thirteenth century the Cistercian *Statutes* and *Libellus diffinitionum* forbade the care of lepers in houses of the order and discouraged lepers from living near Cistercian abbeys: Josephus-Mia Canivez, *Statuta Capitulorum Generalium Ordinis Cisterciensis ab anno 1116 ad annum 1786*, 8 vols. (Louvain, 1933–41), 2:(1204)5; and Bernard Lucet, *Les codifications cisterciennes de 1237 et de 1257* (Paris, 1977), Dist. 10, 19 (on lepers), 12 (on pilgrims). Concerning Cistercian hospitality, see Jutta Maria Berger, *Die Geschichte der Gastfreundschaft im Hochmittelalterlichen Mönchtum: Die Cistercienser* (Berlin, 1999); and Julie Kerr, *Monastic Hospitality: The Benedictines in England, c. 1070–c.1250* (Woodbridge, 2007).

10. André Vauchez, "Assistance et charité en occident, XIIIe–XVe siècles," in *Domanda e consumi: Livelli e strutture (nei secoli XIII–XVIII)* (Florence, 1978), 151–62, at 152. See also François-Olivier Touati, *Maladie et société au Moyen Âge: La lèpre, les lépreux et les léproseries dans la province ecclésiastique de Sens jusqu'au milieu du XVIe siècle* (Brussels, 1998), 187–246; Annie Saunier, *"Le pauvre malade" dans le cadre hospitalier médiéval: France du nord, vers 1300–1500* (Paris, 1993), 5–52; and Carole Rawcliffe, *Leprosy in Medieval England* (Woodbridge, 2006), 104–54.

11. See the figures assembled by François-Olivier Touati, *Archives de la lèpre: Atlas des léproseries entre Loire et Marne au Moyen Âge* (Paris, 1996), 16–23. Also Ferdinand Lot, "L'état des feux de 1328,"

grew from approximately 80,000 to 200,000 people. By midcentury Orléans held 25,000 souls, Chartres 10,000, and cities like Sens, Troyes, Provins, and Meaux counted populations of 5,000 to 10,000, numbers that swelled further during the annual fairs.[12] At the same time the foundation of new towns and the extension of suburban spaces contributed to the multiplication of parishes. Urban and suburban growth attendant with mobility and migration affected everyone, the wealthy and well connected, the vagrant and the laborer, the sick and poor. Under these conditions, institutionalized charity was crucial. By the mid-twelfth century all of the major urban centers of northern France had at least one formal hospital, and often larger cities such as Paris had many more dedicated to specific ailments including leprosy, blindness, ergotism, and so forth.[13] Troyes, Provins, Bar-sur-Aube, Tonnerre, and Auxerre, for example, each had urban hospitals dedicated generally to the care of the sick along with several smaller hospices inside and outside the town walls, which cared for the poor and traveling sick.[14] By the end of the century new hospitals of the Order of the Holy Spirit appeared in many of these towns as well, dedicated specifically to caring for "miserable persons" like pregnant women and foundlings.[15]

New hospitals and leper houses served acute social needs. This was noticeably the case as leprosy became endemic in the European population over the course of the twelfth century. Leper hospitals, both well-endowed institutions and smaller leprosaria, appeared in staggering numbers across Europe, and with particular density in northern France. In the archdiocese of

---

BEC 90 (1929): 51–107, 256–315; and Guy Fourquin, *Le domaine royal en Gâtinais d'après la prisée de 1332* (Paris, 1963).

12. Philippe Dollinger, "Le chiffre de la population de Paris au XIVe siècle: 210,000 ou 80,000 habitants?" *Revue historique* 116 (1956): 35–44; and Raymond Cazelles, "La population de Paris avant la peste noire," *Comptes-rendus des séances de l'académie des inscriptions et belles-lettres* 110 (1966): 539–50.

13. See Sharon Farmer, *Surviving Poverty in Medieval Paris: Gender, Ideology, and the Daily Lives of the Poor* (Ithaca, 2002), 85–92, on the varieties of hospitals. Dorothy-Louise Mackay, *Les hôpitaux et la charité à Paris aux XIIIe siècle* (Paris, 1923), 87–88, lists sixteen hospitals ringing the city and within its walls, including two hospices for widows and the *Filles-Dieu*, as well as four leprosaria. I thank Sharon Farmer for this reference.

14. On the growth of hospitals and life inside, see Adam J. Davis, "Preaching in Thirteenth-Century Hospitals," *Journal of Medieval History* 36 (2010): 72–89.

15. Touati, *Maladie et société*, offers a near exhaustive catalogue, supplemented by his *Archives de la lèpre*. For comparative examples of the growth of hospitals in Europe, see Gisela Drossbach, ed., *Hospitäler im Mittelalter und Früher Neuzeit: Frankreich, Deutschland und Italien: Ein Vergleichende Geschichte. Hôpitaux au Moyen Âge et aux temps modernes: France, Allemagne et Italie: une histoire comparée* (Munich, 2007); and Sethina Watson, "The Origins of the English Hospital," *Transactions of the Royal Historical Society* 16 (2006): 75–94; also Anne E. Lester, "Lost But Not Yet Found: Medieval Foundlings and Their Care in Northern France, 1200–1500," *Proceedings of the Western Society for French History* 35 (2007): 1–17.

Sens alone, François-Olivier Touati counted no fewer than 395 leprosaria.[16] In Champagne, the comital family took the lead in supporting such communities. In 1123, Count Hugh (r. 1093–1125) founded the leper hospital of Les Deux-Eaux, three kilometers outside of Troyes, which grew from a community of the infirm living under the care of a priest and a female recluse.[17] The count's benefaction transformed it into one of several well-endowed institutions specifically for lepers, who took formal vows, much like monks and nuns, upon entry into the community. Similar "grandes léproseries" were built throughout the twelfth century, including St.-Lazare in Blois, Le Grand-Beaulieu in Chartres, St.-Lazare of Pontoise, St.-Lazare of Paris, St.-Lazare of Meaux, le Popelin of Sens, Pontfraud, St.-Florentin, and St.-Lazare of Orléans.[18]

By the turn of the thirteenth century, informal hospices for lepers and the poor dotted the roadsides and fringed villages and hamlets. Often founded on aristocratic estates, these hospices reveal local impulses for practical charity.[19] They fulfilled needs that could not be met by the larger urban foundations. In 1257, Count Thibaut V made provision in his testament to give twenty pounds each to the hospitals in his castles in Champagne and ten pounds to the leper communities in the same castles.[20] The lords of Ramerupt and Jaucourt, the counts of Brienne and the lords of Dampierre—all vassals of the count—founded and patronized small leprosaria within their castles as well, perhaps in emulation of comital largess, but also no doubt as part of their seigneurial responsibilities, as a manifestation of their capacity for lordly giving.[21] Care for the sick at the local level was a defining aspect of paternalism inherent in aristocratic identity. Care crossed confessional lines as well. Provins, for example, boasted a separate leper house for the Jewish

---

16. Touati, *Archives de la lèpre*, 29; and idem, *Maladie et société*, 247–307.

17. M. Harmand, "Notice historique sur la léproserie de la ville de Troyes," *MSA* 7 and 8 (1848): 429–680, pièces justificatives, 519–54.

18. The counties of Blois-Champagne were still united during Thibaut II's rule, thus he was referred to as the "founder" of the Le Grand-Beaulieu in Chartres and St.-Lazare of Blois. Touati, *Archives de la lèpre*, 25–27 and 41–48.

19. On these distinctions, see ibid., 35–41.

20. *Layettes*, 3:391–92, no. 4387; in English, see Theodore Evergates, ed. and trans., *Feudal Society in Medieval France: Documents from the County of Champagne* (Philadelphia, 1993), 70–72, no. 53.

21. Each of these local lords patronized the leper houses near their castles. The lords of Dampierre were patrons to the houses along the northern border of the county in Châlons, Vitry, and at St.-Dizier (AD Marne, 70 H and 71 H), as were the counts of Brienne. The lords of Ramerupt were the founders and patrons of the leper house in Ramerupt; see Touati, *Archives de la lèpre*, 363; AD Aube, G 408 (1282). The lords of Jancourt patronized the lepers at both Ramerupt and Bar-sur-Aube: AD Aube, 3 H 4038 (1272). See also Henri d'Arbois de Jubainville, "Les premiers seigneurs de Ramerupt," *BEC* 22 (1861): 440–58, at 448–49. Most of these leper communities came to be associated with Cistercian nunneries; see appendix.

population of the town, which enjoyed the count's protection.[22] By the end of the century, burghers in the Champagne fair towns began to gift their urban or suburban residences for the creation of small hospitals within the city walls.[23]

These houses must have been modest affairs, but they were ubiquitous by the thirteenth century. When the knight Hegan of Ervy drew up his will before departing for the Holy Land in 1190, among numerous small gifts he set aside 20 *s*. for each of the leper houses along the road between Pontigny and Troyes.[24] The route that connects the famous Cistercian abbey to the comital capital stretches only sixty kilometers. Hegan's generosity suggests that there was a leper house every three kilometers. The amount of the knight's bequest and the frequency of the houses implies that these were humble places, housing only a few lepers who subsisted on what charity they could gain, but certainly not cut off from the local community or from the salvation-consciousness of pious knights, merchants, pilgrims and penitent crusaders like Hegan, who would have frequently passed by.[25]

Informal hospices for lepers had much in common with houses set aside for the care of the poor and infirm. *Domus-Dei* or *maisons-Dieu,* as they were known, sheltered the sick and poor, but also housed travelers, wayfarers, and other strangers unhinged from the local community.[26] Pilgrims and penitents, who have assumed a voluntary exile and who chose to live for a time as *pauperes Christi* could also have found shelter in *domus-Dei*. It would be unwise, however, to make rigid distinctions about afflictions and the care given in these houses. Nor should we be too restrictive in our thinking about leprosy and its medieval definitions. To be called a leper connoted something more than ailments and symptoms; it suggested a state of mind

---

22. François-Olivier Touati, "Domus judaeorum leprosorum: Une léproserie pour les juifs à Provins au XIIIe siècle," in *Foundations et oeuvres charitables au Moyen Âge,* ed. Jean Dufour and Henri Platelle (Paris, 1999), 97–106.

23. Henri d'Arbois de Jubainville, "Études sur les documents antérieurs à l'année 1285, conservés dans les archives des quatre petits hôpitaux de la ville de Troyes," *MSA* 21 (1857): 49–116. And *Testaments Saint-Quentinois du XIVe siècle,* ed. Pierre Desportes (Paris, 2003), 124–27, no. 44 (1254).

24. Maximilien Quantin, ed. *Recueil de pièces pour faire suite au cartulaire général de l'Yonne (XIIIe siècle)* (Auxerre, 1873), 424–25, no. 420; in English, see Evergates, *Feudal Society,* 68–69, no. 51.

25. On the integration of such houses, see Rawcliffe, *Leprosy,* 252–343; and Sethina Watson, "City as Charter: Charity and the Lordship of English Towns, 1170–1250," in *Cities, Texts and Social Networks, 400–1500: Experiences and Perceptions of Medieval Urban Space,* ed. Caroline Goodson, Anne E. Lester, and Carol Symes (Aldershot, 2010), 235–62.

26. See Marcia Kupfer, "Symbolic Cartography in a Medieval Parish: From Spatialized Body to Painted Church at Saint-Aignan-sur-Cher," *Speculum* 75 (2000): 615–67, at 629–31; Alain Saint-Denis, *L'Hôtel-Dieu de Laon, 1150–1300: Institution hospitalière et société aux XIIe et XIIIe siècles* (Nancy, 1983); and Leon Le Grand, "Les maison-Dieu et léproseries du diocèse de Paris au milieu du XIVe siècle," *Mémoires de la Société de l'histoire de Paris et de l'Île-de-France* 25 (1898): 47–178.

that was penitential and ideally monastic once one joined a community. It designated a state of being that was at once physical and spiritual. Certainly there were differences between the ambulatory and the bed-ridden, the sick and chronically ill, but the taxonomies employed in the greater hospitals of the later Middle Ages did not apply in these smaller communities. Rather, as semi-religious institutions *domus-Dei* sheltered those in need as the poor of Christ and the poor in Christ, a broad and generous spiritual designation. Because such institutions offered both spiritual and physical care, a priest, either from the local parish or connected to a house of canons, undertook the care of souls (*cura animarum*) for those within.[27]

The proliferation of small charitable foundations, whether leper houses or *domus-Dei,* saw the integration of lepers—in the broadest sense—and the poor into the everyday lives of men and women who inhabited the county and traveled its roads. When plotted on a map these smaller communities align precisely along the major trade routes and circulation patterns that cut through the region.[28] With respect to physical care, *domus-Dei* and smaller leper hospices filled the gaps of the larger well-endowed institutions like Les Deux-Eaux, and as such they mapped a new and expanded cartography of charity and caregiving onto the landscape. As Marcia Kupfer has remarked, because of their location on the outskirts of towns and along roadways, these smaller institutions "reorganized tracts of land in the interstices between town and village...they helped tie desolate outlying areas to centers of population never more than two or three kilometers away."[29] This was precisely the effect of founding Cistercian nunneries in leper houses and *domus-Dei,* for they too served to reorganize and reform suburban space in line with the ideals of apostolic charity.

Apostolic Charity and Its Regulation

As the numbers of formal and informal hospitals and leper houses increased over the course of the twelfth and thirteenth centuries, the challenge of regulating these establishments grew ever more acute.[30] The accretion of conciliar

---

27. See Marcia Kupfer, *The Art of Healing: Painting for the Sick and the Sinner in a Medieval Town* (University Park, PA, 2003), 39–41.
28. See Touati, *Archives de la lèpre,* 71; and Mackay, *Les hôpitaux et la charité,* 87–93.
29. Kupfer, "Symbolic Cartography," 631.
30. See, for example, Daniel Le Blévec, *La part du pauvre: L'assistance dans les pays du Bas-Rhône du XIIe siècle au milieu du XVe siècle,* 2 vols. (Rome, 2000); Gisela Drossbach, "Das Hospital—eine kirchenrechtliche Institution? (ca. 1150–ca. 1350)," *Zeitschrift der Savigny-Stiftung für Rechtsgeschichte-Kanonistische Abteilung* 87 (2001): 510–22; and Pierre de Spiegeler, *Les hôpitaux et l'assistance à Liège (Xe–XVe siècles): Aspects institutionnels et sociaux* (Paris, 1987), 105–43.

legislation drawn up during the decades on either side of 1200 reveals the growing complexities of administering to the poor and sick, and to lepers in particular. How secular or religious were these communities to be? And what was the relationship between physical ailment and spiritual health? In 1179, the prelates who gathered in Rome for the Third Lateran Council offered a programmatic answer. With canon 23 the council decreed that groups of lepers, who had come together to live a common life, should be "able to establish a church for themselves with a cemetery and [celebrate the mass with] their own priest."[31] This decree has often been interpreted as a mandate for the exclusion of lepers, who it seemed were to be relegated to their own houses and churches. But this was not what the reformers intended. They provided explicitly for the spiritual administration of these communities, and they did so "in accordance with apostolic charity" (*de benignitate apostolica*).[32] The canon began by invoking 1 Corinthians 12, which chastises those who do not pay greater honor to the weaker members of society. Yet these new communities should take care "not to harm the parochial rights of established churches." To ensure their material and financial success, Pope Alexander III declared that all leper houses "should not be compelled to pay tithes for their gardens or the pasture of their animals," echoing the exemptions enjoyed by the Cistercians by the late twelfth century.[33] As Joseph Avril has argued, the Third Lateran Council's decree made leper houses into quasi-monastic communities with spiritual rights and regulations.[34] Many of the new statutes drawn up for local hospitals in northern France closely resembled monastic rules.[35]

The reforms initiated in Rome in 1179 were reiterated in the following decades. Smaller councils held in Paris in 1212 and in Rouen in 1214 dealt with the question of hospital administration more specifically and addressed how to put such reforms into effect. Bishops in attendance at these councils

---

31. "ut ubicumque tot simul sub communi *vita* fuerint congregati, qui ecclesiam sibi cum coemeterio constituere et proprio gaudere valeant presbytero"; "Third Lateran Council—1179," in *Decrees of the Ecumenical Councils,* ed. Norman P. Tanner, 2 vols. (Washington, DC, 1990), 1:222–23.

32. Ibid., 1:222. The language of the canon is at odds with its interpretation. See, for example, Robert I. Moore, *The Formation of a Persecuting Society: Authority and Deviance in Western Europe 950–1250,* 2nd ed. (Oxford, 2007), 49–54. More recently this interpretation has been amended in Rawcliffe, *Leprosy,* 257–59.

33. "Caveant tamen ut iniuriosi veteribus ecclesiis de iure parochiali nequaquam exsistant. . . . Statuimus etiam ut de hortis et nutrimentis animalium suorum, decimas tribuere non cogantur." "Third Lateran Council—1179," 1:222–23.

34. Joseph Avril, "Le IIIe concile de Latran et les communautés de lépreux," *Revue Mabillon* 60 (1981): 21–76.

35. See Leon Le Grand, *Statutes d'hôtels-Dieu et de léproseries: Recueil de textes du XIIe au XIVe siècle* (Paris, 1901).

recognized that the care of the poor, sick, and pilgrims often fell to monastic houses, but they legislated that all those who served in such houses must wear a religious habit to distinguish themselves from their secular counterparts. They affirmed that alms given for the sick must be used for that purpose, to provide what was needed.[36] The local French councils also recognized that it was women, and nuns in particular, who cared for lepers and the sick. Indeed the canons addressed to "those who remain in houses of lepers and hospitals, ministering to those who are sick and to pilgrims" all appear under rubrics pertaining to nuns and decree that all such women must renounce whatever was their own, take a vow of continence, and obediently promise faith and devotion to the bishop.[37] To the prelates and compilers of the canons, the obligations and vows of women in leper houses were so similar to that of professed nuns that their legislation fell under the decrees for nuns (*ad moniales*).

The local French councils that broached these issues were preparatory for the great council of 1215 convened under Pope Innocent III's direction. Calling to the Lateran over 400 European bishops, and 800 other prelates and leading secular princes and nobles, Innocent's aim was nothing short of reconfiguring the relationship between lay society and the church. The Fourth Lateran Council followed the agenda tested earlier in northern France and addressed major issues of social and religious significance.[38] New canons legislated a staggering variety of practices including the prohibition of usury, the institution of a definition of marriage, the obedience of the secular clergy, uniformity in the regular life, a response to heresy, and a renewed call to crusade. The council did *not*, however, address a single canon to the reform of women religious or to nuns specifically. As for hospitals and the care of the sick, Innocent departed from the practical administrative concerns addressed locally among northern French bishops and approached illness as a theological problem. The perspective was again that of the New Testament. Returning to 1 Corinthians 12, Innocent and his advisors stressed the idea that the health of the body mirrored that of the soul, noting that both were part of the larger social body of the Christian

---

36. J. D. Mansi, ed., *Sacrorum conciliorum nove et amplissima collectio*, 53 vols. (Venice, Florence, and Paris, 1759–89), vol. 22, cols. 835–36, 906, and 913.

37. The canons of the councils of Paris and Rouen are nearly identical on this matter, though they are listed separately in the manuscript sources. "De iis qui manent in domibus leprosorum et hospitalibus, ut infirmis et peregrinis ministrent"; ibid., cols. 835–36 and 913.

38. On Robert of Courson and the reforms emanating from Paris, for example, see John W. Baldwin, *Masters, Princes and Merchants: The Social Views of Peter the Chanter and His Circle,* 2 vols. (Princeton, 1970), 1:315–43.

community, bound by charity and mutual affection. The legislation on the care of the sick was conceptually tied to new doctrines arising out of the same council, specifically the necessity of annual confession for Christians to maintain the well-being of the soul and hence the health of the body, thus further entwining sickness, charity, and penance.

Canons 21 and 22 of Lateran IV together defined the relationship between the priest and the individual and the relationship of the community as a whole. Canon 21 famously made annual private confession to a priest a required penitential exercise for all Christians. The care the priest offered was couched in a familiar simile:

> The priest shall be discerning and prudent, so that like a skilled doctor he may pour wine and oil over the wounds of the injured one. Let him carefully inquire about the circumstances of both the sinner and the sin, so that he may prudently discern what sort of advice he ought to give and what remedy to apply, using various means to heal the sick person. Let him take the utmost care, however, not to betray the sinner at all by word or sign or in any other way.[39]

Illness was thus linked symbolically to sin, or, rather, sinning made one ill in the spirit. Illness was also a metaphor for the diseased and corrupted soul. Its care existed in the relationship between the individual and their physician/priest and the ability to cure the self through contrition and repentance.

Canon 22, which followed, made it clear that the reverse was also true: sickness could be a sign of sin, in which case physical health could be restored only if spiritual health was seen to first:

> As the sickness of the body may sometimes be the result of sin—as the Lord said to the sick man whom he had cured, *Go and sin no more, lest something worse befall you*—so we by this present decree order and strictly command physicians of the body, when they are called to the sick, to warn and persuade them first of all to call in physicians of the soul so that after their spiritual health has been seen to they may respond better to medicine for their bodies; for when the cause ceases so does the effect. This among other things has occasioned this decree, namely that some people on their sickbed, when they are advised by

---

39. "Fourth Lateran Council," in Tanner, *Decrees of the Ecumenical Councils,* 1:245; Kupfer, *Art of Healing,* 133–36.

physicians to arrange for the health of their souls, fall into despair and so the more readily incur the danger of death.[40]

Together these two canons portrayed physical sickness as a spiritual state that depended for its cure on penance. Thus the sick, and lepers in particular, whose sickness rarely if ever abated, became semi-permanent penitents, marked by the corrupted nature of their bodies. Care of the sick became part of a broader penitential theology as suffering from illness became dependant on one's spiritual state and made necessary the role and intercession of a priest. Simply convalescing in a small *domus-Dei* was no longer sufficient; one needed to be contrite, to adopt a penitential state of mind.[41]

Although Lateran IV's prescriptions for the care of the sick were more theological than practical, they were a powerful mandate for the reform of those who served them. The thrust of the conclusion—that the laity had much in common spiritually with the sick—lay at the heart of the religious changes animating the thirteenth century. Instituting annual confession was a way of incorporating the penitential movement into the sacramental practices of the church. It also meant, however, that the actual care of the sick became more religiously oriented than before. This followed the canons of Lateran III, but also suggested that hospitals, hospices, and leper houses were to be places that cared foremost for the soul.

That Cistercian nuns could help in this process seems to have been a growing perception on the part of bishops and the laity alike. Two generations of bishops implemented the conciliar degrees that made up the reform agenda articulated between 1179 and 1215: those schooled with Innocent III in Paris, trained in the circle of Peter the Chanter; and those who came to office in the decades after 1215. The first generation shared common ideas about moral theology, the penitential aspects of crusading, the evils of usury, and the principles of reform shaped in the schools of Paris during the 1170s and 1180s.[42] After 1215, it was Innocent's ideas and example that profoundly influenced a second generation of reformers. They had come of

---

40. "Fourth Lateran Council," 245–46.
41. See Kupfer, *Art of Healing,* 134; and more generally, Mary C. Mansfield, *The Humiliation of Sinners: Public Penance in Thirteenth-Century France* (Ithaca, 1995), 65–78.
42. This included prelates like Peter of Corbeil (archbishop of Sens, d. 1210), William of Donjeon (archbishop of Bourges, 1200–1219, who had been the Cistercian abbot of Chaalis), and bishops Gérard of Châlons-sur-Marne (1203–1215), Albaric of Reims (1207–1218), and Hervé of Troyes (1203–1223). Other prelates of this generation shared similar ideals about reform, even if they had not been schooled with Innocent III, most prominently Eudes of Sully, bishop of Paris (1197–1208), Philippe of Dreux, bishop of Beauvais (1179–1217), and Renard, bishop of Chartres (1182–1217). Contemporaries from this group also became influential preachers and papal legates, including Fulk

age in a world following Lateran IV and were for the most part local men elevated to their sees in the late 1220s and 1230s.[43] As a result, a cadre of reformers trained in the theology of Paris and in the doctrine of the great reforming councils was in place to implement the reform of hospitals and hospices by yoking them to the institutionalization of religious women as they became Cistercian nuns. This was also a way to reform and legitimize the kinds of care many religious women were already providing in local *domus-Dei* and leper houses.

Cistercian Nuns and Their *Domus-Dei*: The Reform of Charity

The effects of the reform councils can be traced through the institutionalization and expansion of Cistercian nunneries between the 1230s and 1250s. While occasionally other monastic orders accepted the administration of older hospitals, it was far more common for such care to fall to Cistercian nuns and to women more generally.[44] By the middle of the thirteenth century a culture of caregiving characterized many of the new Cistercian nunneries of Champagne, and bishops and patrons alike fostered this association.[45] Of the forty Cistercian nunneries founded in the archdioceses of Sens and Reims after 1200, fourteen or approximately one-third of all foundations were connected to hospitals and *domus-Dei* (see appendix). As described in chapter 1, many of these new nunneries grew out of communities of women living together and ministering to the poor and sick in small hospices, which were then reformed as Cistercian nunneries. Yet Cistercian reform and institutionalization did not sever the initial ties with local hospices or the practice of charity. In most cases, an original affiliation with a hospice or hospital continued after the women were incorporated into the order and recognized as Cistercian nuns.

---

of Neuilly (d. 1202), Jacques de Vitry (d. 1240), Robert of Courson (d. 1219), and Stephen Langton (d. 1228).

43. This generation included men such as Peter of Cuisy (bishop of Meaux, 1223–1255), Jacques de Bazoches (bishop of Soissons, 1219–1242), Gauthier of Cornut (archbishop of Sens, 1222–1241), Robert of Troyes (1223–33), Nicholas of Brie (bishop of Troyes, 1233–1269), and Robert of Thourotte (bishop of Langres, 1232–1240, then Liège, 1240–1246).

44. Exceptions to this pattern existed. In 1201, for example, Peter of Corbeil, archbishop of Sens, consolidated the smaller local leper houses in his parishes into two large leprosaria: St.-Lazare in Melun for men and St.-Lazare in Corbeil for women. See *Cartulaire de l'église Notre-Dame de Paris*, 4 vols., ed. B. Guérard (Paris, 1850), vol. 1, nos. 86, 87; and Avril, "Le IIIe concile du Latran et les communautés de lépreux," 47–51. More generally, see Touati, *Maladie et société*, 247–306, and 631–84.

45. See, for example, Paul Bertrand, *Commerce avec dame pauvreté: Structures et fonctions des couvents mendiants à Liège (XIIIe–XIVe s.)* (Liège, 2004), 471–49; and Walter Simons, *Cities of Ladies: Beguine Communities in the Medieval Low Countries, 1200–1565* (Philadelphia, 2001), 76–80.

Moreover, over the course of the thirteenth century, several Cistercian nunneries accepted the administration of additional leper houses and *domus-Dei*. In the eyes of bishops and patrons, Cistercian female spirituality was tied to the reform of charity and the apostolic ideal of caring for the poor and sick.

It was precisely this notion of reform in the practical and spiritual sense that guided Jacques de Bazoches, the bishop of Soissons (1219–1242), when he reformed the leper house of Berneuil, not far from Compiègne. The leper community had squandered their goods through bad management and needed new oversight and administration.[46] With the advice of "good men" from the parish, Jacques gave a group of devout women the old leper house and most of the lands connected to it and moved the original community of lepers to another house nearby. After transferring these properties and settling the women in their new role, he saw to it that they were soon incorporated into the Cistercian order as the nuns of La Joie Notre-Dame. Even with this new foundation, the care and administration of the lepers continued to be the nuns' obligation.[47]

A similar process of reform through the creation of a new Cistercian nunnery linked to an existing hospital took place at Ramerupt, a small hamlet in the center of the county. There a *domus-Dei* and a leprosarium—two distinct institutions—predated the nunnery's foundation, but in 1229 the community of women serving in the *domus-Dei* of Ramerupt began to be reorganized into a more formal religious house.[48] Records of a prolonged dispute between the women and the canons of St.-Pierre of Troyes concerning the tithes owed by the lepers makes clear that the nuns had been administering the *domus-Dei* themselves. The leper house had originally been founded in the tithing of the cathedral canons, and they believed they should still benefit from the lepers' dues. Yet between the beginning of the dispute and its conclusion, the women of Ramerupt and the hospitals they oversaw were incorporated into the Cistercian order as the nunnery of Notre-Dame de La Piété. In 1235 monks from Clairvaux and Boulancourt intervened on the women's behalf. They argued that the nuns, by virtue of their affiliation with the order, were exempt from paying tithes on their properties and thus were

---

46. "dictis leprosis, qui male vivendo bona sua dilapidabant, de bonis suis atque eorumdem leprosorum necessaria ministrarent"; Louis Carolus-Barré, "L'Abbaye de la Joie-Notre-Dame à Berneuil-sur-Aisne (1234–1430)," in *Mélanges à la mémoire du Père Anselme Dimier*, ed. Benoît Chauvin, 3 vols. in 6 (Arbois, 1982–87), 2:487–504, at doc. 1, 499–500.

47. Ibid., 499.

48. See Arbois de Jubainville, "Premiers seigneurs de Ramerupt," 458, no. 4 (1189); and Quantin, *Recueil*, 108–9, no. 245; also GC 12, col. 610. The tithes were gifts to the lepers from Milo of Jaucourt, canon of Troyes; see AD Aube, G 3985 (1225) and G 4065 (1229).

entitled to keep the income from the *domus-Dei,* as it was part of their holdings by that time.⁴⁹ Abbess Isabelle de Colaverday, in a charter written in her own hand, agreed to pay the canons 100 *l.* to ensure the nuns' possession of the *domus-Dei.*⁵⁰ In the same year the nuns were given formal administration of the leper house of Ramerupt, a donation that ignited a second dispute with the canons over parish jurisdiction and tithes.⁵¹ A final agreement concerning the two hospitals was reached in 1238–39 after the bishop of Troyes, Nicholas of Brie, and the abbots of Cîteaux, Clairvaux, and Boulancourt weighed in on the matter. It was agreed that the nuns held both the *domus-Dei* and the leper house and all the attached lands. They consented to pay a priest to care for the souls of the sick and to pay annual tithes to the canons, except from the gardens and pastures that provisioned the leper house.⁵² In negotiating this compromise, the bishop of Troyes and the Cistercian abbots had foremost in their minds the "reception of the infirm and the works of charity that often take place in houses of this sort."⁵³ More remarkable still is that this was the first time monks of the order formally defined and defended the connection between nuns and lepers.⁵⁴

The bishops, abbots, patrons, and women who took part in these new foundations created institutional affiliations between Cistercian nunneries and leper houses that were to persist long after the women were formally incorporated into the order. The nuns of La Cour Notre-Dame-de-Michery

---

49. "cum questio verterent inter viros venerabiles G decanum et capituum Trecensis ex una parte et abbatissa et moniales de Pietate Sancte Marie cisterciensis ordinis ex altera super eo quod dictes moniales contradicentibus decano et capitulo domum Dei de Rameruco intraverunt eam qui cum suis possessionibus... Tamdem in hunc modum pro bono pacis fuit compositum inter partes quod dictes moniales tenebunt eandem domum dei cum omnibus suis possessionibus et pertinentiis et hospitalitatem transeuntibus et infirmis et egeris sicut fiebat antequam moniales eamdem domum dei." AD Aube, G 3186 (1235).
50. AD Aube, G 3186 (Epiphany, 1235).
51. On Erard's donations, see Arbois de Jubainville, "Premiers seigneurs de Ramerupt," 448–51; and A. Prévost, *Le diocèse de Troyes: Histoire et documents,* 3 vols. (Dijon, 1923), 1:217.
52. "Abbatissam et eius conventum de Pietate Beata Marie juxta Ramercum moveant questionem pertindo ab eis quod de domo leprosorum de Ramercum reddient ipius decime sicut hactenus fuit reddite et quod leprosi in eadem domo recipiant sicut hactenus recepti fuit et quod provideat... leprosies competent secundum possibilitate domus illius et si adquiserit predicte moniales terras ut vineas in decimatione ipsorum in de habeant decimas. Nos conpromissionem super hiis factam a partibus supradictis in viros venerabiles." AD Aube, G 3186 (December 1238) and (September 1239).
53. "dicte domui leprosorum quo ad receptionem infirmorum et alia caritatis opera que in huiusmodi domibus sepe fieri solent." AD Aube, G 3186 (1239).
54. Strikingly, this conclusion contradicted Cistercian legislation on the topic. In 1237 the *Libellus diffinitionum* ordered that "De Leprosis pro quibus petitur ut permittantur habitare prope domos ordinis nostri, omnino ne fiat interdicitur." Lucet, *Codifications* (Paris, 1977), Dist. 10: 19(1237), 17(1257). The abbess was still administering the leper house in 1342 when she helped settle a dispute between the canons and the lepers. See AD Aube, G 3186 (6 July 1342).

grew out of a group of women caring for lepers in a small leprosarium at Viluis. After the nunnery became part of the Cistercian order, the nuns continued to care for lepers in the grange up the road until the fourteenth century.[55] The lepers were mentioned in a papal confirmation of the abbey's holdings in 1245.[56] And again, in 1267, the lepers were noted when the women were admonished to limit their number to forty in response to mounting economic pressures.[57] Caring for lepers was not simply the source of the nunnery's foundation; it was a sustained focus of the nuns' piety and spiritual vocation. The women were still caring for lepers when they came under papal investigation in 1286 for defaulting on the payment of a crusade tax.[58]

Similar administrative and spiritual arrangements occurred throughout the region. The care of lepers and the sick and poor became part of the institutional definition of many Cistercian convents, and this association determined how they functioned as religious communities. The nunnery of St.-Jacques de Vitry, originally founded in the *domus-Dei* of Vitry in 1233, oversaw the needs of the sick and poor and administered the financial affairs of the house, specifically the tithes collected or donated to the lepers.[59] In 1289, the abbess of St.-Jacques de Vitry and the bishop of Châlons disputed the control of another leper hospital, this time at Montmirail. Both claimed jurisdiction over the property and income from alms donated to the lepers. The dispute was first heard before the Jours de Troyes, the highest court in Champagne, where the judges ruled in favor of the nunnery's claim. The bishop of Châlons then appealed the case to Paris. In 1290, when the abbess explained to the Parlement of Paris that a decision had been reached in Troyes the year before, the Parisian judges restored the leper hospital to her control.[60] By 1290 the connection between Cistercian nuns and lepers was enforced both in custom and by law.

---

55. See Maximillien Quantin, ed., *Cartulaire général de l'Yonne: Recueil de documents authentiques pour servir à l'histoire des pays qui forment ce déparatement,* 2 vols. (Auxerre, 1854–60), 2:436 (no. 182); AD Yonne, H 563; and chap. 1, n. 90.

56. "grangiam sitam ante leprosarium de Viluis, cum pertinenciis suis"; Quantin, *Recueil,* 234, no. 503.

57. Ibid., 316, no. 640. See also Touati, *Maladie et société,* 683.

58. AD Yonne, H 787, fols. 21r–22r. See epilogue, 203.

59. "Ego Heimardus Sancti Petri de Montes Cathalaunensis humilis prior notum facio omnibus presentes litteras inspecturis quod ego de consilio boni viri J archidiaconus Cathalaunensis cives abbatis gerens in spiritualibus concessi quod vir illustris Th. Campanie et Brie comes palatines in porprisis domus Dei de Vitriacis quamdam abbaciam monialium cisterciensis ordinis salvo in omnibus iure...et aliarum ecclesiarum prochialium possit construere." AD Marne, 71 H 4 (1233) and (1265).

60. *Olim,* 2:292, xii, and 301, viii; and John F. Benton, "Philip the Fair and the *Jours de Troyes,*" reprinted in his *Culture, Power and Personality in Medieval France,* ed. Thomas Bisson (London, 1991), 191–254, at 203.

By the mid-thirteenth century, patrons and bishops not only founded nunneries in older hospitals, *domus-Dei,* and leper houses but they often gave over these institutions to Cistercian nuns. This was not wholly novel. Monastic houses had been given the responsibilities of hospital administration in the past when the possibility of independently maintaining the sick grew difficult or when the original institution fell into poverty or disrepair. But the number of instances when hospices were given to Cistercian nuns is striking and suggests a preference for the care women offered. In 1240, the Cistercian nuns of Benoîtevaux accepted the administration of the leper house of Reynel and agreed to provide care for the sick in residence.[61] A year earlier, in 1239, Jacques, the priest of St.-Benoît and prior of St.-Sépulchre near Troyes, gave the nuns of Notre-Dame-des-Prés the *domus-Dei* of St.-Julian in Mergey on the condition that they continue to maintain it as a site for hospitality and care for those in need.[62] In 1247 Gilles, the archbishop of Sens, oversaw the transfer of the *domus-Dei* at Malay-le-Roi to the Cistercian nuns of La Joie-lès-Nemours. Guy de Lucrator of Malay-le-Roi had founded the hospice and gave it to the nuns, perhaps as an endowment. His charter was precise on matters usually left silent: not only were the nuns to administer to the sick, but they were also to hold the lands and rights attached to the hospital and pay the annual fees and board to maintain a priest in residence. The nuns agreed to assume these cares and consented to provide eight beds for the poor.[63]

Although bishops often oversaw these institutional affiliations, nuns seem to have initiated many of these connections as well. In 1256, for example, Abbess Johanna of Marcilly petitioned the bishop of Autun to transfer her community from the inhospitable location where the nunnery had been founded to the leper house of Cerce, which Johanna explained was equipped with buildings and sufficient lands to support the nuns.[64] The bishop consented,

---

61. AD Haute-Marne, 25 H 8 (August 1240). There are earlier documents in this series that record the debts the lepers had contracted and their poverty. See also Jean Salmon, "L'Abbaye de Benoîtevaux, regard et évocation," *Bulletin de la Société historique et archéologique de Langres* 17 (1980): 321–27.

62. "tali tenore adjuncto quod ipse moniales secundum facultatem et possibilitatem domus hospitalitatem ibidem observare tenentur." AD Aube, 23 H 232 (September 1239). Nicholas of Brie, bishop of Troyes, oversaw the transfer.

63. AD Yonne, H 211 (vigil of Saint Andrew, 1247), edited in Quantin, *Recueil,* 241, no. 513; and AD Yonne, H 211 (December 1248).

64. "Notum facimus universis quod cum nos in predicto loco de Marcille minime fertili, multum sicco atque propter situm loci ipsius religioni minus apto, substineremus incommoditates non modicas et intolerabiles evidenter,... significamus incommoditates predictas, inter quas eidem dignum duximus declarandi quod propter karitatem nemorum et lapidum et ipsius loci inhabilitatem ad edificandum, tam pauca essent edificia quod insufficentia habitatione nostre penitus inutilia merito possent dici.... rogamus humiliter et devote, quatenus locum commoditatibus non carentem,

but only on the condition that the women continued to take in and care for the lepers of the parish and that they recognize the authority of the bishop over them in that capacity.[65] While these donations and transfers created institutional affiliations between nunneries and hospitals, they also provided a novel way for patrons to give property and rents to the nuns. These were in effect reused donations. What had originally been set aside to found and fund a hospital was now used, or in fact reused, to endow a new Cistercian nunnery. The example of Marcilly points to the fact that many new religious houses were founded on marginal lands, in places that could not sustain a community because they could not be plowed, could not produce sufficient yields, and could not be maintained adequately. Combining new nunneries with existing hospitals allowed spiritual benefits to accrue to initial donors while also benefiting the administration of both foundations.

The practical motives for such associations were clear, and these new institutions—the nunneries and their reformed hospices—achieved a reform that had clear social benefits. Indeed, for the most part nuns provided care for the sick and administered the properties they were given with competence. In many cases, when the documents survive, it is clear that the nunneries continued to oversee their affiliated hospitals and *domus-Dei* well into the fourteenth century. What made this reform possible and desirable, however, was a reorientation in the perception of the poor, sick, and leprous, so that their care became an avenue for salvation and a form of *imitatio Christi* for both the sick and the nuns. Care for the poor and sick in these Cistercian convents linked penitential piety with an institutional religious life in a new and powerful way, fostering a particular kind of Cistercian female spirituality.

Those Touched by God

To care for the poor and sick in the vein of apostolic charity—to wash feet, kiss sores, comfort those in distress—demanded a new perspective toward men and women traditionally excluded from medieval society. The texts of the Gospels provided the model for this interpretation, for Christ had personally touched, healed, consoled, and comforted the sick, poor, and leprous. The effect of this apostolic inflection was a creative restructuring of

---

videlicet locum, domum et possessiones leprosarie de Sarces, sue diocesis, cum omni emolumento et onere eorumdem, nobis ad edificandum et ad transferendum mos ibidem." Quantin, *Recueil,* 265–66, no. 562.

65. Ibid.; and Alexandre Parat, "L'Abbaye de Marcilly," *Bulletin de la Société des sciences historiques et naturelles de l'Yonne* 79 (1925): 339–57, at 342.

the ways medieval society interacted with some marginal groups during the thirteenth century. Cistercian nuns cared for a wide variety of "miserable persons" (*minores et miseratos*) in that they housed widows, orphans, pilgrims, and the transient poor as well as lepers.[66] All who suffered in this way were classified as the poor of Christ (*pauperes Christi*). Yet lepers in particular carried a specific set of social and religious associations, and their care featured prominently in the conversion narratives, saints' lives, and exempla texts of the period.

Through the lens of apostolic charity, lepers emerged as figures of particular penitential significance. The visible signs of leprosy, wrought by ulcers and sores on the skin, hands, and face, marked out those who suffered from its effects. Theological interpretations of the disease, which informed its perception and treatment, were based primarily on two sets of biblical texts. Old Testament texts cast leprosy as a punishment from God for sin (Lev. 13:45, Num. 12:1–5, and 2 Kings 5:21–27). According to Leviticus 13:45, "the leper shall remain unclean as long as he has the disease; he shall dwell alone in a habitation outside the camp." But this kind of social exclusion contrasted with Christian interpretations of Isaiah 53:3–6: "He was despised and rejected by men: a man of sorrows—like a leper [*quasi leprosum*]—as one from whom men hide their faces... upon him was the chastisement that made us whole, and with his affliction we are healed." By the thirteenth century medieval theologians interpreted this passage through their reading of the Gospels: the Man of Sorrows who was like a leper prefigured Christ's redemptive suffering in this world. Such a reading paralleled episodes from the Gospels in which Christ ministered to lepers, and by touching and kissing those seen as repulsive, he made them whole (for example, Matt. 8:2, 11:5; Luke 4:27, 16:19–31; John 11–12).[67]

Although Leviticus 13:45 provided a proof text for the exclusion of lepers, which may later have encouraged their segregation, the Gospels gave new meaning to leprosy.[68] In these texts leprosy was associated with the special

---

66. The nuns of La Cour Notre-Dame cared for eighteen children and lepers in the grange at Viluis by 1282; see AD Yonne H 787, fols. 22v–23r. The nunneries in the congregation of Savigny visited by Stephan of Lexington cared for similar groups of miserable persons. See P. B. Griesser, ed., "Registrum Epistolarum Stephani de Lexinton abbatis de Stanlegia et de Savigniaco," *Annalecta Sacri Ordinis Cisterciensis* 2 (1946): 1–118; and 8 (1952): 181–378.

67. On the interpretations of Isaiah 54:3–4 and Leviticus 13–14, see Nicole Bériou, "Les lépreux sous le regard des prédicateurs d'après les collections des sermons *ad status* du XIIIe siècle," in *Voluntate Dei leprosus: Les lépreux entre conversion et exclusion aux XIIème et XIIIème siècles,* ed. Nicole Bériou and François-Olivier Touati (Spoleto, 1991), 35–80, at 36–37 and 68–70; and Rawcliffe, *Leprosy,* 104–54.

68. Avril, "Le IIIe concile de Latran et les communautés de lépreux."

mark of God. Lepers were chosen by God—much like Job, the Man of Sorrows, Lazarus, and Christ himself—to suffer in this life and proceed directly to heaven in the next. This interpretation—complex and contradictory as it was—became a common theme in sermons, reform texts, and hagiography. Hugh of Floreffe explained in his *Life of Yvette of Huy* that the "devastating fire of leprosy acted as a purgatory, punishing [the leper's] sins so that [they] could pass from this world to the Father, holy in mind and body; all the corporal sins committed before consumed through pain and correction."[69] Jacques de Vitry, Gilbert of Tournai, and Humbert of Romans all used the language of suffering, purgatory, and redemption to describe the spiritual status of lepers in this world.[70] It was their earthly suffering, lepers were told, that granted them a special place after death—like that enjoyed by Lazarus—in the bosom of Abraham (Luke 16:19–31).[71] Preachers indulged the nurturing and feminine aspect of this image and employed it as an extremely effective metaphor to describe what awaited lepers in the next world. Gilbert of Tournai consoled in a sermon that after their death they would be nursed by Christ, just as a mother holds a small child in her bosom and lets him fall asleep on her knee.[72]

By the thirteenth century, caring for lepers was constructed as a way to interact with those who suffered like Christ and who were in turn Christlike. Sermons, exempla, and more elaborate stories, like the legend of Saint Julian

---

69. "ita quod, ut arbitror, ignis iste vastatorius, id est, lepra, purgatoria ei peccatorum suorum effecta sit poena, ut sancta mente et corpore transiret de hoc mundo ad Patrem, consumptis peccatis omnibus per correptionem et poenam, quae praecessit, corporis." *VBJ*, chap. 28, para. 86.

70. Bériou, "Les lépreux sous le regard des prédicateurs," 52–65. See in *Voluntate Dei leprosus*: Gilbert of Tournai writes, "Et si paciencer sustineatis, infirmitas pro martyrio uobis erit et aliud purgatorium non habebitis" (sermon 3, "Ad leprosos et abiectos," line 101); Jacques de Vitry writes similarly, "Tolerabilius quidem esset ut per mille annos affligeretur homo in hoc seculo quam per diem unum in purgatorio ubi, teste Augustino, minor pena acerbior est quam aliqua pena que posset excogitari in hoc seculo" (sermon 1, "Ad leprosos et alios infirmos," lines 40–43).

71. "Quidam portantur in sinum Abrahe, id est usque ad familiare secretum Dei sicut ille mendicus, et in eo alii pauperes et leprosi sancti ab angelis portabuntur in sinum Abrahe. Mt. VII, dicit quedam interlinearis "Sinus Abrahe est requies beatorum pauperum." Gilbert of Tournai, sermon 3, "Ad leprosos et abiectos," lines 224–28, in *Voluntate Dei leprosus*.

72. The language Gilbert of Tournai used gives some indication of the nature of care provided to lepers. "Hec est gestacio deliciosa, Ysa. LVI: Ad ubera portabimini et super genua blandientur vobis, sed sicut littera LXX dicit: 'Paruuli eorum in humeris portabuntur et super ubera consolabuntur.' Loquitur sub metaphora mulieris portantis filium paruulum, quem modo ponit in sinu ad suggendum, modo super genua ad dormiendum. Ihesus enim talium non tantum pater est, immo mater, ut quos gestauerit in utero et latere suo modo foueat in sino suo, Ysa. XLVI: Israel, qui portamini a meo utero, qui gestamini a mea uulua." Ibid., lines 233–41. See Humbert of Romans, sermon 1, "Ad fratres et sorores in dominibus leprosorum," lines 40–73, for comparisons. This is precisely the same imagery used to describe the consolation Alice of Schaerbeek received from Christ after she contracted leprosy; see *VAS*, 10.

the Hospitaller, often ended with Christ appearing in the guise of a leper.[73] A well-known story folded into many thirteenth-century sermons, which enjoyed particular currency in Champagne, recounted how Count Thibaut II (r. 1125–1152) cultivated a special relationship with a leper who lived outside of the town of Sézanne, whom the count regularly visited. During these encounters Thibaut II would wash the leper's feet and give him alms and the kiss of peace. After one such intimate visit, the count's men informed him that the leper he had cared for over the years had in fact died several months earlier. It was then revealed that the leper Thibaut had just seen was not his leper, but in fact Christ in the form of the leper. The count's sustained generosity showed him to be a man touched by God, worthy of a close relationship with Christ. The story was copied into the exempla collections of Caesarius of Heisterbach, Jacques de Vitry, and Thomas of Cantimpré and provided a local illustration of the importance and rewards of bestowing charity, alms, and the kiss of peace upon those who suffered.[74]

Many stories involving lepers turned on the intimate physical contact extended to the sufferer. Caesarius of Heisterbach included two vivid miracles involving lepers in the *Dialogue on Miracles,* which circulated widely among Cistercian monks and nuns: one told of a French bishop who was forced to lick a sore on a leper's nose, and another described how the bishop of Salzburg was compelled to eat the vomit of a leper because it contained the bread of the Eucharist he had just administered.[75] Through an emphasis on the physicality of these interactions, Caesarius conveyed both the disgust and fear that could be associated with lepers as well as the miraculous potential such interactions promised, for each exemplum concluded with the leper manifesting himself as Christ and thus inverting the original association. Listeners were called upon to reorient their perspective toward those suffering in their midst.

---

73. See Carolyn T. Swan, *The Old French Prose Legend of Saint Julian the Hospitaller* (Tübingen, 1977). The romance *Ami and Amile* also invokes many parallels between the suffering of lepers and the suffering of Christ. See Jean Dufournet, ed. *Ami et Amile: Une chanson de geste de l'amitié* (Paris, 1987).

74. Caesarius of Heisterbach, *Dialogus Miraculorum,* ed. Joseph Strange (Cologne, 1851), bk. 8, chap. 31, p. 105; in English, Caesarius of Heisterbach (1220–1235), *The Dialogue on Miracles,* 2 vols., trans. H. von E Scott and C. C. Swinton Bland (New York, 1929), 2:30–34; and Jacques de Vitry, *The Exempla or Illustrative Stories from the Sermones Vulgares of Jacques de Vitry,* ed. Thomas Frederick Crane (London, 1890; reprint, New York, 1971), 43–44, no. 94. The story also appears in Thomas of Cantimpré (c. 1200–1270), *Bonum universale de apibus* (Douai, 1627), 254–55, with slight variation. MAT, MS 1750, part of the collection from Clairvaux, is a small portable volume containing excepted sermons and exempla of Jacques de Vitry, most likely intended as a priest's or preacher's handbook. See fol. 12r for the miracle involving Count Thibaut.

75. Caesarius of Heisterbach, *Dialogus Miraculorum,* bk. 8, chaps. 32–33, pp. 105–8.

Such reorientation often occurred first among women, who in turn provided a model that motivated others to greater charity, most often their husbands. Indeed, Jacques de Vitry was one of the first to record what became a popular story of a noblewomen who had great compassion for the sick and especially for lepers, although her husband could not tolerate them. One day, as Jacques recounted, a leper came to the noblewoman's door and pleaded to be let inside. He was unrelenting in his petitions until the woman finally gave in, carried the leper in her arms into the house, and put him to rest in her husband's bed. Moved by compassion, she put a pillow under his head and covered him with a fur blanket. Just at that moment her husband returned exhausted from the hunt. He then entered his bedroom and found the chamber smelling sweetly of a paradisiacal perfume and the leper nowhere insight. In awe of this miracle, the woman told her husband everything that happened, and he, in turn, converted to a life of religion and charity.[76] Jacques de Vitry incorporated versions of this story into the sermons he preached to hospital workers, and Stephen of Bourbon included a variation of it in his preaching compendium for Dominicans.[77] In this story, not only was the leper's suffering meant to evoke Christ in that the leper was revealed to be Christ, but the noblewoman's sacrifice of her persona and her reputation—carrying the leper in her own arms, or in later versions, bathing and feeding him—and the risk of her husband's wrath make her Christlike in her capacity for charity. Indeed, this was the sentiment that Jacques de Vitry emphasized throughout his sermons to hospital workers, many of whom were married women or spouses: in providing for those in need, men and women provided for Christ himself. As Jacques wrote: "You have renounced the world and taken on the habit of religion so that by giving not only your possessions, but also yourselves, through works of mercy, every day you refresh Christ in his members."[78] This was a direct reference to the Gospel of Matthew (25:35): "Whoever therefore through these works shows charity to his neighbor applies that charity to God." Such examples became living models of the kind of apostolic charity episcopal reformers had in mind as they drafted conciliar degrees about hospitals and the care of the sick.

---

76. See Jacques de Vitry, *Exempla,* ed. Crane, 44–45, no. 95; and MAT, MS 1750, fol. 12r–v. See also Sharon Farmer, "The Leper in the Master Bedroom: Thinking through a Thirteenth-Century Exemplum," in *Framing the Family: Narrative and Representation in the Medieval and Early Modern Periods,* ed. Rosalynn Voaden and Diane Wolfthal (Tempe, AZ, 2005), 79–100, translated at 81–82.

77. Farmer, "Leper in the Master Bedroom," 81–85, citing Jacques de Vitry's sermons "Ad hospitalarios et custodes infirmorum," BNF MS lat. 3284, fols. 101v–107v. *Anecdotes historiques, légendes et apologues tirés du recueil inédit d'Étienne de Bourbon dominicain du XIIIe siècle,* ed. A. Lecoy de la Marche (Paris, 1877), 132, no. 154.

78. Farmer, "Leper in the Master Bedroom," 83.

Inherent in all these miracle stories was an unease that thirteenth-century preachers and audiences harbored toward lepers, while also conveying the haunting idea that the degraded and diseased could be Christ himself.[79] Because lepers lived in a continuous state of self-mortification and humiliation, they came the closest to the true imitation of Christ, for theirs was a living suffering that in the end could bring salvation. This may have been the consolation offered to those suffering from the disease, but for the men and women who cared for lepers and the sick, physical intimacy also gave them a special proximity to those touched by God. Sacrificing oneself for the needs of the poor and sick—by offering one's home, one's bed, one's care as the exempla stories recounted—was the ultimate expression of apostolic charity and Christian love.

Exemplars and Models

Those who chose to care for lepers and the sick participated in the ideal of the *imitatio Christi* in a particularly powerful way. While mendicant friars pursued this ideal through poverty, itinerancy, and preaching, and crusaders sought it through pilgrimage and the militant defense of Christ's patrimony, by the thirteenth century the care of the sick and poor emerged as a gendered expression of this imitation. Overwhelmingly, it was women who aspired to this model of Christ and constructed its practice through self-sacrificing care, bestowed especially toward lepers. While there were exceptions to this gendered dichotomy—for example, Saint Francis and Saint Louis both ministered to lepers—women dominated the practice.[80] Moreover, Cistercian nuns laboring in leper houses and *domus-Dei* benefited from the examples of other holy women whose *vitae* they would have encountered in the Cistercian context and who they were encouraged to emulate.

Beginning in the thirteenth century, monks and canons connected to a network of Cistercian abbeys in the Low Countries centered on the diocese of Liège began to produce an impressive corpus of female hagiography detailing the lives of religious women, beguines, and professed Cistercian

---

79. See Catherine Peyroux, "The Leper's Kiss," in *Monks and Nuns, Saints and Outcasts: Religion in Medieval Society: Essays in Honor of Lester K. Little,* ed. Sharon Farmer and Barbara H. Rosenwein (Ithaca, 2000), 172–88.

80. While men cared for lepers within leprosaria, they did not go out to smaller communities of lepers and found religious houses in connection with a caregiving mission. Herein lies the gendered distinction in behavior and devotion. Daniel Le Blévec, for example, found almost no evidence of mendicant involvement in hospitals in southern France. See Le Blévec, *La part du pauvre.* Nevertheless, see François-Olivier Touati, "François d'Assise et la diffusion d'un modèle théreputique au XIIIe siècle," *Histoire des Sciences Médicales* 16 (1982): 175–84.

nuns.[81] Copies of these *vitae* and stories of the saintly women spread rapidly into Germany and northern France. Much of this hagiography described the social origins and pious works of women struggling to meet their responsibilities to home and family, while committed to a spiritual ideal that hinged on service to others.[82] Throughout the *vitae* from Liège, caring for lepers functioned as a turning point in the process of converting to a life of religion. In choosing to care for lepers or contracting the disease, women were able in clear and decisive terms to separate themselves from lay society and to escape the social constraints of marriage, re-marriage, and motherhood. The *vita* of Yvette of Huy (1158–1228) is explicit about the conversion process involved in caring for lepers. Indeed, following the death of her husband, Yvette's initial transformation toward a life of religion came with her decision to live among a group of lepers beyond the walls of Huy, along the Meuse River, in an old leprosarium that had been neglected by laymen and local priests alike.[83] She remained with the lepers for eleven years and cared for them personally at great cost to her social and physical well-being. She would lay them in bed and help them rise in the morning, giving them the most "faithful service, with all care and reverence, for she believed that Christ is in all things and was seen to revere Christ in each of them."[84]

Serving lepers was also predicated on achieving an ideal of humility that could be attained only through daily service in public to the lowest members of society. Yvette's *vita* was explicit on this account, noting that there was a special grace that God gave to the most humble, the meek, and the infirm. It was this grace that Yvette sought.[85] Her sacrifice was described as even more profound for God did not afflict her with the disease. Rather, she chose to submit herself to its effects purposefully. She sought out "a misery greater

---

81. See Chrysostomo Henriquez, *Quinque Prudentes Virgines sive B. Beatricis de Nazareth, B. Aleydis de Scharenbecka, B. Idea de Nivellis, B. Idea de Lovanio, B. Idea de Levvis, Ordinis Cisterc. Praeclara gesta, ex antiquis M.S. eruta* (Antwerp, 1630); Simone Roisin, *L'hagiographie cistercienne dans la diocèse de Liège au XIIIe siècle* (Louvain, 1947); Simons, *City of Ladies;* and Ernest McDonnell, *Beguines and Beghards in Medieval Culture: With Special Emphasis on the Belgian Scene* (New Brunswick, NJ, 1954), 40–58, 101–19, 170–86, 320–40.

82. Concerning this struggle, see the remarks by Roisin, *L'hagiographie cistercienne,* 85; and Carpenter, "Juette of Huy," 57–60.

83. *VBJ,* chap. 10, para. 33.

84. "et cuncta sancta obsequia fideliter exhibentem,... et reverentia ut in omnibus esse Christum crederet, et Christum revereri videretur in singulis." *VBJ,* chap. 10, para. 35.

85. "Denique ut humilis humilior fieret adhuc, (humilibus Deus dat gratiam) coram humilibus, id est, leprosis, et decumbentibus humiliare se voluit, cunctorum necessitatibus humiliter subserviens, ut semper eam humiliorem efficeret intus quotidiana servitus, foris repraesentatio ministerii vilis." *VBJ,* chap. 10, para. 33.

than all other miseries, that is, to serve and live with lepers."[86] In so doing, she cultivated a new religious identity separate in every way from the social world she had known. And, as described previously, in the years before her death Yvette began to wear the customary Cistercian tunic beneath her clothes, close to her flesh.[87] In her own way both through her actions and her dress she saw herself affiliated in spirit with the pious ambitions of the Cistercian order.

In many female *vitae* ministering to lepers and the poor also functioned as a way for women to set themselves in opposition to the profit economy. In several examples women took up residence among lepers with the hope of cleansing themselves from a past tainted by associations with business, investments, and financial gain. The ideal of inverting one's original identity and social status through a deliberate act of self-abasement is a notable and recurring theme throughout these texts. Thus, when a leper asked Margaret of Ypres for alms on the street after she had already given away all of her possessions, her response was to become a member of the urban poor (*pauperculae*): she begged alms, which she then donated to the leper.[88] A compulsion to be one of the poor of Christ, so that "naked she might follow the naked Christ," likewise compelled Mary of Oignies to beg, until she was restrained by her companions. While Jacques de Vitry's point may have been to reinforce the cloistered lifestyle for religious women, his depiction of Mary's desire to take part in the apostolic life and assume the status of the poor of Christ is the focus of his description.[89] In a similar manner Yvette of Huy, riddled with anxiety over previous business investments, opened her house to beggars and the poor. Giving away all her goods, she sought "privately and publically, to share every suffering of each one," to become one of the poor herself.[90] Some women, however, like Juliana of Mont-Cornillon, were forced through real necessity into mendicancy.[91] To beg and to be like the poor were intensely humbling practices, and that was part of the religious appeal. Poverty, like caring for

---

86. "tantam appetere miseriam, et miseriam omnibus miseriis graviorem, videlicet servire, et cohabitare leprosis." *VBJ,* chap. 10, para. 34.

87. *VBJ,* intro, para. 2.

88. Thomas of Cantimpré, *Vita Margarete de Ypres,* ed. G. Meersseman, "Les frères prêcheurs et le mouvement dévot en Flandre aux XIIIe s.," *Archivum Fratrum Praedicatorum* 18 (1948): 69–130, edition of the *vita,* 106–30, at 117. The Dominican Thomas de Cantimpré is the most likely author of the *vita* of Margaret of Ypres, which was probably written between 1240 and 1244.

89. *VMO,* chap. 2, para. 45, for Mary's begging; and para. 52 for the taint of money accrued in the world. For the anxiety attending these women over money acquired through credit or business transactions, see also *VIN,* para. 4.

90. "nunc privatim, nunc publice, ut quasi seipsam pati in singulorum passionibus singulis factis ostenderet." *VBJ,* chap. 9, para. 31. See chap. 9, paras. 25–31, generally.

91. *VJC,* chap. 6, para. 31.

lepers, was another way for religious women to reject their social status, their associations with the urban bourgeoisie, and their natal families.[92] Through caregiving and begging alms religious women became linked physically and spiritually to God's chosen people: the poor and the leprous. This association, in turn, heightened the efficaciousness of women's prayers and intercessions, while it propelled them to create a new religious identity distinct from the world they had known before.

The *vitae* and miracle stories relating to lepers and to the women who cared for them passed from the Low Countries to Champagne through many channels. Some were no doubt carried on the tongues of merchants and travelers from Douai, Ypres, and Liège, who had stalls at the Champagne fairs.[93] Other stories certainly circulated with groups of Cistercian monks and nuns who came to Champagne to aid in founding new monastic houses. Recall that in 1221, when Blanche of Navarre founded Argensolles at the advice of the saintly *conversus* Arnulf of Villers, the story of Arnulf's vision traveled from Liège back to Champagne with a Cistercian monk of Larrivour who was a spiritual advisor to the countess.[94] Such travel and storytelling among Cistercian men and women fostered the creation and dissemination of a common corpus of texts. But religious women and nuns traveled between communities as well, bringing with them their own store of edifying tales. Argensolles, for example, began with thirty-five nuns from the Cistercian nunnery of Val-Notre-Dame outside of Liège. The first abbess of Argensolles was Ida, who had been the prioress of Val. According to a later copy of her *vita* she resisted the initial attempt to elect her as prioress and begged God for an illness that would keep her from such responsibilities.[95] After some time she became afflicted with leprosy, though in due course she received a cure from God.[96] Ida's story and that of her contemporaries gave textual form to the Cistercian ideal of charity and self-sacrifice as an expression of piety.

The hagiographical material produced mainly in the diocese of Liège would have resonated powerfully with religious women and Cistercian nuns in Champagne, who would have heard these stories from priests, monks,

---

92. See Carpenter, "Juette of Huy," 60–69; and Meersseman, "Les frères prêcheurs," 70–106.

93. For the impact of these women on contemporary society beyond the Low Countries, see Miri Rubin, *Corpus Christi: The Eucharist in Late Medieval Culture* (Cambridge, 1991), 164–76.

94. See chap. 1, 28–29.

95. E. Héron de Villefosse, ed., "Vie manuscrite de la bienheureuse Ide, première abbesse du monastère d'Argensoles (Marne)," *Revue de Champagne,* 2nd ser., 1 (1889): 481–98.

96. Ibid., 488.

and local confessors.[97] While it may be difficult to imagine the daughters or sisters of the aristocracy of Champagne engaging in the kind of personal care of the sick and poor that is typically associated with women like Mary of Oignies or Elizabeth of Hungary, it was precisely the inversion of social status that made their actions penitential.[98] Moreover, because of their association with the body, women were seen as particularly capable of such physical suffering.[99] There were contemporary models for such behavior. John of Montmirail, a knight and fief-holder close to the count and king, cared for lepers and the sick later in his life, as did his daughter Elizabeth.[100] Many other women of high status undertook such acts of penance, and it is certainly plausible that northern French aristocratic women did the same. Indeed the social context and foundation history of many of the Cistercian convents offer a critical setting within which to interpret these spiritual texts that depict devout women as exemplars of the Christian life. The texts also offer insight into what emerged as a distinct form of Cistercian female spirituality, predicated on humility, self-sacrifice, and an ideal of charity that was deeply rooted to service in the world and within one's community.

Female Piety and Cistercian *Caritas*

For Cistercian nuns, caring for lepers and the poor was spiritually efficacious on multiple levels. Within the monastic life penitential acts such as physical caregiving aided the process of retraining the body and the mind to direct an individual nun toward Christ. Attending to a leper house or *domus-Dei* was an act of discipline that accorded well with prescriptions for manual labor emphasized in the Cistercian customaries. It also reflected an orientation

---

97. See, for example, MAT, MS 1750 (sermons and exempla of Jacques de Vitry) and MS 401 (a compendium of saints' lives, including those of Mary of Oignies and Saint Francis); both were part of the collection of Clairvaux.

98. See Anneke B. Mulder-Bakker, ed., *Mary of Oignies: Mother of Salvation,* trans. Margot King and Hugh Feiss (Turnhout, 2006), 14–15; and Herbert Grundmann, *Religious Movements in the Middle Ages: The Historical Links between Heresy, the Mendicant Orders, and the Women's Religious Movement in the Twelfth and Thirteenth Century with the Historical Foundations of German Mysticism,* trans. Steven Rowan (Notre Dame, IN, 1995), 75–88 and 137.

99. See Caroline Walker Bynum, *Holy Feast and Holy Fast: The Religious Significance of Food to Medieval Women* (Berkeley, 1987), 260–76; idem, "The Female Body and Religious Practice in the Later Middle Ages," in her *Fragmentation and Redemption: Essays on Gender and the Human Body in Medieval Religion* (New York, 1991), 181–237; and Ellen Ross, "'She wept and cried right loud for sorrow and pain': Suffering, the Spiritual Journey, and Women's Experience in Late Medieval Mysticism," in *Maps of Flesh and Light: The Religious Experience of Medieval Women Mystics,* ed. Ulrike Wiethaus (Syracuse, 1993), 45–59.

100. See chap. 5, 159.

toward penitence and works of mercy advocated by many thirteenth-century preachers. The connection to leper houses was an institutional accommodation for the ideals of penitential spirituality that remained present and practiced in many Cistercian nunneries.[101]

It may be that in many of the smaller Cistercian convents attached to leper houses and *domus-Dei,* women would have served for a year or more, perhaps as *conversae,* before turning to a life of more profound contemplation and taking vows as nuns. As the *vitae* of religious women made clear, such service was also an act of humility, an action that literally remade the person who took up such care. Humility was one part of attaining the religious life, one step on the way to finding God's grace. Certainly not all women practiced heroic acts of radical asceticism or charity, but the efforts of reconceptualizing the place of lepers and the sick, their care and administration, helped to reorient the mind. Humility as an external practice led nuns to the internal transformation of the self.[102] Moreover, as Megan Cassidy-Welch has argued, such action, both literally practiced and metaphorically indulged within the cloister, served to remake nuns, to transform them from lay persons into those with a special connection and commitment to the divine. Through the imitation of Christ's ministry and suffering on earth, a nun focused her imagination more intensely on Christ's humanity, His suffering, and in turn His salvation. This meant training the body in concert with training the mind.[103] The result was a nun who would more closely resemble Christ in outward caregiving and in her inner spiritual state. For Cistercian nuns, care for lepers and the poor was directly connected to the creation and cultivation of a new—more Christlike—self.

An emphasis on humility and nurturing appears in several of the surviving sermons to Cistercian nuns from the middle of the thirteenth century.[104]

---

101. The pervasive association of leprosy with moral degeneracy and specifically sexual sins may have found possibilities for redemption, much as the sins of prostitutes could be redeemed, in the convents of Cistercian nuns. Moreover, sexual sins, as much as profit, were urban concerns further heightening the connection between towns and cities and the leper houses and Cistercian nunneries—locales of redemption—on their margins.

102. See Amy Hollywood, "Inside Out: Beatrice of Nazareth and Her Hagiographer," in *Gendered Voices: Medieval Saints and Their Interpreters,* ed. Catherine M. Mooney (Philadelphia, 1999), 79–98, esp. 84, and 92–93.

103. Megan Cassidy-Welch, *Monastic Spaces and Their Meanings: Thirteenth-Century English Cistercian Monasteries* (Turnhout, 2001), 98.

104. See, for example, Jacques Foviaux, "Les sermons donnés à Laon, en 1242, par le Chanoine Jacques de Troyes, futur Urbain IV," *Recherches Augustinennes* 20 (1985): 203–56. The second sermon he preached to the nuns of Le Sauvoir-sous-Laon concerned the theme of lactation as a metaphor for the nourishment of God based on the prophesy of Hosea 2:14. Similar themes appear in the sermons preached to the beguines of Paris toward the end of the thirteenth century. See Nicole

A manuscript from Clairvaux preserves a collection of sermons by Jacques de Vitry that emphasize the importance of manual labor and chastity for Cistercian women. One in particular focuses on humility for nuns specifically achieved by caring for the infirm. Building on this Jacques makes reference to Job 22:29, "For God abases the proud but he saves the lowly." In heaven, he explained, "religious convents are beds for the consolation of the meek and infirm."[105] Ministering to the sick and poor, administering hospices, and nursing lepers came to define a prominent aspect of the social and spiritual role of Cistercian nuns. Active caregiving that brought Cistercian nuns outside their cloisters was also one of the ways that the laity would have seen such women at work, dressed in white habits, on the margins of their towns, consoling those who had been excluded from urban centers.

It would be misguided to think that these were wholly abstract concepts and connections. The notion of service to Christ and imitation of Christ and particularly the acceptance of one's humanity were concepts that infused many of the works of Bernard of Clairvaux, but particularly his sermons on the *Song of Songs*. Bernard explained to his listeners that "as the Son of God used his humanity to save the world, so ordinary men and women could use their humanity to imitate His divinity and so save themselves (and others)."[106] Bernard's sermons were particularly favored in Cistercian convents.[107] The care and oversight Cistercian nuns extended to the poor and sick brought them into contact with men and women excluded and marginalized from society. The origins of Cistercian convents in connection to hospices, leper houses, and *domus-Dei* and within the penitential and apostolic religious movements facilitated the institutionalization and reform of those who had been on the margins. For those religious women who were reformed as

---

Bériou, "La prédication au béguinage de Paris pendant l'année liturgique 1272–1273," *Recherches augustinennes* 13 (1978): 105–229.

105. As was common, the entire sermon was built around a Bible passage. Here Jacques de Vitry focused on 2 Kings 4:9–11: "Animaduerto quod vir Dei sanctus est iste, qui transit per nos frequenter; faciamus ei cenaculum paruum, et ponamus ei in eo lectulum, et mensam, et sellam, et candelabrum, ut cum venerit ad nos, maneat ibi." This imagery clearly paralleled the type of hostels and leper houses that Cistercian nuns administered to during this period. He made this parallel clear by stating, "In cenaculo religiosi conventus est lectulus ad consolationem pusillanimum et infirmorum." From "Sermo ad moniales albas cisterciensis ordinis vel alias albas," 19, in Jean Longère, "Quatre sermons ad religiosas de Jacques de Vitry," in *Les religieuse en France au XIIIe siècle,* ed. Michel Parisse (Nancy, 1989), 215–300, at 286. As stated earlier, this sermon appears in a manuscript in the collection of Clairvaux, now MAT, MS 228, fols. 118ra–19vb. It also appears in another Clairvaux manuscript containing exempla of Jacques de Vitry (MAT, MS 1750, sermon 30, fol. 32r–v).

106. Bernard of Clairvaux, *Sancti Bernardi Opera,* ed. Jean Leclercq, H.-M. Rochais, and C. Talbot, 8 vols. (Rome, 1957–77), vol. 2, serm. 66, p. 185. In English, idem, *On the Song of Songs III,* trans. Killiam Walsh and Irene M. Edmonds (Kalamazoo, MI, 1979), 202.

107. *VJC,* bk. 1. chap. 6.

Cistercian nuns, these new institutions transformed the care of the poor and sick into a sanctioned vocation and pious monastic practice. In this sense Cistercian women took seriously the notion that *caritas* extended to the full social body of the church. Whereas Cistercian monks, as Martha Newman has described, understood *caritas* to extend to their responsibilities in positions of power outside the cloister, Cistercian women interpreted *caritas* as a practice that applied to everyone, but particularly to the wretched, the *pauperes Christi,* who would be the first to find salvation.[108]

---

108. Newman, *Boundaries of Charity.*

CHAPTER 5

One and the Same Passion
Convents and Crusaders

Late in the summer of 1192, ships began to return to the southern ports of France and Italy bearing crusaders and pilgrims who had defended the Holy Land after the city of Jerusalem had fallen to Saladin. Among the knights, lords, squires, and retainers was an Englishwoman of middle age, Margaret of Beverley, sometimes known as Margaret of Jerusalem, who had undertaken a pilgrimage in the mid-1180s only to be caught up in the warfare of the Third Crusade. Margaret had been born in Jerusalem in the mid-twelfth century when her parents were on pilgrimage. She returned with them to England as an infant and grew up in Beverley, caring for her younger brother Thomas after their parents died. When Thomas entered the entourage of Thomas of Becket, archbishop of Canterbury, and then joined the Cistercian order as a monk at Froidmont in France, Margaret returned to the East.

Shortly after arriving in Jerusalem as a pilgrim, Margaret participated in the fifteen-day defense of the city, taking up arms to fight alongside the Christian crusaders. When Jerusalem fell in the summer of 1187, she was taken captive by Saladin's forces and ransomed—only to be taken captive again and this time forced to perform hard labor for the Muslims for fifteen months. Finally, by chance, she was among a group of Christians freed through the generosity of a Christian merchant from Tyre. She suffered Muslim captivity one final time, after which she made her way to the shrine of Saint Margaret of Antioch to give thanks for her release. From there, she undertook a longer pilgrimage down the Levant coast, living in poverty and suffering for Christ.[1] As she traveled throughout the Holy Land she wore only a rough tunic and carried a small Psalter, her sole possessions.[2] Traveling by foot, clad in a manner that anticipated a monastic conversion, she fulfilled her pilgrimage and visited other shrines in the Holy Land. She arrived in Acre in the summer of 1191, as Richard I, king of England, concluded the treaty with Saladin that brought the Third Crusade to a close.[3] After this she traveled from Acre to Compostella, then to Rome, and finally to the Cistercian abbey of Froidmont in the diocese of Beauvais to find her brother.[4] Shortly after their reunion, she joined the Cistercian nunnery of Montreuil-les-Dames outside of Laon, where she lived for eighteen years as a Cistercian lay-sister (*conversa*) until her death sometime around 1214.[5]

What is known about Margaret's extraordinary life comes from the *vita* that Thomas of Froidmont (d. 1225) composed for his sister in prose and verse during the years after her death.[6] She offered an example of the new spirituality of suffering and sacrifice for Christ, and the verse text may have been composed partly for liturgical use to commemorate her death.[7] Thomas lauded his sister foremost for the suffering she endured in the East, fighting for Christ, surviving as a captive and a poor pilgrim, and after her return to France living as a *conversa* in the Cistercian order. As Christoph Maier has argued, suffering emerges as a main theme in her *vita,* specifically "sacrificial suffering... represented by her willingness to accept the mortal dangers

---

1. For the narrative of these events, see Thomas of Froidmont, *Hodoeporicon et pericula Margarite Iherosolimitane,* in Paul Gerhard Schmidt, "'Peregrinatio periculosa.' Thomas von Froidmont über dei Jerusalemfahrten seiner schwester Margareta," in *Kontinuität und Wandel: Lateinische Poesie von Naevius bis Baudelaire: Franco Munari zum 65. Geburtstag,* ed. Ulrich Justus Stache, Wolfgang Maaz, and Fritz Wagner (Hildeshein, 1986), 461–85.

2. Ibid., 481, vv. 133–38.

3. Ibid., 483–84, vv. 195–204.

4. Ibid., 484, vv. 208–20.

5. "Ingressa est igitur monasterium Virginum, cui nomen est Monasteriolum, in episcopatu Laudunensi, *conversa,* ibique per annos duodeviginti conversata est, frequenter atque fortiter salutando Mariam, que multum laboravit in nobis, maxime quando ipsius animam mortis Christi amaritudo amarissima pertransivit." Ibid., 474–75; on the date of her death, see 471, n. 19.

6. On the manuscript tradition, see the remarks ibid., 467–69, esp. n. 18. A copy of the *vita* appears to have been among the manuscripts in the Collection Clairvaux, although it is no longer extant.

7. See M. de Florival, "Un pèlerinage au XIIe siècle: Marguerite de Jérusalem et Thomas de Froidmont," *Bulletin de la Société académique de Laon* 26 (1882–1884): 35–69. On the composition of rhymed verse among the Cistercians generally, see William D. Paden, "*De monachis rithmos facientibus:* Hélinant de Froidmont, Bertran de Born and the Cistercian General Chapter of 1199," *Speculum* 55 (1980): 669–85.

of war and her readiness to endure captivity and poverty," all of which she "suffered in the spirit of following Christ (*consecutio Christi*)."[8] In Thomas's words, "she took the cross, so that she could follow Christ as a Christian, going across the sea to accomplish this."[9] As the *vita* makes clear, her vows as a lay sister allowed her to prolong her experience of suffering on crusade. Service in the monastic life was constructed as analogous to service on crusade; it was to suffer for Christ in a different way and in a different context. At Montreuil-les-Dames Margaret cultivated an ardent devotion to the Virgin Mary, for as Thomas explained, "Mary and Christ had suffered one and the same passion at the Crucifixion; in one flesh and one spirit."[10] For Margaret, devotion to the Virgin in the cloister was on a continuum with her devotion to Christ realized through her pilgrimage to the East.

While Margaret's life was clearly exceptional, the devotional ideals she embodied were becoming increasingly common in the early decades of the thirteenth century, particularly among families of men and women who took part in the crusade movement. Indeed, over the course of the thirteenth century, female Cistercian communities came to play an increasingly important role in the development of crusade piety and commemoration. In this way, the broader context of the crusade movement shaped the scope and significance of Cistercian female spirituality profoundly. These developments have often gone overlooked because most crusade histories follow those who departed for the East and neglect the devotional practices of the female kin left behind. Yet as Margaret of Beverley makes clear, to separate the suffering of the cloister from the sufferings of the campaign is to miss the carefully constructed nature of thirteenth-century crusade spirituality as it came to incorporate the home front within its larger ideals. It also overlooks the ways in which the Cistercian order had become deeply involved in crusading and commemoration.

Over the course of the thirteenth century—motivated largely by repeated failures in the East—crusading as a religious movement began to be redefined as popes and preachers encouraged the participation of women

---

8. Christoph T. Maier, "The Roles of Women in the Crusade Movement: A Survey," *Journal of Medieval History* 30 (2004): 61–82, at 65.

9. "Hic autem adolescentie complevit annos, et adulta baiulans sibi crucem, ut Christum Christiana sequeretur, pergere profecta (?) est in transmarina." Thomas of Froidmont, *Hodoeporicon*, 473.

10. "Equidem cum sit una passio Marie cum Christo, una caro, spiritus unus, ex quo ei dictum est, Dominus iterum inseparabiliter perse... it promissum ei donum." Ibid., 475; also Maier, "Roles of Women," 65–66. On compassionate suffering, see Amy Neff, "The Pain of *Compassio*: Mary's Labor at the Foot of the Cross," *Art Bulletin* 80 (1998): 254–73.

at home in the West.[11] This was a departure from earlier practices. In the decades before 1200, and specifically during the Second and Third Crusades, which responded to territorial losses in the Holy Land, the ecclesiastical hierarchy had attempted to streamline crusade armies to make them more effective militarily. The early rhetoric of the call to crusade as articulated in sermons and letters emphasized the participation of men, specifically men of the knightly class. As a consequence, during the twelfth century crusading was articulated as a gendered pursuit that excluded women, while it simultaneously prescribed and reinforced aristocratic masculinity through taking the cross.[12] Although some women did go to the Holy Land before 1200, they were not called upon to take a crusade vow or to participate in crusading. Indeed, Margaret went as a pilgrim, though, as Thomas notes, in defending Jerusalem and enduring captivity she became in effect a crusader, suffering for Christ.

With the loss of Jerusalem to Saladin in the autumn of 1187, however, popes and preachers in the West began to broaden their definition of a crusade, setting it within a wider conception of penance and religious reform.[13] It was increasingly believed that spiritual failings among the faithful of Christendom were responsible for the repeated military failures in the East. God's favor had been lost. Influenced by the reform ideals of the Parisian masters in the circle of Peter the Chanter, during the first two decades of the thirteenth century Pope Innocent III and his successors refined the meaning of crusade participation.[14] Throughout the preaching campaigns that followed Innocent III's famed bull *Quia maior* (19–29 April 1213) that called

---

11. See Maier, "Roles of Women," 61–64; also Deborah Gerish, "Gender Theory," in *Palgrave Advances in the Crusades,* ed. Helen J. Nicholson (New York, 2005), 130–47; and Susan B. Edgington and Sarah Lambert, eds., *Gendering the Crusades* (New York, 2001). On the roles of women more generally, see Sabine Geldsetzer, *Frauen auf Kreuzzügen, 1096–1291* (Darmstadt, 2003); Christine Dernbecher, *"Deum et virum suum diligens": Zur Rolle und Bedeutung der Frau im Umfeld der Kreuzzüge* (St. Ingbert, 2003); and Natasha R. Hodgson, *Women, Crusading and the Holy Land in Historical Narrative* (Woodbridge, 2007).

12. See Sarah Lambert, "Crusading or Spinning," in Edginton and Lambert, *Gendering the Crusades,* 1–15; and Helen J. Nicholson, "Women on the Third Crusade," *Journal of Medieval History* 23 (1997): 335–49. For the masculine emphasis in sermons before 1200, see Constance M. Rousseau, "Home Front and Battlefield: The Gendering of Papal Crusading Policy (1095–1221)," in Edginton and Lambert, *Gendering the Crusades,* 31–44, at 31–35. On masculine identity, see Katherine Allen Smith, "Saints in Shining Armor: Martial Asceticism and Masculine Models of Sanctity, ca. 1050–1250," *Speculum* 83 (2008): 572–602; and Ruth Mazo Karras, *From Boys to Men: Formations of Masculinity in Late Medieval Europe* (Philadelphia, 2002).

13. See Rousseau, "Home Front and Battlefield," 35–36.

14. Jessalynn Bird, "Innocent III, Peter the Chanter's Circle and the Crusade Indulgence: Theory, Implementation, and Aftermath," in *Innocenzo III: Urbs et Orbis. Atti del congresso internazionale Roma, 9–15 settembre 1998,* ed. Andrea Sommerlechner, 2 vols. (Rome, 2003), 1:503–24.

the Fifth Crusade, crusading began to be described as a religious undertaking that depended upon the participation of all Christians.[15] Preachers spoke to great crowds, calling everyone in attendance to take vows: men, women, children, the poor, the old and infirm, but the latter, those who could not fight, were encouraged to commute their vows into monetary payments that would fund military men to go in their stead. Preachers occasionally spoke directly and enthusiastically to groups of women, extolling them to encourage their husbands and sons to take vows. While preaching in Genoa late in the summer of 1216, Jacques de Vitry proclaimed that in this way women too could become crusaders.[16] Jacques recognized not only that such women were "fervent and devout," but also that they controlled considerable wealth that could benefit the crusade cause. Moreover, their acceptance of the cross encouraged their husbands to follow their example.[17] Some women did on occasion accompany their husbands and male kin on crusade or simply took vows and went themselves. Yet it was far more common for women to take vows that would be commuted into monetary payments to provide a subsidy for a knight or contribute to the general funds raised to support the crusading army.[18] Over the course of the thirteenth century, vow commutations became one of the standard ways of funding campaigns to the East. The impact of this policy in the West was profound. Indeed, once taken, the crusade vow also entailed a commitment to spiritual conversion and penance, even if such penance was not carried out through a pilgrimage to Jerusalem. And those who commuted their vows were accorded the benefits of the crusade indulgence, which in its most powerful form promised "full remission of the penance enjoined for confessed sins."[19]

Yet, ironically, because there was a call to integrate women into the crusade movement, gendered participation was further circumscribed. Christoph

---

15. Rousseau, "Home Front and Battlefield," 35–36; and James Powell, *Anatomy of a Crusade, 1213–1221* (Philadelphia, 1986), 20–21, 51–65.

16. "Multitudo autem mulierum divitum et nobilium signum crucis recepit: cives mihi equos abstulerunt, et ego uxores eorum crucesignavi." Jacques de Vitry, *Lettres (1160/1170–1240),* ed. R. B. C. Huygens (Leiden, 1960), Letter 1, lines 152–4, pp. 71–78, at 77; also the comments in James Powell, "The Role of Women in the Fifth Crusade," in *The Horns of Hattin: Proceedings of the Second Conference of the SSCLE Jerusalem and Haifa, 2–6 July 1987,* ed. B. Z. Kedar (London, 1992), 294–301.

17. "Adeo enim ferventes et devote erant." When the men of Genoa found that their wives and sons had accepted the cross, "postquam verbum predicationis audierunt signum crucis cum magno fervore et desiderio receperunt." Jacques de Vitry, *Lettres,* 77.

18. See Christoph T. Maier, *Preaching the Crusades: Mendicant Friars and the Cross in the Thirteenth Century* (Cambridge, 1994), 135–60; and Michel Lower, *The Barons' Crusade: A Call to Arms and Its Consequences* (Philadelphia, 2005), 13–36.

19. Bird, "Innocent III, Peter the Chanter's Circle and the Crusade Indulgence," 507; also Powell, *Anatomy of a Crusade,* 20–21.

Maier has argued that "Pope Innocent III's reforms led to a situation in which gender roles became more and more clearly defined, especially when taking into account the home front as an integral element of the crusade *movement*."[20] Vow redemptions became a way of allowing women to participate spiritually in the movement while simultaneously ensuring that they would remain at home. From 1215 forward, women's participation was intended to support, enhance, and even mirror—in spiritual and metaphoric terms—male actions in the East. While crusading became gendered in explicit ways, the experiences of devotion were nonetheless further intertwined with the shared ideal of penance and suffering meant to recall Christ's own redemptive sacrifice.

The Cistercian convents of Champagne developed within this gendered framework. Indeed in many cases male aristocratic support for Cistercian convents was closely tied to the spirituality of crusading that pervaded Champagne throughout the thirteenth century. In this context the piety of Cistercian nuns supported and paralleled the penitential sacrifices that distinguished the crusade movement, allowing women to share in and support the suffering of crusaders and the movement as a whole. Crusaders and their families cultivated relationships with Cistercian convents in part to benefit from the penitential piety and prayers such religious women offered. The Cistercian convents housed female members of crusader families, functioned as sites of liturgical worship in support of crusade expeditions, and served as family necropolises for returning or deceased crusaders who were remembered and commemorated by Cistercian nuns and by the Cistercian order as a whole. Over the course of the thirteenth century, as the crusade movement changed to take on aspects of the *imitatio Christi,* both religious endeavors—crusading and the active piety of Cistercian nuns who cared for the poor and sick—became expressions of a broader religious orientation focused on Christ's sacrifice, on Jerusalem, and on a theology of redemption.

A striking number of aristocratic families participated in both the crusades and the patronage of Cistercian convents. For those who left for the East on crusade, penitential piety was practiced through pilgrimage and holy war; they went literally to walk in the way of Christ.[21] For those who remained at home—primarily women—prayer, processions, crusader liturgies, and works of mercy characterized a piety of penance that allowed them to become "poor for the poor Christ," and thereby "to return, under the

---

20. Maier, "Roles of Women," 74.
21. Another phrase to describe this imitation was conforming (*conformari*) to Christ, which included following Christ unto death. See Christoph T. Maier, *Crusade Propaganda and Ideology: Model Sermons for the Preaching of the Cross* (Cambridge, 2000), 59–60.

habit of religion, to the house of the poor Christ."[22] Ultimately both practices worked for the same ends: the triumph of Christianity and a rearticulation of its ideals based on a shared imitation of Christ. By the third decade of the thirteenth century, harnessing the prayers and holiness of Cistercian nuns was a powerful way for many crusader families to advance these aims and ideals. For those women inside the convents, this also became a way of participating in the crusades.

A Crusading Aristocracy and the Cistercian Order

From the inception of the crusades in 1095, the idea of taking back Jerusalem from the Muslims met strong support in Champagne. The aristocracy of the county contributed an endless supply of nobles and knights to fight and, after 1204, to settle in the East, both in the Holy Land as well as in the Peloponnese. The counts of Champagne took part in every campaign launched to the East between 1095 and 1270, and in 1226 Thibaut IV briefly joined the French king on the Albigensian Crusade in southern France. Generations of the region's barons and their knights and retainers took part in these expeditions, and their combined efforts marked out Champagne's unceasing commitment to the pious cause.[23]

The Cistercians too were powerful advocates of the crusades. In 1146–47 Bernard of Clairvaux preached a tireless tour across Europe, rallying recruits for the Second Crusade. In a letter to Pope Eugenius III he noted that the impact of his sermons was so great that "towns and castles [were] emptied, and now one may scarcely find one man among seven women, so many women [were] widowed while their husbands [were] still living."[24] Bernard likewise promoted the Knights Templar, who drew their first members from

---

22. Bernard of Clairvaux, *Sancti Bernardi Opera*, 8 vols., ed. Jean Leclercq, H.-M. Rochais, and C. Talbot (Rome, 1957–77), 8:437 (Ep. 459); see also William J. Purkis, *Crusading Spirituality in the Holy Land and Iberia c. 1095–c. 1187* (Woodbridge, 2008), 98–101.

23. See A. Prévost, "Les champenois aux croisades," *MSA* 85 (1921): 109–86; Jean Longnon, *Les compagnons de Villehardouin: Recherches sur les croisés de la Quatrième Croisade* (Geneva, 1978); Yvonne Bellenger and Danielle Quéruel, eds. *Les champenois et la croisade: Actes des quatrièmes journées rémoises, 27–28 novembre 1987* (Paris, 1989); Theodore Evergates, "The Origin of the Lords of Karytaina in the Frankish Morea," *Medieval Prosopography* 15 (1994): 81–113; Peter Lock, *The Franks in the Aegean, 1204–1500* (London, 1995); Danielle Quéruel, ed., *Jean de Joinville: De la Champagne aux royaumes d'outre-mer* (Langres, 1998); and Caroline Smith, *Crusading in the Age of Joinville* (Aldershot, 2006).

24. *Sancti Bernardi Opera*, 8:141 (Ep. 247). Generally, E. Willems, "Cîteaux et la Seconde Croisade," *Revue d'Histoire Ecclésiastique* 49 (1954): 116–52; Michael Gervers, ed., *The Second Crusade and the Cistercians* (New York, 1992); and Purkis, *Crusading Spirituality*, 86–119.

the ranks of the Champenois aristocracy.[25] Cistercian sermons and letters set the tone for crusade preaching and crafted a vocabulary of recruitment, which flourished through the end of the twelfth century.[26] Moreover, beginning in 1143 Bernard also preached against the "heretics" in the county of Toulouse. In sermons and chronicles the abbot of Clairvaux and the Cistercians who followed him crafted a rhetorical program that defined heresy and helped to propel the crusade in southern France.[27] During the thirteenth century the Cistercians remained a powerful presence in the crusade movement. They established monastic houses in the Holy Land and in the Peloponnese, and abbots of the order continued to give crusade sermons, even as their efforts were eclipsed by the voices of more persuasive preachers trained in this art as secular canons or friars.[28]

The links between crusaders and Cistercian female foundations, however, provide insight into the expansion of crusading as a movement as it incorporated the home front in a specific institutionalized form. This is not to suggest that the aristocracy and crusading families of Champagne patronized Cistercian nunneries instead of other houses, but rather that what we see is a new and concerted effort to support these particular female communities. The context of the crusades, in turn, informed the practices and spirituality of Cistercian nuns in profound ways. In 1202, when Geoffrey IV, count of Perche, fell ill and died before he could complete the Fourth Crusade, he instructed his widow Mathilda of Brunswick to found a religious house for the remission of his vow. Two years later, in 1204, she founded the Cistercian nunnery of Les Clairets to the west of Chartres.[29] Whether it was Geoffrey or Mathilda who made the final decision to support a house of Cistercian women, such a choice was understood to function as a penitential act

---

25. See Bernard of Clairvaux, "Liber ad milites templi: De laude novae militiae," in *Sancti Bernardi Opera*, 3:213–239; and Malcom Barber, *The New Knighthood: A History of the Order of the Temple* (Cambridge, 1994).

26. Purkis, *Crusading Spirituality*, 111–19.

27. See Beverly Mayne Kienzle, *Cistercians, Heresy and Crusade in Occitania, 1145–1229: Preaching in the Lord's Vineyard* (Rochester, NY, 2001); and Mark Gregory Pegg, *A Most Holy War: The Albigensian Crusade and the Battle for Christendom* (Oxford, 2008), 50–118.

28. See Elizabeth A. R. Brown, "The Cistercians in the Latin Empire of Constantinople and Greece, 1204–1276," *Traditio* 14 (1958): 63–120; and Bernard Hamilton, "The Cistercians in the Crusader States," reprinted in his *Monastic Reform, Catharism and the Crusades, 900–1300* (London, 1979), 405–22. On Cistercian preaching, see Alfred Andrea, "Adam of Persigne and the Fourth Crusade," *Cîteaux* 36 (1985): 21–37; and Penny J. Cole, *The Preaching of the Crusades to the Holy Land, 1095–1270* (Cambridge, MA, 1991), 80–141.

29. *GC* 8, col. 1324; and cols. 349–50, instr. 78–79; and Vicomte Hector de Souancé, ed., *Abbaye royale de Notre-Dame des Clairets: Histoire et cartulaire, 1202–1790* (Nogent-le-Rotrou, 1894), esp. 1–2, and nos. 3–5.

commensurate with crusading. In the same year, 1204, Mathilda of Garlande carried out her husband's, Matthew of Montmorency, last wishes after he died (1203) on the Fourth Crusade and founded a house of Cistercian nuns at Porrois, also known as Port-Royal-des-Champs, just north of Paris.[30] In a similar vein, Brigitte Pipon has suggested that Jean II, lord of Nesle (1197–1239), founded the Cistercian nunnery of L'Abbaye-aux-Bois in the diocese of Beauvais (between Roye and Noyon) in April 1202 precisely during the interval between taking a crusade vow in February 1200 and departing in 1203. Pipon posits that Jean may have chosen to create a female house with his wife, Eustachie of St.-Pol, or another female family member in mind.[31] The early Cistercian female foundations created in connection with the Fourth Crusade marked the beginning of a trend that became even more pronounced in the following generation.

These foundations were both acts of penance and provision. Foundation gifts, often portions of familial estates or rents, functioned like alms that would support a community of nuns in perpetuity, thus serving as a final penitential bequest before the men left for the Holy Land. These new foundations also provided for the souls and on occasion the bodies of the crusaders' female kin, if they chose to profess within the community. Enguerrand de Boves was a seasoned crusader when he departed on the Fifth Crusade in 1219. In the same year, perhaps thinking of his own soul and surely that of his wife, he founded the Cistercian nunnery of Le Paraclet, endowing it with a vast portion of his estates as well as rents, mill rights, and annual yields of eels from his mill ponds.[32] By September 1219 he had arrived in Egypt and took part in the siege of Damietta. He was in Syria in 1222, but soon thereafter returned to France and died the following year.[33] As this example illustrates, such foundations were undertaken in the years or months before departure and were significant economic and religious decisions for families

---

30. See *Cartulaire de l'Abbaye de Porrois au diocèse de Paris, plus comme sous son nom mystique Port-Royal,* ed. Adolphe de Dion (Paris, 1903), 25, no. 1, 29–30, no. 4; and Longnon, *Les compagnons de Villehardouin,* 116–18.

31. Brigitte Pipon, *Le chartrier de l'Abbaye-aux-Bois (1202–1341): Étude et édition* (Paris, 1996), 42–43, and 95–96, no. 1. Contrast with Longnon's remarks on Jean of Nesle in *Les compagnons de Villehardouin,* 149. Although Longnon consulted a vast array of cartularies to compile his study, he did not use Abbaye-aux-Bois's cartulary (housed in the collection of the Newberry Library of Chicago since 1986), and in turn he omits this foundation at a key moment before Jean of Nesle's departure.

32. Le Paraclet is not to be confused with the twelfth-century abbey founded by Abelard and Heloise. See *GC* 10:339–41, instr. 65; see also Amiens, AD de la Somme, 65 H 88★, for the cartulary. Enguerrand's brother Robert de Boves, lord of Fouencamps, also donated to the Le Paraclet before his departure in 1219; see Longnon, *Les compagnons de Villehardouin,* 123–24.

33. See Powell, *Anatomy of a Crusade,* 219.

and local communities. They were intended to communicate the departing lord's spiritual and penitential commitment, while at the same time rendering his familial lordship and status present in the new institution.

Cistercian Convents and Crusader Patronage: Five Case Studies of a Movement

From the mid-1220s, members of the crusading aristocracy of Champagne and its neighboring principalities began founding new female Cistercian houses or playing a role in their patronage when they prepared to go to the East and when they returned from crusade. Crusader patronage was precisely the kind of aristocratic support the Cistercian order sought when it directed female communities to be "endowed and enriched." Crusading may also help explain the proliferation of Cistercian convents in Champagne, for such foundations reinforced the heightened sense of religious devotion evident during these decades. The provisions of five aristocratic families illustrate the connection between Cistercian convents and crusading. Indeed, by considering the strategies of families rather than the ambitions solely of the nuns or crusaders, the shared elements of thirteenth-century devotion become much clearer.

Over the course of the twelfth century, the Dampierre family became one of the most powerful and prominent lordly households in the county, attaining high positions in the church and the constableship of Champagne. They contracted favorable marriages with the noble house of Bourbon and the counts of Flanders and controlled not only their familial properties at Dampierre, but also the attached lordships of St.-Dizier and St.-Just to the northeast of the county. The Dampierres produced several crusaders, including Guy II, who took part in the Third Crusade, and William III, who traveled with Louis IX to the East in 1248.[34] In 1226, William II (d. 1233) with his wife, Margaret, the countess of Flanders, founded the Cistercian nunnery of St.-Dizier on their familial property, and their sons, William III (d. 1251) and John (d. 1259), confirmed the foundation and continued to patronize

---

34. This branch of the Dampierre family must be distinguished from those of Dampierre-le-Château, although the latter lordship also boasted crusaders, notably Renard II of Dampierre (d. 1234), who spent nearly thirty years in Muslim captivity in the East until he was ransomed in 1231. On the Dampierre-St.-Dizier family, see Theodore Evergates, *The Aristocracy in the County of Champagne, 1100–1300* (Philadelphia, 2007), 226–29; and Charles Savetiez, "Maison de Dampierre-Saint-Dizier," *Revue de Champagne et de Brie* 17 (1884): 10–12, 113–25, 210–20, 283–90, 361–68, 465–71; 18 (1885): 66–72.

it during their lifetimes.[35] Although William II and Margaret of Flanders founded several other Cistercian nunneries in the county of Flanders (most famously that of Flines), it was at St.-Dizier on his familial property that William II chose to be buried.[36] This was a family that articulated specific forms of piety and patronage and through their choices created a collective expression of religious devotion that bound together crusading and Cistercian female spirituality.

Hugh V of Châtillon (d. 1248), the lord of St.-Pol, was, like the lords of Dampierre, one of the more powerful barons in Champagne. Hugh's lands lay to the northwest of the county, close to the orbit of Paris. The Châtillon were also a family of crusaders: Hugh V's grandfather, Gaucher II, died on the Second Crusade; his father, Gaucher III (d. 1219), and uncle, Guy III, were both familiars of Philip II of France and accompanied the king on the Third Crusade. Guy died in Acre in 1191. Gaucher then inherited the lordship and, after his marriage to Elizabeth of St.-Pol, augmented his holdings with that of St.-Pol. He fought with Philip II in Normandy and in 1214 at Bouvines, and took part in the Albigensian Crusade, yet he also remained close to the count and countess of Champagne. In 1226 Gaucher III's eldest son, Guy IV, died on campaign in the south of France in the company of his lord, Count Thibaut IV, during the final phase of the Albigensian Crusade.[37] The second son, Hugh V, inherited the lordships of Châtillon and St.-Pol as a mature adult following his brother's death.[38] In the same year, 1226, Hugh founded the Cistercian nunnery of Pont-aux-Dames on a bridge in Couilly where there had been a *domus-Dei*. Six years later, in 1232, he founded L'Amour-Dieu near Troissy, which also grew out of a preexisting *domus-Dei*.[39] Hugh V had

---

35. GC 9:973; AD Marne, 71 H; and Anne-Marie Couvret, "Charte de Jean de Dampierre pour l'Abbaye Notre-Dame de Saint-Dizier," *Cahier Haut-Marnais: Revue de sciences, de lettres et d'art* 131 (1977): 157–59.

36. See below, 166.

37. Just before his death he made a donation of 10 *l.* annually for the construction of a chapel in the *domus-Dei* of Troissy, which would become the nunnery of L'Amour-Dieu. AD Marne, 69 H 21 (August 1225).

38. See Evergates, *Aristocracy,* 176–78, 221–23; and André Duchesne, *Histoire de la maison de Chastillon sur Marne* (Paris, 1621), 60, 98–101. Also Jean-Noël Mathieu, "A propos des châtelains de Châtillon-sur-Marne," *MSM* 107 (1992): 7–27; and Jean-François Nieus, *Un pouvoir comtal entre Flandre et France: Saint-Pol, 1000–1300* (Brussels, 2005), 163–66, on Hugh V. The Châtillon resembled many other aristocratic lineages that pursued crusading over generations. See Elizabeth Siberry, "The Crusading Counts of Nevers," *Nottingham Medieval Studies* 34 (1990): 64–70.

39. GC 8:1624, instr. 558 (Pont-aux-Dames); GC 9:481–82, instr. 58–60, 62–63 (L'Amour-Dieu). Also, Claude-Hyacinthe Berthault, *L'Abbaye de Pont-aux-Dames, ordre de Cîteaux; Assise en la paroisse de Couilly, châtellenie de Crécy, élection et diocèse de Meaux-en Brie, 1226–1790* (Meaux, 1878); and Robert Martin, "Aux sources de l'Abbaye de Pont-aux-Dames," *Bulletin de la Société littéraire et historique de la Brie* 40 (1984): 17–36.

a reputation as a great baron and cultivated close ties with the royal family.[40] It appears that he intended to go on crusade with Louis IX in 1248 but died before departing.[41] He would have accompanied his nephew Gaucher, the lord of Montjay. The younger Gaucher drew up a detailed testament before his departure that made elaborate provisions for the poor should he die in the East. He delegated two Cistercian abbots to distribute tunics and shoes annually to the poor on his behalf. Gaucher died 5 April 1250 at the battle of Mansourah in Egypt at the age of twenty-eight.[42] Thus the Châtillon family pursued Cistercian patronage and crusading over three generations.

When Hugh V of Châtillon founded the nunnery of L'Amour-Dieu in 1232 he did not act alone. The decision to create a Cistercian nunnery was made in conjunction with Philip of Mécringes, whom Hugh described as "[his] beloved lord and knight."[43] Indeed, Hugh granted the rights to the small *domus-Dei* on his property at Troissy to Philip, and it was Philip who made the decision to convert it into a community of Cistercian nuns, with Hugh's approval.[44] In this way the men were joint founders of L'Amour-Dieu. While similar to Hugh V's previous foundation at Pont-aux-Dames in that both houses grew from a preexisting *domus-Dei* incorporating the sick and the women already there in residence who cared for them, Philip's decision also had a precedent. In 1229 Philip had founded La Piété near Ramerupt in the diocese of Troyes. There too the community grew out of a group of women who lived together as penitents associated with the local hospital.[45] La Piété was founded on lands close to the lordship of Erard of Brienne, another prominent baron in Champagne and a well-known crusader. In 1236, Erard began what would become a sustained relationship with the nunnery, though his family would also donate to other Cistercian convents near Brienne.[46] In 1229, the same year that Philip de Mécringes founded La

---

40. See Jean of Joinville, *Vie de Saint Louis,* ed. Jacques Monfrin (Paris, 1995), para. 96.

41. See Evergates, *Aristocracy,* 179, 223. Hugh inventoried his property before his planned departure: Jean-François Nieus, "Un example précoce de repertoire féodale: Le livre des fiefs de la châtellenie d'Encre (nord de la France, ca. 1245)," *Bulletin de la Commission Royale d'Histoire* 168 (2002): 1–70.

42. Gaucher's will is AD Nièvre, 43 H 5 (marked on reverse H 164, no. 20), which has been transcribed and edited by H. de Flamare, "La charte de depart pour la Terre-Sainte de Gaucher de Châtillon," *Bulletin de la Société Nivernaise* 13 (1886–89): 174–82.

43. "dilecto meo domino Philippo de Mescringes militi"; AD Marne, 69 H 24 (1232). See also GC 9:481–42, instr. 58–60, 62–63; and Albert Noël, "L'Abbaye de l'Amour-Dieu de l'ordre de Cîteaux (1232–1802)," *Revue de Champagne et de Brie* 1 (1876): 144–53.

44. AD Marne, 69 H 24 (April 1239).

45. See GC 12:609–10; and BNF, Collection Duchesne, 4:35–41; also chap. 4, 130–31, in this book.

46. AD Aube, G 3186 (August 1235); and Anne Bondeelle-Souchier, "Les moniales cisterciennes et leurs livres manuscrits dans la France d'ancien régime," *Cîteaux* 45 (1994): 193–337, at 275–76.

Piété, Marie, countess of Brienne, founded the Cistercian nunnery of Le Jardin near Sézanne. A succession of crusading lords in Champagne, including Hugh of Broyes, Hugh of Conflans, and the counts themselves were patrons of Le Jardin and appear in the nunnery's necrology.[47] Thus in the years following the Albigensian Crusade (1209–1229) and the Fifth Crusade (1223) but before the Baron's Crusade (1239), the aristocracy of Champagne carefully cultivated the piety of Cistercian nuns.

Bonds of lordship, like those of marriage, could connect and influence patterns of patronage as well. Philip of Mécringes was only a lesser knight, but his service and piety connected him to the barons of the region. Indeed, Philip held his fief at Mécringes from Jean of Montmirail and Jean's heirs.[48] Jean I of Montmirail, like Hugh of Châtillon, was a member of the upper aristocracy of northern France with ties to the counts of Champagne and King Philip II, in whose court he was raised. In the mid-1180s he married Helvide of Dampierre, thus entwining the two families further in a common knightly and pious culture. He accompanied Philip II on the Third Crusade and in the 1190s fought alongside his king in Normandy. He may have considered taking part in the Fourth Crusade but instead turned to pious pursuits and a life of monastic spirituality.[49] He was particularly moved by the plight of lepers and offered considerable patronage for their care, establishing a leper house in Montmirail in 1203. In 1210, John abandoned his wife of twenty-five years and his five children and entered the Cistercian abbey of Longpont. After his death in 1217, his tomb became the site of miracles, and two monks of Longpont composed a *vita* in support of his canonization (ca. 1230).[50] His heirs Jean II of Montmirail and Matthew of Oisy founded two Cistercian nunneries after their father's death: La Grâce in 1223 in the diocese of Troyes, and Belleau nearby in 1242.[51]

---

47. A few charters survive in BNF, Collection Champagne, 151:9–25; see also Léonce Lex, "Martyrologe et chartes de l'Abbaye Notre-Dame du Jardin lez Pleurs (Marne)," *MSA* 21 (1884): 365–93.

48. According to Noël, "L'Abbaye de L'Amour-Dieu," 144, Philip of Mécringes was known for his piety. In addition to the nunneries, he donated land and rents to the *domus-Dei* that Jean and Helvide of Montmirail founded in 1208. The editors of the *Acta Sanctorum* also include a charter of donation from Philip and his wife, Flandrina, and his brother Ausericus in 1210 for the *domus-Dei* of Montmirail; see *AASS*, September, 8:206 D.

49. See Evergates, *Aristocracy*, 92–96, 175–76, 236–38; Alexandre Clemet Boitel, *Histoire du bienheureux Jean, surnommé l'humble, seigneur de Montmirail-en-Brie* (Paris, 1859); and M. R. Mathieu, *Montmirail en Brie: Sa seigneurie et son canton* (Paris, 1975), 60–82.

50. "*Vita* de B. Joanne de Monte Mirabili," *AASS*, September, 8:186–255; and Alain-Charles Dionnet, "La cassette reliquaire du Bienheureux Jean de Montmirail," *Revue Française d'héraldique et de sigillographie* 65 (1995): 89–107.

51. Matthew of Montmirail founded the Cistercian nunnery of Belleau in 1242; *GC* 12:534. He and his wife were also patrons of the nunneries of Ormont and La Grâce; *GC* 12:506, 534.

Peter of Jaucourt was also part of this network of knightly patronage that combined crusade piety with the support of Cistercian female communities. Peter, it will be recalled, held lands and fiefs just outside of Bar-sur-Aube and had founded Val-des-Vignes near his castle of Jaucourt in 1232.[52] He appeared in the statutes of the order in 1231 requesting a mass to be sung after his death. In 1236 he petitioned the Cistercian General Chapter for the official incorporation of Val-des-Vignes.[53] Peter also had close ties to King Louis IX as well as the counts of Champagne and served as the chamberlain for Countess Blanche of Navarre in 1216 and later as the panetier of Champagne in 1234.[54] Peter's son, Erard of Jaucourt, accompanied Louis IX on his final crusade in 1270 and died in the same year with his king. Before his departure, the lord of Jaucourt drew up a will bequeathing a portion of his goods to the nuns and depositing a copy of his testament with the women at Val-des-Vignes.[55] Within the year Erard's body was returned to the nunnery, where he was buried beside his father Peter.[56]

All of these foundations—eight in total—represent a choice on the part of crusaders and their families in Champagne at a particular point in the evolution of the crusade movement to found and support a specific kind of female spirituality connected to the Cistercian order.[57] This was not done at the expense of other patronage. Indeed, all of these families maintained ties with older houses of monks and nuns, such as Clairvaux, Pontigny, Montier-la-Celle, the Paraclete, and Notre-Dame-aux-Nonnains, and patronized the military orders, the order of Calatrava and the Trinitarians, as well as local hospitals and houses of friars once the latter arrived in

---

52. See Evergates, *Aristocracy*, 188–89; and AD Aube, 3 H 4082 (August 1236), 3 H 4011 (December 1242), and 3 H 4037 (January 1243). Peter's brother, Thomas of Jaucourt, also gave to the nuns: AD Aube, 3 H 4071 (October 1237).

53. Josephus-Mia Canivez, *Statuta Capitulorum Generalium Ordinis Cisterciensis ab anno 1116 ad annum 1786*, 8 vols. (Louvain, 1933–41), 2:(1231)19 and (1236)67.

54. See Henri d'Arbois de Jubainville, *Histoire des ducs et des comtes de Champagne*, 7 vols. (Paris, 1859–69), 4.2: 545–46.

55. AD Aube, 3 H 4036, which was reconfirmed and augmented by his wife and sons after his death in 1272; AD Aube, 3 H 4038.

56. Alphonse Roserot, *Dictionnaire historique de la Champagne méridional (Aube) des origins à 1790*, 3 vols. (Langres, 1942–48), 1:146, and table 10.

57. These examples could be multiplied among the upper aristocracy: Philip of Nemours, for example, founded La Joie-lès-Nemours and was a close companion of Louis IX, accompanying the king on crusade in 1248. (See above, chap. 3, 102–7.) Moreover, the counts of Champagne and Louis IX patronized and founded Cistercian nunneries during this period. See Anselme Dimier, *Saint Louis et Cîteaux* (Paris, 1954).

Champagne.⁵⁸ But the foundation of new Cistercian convents, particularly those connected with preexisting hospitals and *domus-Dei,* offered crusader families the combined benefits of the prayers of penitential women who had become Cistercian nuns and the more traditional institutional affiliation with the Cistercian order, which had supported crusading for generations.

These nunneries also received the female family members of crusaders, typically daughters and sisters of men who traveled to the East. In 1233, just after the foundation of La Piété, Beatrice of Dampierre took the habit and professed as a nun there. A generation later, Sybile, one of Erard of Brienne's daughters, became the abbess of the same nunnery.⁵⁹ Likewise, when Enguerrard of Boves and his wife founded Le Paraclet in 1219, their daughters Marguerite and Isabelle became the first abbess and prioress of the community.⁶⁰ Jean of Montmirail's eldest daughter Elizabeth seems to have shared his spiritual pursuits and charitable concern for lepers, for she took vows and professed at the *domus-Dei* of Montmirail which her father had founded.⁶¹ In what may have been a similar display of filial devotion, Erard of Jaucourt's daughter Alix became a nun at Val-des-Vignes after his death and eventually served as abbess of her family's foundation.⁶² Jonathan Riley-Smith has argued for the role of female family members in encouraging crusading among their male kin.⁶³ When for political or dynastic reasons men could not take the monastic habit, crusading was a viable alternative that found its parallel in female profession.⁶⁴ This pattern suggests a gendered understanding of penitential spirituality: male relatives would travel to the East and incur the

---

58. See Arbois de Jubainville, *Histoire,* 4.2:604–26; and "Chartes de la commanderie de Beauvoir de l'Ordre Teutonique," in *Collection des principaux cartulaires du diocese de Troyes,* ed. Charles Lalore, 7 vols. (Paris, 1875–90), 3:177–328.

59. See *GC* 12:610–11. See also Henri d'Arbois de Jubainville, "Les premiers seigneurs de Ramerupt," *BEC* 22 (1861): 440–58, at 450, who notes that Sybile's brother, Erard II, lord of Ramerupt, accompanied Louis IX on crusade and died in 1250 at the battle of Mansourah.

60. *GC* 10:1345.

61. Mathieu, *Montmirail en Brie,* 69.

62. Roserot, *Dictionnaire historique de la Champagne,* 1:146, and table 10.

63. Jonathan Riley-Smith, "Family Traditions and Participation in the Second Crusade," in Gervers, *The Second Crusade and the Cistercians,* 101–8; and Riley-Smith, *The First Crusaders: 1095–1131* (Cambridge, 1998), 5, 93–105.

64. Louis IX and his sister Isabelle, who founded the Franciscan nunnery of Longchamp and may have hoped to live as a Franciscan herself, exemplify this dual notion of piety. On this see William Chester Jordan, *Louis IX and the Challenge of the Crusade* (Princeton, 1979), 9–10; and idem, "Isabelle of France and Religious Devotion at the Court of Louis IX," in *Capetian Women,* ed. Kathleen Nolan (New York, 2003), 209–23. In January 1286, Jean de Joinville's sister, Héluyse de Joinville, founded a Franciscan nunnery, Ste.-Claire à Montigny. See Jules Finot, "Héluyse de Joinville, soeur de l'historien Jean de Joinville (1264–1312)," *BEC* 37 (1876): 528–40.

hardships and suffering attendant with crusading, while female relatives would join a Cistercian nunnery, perhaps serving for a time among the poor and sick and then taking strict vows to live as a professed nun. Both forms of religious profession were united in their pursuit of the *imitatio Christi*.

Departure, Prayer, and Commemoration

As crusaders and their families fostered an ongoing relationship with Cistercian nunneries throughout the duration of the crusades, they did so with an eye to more immediate consequences. Once a crusader had taken the public vow to go to the East, preparations had to be made for the journey and for the contingency that one might not return. Thus, like Gaucher of Montjay, nephew of Hugh V of Châtillon, many crusaders drew up wills providing for their estates, their families, and the final salvation of their souls. Because crusading itself was a penitential experience, "preparations for the crusade were always marked by acts of penitence."[65] In addition to gifts to the nuns, many crusaders offered donations to the poor and sick and to lepers in particular, who symbolized the poor in Christ or the Man of Sorrows in this world.[66] The hope may have been that such acts of pious charity would ensure the completion of the greater, more arduous penitential undertaking.

By the thirteenth century specific rituals of departure developed that underscored the solemn penitential nature of crusading.[67] On these occasions—during the weeks preceding the leave-taking and on the day itself—crusaders publicly reconfirmed their vows, took part in ceremonies for blessing and bestowing the pilgrim staff and wallet, and heard prayers and hymns intoned for their success on crusade and safe return as they bid farewell to loved ones and their familial estates. Departure functioned as a solemn liturgical event, which purified crusaders and prepared their families for the sacrifices and hoped-for salvation that was to follow. Many crusaders began their journeys from the gates of a monastery or nunnery, leaving a holy space for the Holy Land. Louis IX undertook such a ritual of departure over the course of several

---

65. Jonathan Riley-Smith, *The Crusades, Christianity and Islam* (New York, 2008), 34, and generally 29–44, on the crusades as penitential wars.

66. See the gifts listed in M. Harmond, "Notice historique sur la léproserie de la ville de Troyes," *MSA* 8–7 (1847–48): 429–669, at 550–51 (1215) and (1217); and 564 (1239); also Annie Saunier, *"Le pauvre malade" dans le cadre hospitalier médiéval: France du nord, vers 1300–1500* (Paris, 1993), 28.

67. See William Chester Jordan, "The Rituals of War: Departure for Crusade in Thirteenth-Century France," in *The Book of Kings: Art, War, and the Morgan Library's Medieval Picture Bible*, ed. William Noel and Daniel Weiss (London, 2002), 99–105; and Jordan, "Crusader Prologues: Preparing for War in the Gothic Age," in *The Christian Culture Lecture* (Notre Dame, 2009); also Riley-Smith, *First Crusaders*, 139–43.

days as he prepared to leave Paris at the beginning of June 1248. Barefoot and humble, he processed first to St.-Denis, where he received the oriflamme, the battle standard of Charlemagne, and from there to smaller churches in the city, ending with a final ceremony at the gates of the Cistercian nunnery of St.-Antoine-des-Champs.[68] Joinville describes a similar penitential departure in 1248 when he left the Cistercian monastery of Cheminon after receiving the abbot's blessing and the pilgrim's script and staff from the abbot's hands.[69] When Guy of Dampierre joined Louis IX's crusade in 1270, he and his contingent of knights departed from the Cistercian nunnery of Flines in Flanders, which had been founded by his mother, stopping at the abbey of Clairvaux as he traveled south to the Mediterranean.[70] The details of such rituals are rarely recorded, but it seems reasonable that those families who founded and patronized Cistercian nunneries on their own familial estates or in their houses would have used these new institutions as points of departure, bidding farewell to family who gathered outside the abbey gates and to female kin professed inside. Specific hymns and crusader songs were composed for just such events, combining the penitential solemnity of the ritual with the lyrics of loss and longing to make it clear that both crusaders and those at home sacrificed themselves for this greater cause.[71]

Departing from a monastery and nunnery highlighted what preachers made clear was crucial to the success of the crusade: penitential prayers and processions on the part of those who remained at home.[72] Prayers both for individuals and for the undertaking as a whole were a particularly important manifestation of the crusade movement. Prayers could take the form of individual devotions or communal liturgical services. Cistercian nuns were keen practitioners of both types of prayer. It had been widely recognized by the thirteenth century that the prayers of pious women were especially efficacious, as female hagiography and the countless exempla stories of Jacques

---

68. Jordan, "Rituals of War," 101; and idem, *Louis IX,* 109–10.
69. Joinville, *Vie de Saint Louis,* para. 122; and Smith, *Crusading in the Age of Joinville,* 103–8, 139–49.
70. See Thomas Coomans, "Moniales cisterciennes et mémoire dyanstique: Église funéraires princières et abbayes cisterciennes dans les anciens pays-bas médiévaux," *Cîteaux* 56 (2005): 87–145, at 124.
71. See Jordan, "Rituals of War," 102–3; and Margaret Switten, "Singing the Second Crusade," in Gervers, *The Second Crusade and the Cistercians,* 67–76. Also *Les chansons de croisade,* ed. J. Bédier and P. Aubry (Paris, 1909); and for Champagne, see William Chester Jordan, "The Representation of the Crusades in the Songs Attributed to Thibaud, Count Palatine of Champagne," *Journal of Medieval History* 25 (1999): 27–34.
72. See Christoph T. Maier, "Crisis, Liturgy and the Crusade in the Twelfth and Thirteenth Centuries," *Journal of Ecclesiastical History* 48 (1997): 628–57; and Bird, "Innocent III, Peter the Chanter's Circle, and the Crusade Indulgence."

de Vitry and Caesarius of Heisterbach made clear.[73] Women's prayers had the power to free captive crusaders, convert non-Christians, and save the damned from purgatorial suffering.[74] While it was common in donation charters to ask for nuns to pray for the souls of donors and their family members, knights also asked that Cistercian nuns celebrate anniversary masses for their souls specifically according to the practices of the Cistercian order. When the knight Giles de Genduno drew up his final testament, he bequeathed a portion of his properties and rents to the Cistercian nuns of Clairmarais outside Reims, asking that they remember him in prayer according to the customs of the Cistercian order.[75] Likewise, William de Lézinnes, a member of the crusading family of Villehardouin, gave the Cistercian nuns of Notre-Dame-des-Prés outside of Troyes all that he possessed in the parish of Savoie in return for an anniversary mass in his honor following the manner of the General Chapter.[76] The prayers of the order itself were understood to be profoundly powerful.

Prayers, both private and corporate, as well as processions and liturgical rites became a fundamental manifestation of crusade participation on the home front. While the laity was called upon to take part in monthly processions and offer personal prayers designed to support the crusades generally, the Cistercian order took the lead in channeling the voices of its monks and nuns to benefit crusaders individually and as a group.[77] After the defeat of the crusader forces at the battle of Hattin in 1187, the Cistercian order augmented their liturgy to include regular corporate prayers to support the crusades and specific prayers for those who died in the East.[78] As Christoph Maier has argued, Cistercian liturgical support most likely grew out of Pope Gregory VIII's precepts outlining the content of such prayers and calling on Christendom as a whole to do more in the service of the Holy Land.[79]

---

73. See Barbara Newman, "On the Threshold of the Dead: Purgatory, Hell, and Religious Women," in her *From Virile Woman to WomanChrist: Studies in Medieval Religion and Literature* (Philadelphia, 1995), 108–36; and Jo Ann McNamara, "The Need to Give: Suffering and Female Sanctity in the Middle Ages," in *Images of Sainthood in Medieval Europe*, ed. Renate Blumenfeld-Kosinski and Timea Szell (Ithaca, 1991), 199–221.

74. See Nicole Bériou, *L'avènement des maîtres de la Parole: La prédication à Paris au XIIIe siècle*, 2 vols. (Paris, 1998), 1:847, no. 105.

75. "in crastino dicti festi fiat anniversarium eius ibidem secundum consuetudinem ordinis Cisterciensis"; AD Aube, 3 H 3752 (November 1234).

76. "Etiam illae concesserunt mihi et meis quod ipsae facient anniversarium nostrum in perpetuum, prout conceditur a capitulo generali"; AD Aube, 23 H 300 (1240).

77. See Maier, "Crisis, Liturgy and Crusade," 634–35.

78. Canivez, *Statuta*, 1:(1190)122. Although dated to 1190, this statute makes reference to earlier practices.

79. Maier, "Crisis, Liturgy and Crusade," 632–33.

The Cistercians further elaborated on these instructions in 1190 when the General Chapter decreed that each priest of the order should celebrate a mass of the Holy Spirit for "kings, princes and the crusaders" and that those who died on crusade should be commemorated in daily masses for the dead.[80] These liturgical rounds were amplified again during the thirteenth century as Innocent III attempted to make liturgical support "a permanent element of the crusade."[81] In 1248, all the Cistercian houses in the French kingdom were called upon to offer special prayers and a weekly procession within their cloisters for the success of Louis IX's expedition.[82] In that year and again in 1269 the king and other crusaders who accompanied him on his final expedition specifically petitioned female communities for their prayers before they departed and for anniversary masses should they die on campaign.[83] After Louis IX's death in Tunis in 1270, the Cistercian order composed the first monastic liturgy in his honor.[84] A year later, the abbot of Royaumont received permission from the General Chapter to establish an anniversary for the king at the monastery, although Louis would only be officially canonized in 1297. In the office composed for Louis he is praised, in the common idiom of monastic spirituality, as a *miles Christi,* a soldier of Christ.[85] Yet the Cistercian office for Louis in particular emphasized Louis's crusades as a spiritual endeavor, a kind of exile that paralleled the monastic vocation and that described Louis as eager to follow in the footsteps of Christ (*sollicitus Christi sequi vestigia*).[86] The liturgical prayers for the crusades outlined in the Cistercian statutes were intoned in every house in the order, including its nunneries.

Closely connected with prayers for crusaders was their commemoration and remembrance after death. Although the Cistercian order initially banned lay burial within its churches, cloisters, and monastic spaces, by the thirteenth century this practice had become commonplace in many houses.[87]

---

80. Canivez, *Statuta,* 1:(1190)122. These stipulations were augmented further in (1194) 172, (1196) 208, and (1197) 210.
81. Maier, "Crisis, Liturgy and Crusade," 633.
82. Canivez, *Statuta,* 2:(1248) 289, 316, 361, 377.
83. Dimier, *Saint Louis et Cîteaux,* 122–24. See also Louis Carolus-Barré, "L'Abbaye de la Joie-Notre-Dame à Berneuil-sur-Aisne (1234–1430)," in *Mélanges à la mémoire du Père Anselme Dimier,* 3 vols. in 6, ed. Benoît Chauvin (Arbois, 1982–87), 2:487–504.
84. See M. Cecilia Gaposchkin, *The Making of Saint Louis: Kingship, Sanctity, and Crusade in the Later Middle Ages* (Ithaca, 2008), 125–39. The earliest copy of the office survives in a Cistercian breviary from ca. 1300: MAT, MS 1973, fols. 224va.–26vb.
85. Gaposchkin, *Making of Saint Louis,* 135.
86. Ibid., 132.
87. See Jackie Hall, "The Legislative Background to the Burial of Laity and Other Patrons in Cistercian Abbeys," *Cîteaux* 56 (2005): 363–71; and Jackie Hall, Sheila Sneddon, and Nadine Sohr,

Cistercian abbeys, and the monastery of Clairvaux in particular, served as a coveted final resting place for generations of the northern French nobility and crusading elite. Several of the queens of France choose Cistercian monasteries and nunneries as their final place of rest during the thirteenth century.[88] Returning crusaders who sought burial in Cistercian houses occasionally augmented their final donations with additional gifts of portable altars taken on crusade or pieces of the True Cross in return for the pious prayers of the order.[89] Such gifts, in turn, brought fragments of the crusade experience and the Passion relics into the monastic cloister, further allying the monastic space with the space of the Holy Land, allowing even those returned crusaders to be buried symbolically and spiritually near Jerusalem.

In many cases the newly founded Cistercian convents served as burial places for crusaders and their families. Hugh V of Châtillon (d. 1248) was buried beside his wife, Marie of Avesnes (d. 1241), in the nunnery of Pont-aux-Dames.[90] Likewise, when Erard of Jaucourt died in 1270 on crusade, his body was returned to France and laid to rest next to that of his father, Peter of Jaucourt, in the nunnery of Val-des-Vignes.[91] William of Dampierre too was buried in his foundation of St.-Dizier—a choice articulated in the charters he and his wife, Margaret of Flanders, produced when the nunnery was founded. This decision was striking because Margaret had already founded several Cistercian nunneries in Flanders, which were larger and better endowed than St.-Dizier. Yet William seems to have intended upon death to return to his familial holdings to be commemorated there. It may have been his intent that his sons lie beside him after their deaths as well.[92] The heirs of Erard of

---

"Table of Legislation," *Cîteaux* 56 (2005): 373–413. Also, Megan Cassidy-Welch, *Monastic Spaces and Their Meanings: Thirteenth-Century English Cistercian Monasteries* (Turnhout, 2001), 217–41.

88. See Hall, "Legislative Background"; and Coomans, "Moniales cisteriennes et mémoire dynastique"; also Elizabeth A. R. Brown, "Authority, the Family, and the Dead in Late Medieval France," *French Historical Studies* 16 (1990): 803–32.

89. For the portable altar, see *Recueil des chartes de l'Abbaye de Clairvaux au XIIe siècle,* ed. Jean Waquet, Jean-Marc Roger, and Laurent Veyssière (Paris, 2004), 358–9, no. 288 (1191). For a fragments of the True Cross at Clairvaux, see Anatole Frolow, *La relique de la vraie croix: Recherches sur le développement d'un culte* (Paris, 1961); and Charles Lalore, *Le trésor de Clairvaux du XIIe au XVIIIe siècle* (Paris, 1875).

90. Duchesne, *Histoire de la maision de Chastillon-sur-Marne,* 101.

91. Roserot, *Dictionnaire historique de la Champagne,* 1:143–46. For mention of his testament, drawn up before he departed "transmarinum iter," see AD Aube, 3 H 4038 (April 1270).

92. "post mortem eliget sepulturam"; AD Marne, 71 H 6 (1242). The charter was created after William's death in the name of his wife, Margaret. By contrast, Coomans believes that William's tomb was at Flines. See Coomans, "Moniales cisterciennes et mémoire dynastique," 123–28. Yet Abbé E. Hautcoeur earlier called into question the history of William's place of burial: E. Hautcoeur, *Histoire de l'Abbaye de Flines* (Paris, 1874), 418–19. The St.-Dizier charter may clarify these questions.

Ramerupt likewise used the nunnery of La Piété as a family necropolis.[93] By contrast, Jean of Montmirail was buried at Longpont, and his tomb became the site of miraculous cures. His wife, Helvide of Dampierre, lived for eight years after his death and was buried at the Cistercian house of Vauclair.[94] Cistercian prayers for the dead, particularly the crusading dead, were devoutly cultivated among the aristocracy of Champagne. Moreover, by the thirteenth century the prayers of women—especially Cistercian nuns—were perceived as profoundly efficacious.[95] Burial in a Cistercian abbey became a mark of one's social and religious status and the penitential quality of one's life.

A Shared Imitation

In addition to prayers and commemoration for those dead and departed, the Cistercian convents of Champagne also functioned as sites of penitential piety where the suffering of Christ was invoked both within the cloister and beyond its walls. The nunneries, as addressed in chapter 4, were places where women took part in the *imitatio Christi* and in turn came to share this imitation with male crusaders. To a degree, the practice of penance and self-sacrifice had always been associated with the austerity of the Cistercian way of life, which emphasized a rigorous interpretation of the *Rule of Benedict,* a commitment to manual labor, and submission to the monastic virtues of humility and obedience. Moreover, Cistercian spirituality was predicated on an understanding of imitation and intimacy with the humanity of Christ on earth. These themes appear throughout Bernard of Clairvaux's writings, particularly his sermons on the *Song of Songs,* which explain why God took the form of man and suffered in the physical world. The incarnation was an example for all Christians of how to live in the flesh and how to attain salvation in the hereafter.[96] For Bernard, writing in a twelfth-century context, the cloister was the preferred space of divine imitation, to be esteemed even over the act of crusading. As he wrote to the sister of the knight Henry of Stopho,

---

93. See William Mendel Newman, *Les seigneurs de Nesle en Picardie (XIIe–XIIIe siècle), leurs chartes et leur histoire: Étude sur la noblesse régionale ecclésiastique et laïque,* 2 vols. (Philadelphia, 1971), 1:198, no. 18. I thank Ted Evergates for this reference.

94. See Boitel, *Histoire du bienheureux Jean;* and Dionnet, "La cassette reliquaire du Bienheureux Jean de Montmirail." I have not been able to find Philip of Mécringes's burial place, though a sister or possibly a daughter, Agnes of Mécrignes, professed as a nun at the Paraclete (Aube) and was buried there.

95. See Michel Lauwers, *La mémoire des ancêtres, le souci des morts: Morts, rites, et société au Moyen Âge (diocèse de Liège, XIe–XIIIe siècles)* (Paris, 1997), 426–59.

96. See Marsha L. Dutton, "Intimacy and Imitation: The Humanity of Christ in Cistercian Spirituality," in *Erudition at God's Service,* ed. John R. Sommerfeldt (Kalamazoo, MI, 1987), 33–69.

explaining her brother's decision to profess as a Cistercian monk rather than go on crusade, Bernard said that in doing so, Henry had "turned his face toward that true Jerusalem" by adopting the contemplative life in contrast to traveling to the earthly Jerusalem.[97] According to Bernard the true *imitatio Christi* was to be found in the cloister. In this sense imitation was open to all Christians because everyone lived in the flesh and had to comprehend the relationship between their corporal and divine natures. As Bernard explained, the Son of God used His humanity for the salvation of the world, so ordinary men and women could use their humanity to imitate Him and thereby save themselves and others.[98] This imitative ideal—to know Christ by living like Christ through daily activities both in the cloister and through one's labor—was fundamental to Cistercian spirituality and, by the thirteenth century, to the ideal of living in a Christlike world.[99] Bernard's ideas profoundly informed the thirteenth-century understanding of the *imitatio Christi* in all of its complex manifestations.

Within a gendered context, moreover, beginning in the late twelfth century the conflation of crusading and the Cistercian lifestyle came to be articulated even more explicitly. Certainly one of the clearest examples of this was the *vita* of Margaret of Beverley described earlier.[100] Margaret's move from a penitential pilgrim-crusader to a lay sister existed along a continuum focused on a life in service to Christ and in suffering for Him. By the thirteenth century, a similar process of identifying suffering on crusade with self-sacrifice at home occurred in many of the Cistercian nunneries of Champagne. This was particularly the case for those houses founded in *domus-Dei* or informal hospitals where nuns and *conversae* took it upon themselves to care for the poor and sick, who represented "the poor in Christ" in their midst. Through the acts of personal caregiving and compassion, clothing and feeding the poor and sick, washing their feet, and tending their sores, the women of these convents practiced a penitential piety that was a form of *imitatio Christi*. Such actions, coupled with the renunciation of family and social ties, wealth and worldly connection that were part of the monastic profession, allowed nuns to attain the spiritual imitation Bernard of Clairvaux had lauded. By giving of themselves in the cloister through prayer, liturgy, and devotion to the Virgin Mary and Christ, and in the hospice through ministry to the poor

---

97. *Sancti Bernardi Opera*, 7:157–58 (Ep. 64). See also Purkis, *Crusading Spirituality*, 99–103.
98. Bernard of Clairvaux, *Sermones Super Cantica Canticorum 36–86*, serm. 66, 185, in *Sancti Bernardi Opera*, vol. 2; in English, see Bernard of Clairvaux, *On the Song of Songs III*, trans. Killian Walsh and Irene M. Edmonds (Kalamazoo, MI, 1979), 202.
99. See Pegg, *A Most Holy War*, 48–49, 189.
100. See above, 147–50.

and sick, these women could give to Christ and for Christ in a way that also paralleled the sacrifices and piety of crusaders, who had themselves vowed to walk in the way of the Lord. Both forms of piety had become an expression of the shared *imitatio Christi* ideal.[101]

By the 1230s and 1240s, theologians and preachers such as Jacques de Vitry and Thomas of Cantimpré praised Cistercian nuns and penitential women, describing their actions in vivid detail and acknowledging them as living martyrs. Their prayers, punishing asceticism, and self-sacrifice cast them as an antidote to the heresy that ran rampant in southern France, making them "soldiers for God in their true humility."[102] The heights of their voluntary suffering, self-mortification, and selfless charity meant that they had effectively become martyrs, suffering like Christ in this life for the salvation of others in the next.[103] This was a martyrdom that at times specifically evoked crusading as its goal or parallel. In 1211, when Mary of Oignies heard that the "holy martyrs of Christ" had been killed at Montgey in southern France "by the enemies of the cross of Christ, she saw the holy angels rejoicing and carrying the souls of those who had been killed immediately to the supernal joys without purgatory." She so longed to join them that "she could barely be restrained" and was only stopped from doing so by social convention.[104] In a similar manner, Yvette of Huy, who tended lepers before becoming a recluse, was described as "Christ's fighter" and part of the "army of God" for her physical labors among the sick.[105] Women also explicitly chose to suffer a living martyrdom at home in the service of the crusade effort. In perhaps the most visceral example of this calculus of suffering, in 1247, Alice of Schaerbeek (d. 1250), a Cistercian nun suffering from leprosy, gave Louis IX the spiritual merit she accrued from the loss of her right eye to ensure the success of his crusade in Damietta.[106] Religious women had many examples of suffering and martyrdom that allowed them to share in the crusade experience without departing for the East.

---

101. For a similar example, see Catherine M. Mooney, "*Imitatio Christi* or *imitatio Mariae*? Clare of Assisi and Her Interpreters," in *Gendered Voices: Medieval Saints and Their Interpreters*, ed. Catherine M. Mooney (Philadelphia, 1999), 52–77.
102. *VMO*, para. 2. See also McNamara, "The Need to Give," 204–18.
103. Dyan Elliott, *Proving Woman: Female Spirituality and Inquisitorial Culture in the Middle Ages* (Princeton, 2004), 70.
104. *VMO*, para. 83. Here the field of battle is wrongly identified—it should be Montgey; see Pegg, *A Most Holy War*, 112–13.
105. See *VBJ*, paras. 110, 121.
106. *VAS*, chap. 27, 24. The language of martyrdom pervades Alice's *vita*, particularly the equation of suffering from leprosy as a kind of living martyrdom. See chaps. 8 and 33.

The penitential piety cultivated in the new Cistercian convents of Champagne was taken up in part to recall Jerusalem and to bring the suffering and sacrifices of male kin in the East closer to home, just as the Virgin Mary, it was believed, had suffered equally with Christ at His passion. Cistercian penitential piety also meant that the prayers nuns offered for crusaders were particularly potent. By the middle of the thirteenth century such prayers had become a necessary component of crusading as the movement expanded to include the home front in the hope of channeling an outpouring of piety to lead the Christian armies to success in the East. When victory did not follow, the prayers and penances of the nuns of Champagne would have been all the more comforting to those who were laid to rest within their abbey walls. The forms of suffering cultivated by crusaders and nuns were distinctly social, taken on as a shared imitation of Christ. In turn, this imitation bound men and women together as part of a larger moral community, which sought the perfection of Christian society in the present.[107]

---

107. On social suffering, see the dedicated issue of *Daedalus* 125 (1996); and Arthur Kleinman, "'Everything That Really Matters': Social Suffering, Subjectivity, and the Remaking of Human Experience in a Disordering World," *Harvard Theological Review* 90 (1997): 315–35.

A Space Apart

Gender and Administration in a New Social Landscape

Late in the spring of 1290 Alice, abbess of the Cistercian convent of St.-Jacques de Vitry, traveled to Paris and appeared before the Parlement of Paris, the high court of the realm, during its Pentecost session. Representing her convent and its interests—financial and spiritual—she pleaded her case for their rightful possession of the leper house of Montmirail. A few years earlier, possibly in 1287 or 1288, the masters of the high court of Champagne known as the Jours de Troyes had confirmed the nunnery's claim to the leper house, a decision the bishop of Châlons contested. Indeed, the following autumn, unsatisfied with the ruling in Troyes and hopeful of a more favorable outcome, the bishop brought a complaint before the Parlement of Paris in the session of St. Martin arguing that the royal officials had wrongly transferred possession of the hospital to the nuns. Ignorant of the previous ruling made in Troyes, the Paris masters then judged in the bishop's favor, annulling the original transfer. Thus during the following Parlement of Pentecost in 1290, Abbess Alice came to Paris herself and testified personally, pointing out that she had not been called to Paris for the earlier hearing and noting that the court in Troyes had made a formal decision two years earlier that Paris judges could not legally reverse. The Parisian masters thus returned possession to the abbess and the nunnery.[1]

---

1. See *Olim,* 2:292, no. 12, and 301, no. 8; and John F. Benton, "Philip the Fair and the Jours de Troyes," reprinted in his *Culture, Power and Personality in Medieval France,* ed. Thomas N. Bisson (London, 1991), 191–254, at 203.

We know almost nothing about Abbess Alice. She appears in the court records at Paris and, several years later, in the settling of another dispute with the abbot of Moncel, a Premonstratensian house not far from the abbey of St.-Jacques, but otherwise the documents are silent.[2] No family is listed, no age, no date of profession; all we know of her is through her few remaining administrative acts on behalf of her convent. Nothing is recorded of her trip to Paris: whether she traveled in the company of another nun or a lay brother, if by foot or palfrey, and where she stayed when she reached Paris or how long the proceedings took. Yet she was well aware of changes taking place in the county of Champagne and was able to react accordingly. The last decades of the thirteenth century witnessed challenges in the region that few would have expected. In 1285, Philip IV the Fair married Countess Jeanne of Navarre, heiress to Champagne, and the principality was formally joined to the kingdom of France. From then on Champagne was subject to royal taxation, and the high court of Troyes came to be staffed by Parisian masters and was slowly subordinated to the Parlement of Paris. Much official business was removed to Paris, and abbesses and their communities responded in turn.[3]

Administration emerged in the later half of the thirteenth century as a serious concern for most Cistercian institutions. In the 1220s and 1230s, initial gifts and grants of land and hospitals had provided religious women with buildings and small chapels, but smaller piecemeal gifts and sales of garden plots, urban apartments, and local rents allowed the nuns to persist at a level of sufficiency that accorded with the apostolic ideal of poverty. Through their participation in the land and rental market of the later thirteenth century, the Cistercian convents also took part in the broader social and economic changes affecting northern France. Indeed, the secular interactions the nuns pursued, particularly in the administration of their properties and assets, reflect significant changes in the social mobility of the county and in the economy especially as the burdens of taxation became encumbered by royal crusading obligations. The properties the nuns acquired and administered also reflected the transformation of the urban and suburban landscape as it was carefully parceled out into smaller and smaller pieces of property that were sold off or capitalized in a process that reveals the strains placed on the region's aristocracy. In this context the Cistercian nunneries thrived for a time and through careful purchases and sales created a space apart, a space of refuge and a space of charity within the Champenois landscape. The surviving documents that

---

2. She is not named in the *Olim* but mentioned in *GC* 9:974.

3. On these events, see Benton, "Philip the Fair and the *Jours de Troyes*"; and Theodore Evergates, *The Aristocracy in the County of Champagne, 1100–1300* (Philadelphia, 2007), 56–62.

comprise the nunneries' archives reflect the administrative abilities of Cistercian nuns and their commitment to a life of sufficiency that allowed them to dispense charity and that allowed the convents to persist as institutions that served specific spiritual and economic needs.

Gender and Administration

On the whole the Cistercian convents were relatively well administered throughout the thirteenth century. No houses fell into crippling debt until the close of the century, though at crucial junctures several were admonished to limit the number of nuns to twenty or forty depending on the abbey.[4] In many cases what successes the Cistercian convents enjoyed correlated to the administrative abilities of particularly competent abbesses. Several of these women came from noble families and brought with them social capital as well as experience managing estates. In Champagne, where partible inheritance was the normal practice, many women had exercised a degree of control over their own personal wealth. Abbesses appear in the documents relatively infrequently, however. When they officiated a transaction or executed a charter in their own name, it often pertained to a matter under dispute that found resolution through arbitration and compromise or in a high court. An abbess personally represented the interests of her nunnery as an institution and the nuns as a corporate body. For an effective compromise to be enacted, the abbess needed to be present to give her consent and to ratify the agreement with her seal.

Champagne lacks the detailed visitation records often produced by bishops and abbots of other regions. Nothing like the dense register of Archbishop Eudes Rigaud exists for Champagne, though Eudes himself traveled through the county from time to time. In 1249 he visited his sister, Marie, who was the abbess of the Paraclete and oversaw the financial and religious well-being of the nunnery.[5] Moreover, no account books survive for Cistercian convents—if

---

4. See Maximilien Quantin, ed. *Recueil de pieces pour faire suite au cartulaire générale de l'Yonne (XIIIe siècle* (Auxerre, 1873), 316, no. 640 (1267), limiting the number of nuns at La Cour Notre-Dame-de-Michery to forty. In 1289, when submitting a plea of poverty to the papal legate, Notre-Dame-des-Prés supported forty-one nuns; AD Aube, 23 H 14 (9 November 1289). In 1298 the Cistercian General Chapter ordered Val-des-Vignes to limit its numbers to twenty nuns, three *conversae,* one chaplain, and one confessor; AD Aube 3 H 4003 (1298).

5. The nunnery cast its accounts on 11 June 1249, while Eudes was present. At this time the nunnery had fallen into receivership and had debts totaling 180 *l.* See "Cartulaire de l'Abbaye du Paraclet," in *Collection des Principaux Cartulaires du diocèse de Troyes,* ed. Charles Lalore, vol. 2 (Paris, 1875–90), xii–xxiii, and 222–24, no. 246 (1249); John F. Benton, "The Paraclete and the Council of Rouen of 1231," in his *Culture, Power and Personality,* 411–16; and Adam J. Davis, *The Holy Bureaucrat: Eudes Rigaud and Religious Reform in Thirteenth-Century Normandy* (Ithaca, 2006).

they were drawn up at all—until the very end of the medieval period.[6] Rather the mechanisms of management and oversight must be reconstructed piecemeal from the interstices of procedure alluded to within the charters. By noting when a document was written, who created it, at whose request, and before what groups of people, the contours of how the nuns controlled their property and how they purchased, sold, and disputed their possessions comes into view. It is certainly clear that decisions were made about acquiring lands, particularly purchasing lands and rents, creating annuities, and letting other lands out to lease. Whether it was an abbess, the convent as a community, or lay brothers who were behind such decisions is difficult to know and doubtless depended on the circumstances. As the charters show, there was a remarkable degree of cooperation among religious men and women on a daily basis. This included not only priests charged with administering to the spiritual needs of the nuns or lay brothers who aided in monastic affairs, but also local clerics, deans, masters, and lay advisors who helped Cistercian nuns navigate changes in secular administration, the court system, alms collection, document production, and record keeping. It was precisely these networks that transformed a religious movement into permanent monastic institutions in Champagne.

For lesser matters concerning day-to-day administration, Cistercian nuns often relied on male clerics with ties to their convents.[7] Most administrative activities, like rent collection, property assessments and repairs, were routine matters that were largely unremarkable and thus went unrecorded. A few charters note or allude to the creation of prebends for clerics and priests. It is clear that some of these individuals were married and thus would not have provided spiritual care for the nuns, but rather would have aided in the secular affairs and daily business of the convents. For example, in 1249 the nuns of Notre-Dame-des-Prés leased lands and a field in Savoie, where they held more extensive property, to William de Savoie, a cleric. In return he paid four measures of wheat and four measures of barley to the nuns annually.[8] William may, in effect, have been administering the nuns' lands in Savoie and

---

6. The Paraclete is the only house for which a detailed account of the nunnery's finances survives. Rent books exist for two local Benedictine houses: the Paraclete, compiled in 1226–27, 1281–82, and 1305–6 (AD Aube, 24 H 5), and Notre-Dame-aux-Nonnains from 1305 (AD Aube, 22 H 59).

7. Whether it was standard for a chaplain or confessor to be attached to a Cistercian nunnery is still unclear. No priests or chaplains are listed among those whom the nuns of Notre-Dame-des-Prés provided for, nor among the community of La Cour in the charters from the 1280s. When the income of Val-des-Vignes was evaluated and the nunnery was forced to limit its number to twenty, the charter also stated that they were permitted one chaplain and one confessor. See AD Aube, 3 H 4003 (1298).

8. AD Aube, 23 H 301 (December 1249).

paying them a portion of the annual yields. He was, however, probably not administering the sacraments, for in 1258 the lands and annual payment obligation passed to William's widow, Isabelle, to hold for the remainder of her life.[9] In a similar fashion, in 1234, the nuns of Argensolles created a prebend for Garias, the provost of St.-Quiriace of Provins. They gave him the use of a mill at Rosson for his lifetime in return for the "help and counsel" he provided in acquiring the same mill.[10]

The nunneries also relied on Cistercian lay brothers (*conversi*) for administration. Here too the references are scant. Larger communities of nuns like Argensolles were allowed from the time of their foundation twenty *conversi* brothers in residence, but references to *conversi* in the charters of the smaller nunneries are rare. In 1268 Renardo, a baker of Bar-sur-Aube, took the habit and joined the nuns of Val-des-Vignes as a *conversus*. He was soon followed by his daughter, whom he provided for with a rent and a donation of 10 *l*.[11] It is possible that he conducted commercial transactions for the nuns, aided in part by his previous experience in Bar-sur-Aube. A clearer indication of the administrative role of a *conversus* emerges from a series of documents in the archives of Notre-Dame-des-Prés. In 1251 the nuns reached a compromise with the canons of St.-Pierre following a dispute over lands in Echenilly in the suburbs of Troyes. Both parties agreed to divide the lands in question and promised to abide by the agreement by swearing on the Gospels. Abbess Isabelle was absent from these proceedings, and in her place she sent a *conversus* named John. He carried with him a charter Isabelle had written and sealed herself, granting him permission and authority to swear to the compromise in her place (see fig. 6).[12]

Among all of the convent records, what is most noticeable by its absence is clear documentation of the roles played by Cistercian monks and abbots. Abbots almost never left records of visitation or direction and rarely took part in property disputes in defense of the nuns under their charge. Even more surprising, given the density of Cistercian houses on the ground in Champagne, is the lack of disputes between male and female houses in the order.

---

9. AD Aube, 23 H 301 (1258).
10. AD Marne, 70 H 10 (October 1234).
11. "cum religiose mulieres abbatissa et conventus vallis vinearum cisterciensis ordinis prope dictam barrum dedint et concesserint Renardo de dicto barro panifici prebendam in habitu seculari tanquam uni de fratribus seu sororibus earumdum infra p[ro]prisum dicte vallis vinearum tam cum quam diu vixit expendendam... decem que libris dicte monete quas sorori Margarete filie sue moniali dicte vallis erogavit." AD Aube, 3 H 4074 (September 1268).
12. AD Aube, G 3101 (June 1251) is a confirmation of the agreement by Abbess Isabelle; AD Aube, G 3101 (June 1251) is the assent of the abbot of Larrivour to the agreement. This is the closest document I have found to administrative oversight by a Cistercian male community.

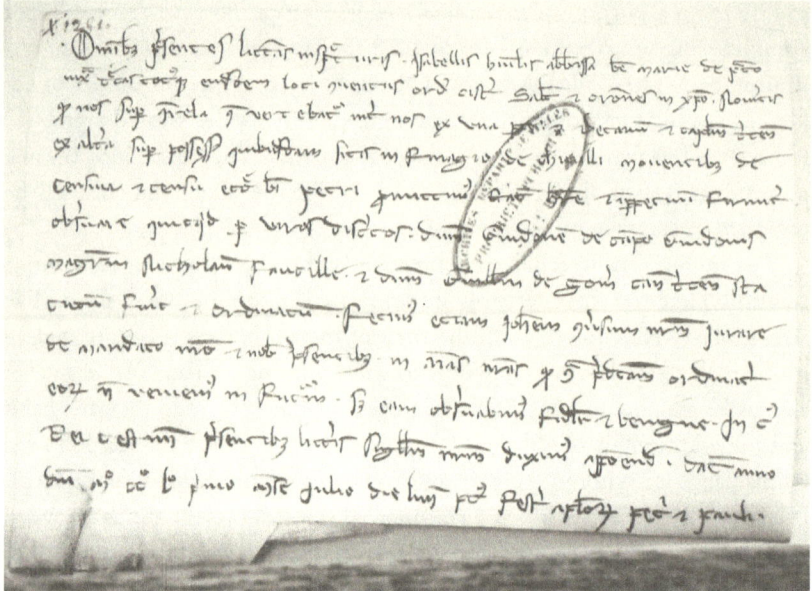

FIGURE 6. Charter from Abbess Isabelle of Notre-Dame-des-Prés, granting permission to the *conversus* John to swear to an agreement in her place. AD Aube, G 3101 (29 June 1251). Photo by the author.

Judging from the documents of practice, Cistercian monks and abbots played virtually no role in the administration of convents or in their economic regulation. The nuns turned elsewhere for such help. In 1231, when the women of Notre-Dame-des-Prés sought institutional recognition from the bishop of Troyes, they did so with the help of the local Benedictine abbots of St.-Martin and St.-Loup, two of the male monasteries in Troyes.[13] Val-des-Vignes was likewise incorporated into the order through the agency of their main knightly patron, Peter of Jaucourt.[14] In 1289, when the nuns of Notre-Dame-des-Prés submitted a plea of poverty to the cardinal legate for exemption from taxation, they acted again with the aid of the deans of the Benedictine abbeys of St.-Martin and St.-Loup and a canon and local guardian of the Friars Minor of Troyes.[15] There were exceptions to this, of course. In matters that pertained to

---

13. AD Aube, G 3101 (August 1231).

14. Josephus-Mia Canivez, *Statuta Capitulorum Generalium Ordinis Cisterciensis ab anno 1116 ad annum 1786*, 8 vols. (Louvain, 1933–41), 2:(1236)67.

15. "Reverendo in Xpisto patri ac domino J., permissione divina tituli Sancti Cecilie presbitero cardinali, apostolice sedis legato, decanus, abbates Sancti Lupi, Sancti Martini monasteriorum et magister Odo de Thoriaco, canonicus Trecensis ac gardianus Fratrum Minorum Trecensium." AD Aube, 23 H 14 (9 November 1289).

the Cistercian order as a whole—taxation or claustration, for example—Cistercian abbots took a more active interest. Otherwise, administratively the nuns appear to have been left to themselves to amass properties, to collect rents and alms, and to live, it was hoped, without scandal.

That Cistercian nuns were successful in this regard is manifest in the charters themselves, that is, in the fact of their survival in significant numbers. Historians often gloss over the realities of physical preservation, but in this case it is indicative of a profound interest in managing the convents' wealth and securing their identity. While none of the Cistercian convents created copies of their records in bound cartularies during the medieval period, many of the convents kept their archives in strikingly good order. Stored in coffers and chests, the documents represented the material histories of their institutions. Their possession safeguarded the well-being of the monastic community and was a mark of the authority of its abbess to control and administer. Indeed, the importance of the physical possession of charters was well recognized. After reforming the leper house at Mont-Cornillon and falling into disfavor with the citizens of Liège, Juliana, her hagiographer observes, "[knew] that great loss and peril threatened her and the whole house if [the charters] fell into" the wrong hands. She thus "ke[pt] the charters herself and faithfully preserve[d] them."[16] Charters were the very fabric of a monastic institution's identity. Creating copies of the charters in bound cartularies would have also been wise as many of the older male Benedictine houses understood, but this was not a common practice for female communities in Champagne until the very end of the thirteenth century.[17] Even the Paraclete, Abelard and Heloise's foundation, did not draw up a cartulary until the 1280s. Likewise, the comital foundations of St.-Étienne and St.-Maclou—which housed the great chancelleries of the principality—did not compile their own cartularies until the 1270s. One wonders also in the case of Cistercian nunneries if a lack of interest in creating cartularies correlated to a disinterest in engaging in the kinds of strategies of power and accountability that the *vita apostolica* and poverty movement had so deliberately eschewed. If so, the disregard for such administrative tools may have signaled a broader critique and disaffection for a society of accounting and profit accumulation more generally.

As the century progressed, however, the nuns began to use their documents in an administrative capacity. Several charters from the later thirteenth century recording the purchase of multiple rents read like rent books, great lists of

---

16. *VJC,* chap. 5, para. 21.
17. On the cartularies as administrative tools, see Robert F. Berkhofer III, *Day of Reckoning: Power and Accountability in Medieval France* (Philadelphia, 2004).

small properties and what they owed.[18] Houses like Clairmarais, which held substantial numbers of urban rents in Reims, drew up rental lists to keep track of their assets (fig. 7).[19] Clairmarais's lists are undated, though the careful hand and rubrics of the parchment place them in the mid-thirteenth century. The entries were relatively simple, noting only what was necessary for the collection of rents due: "For the house which belonged to *la femme Colet Lespicier* on the place Saint Antoine, 12 *d.* and 1 *obolus,* or half penny"; or "Herbert *Cocheles,* 5 *l.* on a *table au change* that was his father's."[20] Some entries were amended or updated: a name crossed out and another written in above in a new hand, often indicating when a daughter or a widow took over payments for a deceased father or husband. Occasionally whole entries are crossed out, whether because they were sold or misreported is not clear. Reflecting a similar administrative impulse, in January 1255 the abbess of L'Amour-Dieu drew up a list of the rents the convent owed and when payments were to be made. The list is written in French, in the first person—"*si sont escrit li cens que nos devons*"—and it appears to be authored by the abbess or a nun on her behalf, accounting what the community owed and to whom it was obligated.[21] These measures were all aspects of management in which women proved to be as competent as men. The difference among the Cistercian houses, however, was that the nuns esteemed a way of life on the edge of sufficiency. The rents they held were typically fixed rents, which in the short term provided useful capital for alms and for the administration and upkeep of their hospitals and leper houses, but by the close of the century would prove to be unwise when inflation and taxation took their toll.

Finally, a major distinction existed between the Cistercian convents of the thirteenth century and many of the neighboring male monastic houses. Cistercian nuns rarely drew up or officiated in the creation of documents—gifts, sales, leases, or rental books—pertaining to their communities. Rather, as each document makes clear in its opening lines, the nuns relied on a host of clerics, episcopal officials, and local deans to draw up these texts. These men oversaw the daily administration of their parishes and in turn were a crucial part of the nunneries' administrative network, though not affiliated with the nuns in any official way. They generated the outgoing copies of charters that laymen kept as well as the incoming copies that were retained by the nuns and formed

---

18. See, for example, AD Aube, 23 H 179 (December 1264) and 23 H 5 (23 June 1268) in the collection of Notre-Dame-des-Prés.

19. AD Aube, 3 H 3783 (undated, mid- to late thirteenth century).

20. AD Aube, 3 H 3783 (undated).

21. AD Marne, 69 H 24 (January 1255). The list is written in a clear, careful hand, not the quick administrative cursive of local officials.

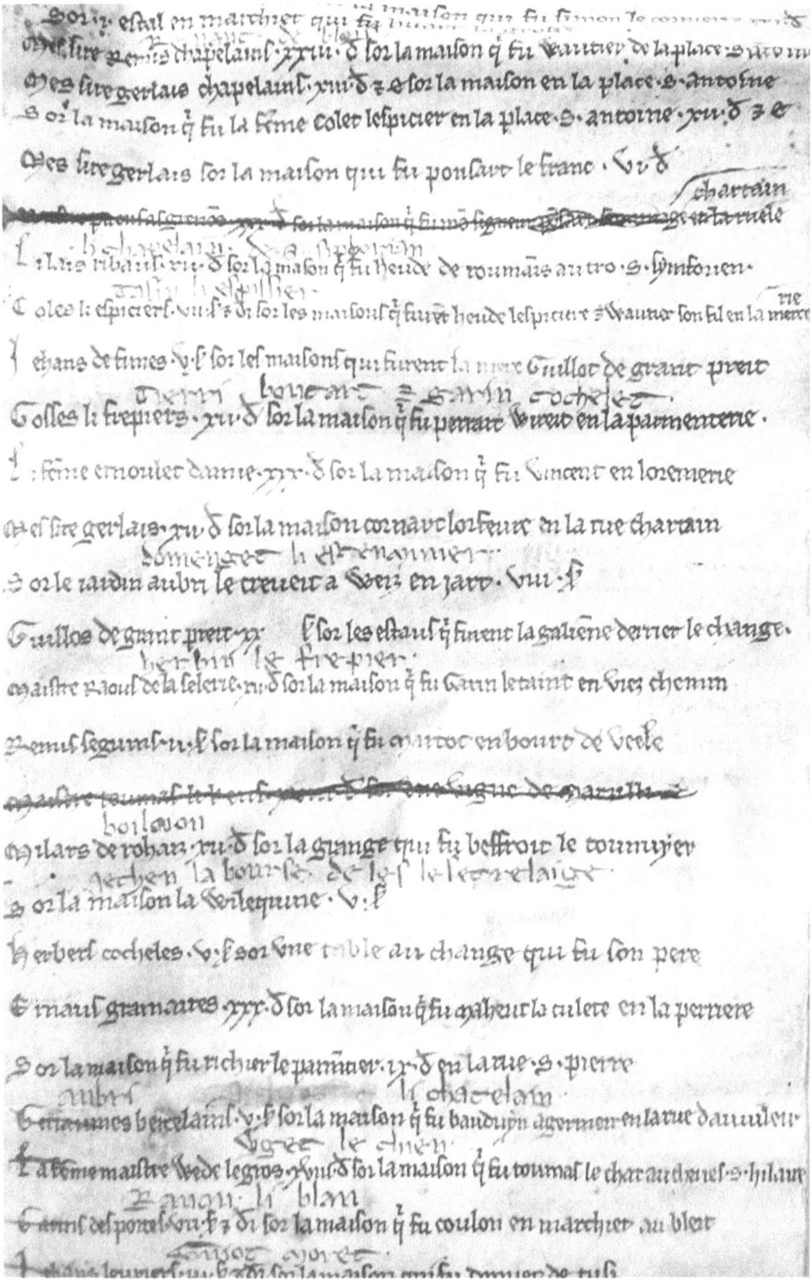

FIGURE 7. Detail, rental list (*censive*) from Clairmarais for properties in Reims. AD Aube, 3 H 3783 (undated, probably mid- to late thirteenth century). Photo by the author.

their archives. The creation of documents by local officials also had the effect of significantly broadening the patronage network that Cistercian nunneries came to cultivate.

Official Acts: The Networks of the Cistercian Convents

The foundation of Cistercian convents in granges, *domus-Dei,* and leper houses revealed a great deal about the origins of these communities, their connections to the *vita apostolica,* and their initial associations with specific bourgeois and aristocratic patrons who often endowed the nuns with their first buildings. The properties and incomes the nuns accumulated reflected the social networks they fostered, particularly with the lesser aristocracy, urban artisans, burghers, single women, and widows. This convergence of support meant that the nuns cultivated a patronage base different from that of older monastic houses, which had benefited mainly from the gifts of the landed aristocracy. The ability of burghers and citizens to enact economic relationships with the nuns was tied to the proliferation of a new form of written record—official charters authenticated by a designated episcopal official or local dean—that made legally binding property transactions accessible to this new class.

Traditionally the production of official records had been the preserve of the aristocracy and the ecclesiastical elite, those men and women with access to writing, to personal chanceries staffed by scribes or clerics, and who employed their own personal seals to make a parchment a legal text. Lesser knights and vassals who hoped to alienate property or fiefs during much of the twelfth century did so under the seal and with the permission of their lords. Likewise, donations made to the church and to abbeys in particular were drawn up under the name of the bishop or the monastic community benefiting from the transaction. By the 1230s, however, this arrangement became increasingly challenging. A princely bureaucracy connected to the comital chancery no longer produced such texts, and many lesser aristocrats began to use their own personal seals to officiate documents.[22] Moreover, after 1234, when Count Thibaut IV inherited the kingdom of Navarre, he was absent from the county for long stretches of time, either in Navarre or on crusade. Two decades later, after the marriage of Thibaut V to Isabelle of France, the daughter of King Louis IX, the count increasingly resided in Paris. Bishops too were often away from their sees on business or on crusade and thus not present in their

---

22. See chap. 2, 50–53.

episcopal courts to officiate such transactions. To compensate for this absence and the continual need to transact official business, the bishop's court evolved into a separate entity, distinct from the *familia* of the bishop who would travel with him on business.[23]

The rise of the bishop's court, known as the officiality court, was part of a larger change in the administration of ecclesiastical property and income. By the thirteenth century a host of different officials, secular and ecclesiastical, emerged who were trained in Roman law and who came to function much like the public notaries of southern Europe.[24] While the towns of Flanders and Picardy maintained urban archives and scribes in the employ of the municipality to draw up and preserve official copies of charters, sales, and testaments, the towns and cities south of the Somme and Meuse rivers—within Champagne—relied upon officials connected to the episcopal court and parish hierarchy, either the bishops' officials or local rural deans, known as deans of Christianity.[25] In Champagne, diocesan officials and rural deans typically authenticated documents with another lay official, often a town mayor or the local *prévôt*, the count's administrative representative, to ensure that the document was valid in both lay and ecclesiastical courts.[26]

Throughout the thirteenth century men and women of Champagne came before one or more trained officials, or often their scribes or clerics, and for a fee they created a legal document recording the terms of a sale or donation, authenticated with the official seal that gave it legal authority. By 1231, the *officiales* of Troyes had their own seals and their own courts. In episcopal centers like Troyes, Langres, and Reims, men and women came before officials and spoke their transactions orally, in public, in an act of performance, describing their gifts and sales and detailing the shape of their urban and suburban properties.[27]

---

23. See Paul Fournier, *Les officialités au Moyen Âge: Étude sur l'organisation, la competence et la procédure des tribunaux ecclésiastiques ordinaries en France, de 1180 à 1328* (Paris, 1880); Robert-Henri Bautier, "L'exercice de la juridiction gracieuse en Champagne du milieu du XIIIe siècle à la fin du XVe," reprinted in his *Chartes, sceaux et chancelleries*, 1:359–436; Louis Carolus-Barré, "L'organisation de la juridiction gracieuse à Paris, dans le dernier tiers du XIIIe siècle: L'officialité et le Châtelet," *Le Moyen Âge* 69 (1963): 417–35; and Olivier Guyotjeannin, "Juridiction gracieuse ecclésiastique et naissance de l'officialité à Beauvais (1175–1220)," in *À propos des actes d'évêques: Hommage à Lucie Fossier*, ed. Michel Parisse (Nancy, 1991), 295–310.

24. See Robert-Henri Bautier, "L'authentification des actes privés dans la France médiévale: Notariat public et juridiction gracieuse," in *Notariado público y documento privado* (7ème Congrès international de diplomatique, Valence, 1986) (Valencia, 1989), 2:281–304.

25. Ibid., 305–18.

26. Ibid., 322–33; and Bautier, "L'exercice de la juridiction gracieuse," 362–65.

27. Guyotjeannin, "Juridiction gracieuse ecclésiastique." See *La diplomatique urbaine en Europe au Moyen Âge: Actes du congrès de la commission internationale de diplomatique, Gand, 25–29 août 1998*, ed. Walter Prevenier and Thérèse de Hemptinne (Leuven, 2000).

These texts were therefore collective endeavors, representative of the language and vocabulary of the official scribe as well as the donor or seller. This exchange was part of a second revolution in textual production that saw not only the recording of information (the movement from memory to written records), but also, more importantly, the standardization of legal forms accessible for the first time to a much broader public.[28]

Over the course of the century charters produced in this way became ever more detailed and precise, capable of serving as administrative tools in their own right. They described the boundaries of a house or vineyard, or rights to rents and tolls, parsing the longitude and latitude of each urban plot, house, and back garden that the nuns purchased. Often the money owed for a sale was paid out before the eyes of the officials, usually at the time the charter was drawn up, and thus the charter was a receipt of sorts. In addition, guarantee clauses that vividly signaled the officials' training in Roman law became a common feature of authenticated documents, insuring that the transaction recorded would persist inviolate and undisturbed. As documents grew more specific and technical they opened the use and benefits of a pragmatic literacy to a wider social group. It was under the seal of the deans of Christianity and the local *prévôts* that urban bakers, butchers, tanners, and widows contracted business. Yet as access to such documents expanded, the texts themselves became more circumscribed and formulaic, always with the goal of eliminating ambiguity.[29] In this way, these texts became documents that facilitated administration while simultaneously giving permanence to a public transaction (see fig. 8).

Cistercian nuns conducted business in these terms, and it is these texts that make up the greater part of their monastic archive, reflecting the importance of their institutions within the religious landscape of Champagne. By the 1240s the physical characteristics of these texts distinguished them as the product of a studied bureaucracy: parchments were cut to a standard size; the script was clear and uniform; the left-side margins were broadened and fixed; and the orthography and word choice were regularized, with one clause following another formulaically. The seal-tags onto which the authenticating wax was pressed were made of reused strips of parchment, not silken threads. The images on the

---

28. In Guyotjeanin's words, "un nouveau système juridique et documentaire," in "Juridiction gracieuse ecclésiastique," 301.

29. See Richard Britnell, "Pragmatic Literacy in Latin Christendom," in *Pragmatic Literacy East and West, 1200–1300* ed. Richard Britnell (Woodbridge, 1997), 3–24; Michael Clanchy, *From Memory to Written Record: England 1066–1307*, 2nd ed. (Oxford, 1993); Karl Heidecker, ed., *Charters and the Use of the Written Word in Medieval Society* (Turnhout, 2000); and David R. Olson and Nancy Torrance, eds. *Literacy and Orality* (Cambridge, 1991).

GENDER AND ADMINISTRATION IN A NEW SOCIAL LANDSCAPE

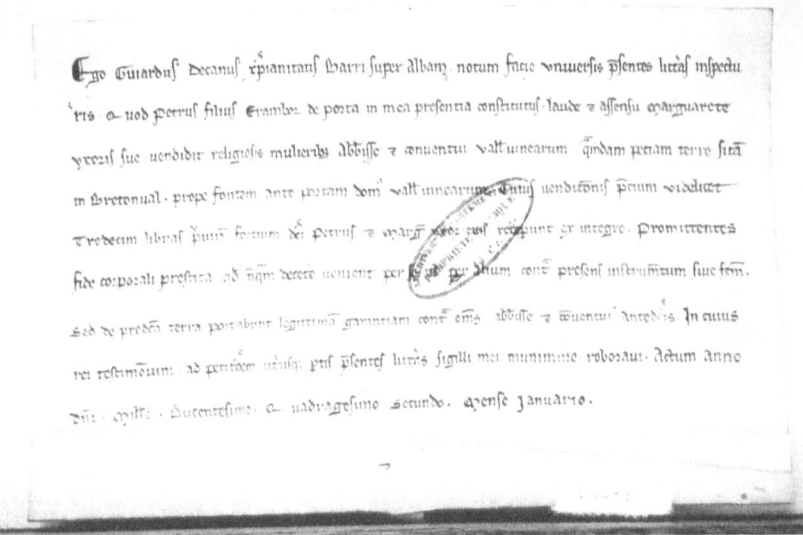

FIGURE 8. Charter officiated by the dean of Christianity of Bar-sur-Aube. AD Aube, 3 H 4077 (January 1242). Photo by the author.

seals were symbolic and heraldic, evoking civic or ecclesiastical authority generally and the office behind the seal, not an individual.[30] The seal of the deans of Bar-sur-Aube, for example, was an image meaningful to a town intimately connected to the river Aube: a bass fish with a hook in its mouth surrounded by several stars, and on the reverse another bass and a hound (fig. 9).[31] The texts conferred authority not by virtue of the action of a gift or sale, but by the physical parchment record that carried a new legal significance.

The men creating such charters—officials of the bishop's court, rural deans, *prévôts*, and mayors—had become a vital part of the nuns' administrative network and their names and seals fill the nuns' archives. In Troyes, for example, Master Thibaut de Pommorio (1240–1242), Master Nicolas (1242–1245), and Master John (1245–1250) were the officials of the episcopal court of Troyes who ratified the vast majority of documents during their successive tenures with the seal of the bishop's court of Troyes (*curia Trecensis*). They were probably deans and almost certainly canons of the cathedral of Troyes. Their

---

30. See, for example, Eef Dijkhof, "Goatskin and Growing Literacy: The Penetration of Writing in the Former Counties of Holland and Zeeland in the Thirteenth Century in Relation to the Changes of the Internal and External Features of the Charters Issued," in Heidecker, *Charters and the Use of the Written Word*, 101–12.

31. See Henri d'Arbois de Jubainville, *Histoire de Bar-sur-Aube sous les comtes de Champagne, 1077–1284* (Paris, 1859), 14–16, 153–54.

FIGURE 9. Charter displaying seals of Alice of Jaucourt, the dean of Christianity, and the *prévôt* of Bar-sur-Aube. AD Aube, 3 H 4038 (April 1272). Photo by the author.

title, master (*magister*), implies that they had received formal university training. In this capacity they were the administrators of the temporalities of the bishop and the diocese more widely, overseeing property transfers pertaining to ecclesiastical houses within the see.[32] Likewise, in the court of Reims men like John de Blois (1233–1252), Michael de St.-Denis (1243–1245), and Gérard de Menney (1245–1250), all of whom were canons at Reims, were employed in the same administrative capacity.[33]

In Bar-sur-Aube and other locales in the southern half of the county the arrangement differed slightly. Here pairs of officials worked in concert, like Girard, the dean of Christianity in Bar, and John the *prévôt* of the same town. The pairings occasionally change, and a dean of Bar is found with a *prévôt* of Chaumont or the mayor of Bar-sur-Aube.[34] The "dean of Christianity" was an archaic title for a rural dean—in this case from the see of Langres—charged with administering the temporal affairs of the diocese. Deans were technically episcopal officials, who were members of the secular clergy but

---

32. On the officials of the ecclesiastical court of Troyes specifically, see Théophile Boutiot, *Histoire de la ville de Troyes et de la Champagne méridionale*, 5 vols. (Troyes, 1870–74), 1:433–38; and Henri d'Arbois de Jubainville, "Études sur les documents antérieurs à l'année 1285, conservés dans les archives des quatre petits hôpitaux de la ville de Troyes," *MSA* 21 (1857): 49–116, at 68–84.

33. See Odile Grandmottet, "Les officialités de Reims aux XIIIe et XIVe siècles," *Bulletin d'Information de l'I.R.H.T.* 4 (1955): 77–106.

34. Arbois de Jubainville, *Histoire de Bar-sur-Aube*, 14–16, gives a list of many of the *prévôts* and deans who officiated charters during the thirteenth century.

unattached to a cathedral chapter.³⁵ Their texts offer a glimpse into the workings of a local ecclesiastical administration that had become instrumental in facilitating the daily transactions of the county in smaller towns like Bar-sur-Aube. This was the day-to-day practice of administered Christianity.

The nuns' records clearly illuminate the bonds created with each of these men over a period of several years, in some cases spanning two decades. These canons, deans, and officials, and the records they produced, were emblematic of the wider social networks the Cistercian nuns benefited from and which connected them to the circles of the urban elite and artisan classes and the civic social structures that prospered during the second half of the thirteenth century. In this way, as the women's religious movement became institutionalized in Champagne under the auspices of the Cistercian order, it never lost its connection to its original social context. Rather the process of institutionalization depended upon the nuns' relationships with local religious men who facilitated their expansion and supported their transformations into permanent communities. It would be these men—deans, masters, and episcopal officials—who most often helped the nuns when they fell into debt or who appear giving to the women in testaments and bequests at the end of their lives. We are afforded a sense of the intimacy of local administration as it persisted outside the confines of an order and its rounds of visitation. These arrangements would endure and later inform the kinds of religious associations and bonds common among men and women like the sisters and brothers of the Common Life, or between local anchoresses and beguines and their confessors and clerical advocates during the fourteenth and fifteenth centuries.³⁶

Consolidation of Property: Gifts, Purchases, and the Production of Space

The vast majority of charters from the 1250s to the 1280s record sales, purchases, and disputes of small pieces of property, rarely more than a few arpents of land, and rental income, most often consisting of houses, rents, and stalls

---

35. See H. Neils, "Les doyens de chrétienté: Étude de diplomatique sur leurs actes de juridiction gracieuse en Belgique au XIIIe siècle," *Revue Belge de Philologie et d'Histoire* 3 (1924): 59–74, at 68–70. The reliance on rural deans was not exclusive to female communities. The very same officials contracted many of the donations and sales to Clairvaux at this time. See *Inventaire Archives de l'Aube*, series H, Clairvaux, 23–27.

36. See John Van Engen, "The Christian Middle Ages as an Historiographical Problem," *American Historical Review* 91 (1986): 519–52, at 541; and idem, *Sisters and Brothers of the Common Life: The Devotio Moderna and the World of the Later Middle Ages* (Philadelphia, 2008); also Jennifer Deane, "*Geistliche Schwestern:* The Pastoral Care of Lay Religious Women in Medieval Würzburg," in *"Brothers and Sisters in Christ": Men, Women, and the Religious Life in Germany, 1100–1500*, ed. Fiona Griffiths and Julie Hotchin (Turnhout, forthcoming).

within the nearest town. These were properties local artisans and townsmen could afford to sell or donate. Episcopal and papal confirmations on occasion offer a snapshot of the holdings some Cistercian nunneries amassed. For the most part, lands were accumulated piecemeal over time. When Pope Innocent IV confirmed the possessions of La Cour Notre-Dame-de-Michery in 1245, the nuns counted among their holdings the convent buildings and all that pertained to it: a grange known as Bosco-Baillet with woods and adjacent lands; a grange called Trande and its adjacent lands and fields; and the grange building at Viluis, which had been their first home, situated next to the leper house of the same name. They also held tithes, lands, vineyards, customary rents (*cens*), fixed rents (*redditus*), lands, and other plots in the local towns, as well as a mill at Champitiol, and pasturage rights nearby.[37] On the whole their domains were small and local, simple plots and farmhouses supplemented by rents and tithes. Indeed, with rare exceptions, the Cistercian convents of Champagne did not engage in the extensive grange agriculture that their Cistercian brethren pursued. In part this option was no longer possible by the mid-thirteenth century, for such lands were not available and were rarely donated by this time. Moreover, the religious goals of Cistercian nuns did not esteem the practice of grange agriculture, production, and marketing, which occasioned the accumulation of wealth rather than its redistribution. Although some nunneries possessed granges and organized their rural holdings in this way, this system was never practiced on the same scale as that of the monks of the order.[38] Rather, Cistercian nuns made a virtue of necessity, using their smaller suburban endowments to inform their spiritual orientation.

The properties that made up a nunnery's holdings were most often the result of the incremental support of local men and women. Michael Drapier, *civis* of Troyes, for example, gave Notre-Dame-des-Prés a single arpent of arable land in the township (*finagia*) of St.-Léger in August 1257 as alms for the remembrance of his daughter Sibille.[39] The charter was simple and the gift meager, but it closed with a rigorous legal formula by which Michael agreed to renounce all rights to the property and promised not to go against the donation by reclaiming the land. Seven years earlier the same nuns of Troyes had John, *officialis Trecensis*, confirm their possession of 15 *s.* of annual rent, which Isabelle la Poire gave them before her death, and that Baudouin

---

37. Quantin, *Recueil*, 233–34, no. 503. For analogous confirmations, see for Notre-Dame-des-Prés, AD Aube 23 H 11 (3 February 1246); and for St.-Jacques de Vitry, AD Marne 71 H 4 (1259) and 71 H 38 (1259).

38. See Constance Brittan Bouchard, *Holy Entrepreneurs: Cistercians, Knights, and Economic Exchange in Twelfth-Century Burgundy* (Ithaca, 1991).

39. AD Aube, 23 H 295 (August 1257)

Rabière and Osanna, his wife, agreed to pay the nuns during their lifetimes to fund an anniversary mass for Isabelle.[40] It was small donations like these that allowed the Cistercian nunneries over the course of the thirteenth century to amass properties near their abbeys, accrue rents in kind and in cash within the nearest towns, and secure small urban and suburban plots that could be rented or sold in turn.

It is clear that Cistercian nuns also took part in the property market thriving in Champagne. By the 1260s and 1270s some nunneries managed significant numbers of purchases, mostly of small properties and annual rents—and occasionally offered strikingly large sums for such acquisitions. Many of the purchases show the nunneries carefully consolidating their holdings in specific locations. For example, after Notre-Dame-des-Prés was granted legal possession of the grange at Chichéry, the initial gift from Stephen of Champguyon, they then received the sizable donation from the knight Hugh of St.-Maurice and his wife of one-quarter of their possessions. The nuns then obtained smaller bequests from lesser townsmen, and in the 1250s and 1260s they began to purchase properties. Donations in alms of small pieces of land, or three or four measures of grain paid annually, or a house in Troyes were most common. In many cases the nuns were quick to lease the urban properties they received. They also took part in the brisk rental market for apartments as well as stalls and shops during the period when the fairs of Troyes were in session. On occasion they accepted gifts, which were often annuities or variants thereof.[41] For example, in 1256, Milo, a draper, and his wife, Osanna, gave the nuns a field and part of a stream to which they held water rights near Pont Hubert, under the condition that the nuns paid Milo and Osanna 20 s. a year for the remainder of their lives. Thus the nuns' received the use of the lands, and Milo and Osanna were provided with a steady income until their deaths.[42] Between 1251 and 1271 the nuns made a series of purchases totaling approximately 900 l.[43] They acquired lands in Echenilly, Rivière-de-

---

40. AD Aube, 23 H 338 (April 1250).

41. On convents and the use of annuities, see William Chester Jordan, *Women and Credit in Pre-Industrial and Developing Societies* (Philadelphia, 1993), 64–66; and Patricia Lewis, "Mortgages in the Bordelais and Bazadais," *Viator* 10 (1979): 23–38. This kind of arrangement may have been what Hugh of St.-Maurice and his wife, Marguerite, intended when they left their gift to the nuns of Notre-Dame-des-Prés, for they stipulated that, should they fall into need, the nuns should provide for them to the extent that it was possible for the community to do so: "et si forte quod absit, ad inopiam devenirent, ipsis tanquam veris patronis domus sue necessaria ministravent." AD Aube, 23 H 9 (June 1234).

42. AD Aube, 23 H 256 (January 1256).

43. AD Aube, 23 H 169 (December 1251), 23 H 16 (1255), 23 H 153 (December 1256 and May 1260), 23 H 269 (December 1263 and May 1266), 23 H 5 (January 1263, October 1264, 23 June 1268), 23 H 178 (March 1263), 23 H 179 (December 1264), 23 H 210 (December 1265), 23 H

Corps, Fontvannes, and Moussy as well as incomes from rents in kind and cash, at times making compound purchases to consolidate their holdings in a particular area.[44]

Like Notre-Dame-des-Prés, Argensolles made purposeful purchases to expand from its initial holdings. Countess Blanche had founded the community in a grange purchased from the monks of Hautvillers and supplemented this initial endowment with 1,000 arpents of woodland, which she had systematically acquired from neighboring knights and landholders. To this she added perpetual donations in kind and cash from rents and tolls from the fair towns.[45] In 1229 Count Thibaut IV augmented his mother's donations with the gift of several mills that he had purchased and donated to the nunnery.[46] This contribution forged a connection between Argensolles and the nearby towns of Épernay and Vertus, where the mills were located. Soon thereafter, in 1233, the commune of Vertus sold the nuns a measure of grain, paid annually.[47] In 1236 the nuns also transacted sales with men and women in Épernay under the seal of the mayor and *échevins* of the town.[48] During the 1250s and 1260s they consolidated their holdings around three main points: in the lands near Argensolles itself, in pasturage rights outside of Épernay, and in banal rights over mills and ovens in the surrounding territories. The connection that the nuns fostered with the nearby towns of Épernay, Vertus, and Châlons broadened

---

244 (May 1267 and July 1271), 23 H 181 (April 1269), 23 H 245 (December 1271). The purchases were conducted in the two currencies of the county and totaled 205 *l. provinois* and 668 *l. tournois*, respectively. From 1222, however, the value of the pound *tournois* was equal to that of the pound *provinois*, so the totals can be compounded.

44. They held 70 arpents of land in Echenilly (AD Aube, G 3101 [July 1251]); 45 arpents of arable land in Rivière-de-Corps as well as annual cents (*cens*) (AD Aube, 23 H 269 [December 1263]); annual rents (*cens*) and a peck of grain at Chichèry (AD Aube, 23 H 5, fol. 25r [January 1264]); 7 *l.* of annual rent from two stalls in Troyes and from other rents in Fontvanne, Prugny, and Vauchassis (AD Aube, 23 H 178 [March 1263]); 50 arpents of arable land and 17 *s.* and 6 *d.* in annual rents at Rivière-de-Corps (AD Aube, 23 H 5, fol. 10r [October 1264]); a house and a quarter of the land and customs at Rivière-de-Corps (AD Aube, 23 H 269 [May 1266]); a house and several arpents of land at Moussey (AD Aube, 23 H 244 [5 May 1267]); several fragments of arpents and rents at Fontvanne (AD Aube, 23 H 5 fol. 38r [23 June 1268]); half a house at Moussey (AD Aube, 23 H 244 [July 1271]); and 3 *quarteria* of fields at Moussey (AD Aube, 23 H 245 [December 1271]). These purchases began just after Pope Urban IV gave the nuns 100 marks of silver to commemorate his mother, who was buried at Notre-Dame-des-Prés. For the donation, see Charles Lalore, "Documents sur l'Abbaye de Notre-Dame-aux-Nonnains de Troyes," *MSA* 38 (1874): 5–236, at 119, no. 191 (9 September 1263).

45. See AD Marne, 70 H 12; *GC* 9, instr. 132–33; and Theodore Evergates, ed. and trans. *Feudal Society in Medieval France: Documents from the County of Champagne* (Philadelphia, 1993), 137–39, no. 104.

46. AD Marne, 70 H 12 (1229). This donation details several smaller purchases that Thibaut incorporated into one larger gift.

47. AD Marne, 70 H 8 (1233).

48. AD Marne, 70 H 6 (March 1236).

the social network of the nunnery beyond the intimate circle of the "faithful and beloved" of the count and countess to include townsmen and women and their daughters. Thus in 1252 Hersanda and Margaret, sisters of Agnes de Porta Mathe of Châlons, donated all their movable goods and property to Argensolles and joined the nunnery.[49] In the following decade Emelina daughter of Peter le Oientier of Épernay also professed at Argensolles.[50] These charters reflect the changing demographics of the nunnery as well as shifts in the composition of its patrimony.

Val-des-Vignes cultivated its domain in a similar way. Although the nunnery received small-scale donations of woodlands and vineyards during the first decade of its history, Peter of Jaucourt functioned as the knightly founder and patron, giving the nuns properties nearby as well as one-sixth of the tithes he held from Chaumont.[51] His wife, Alice, donated 200 measures of wine and oats from the tithes of Condis and Betrenayo.[52] The lands and tithes that Peter gave to the nuns were part of a previous grant from the count. In 1235 Count Thibaut IV had given Peter of Jaucourt (whom the count recognized as one of his "faithful and beloved") lands near Bar-sur-Aube and part of the tithes of Chaumont to augment his fief.[53] Instead of retaining all of these lands for his personal use, Peter reused them, donating a portion to the nuns at Val-des-Vignes. When Count Thibaut IV appeared in the records of Val-des-Vignes it was not as a patron, but rather to confirm the donations his "beloved" Peter and his family had offered from within a fief held from the count.[54]

Yet the majority of the Val-des-Vignes's donations, purchases, and leases involved men and women from neighboring Bar-sur-Aube, from both the upper bourgeoisie, including the mayors of Bar, and the prominent de Porta family, as well as artisan laborers such as bakers, butchers, furriers, and local clerics.[55]

---

49. AD Marne, 70 H 12 (June 1252).

50. AD Marne, 70 H 5 (1264).

51. See AD Aube, 3 H 4077 (October 1232), 3 H 4037 (1232), and 3 H 4037 (October 1232). For Peter of Jaucourt's gift, see AD Aube, 3 H 4082 (August 1236), and the bishop's confirmation, AD Aube, 3 H 4082 (March [Easter] 1240).

52. AD Aube, 3 H 4011 (December 1242).

53. In October 1232 Count Thibaut IV transferred those lands and tithes that had been part of a fief held by Simon of Chaumont and part of a fief of the deceased Flos Barnage to Peter of Jaucourt. See *Layettes*, 2:240, no. 2207.

54. AD Aube, 3 H 4011 (July 1252), in which Count Thibaut IV confirms the donation of the tithes from Chaumont.

55. Erard de Porta and his family, including his son Peter and wife, Margaret, donated and sold lands and vines in Bretonval to the nuns. See AD Aube 3 H 4079 (1231) and 3 H 4077 (January 1242). In the following decade Peter de Porta (perhaps a nephew, the son of the deceased Guichard de Porta) exchanged lands that he held in Bretonval for other lands held by the nuns, and in 1256

The nuns of Val-des-Vignes consolidated their domains in two main waves. In the first, after their founding in Bretonval near the small town of Ailleville outside of Bar-sur-Aube, the nuns steadily consolidated the lands surrounding the nunnery, connecting their buildings to the lands of the nearby leper house.[56] This was done both through donations as well as through small-scale purchases of properties valued at amounts varying from 22 *l.* to 24 *s.*[57] In most cases the small pieces of vineyard and arable land sold to the nuns were allods, that is, unencumbered lands that were not fiefs but were most often in the possession of burghers of Bar-sur-Aube and originally cultivated for their personal needs.[58] Toward the end of the thirteenth century the nuns began to lease small pieces of vineyards back to certain townsmen and women.[59] They also acquired houses in Bar, which they leased back to those individuals making the initial donation somewhat like an annuity.[60]

The second wave of consolidation came in the later 1260s, when the nuns of Val-des-Vignes turned their gaze from Bar-sur-Aube to Chaumont. They acquired arable lands and a grange near the city where they held the tithes

---

Richer de Porta, a canon of St.-Maclou, donated vines near Bretonval. See AD Aube, 3 H 4077 (May 1250) and 3 H 4079 (September 1256). The de Porta family may have played a similar role in relation to Val-des-Vignes as the Champguyon family did for Notre-Dame-des-Prés in Troyes.

56. Seventeen charters in the archive of Val-des-Vignes detail the accumulation of these lands. Many follow a specific formula: "dedi et concessi sanctimonialibus de Valle Vinearum quondam plantam sitam inter Aquilavilla et domum leprosorum de Barro super Album" (AD Aube, 3 H 4037 [January 1243]); or "quondam petiam terrae arabilis sitam inter leprosarium dicti Barri et Aquilavillam" (AD Aube, 3 H 4074 [July 1257]). See also AD Aube, 3 H 4077 (March 1269), 3 H 4038 (December 1271), and 3 H 4039 (May 1274). They purchased lands near the mill of the lepers (AD Aube, 3 H 4037 [January 1246]) and near a place called Postellum, which bordered on the leper house (AD Aube, 3 H 4038 [April 1272] and [April 1273]); see also AD Aube, 3 H 4079 (May 1265), 3 H 4043 (October 1268), 3 H 4073 (December 1272), 3 H 4038 (July 1273), 3 H 4039 (June 1288). In 1275 the nuns began to rent out part of this property near the leper house, most likely in an attempt to compensate for falling rents as the economy began to worsen. Abbess Margaret drew up a new lease for a small piece of vineyard let out to the widow Ermengard: "quondam vineam nostram sitam inter domum leprosorum et Aquilavillam"; AD Aube, 3 H 4043 (July 1275).

57. See, for example, AD Aube, 3 H 4077 (August 1242), purchase for 100 *s.*; AD Aube, 3 H 4118 (1248), purchase for 22 *l.* and 12 measures of grain; and AD Aube, 3 H 4079 (December 1250), sale of property worth 24 *s.* and 1 *d.* of annual rent.

58. The charters of sale stipulate that the lands or vines sold to the nuns were free from all rents, obligations, customs, or services. See, for example, AD Aube, 3 H 4043 (January and November 1257). On the use and configuration of these smaller suburban and urban plots, see Arlette Higounet-Nadal, "Les jardins urbains dans la France médiévale," in *Jardins et vergers en Europe occidentale (VIIIe–XVIIIe siècles)* (Auch, 1989), 115–44.

59. See AD Aube, 3 H 4043 (July 1275), paying 5 *s.* annually; 3 H 4039 (February 1277) paying 12 *d.* annual rent; 3 H 4074 (March 1288) lease of vineyard to Gilete of Bar, a widow described as *dilecta nostra in Christo* in return for 7 *s.* annual rent; and 3 H 4074 (April 1293) lease to Jaqueta of Bar, a widow, in return for 3 *s.* annual rent. The rents paid on these pieces of vineyard were never high, and it is unlikely that the nuns were profiting by this arrangement.

60. See AD Aube, 3 H 4071 (January 1263), and 3 H 4079 (March 1266).

Peter of Jaucourt had originally donated.[61] The acquisition of new lands and rights was stimulated in 1270 when Count Thibaut V donated 20 *l.* in annual rents paid over the course of five years.[62] In the following year the women undertook a series of purchases to acquire the customary rents and rights to justice and seigneurial fees on arable lands and vines in Ailleville, that is, on lands they already possessed.[63] The nuns were consolidating their holdings by effectively creating allodial lands free from all outside exactions or obligations. In this way the women were participating in the capitalization of older feudal rights in an attempt to consolidate their own domains. They also changed—in unintended ways—the social and topographical landscape of Champagne.

Even as Cistercian nunneries acquired rural lands used for cultivation, pasture, or lease, by the second half of the century urban and suburban rents came to dominate their "portfolio" of holdings. This was particularly true for those houses located near larger towns and cities like Val-des-Vignes, Notre-Dame-des-Prés, and Clairmarais. This urban orientation is indicative of the types of income willingly alienated during the second half of the thirteenth century, but it also reveals how the nunneries managed their assets. Rents, collected from customary dues (*cens* and *tailles*), from stalls in the fairs, and from urban and suburban houses, provided a steady income for female communities that did not obligate them to deal with the burdens of direct cultivation or the challenges of employing rural laborers. It may have been that gender played a role in this decision. The perception that nuns should not be seen laboring in the fields or in positions of authority over male *conversi*, which was reinforced in the Cistercian legislation, was probably significant. More convincing is the simple economic reality of the 1260s and 1270s that saw less rural land available for sale and donation and more institutions turning to fixed rents that produced reliable income paid out in yearly assessments. Many communities, but particularly charitable foundations like urban hospitals, poorhouses, and parochial charities, invested in rental properties, which provided the money needed to dispense charity and alms on a regular basis.[64]

---

61. See AD Aube, 3 H 4086 (November 1268) comprising three separate charters all drawn up in the same month reflecting this consolidation; and 3 H 4085 (April 1268). All of these purchases occurred over the course of 1268, involved burghers of Chaumont, and totaled 146 *l.* and 5 *s.*

62. AD Aube, 3 H 4011 (May 1270). In the same charter Count Thibaut V also confirmed that the nuns could acquire lands and rights within his fiefs and rear-fiefs in Chaumont, thus effectively endorsing their new acquisitions.

63. See AD Aube, 3 H 4038 (July and December 1271), 3 H 4112 (May 1271), 3 H 4089 (May 1271), 3 H 4073 (September 1271), 3 H 4036 (April and December 1271), 3 H 4110 (May 1272), and 3 H 4043 (November 1273).

64. See Jean Imbert, *Les hôpitaux en droit canonique* (Paris, 1947), 287–94; and M. Galvin, "Credit and Parochial Charity in Fifteenth-Century Bruges," *Journal of Medieval History* 28 (2002): 131–54.

As Robert Génestal has shown for Normandy, many monastic institutions invested in fixed rents by midcentury, which they used for gifts to the poor at the abbey gates, to maintain the infirmary, and to cover the expenses of rebuilding and repairs to their monastic buildings.[65]

The Cistercian convents acted similarly. The later part of the century coincided with rebuilding campaigns in many of the convents, and annual rents supported such projects.[66] Moreover, a concerted interest in the purchase of rents also speaks to the administrative realities attendant with providing for the dependant hospices, *domus-Dei,* and leper communities that many of the nunneries maintained. Finally, the purchase of rents, particularly fixed income like *cens* and *taille* payments that had once been markers of lordship, functioned as a source of credit for those selling to the nuns.[67] Rents generally sold for ten times their annual value.[68] A seller would receive a lump sum at the time of purchase. In 1268, for example, the knight William of Rosières received 100 *l.* for his sale of numerous small parcels and rents (*censuales*) to Notre-Dame-des-Prés.[69] A year later, just as he departed for crusade, the nuns of Val-des-Vignes paid Erard of Jaucourt 60 *l.* for a similar compounded purchase.[70] It is possible, though rarely explicitly stated, that many of the sales contracted by knights, *armigers,* and their families in 1267, 1268, and 1269 were used to fund the crusade to Tunis that departed with Louis IX in 1270. In this way, the Cistercian nunneries also began—on a modest scale—to play a role in the credit networks of the later thirteenth century.

Alms and *Amortissations*

How did Cistercian nunneries afford to make these purchases? In addition to donations and the small but steady income from rents, nuns also received bequests of alms. Donations in alms are the most difficult assets to trace in the economic histories of monastic houses, for such gifts could often pass unrecorded. Occasionally testaments detail amounts left to communities or individual nuns, but alms were typically one-time gifts of lump sums in cash.[71]

---

65. Robert Génestal, *Rôle des monastères comme établissements de crédit étudié en Normandie du XIe à la fin du XIIIe siècle* (Paris, 1901), 157–210.
66. See chap. 3, 96–102.
67. On urban credit networks, see Galvin, "Credit and Parochial Charity."
68. This was also how fiefs were valued when sold. See Evergates, *Aristocracy,* 26.
69. AD Aube, 23 H 5, fol. 38r (23 June 1268).
70. AD Aube, 23 H 181 (April 1269).
71. See, for example, the testaments in the archives of Clairvaux, AD Aube, 3 H 336 (January 1255, December 1273, and November 1286), which grant 20 or 40 *s.* each to most monastic houses in the vicinity.

Moreover, alms were often donated spontaneously, bestowed to the nuns—literally by hand—on feast days, on the death and burial of a relative, or when a family member took the cross or the monastic habit. By the 1260s and 1270s, as some houses suffered economically, nuns occasionally turned to mendicancy, going out in pairs on feast days to beg for alms in nearby towns, though of course this was forbidden in monastic legislation.[72] The amounts of these collections and their frequency have gone unrecorded.

The convents of Champagne did benefit, however, from several recorded gifts of alms from the kings of France and the counts, those members of society who could bestow charity in an almost universal manner through general donations to numerous religious foundations at one time. Royal gifts of alms often reflected contractual commitments to particular houses and tended to set the fashion for religious patronage.[73] Louis IX regularly bestowed alms to Cistercian convents because the order, and particularly its nuns, held a special attraction for the king and his mother, Blanche of Castile. By the later period of his life Louis IX lavished attention on leper houses, houses of poor women, and a variety of mendicant foundations as well, and it may be that his abiding commitment to the small Cistercian convents along the eastern border of the royal domain fit within the king's identification of religious houses worthy of apostolic charity. The alms that the Champagne nunneries may have received (though it should be said that no charters or receipts confirming these donations are to be found in the women's archives) were part of blanket donations to religious houses throughout the kingdom and the nearby counties, bestowed at regular intervals and typically at Easter.[74] The king's will, drawn up in 1270, made provision for 600 *l.* to be distributed to all the nunneries of the Cistercian order beyond the Parisian

---

72. For example, from the 1260s the nuns of La Cour Notre-Dame-de-Michery went in pairs on feast days to Sens, to Pont-sur-Yonne, to Villeneuve-le-Roi, and even to Paris to beg alms. See AD Yonne H 787, fols. 21–23, and William Chester Jordan, "The Cistercian Nunnery of La Cour Notre-Dame de Michery: A House That Failed," *Revue bénédictine* 95 (1985): 311–20, at 318. When he was abbot of Savigny, Stephen of Lexington also condemned nuns for begging. See P. B. Griesser, ed., "Registrum Epistolarum Stephani de Lexinton abbatis de Stanlegia et de Savigniaco," *Analecta Sacri Ordinis Cisterciensis* 2 (1946): 1–118, and 8 (1952): 181–378, at 251, no. 23.

73. See William Chester Jordan, *Louis IX and the Challenge of the Crusade* (Princeton, 1979), 90–92 and 183–95. For Louis IX's account records, see *RHGF,* 21:261–65 and 22:566–69.

74. See Jordan, *Louis IX,* 183. On royal alms, see Robert-Henri Bautier, "Les aumônes du roi aux maladreries, maisons-Dieu et pauvres établissements hospitaliers du royaume: Contribution à l'étude du réseau hospitalier et de la fossilisation de l'administration royale de Philippe Auguste à Charles VII," in *Assistance et assistés jusqu'à 1610* (Paris, 1979), 37–105; and Xavier de la Selle, *Le service des âmes à la cour: Confesseurs et aumôniers des rois de France du XIIIe au XVe siècle* (Paris, 1995). Aristocratic lords engaged in similar alms bequests, albeit on a smaller scale. See Louis Duval-Arnould, "Les aumônes d'Aliénor dernière comtesse de Vermandois et dame de Valois († 1213)," *Revue Mabillon* 60 (1984): 395–453.

and royal foundations listed by name. This amount can be compared to the 200 *l.* Louis set aside for distribution to the thirty priories of Fontevraud.[75] It is possible that in the years after the king's death, a fraction of these alms reached the Champagne convents, augmenting the income of Notre-Dame-des-Prés, Argensolles, Val-des-Vignes, and many others.

Like his brother King Louis, Alphonse of Poitiers made similar bequests of alms to be widely distributed among the churches within his county and to those religious houses with which he had familial ties.[76] Records of Alphonse's accounts begin to appear with regularity in 1243, and there are references to donations in alms of variable amounts from year to year.[77] Two detailed account records were preserved in the documents of the royal treasury for 1266 and 1267. They list the distribution of alms in Alphonse's name to various religious houses primarily around Paris and Champagne. In 1266 he gave Fontevraud 20 *l.,* Val-des-Vignes 40 *s.* or 2 *l.,* Notre-Dame-des-Prés 40 *s.,* and likewise to the other Cistercian nunneries in the region such as La Cour Notre-Dame-de-Michery and Mont Notre-Dame-lès-Provins.[78]

The effects of these alms are difficult to trace. Alphonse probably never personally visited the Champagne nunneries. His alms were administered either by a brother of the Cistercian order or by a nun from the house receiving the gift.[79] There is little evidence that would lead us to believe that his charity was consistent and could be factored into the nunneries' yearly income with any institutional reliance. Indeed, in the following years, what appeared to be an administrative routine was altered. Another crusade would depart in 1270, and Alphonse was forced to reallocate his resources for that cause. The alms account for 1267 tells a very different story. All of his donations to the Champagne convents from the year before were cancelled (*cancellatum*). Of the houses mentioned above, only the prestigious nunnery of Fontevraud in Anjou proved the exception. The nuns there received a donation of half the previous sum, a mere 10 *l.*[80]

---

75. *Layettes,* 4:419–21, no. 5638. It is difficult to know how many Cistercian nunneries divided the allotted 600 *l.*

76. *Layettes,* 4:119–23, no. 4993.

77. Alphonse, like most feudal lords, took accounts three times a year, at All Saints' Day, Candlemas, and Ascension. For 1243 he paid in alms 70 *l.* 16 *s.* 8 *d.;* 236 *l.* 1 *s.* 8 *d.;* and 90 *l.* 6 *s.* 8 *d.,* respectively. By All Souls' Day of 1247 he had paid out 101 *l.* 9 *s.* 8 *d.;* 271 *l.* 16 *s.* 8 *d.;* and 101 *l.* 17 *s.* 8 *d.,* respectively. Francis X. Hartigan, *The Accounts of Alphonse of Poitiers, 1243–1248: A Quantitative Edition* (New York, 1984), manuscript ed., at 22, 31, 37, 105, 113, and 119.

78. *Layettes,* 4:120–21, no. 4993.

79. For example, "Abbatie de Valle Vinearum juxta Barrum, XL s. tur., per fratrem Petrum quondam subpriorem Sancti Bernardi. Abbatie de Prato Beate Marie juxta Trecas, XL s. tur., per sororem Petronillam de Barro." *Layettes,* 4:121, no. 4993.

80. *Layettes,* 4:210–15, no. 5267. A typical entry reads, "Abbacia de Valle Vignearum juxta Barrum, XL. s. tur.: *cancellatum*"; at 212.

GENDER AND ADMINISTRATION IN A NEW SOCIAL LANDSCAPE   195

The counts of Champagne administered alms in like fashion. In 1257 Thibaut V left bequests to the nunneries of his county that reflected his commitments: to Argensolles (the resting place of his mother) 500 *l.* and to Val-des-Vignes, Notre-Dame-des-Prés, and La Piété at Ramerupt 100 *l.* each.[81] The accounts of the county became more systematic after Philip the Fair, future king of France, became count in 1284. Alms paid to the religious houses within Champagne were recorded for 1285, 1287, and 1288 within the general accounts of the county. During the fairs of St.-Jean and St.-Rémy, royal payments to the nunneries of Troyes ranged in value from 24 *s.* to 20 *l.*[82] These represent the payments of previous contractual donations that originated with Philip IV's comital predecessors consisting of fixed gifts of money from the fairs. The documents in the nunneries' archives give no indication as to the management of these sums. How they were used probably depended on the financial pressures of a given year. Perhaps they were channeled into building expenses or repairs, the purchase of new habits or needed winter coats, or possibly to cover the payment of debts or to consolidate a piece of property and the rights pertaining to it. The latter was perhaps the case for Val-des-Vignes, which engaged in a rash of purchases in the mid-1270s.[83]

Similar to gifts in alms were comital and royal confirmations of gifts and sales made from lands within the count's fiefs and rear-fiefs known as grants of amortization. A charter of amortization bestowed the count's approval, typically granted after a fine or tax was collected, for "the transfer of fiefs into a dead hand (*manus mortua*), incapable of rendering the attached service" obliged by the fief.[84] The dead hand in this case were monastic houses that would not render service for the property. Alienations of fiefs, rear-fiefs, and fief rents to ecclesiastical houses and nunneries specifically meant that such lands and incomes effectively fell out of the comital domain and jurisdiction. Consequently, they could not be taxed, relief and fines could not be garnered,

---

81. Five years before his death Thibaut IV also paid out money for additional stonework for his mother's (Countess Blanche of Navarre) tomb at Argensolles. "Per magistrum Fromundum maçon[em], sen, pro sepultura comitisse Blanche, vii lbs." and "Pro expensa magistri Johannis de Sancto Petro apud Argençoles, pro dicta sepultura, xx s." Listed in the account records of Count Thibaut for 1252 in Auguste Longnon, *Documents relatifs au comté de Champagne et Brie (1172–1361)*, 3 vols. (Paris, 1901–14), 3:13–14. For Thibaut V's will, see *Layettes*, 3:391–92, no. 4387.

82. In 1285 the nuns of Val-des-Vignes received 100 *s.* in alms. See Longnon, *Documents*, 3:30. In 1287 from the fair of St.-Jean, Notre-Dames-des-Prés received 10 *l.* Similar amounts follow for the alms distributions of the Troyes fairs in 1287. In that year Argensolles received 24 *s.* following the fair of Épernay. In total for 1285 the counts dispensed in alms, after the fair of St.-Rémy, 3,637 *l.* 15 *s.* 8 *d.* in diverse alms; the sum remained constant in 1287. See Longnon, *Documents*, 3:30, 45–46, 82–83, and 92.

83. In 1247 Val-des-Vignes received a confirmation and grant of an indulgence to all those who donated alms to the nuns for work on their church: AD Aube, 3 H 4010 (July 1247).

84. Evergates, *Aristocracy*, 76–81, for a discussion of amortization, here at 77.

nor could they be reappropriated by the count. Religious houses and non-noble townsmen or bourgeois were given fiefs and alms or more frequently purchased fiefs and rear-fiefs from the count's knights and retainers. Such acquisitions, particularly once they were amortized or approved by the count, meant that those properties that had once been fiefs in effect became allodial land, that is, they were no longer encumbered by obligations to the counts and could be bought and sold without comital approval.[85]

Over the course of the twelfth and thirteenth centuries a tremendous number of comital fiefs and rear-fiefs had passed into the hands of religious houses and specifically to the Cistercian monasteries and nunneries that flourished in the county. Because there was little way to stem the tide of such alienations, particularly as new religious houses were founded, the counts recognized the expediency of exploiting this practice. In 1224 Thibaut IV and his chancery began to take notice of these transfers and to restrict, regulate, and tax them when they occurred.[86] Although initially the counts approved most donations to religious houses by granting amortizations, in the following forty years it became clear that taxing such transfers was a useful source of income. In 1269 the first general tax on amortizations was assessed and used to finance Thibaut V's crusade with Louis IX. As Theodore Evergates has shown, "the tax applied to all property transferred from fief holders to townsmen and religious houses," which had been alienated during the previous forty years.[87] Canons from St.-Quiriace undertook a great *enquête* and took sworn testimony recorded on parchment rolls detailing the values of the fiefs that had passed out of the count's control.[88] The chancery in turn drafted standardized grants of amortization by which the count confirmed acquisitions made from "[his] fiefs, rear-fiefs, allods or rents through purchase, donation, exchange, or any other mode of acquisition."[89] Fifteen houses are known to have paid for amortizations in 1270, whereas others seem to have

---

85. The count and king frequently retained rights to demand castle guard and to high justice. See, for example, the grant to Notre-Dame-des-Prés: "Pro nobis ac successoribus nostris gardam et justiciam penitus retinentes"; AD Aube, 23 H 12 (11 April 1269). Louis IX similarly retained rights of justice on his donation to La Joie: "Retenta tamen nobis et successoribus nostris in predictis omnimoda justitia alta et bassa, et salvo in aliis jure nostro et in omnibus alieno." Louis Carolus-Barré, "L'Abbaye de La Joie-Notre-Dame à Berneuil-sur-Aisne (1234–1430)," in *Mélanges à la mémoire du Père Anselme Dimier*, ed. Benoît Chauvin, 2:487–504 (Arbois, 1982–87), 503n9.

86. Evergates, *Aristocracy*, 77–79.

87. Ibid., 80.

88. Longnon, *Documents*, 2:xxxix–xl, xliii, and 493–506.

89. Notre-Dame-des-Prés: "aliqua in feodis, retrofeodis, allodiis sive censivis nostris per emptionem, per donationem, per escambium sive permutationem vel alioquoquo modo acquisierint,... laudamus ac etiam confirmamus"; AD Aube, 23 H 12 (11 April 1269). For other examples, see Evergates, *Aristocracy*, 80n155.

negotiated the amount of their taxes.[90] As Thibaut V may have realized, and as his successors and the French kings certainly came to see, comital policies could not stem the tide of alienations, but income through taxation could be one benefit of the changing donation pattern. Indeed, in 1269 Alphonse of Poitiers instituted a similar procedure of taxed amortizations.[91] Likewise, once the county became part of the royal domain, Philip III and Philip IV continued to employ taxation on alienated fiefs, steadily increasing the rates for fiefs acquired as alms or as purchases.[92]

Many of the Cistercian nunneries do not appear to have paid a tax in 1269 but rather were simply granted approval for earlier donations and were frequently given license to acquire property from fiefs in the future. For example, in 1270 Thibaut V allowed Argensolles, his grandmother Blanche of Navarre's foundation, to acquire property yielding income of 100 *l.* annually, but not more than half of any fief.[93] Several months earlier, he granted Notre-Dame-des-Prés a nearly identical charter, except that their acquisitions could not be greater than 30 *l.* in annual income.[94] Likewise, in 1269 the count granted an amortization to Val-des-Vignes that allowed the nuns to acquire property within his fiefs and rear-fiefs, but a year later he restricted this to property totaling an annual revenue of 20 *l.* over the next five years (see fig. 10).[95] Similar grants appear in the archives of St.-Jacques de Vitry and Clairmarais.[96] The king also made concessions to those Cistercian nunneries under his protection. Thus among the charters of La Joie Notre-Dame in Berneuil is a 1270 grant of amortization from Louis IX that is nearly identical to those extended by the count.[97]

The effects of the amortizations were profound. Not only did they allow the counts and the king to raise needed income from taxes—frequently to

---

90. Henri d'Arbois de Jubainville, *Histoire des ducs et des comtes de Champagne,* 7 vols. (Paris, 1859–69), 4:631–32.

91. P. Guébin, "Les amortissements d'Alphonse de Poitiers (1247–1270)," *Revue Mabillon* 15 (1925): 80–106, 133–44, 293–304; 16 (1926): 27–33; and Yves Dossat, "Alphonse de Poitiers et les clercs," in *Les évêques, les clercs et le roi (1250–1300)* (Toulouse, 1972), 361–91. The count of Poitiers employed a canon of St.-Quiriace of Provins, Giles Cannelini, to collect his amortization taxes.

92. Evergates, *Aristocracy,* 80–81. The amounts of the royal tax collection for the *bailliage* of Troyes indicate that in 1294–95 Philip IV raised about 8000 *l.* from amortization taxes paid by sixty-nine religious houses and seventy individuals. See John F. Benton, "The Accounts of Cepperello da Prato for the Tax on *Nouveaux Acquêts* in the Bailliage of Troyes," reprinted in his *Culture, Power and Personality,* 253–73.

93. AD Marne, 70 H 12 (May 1270); Evergates, *Aristocracy,* 80n157.

94. AD Aube, 23 H 12 (11 April 1269).

95. AD Aube, 3 H 4011 (January 1269) and (March 1270).

96. St.-Jacques de Vitry: AD Marne, 71 H 4 (Feast of Saint Lucie, 1268); Clairmarais: AD Aube, 3 H 3718 (1294).

97. Carolus-Barré, "L'Abbaye de La Joie-Notre-Dame," 503n9 (February 1270).

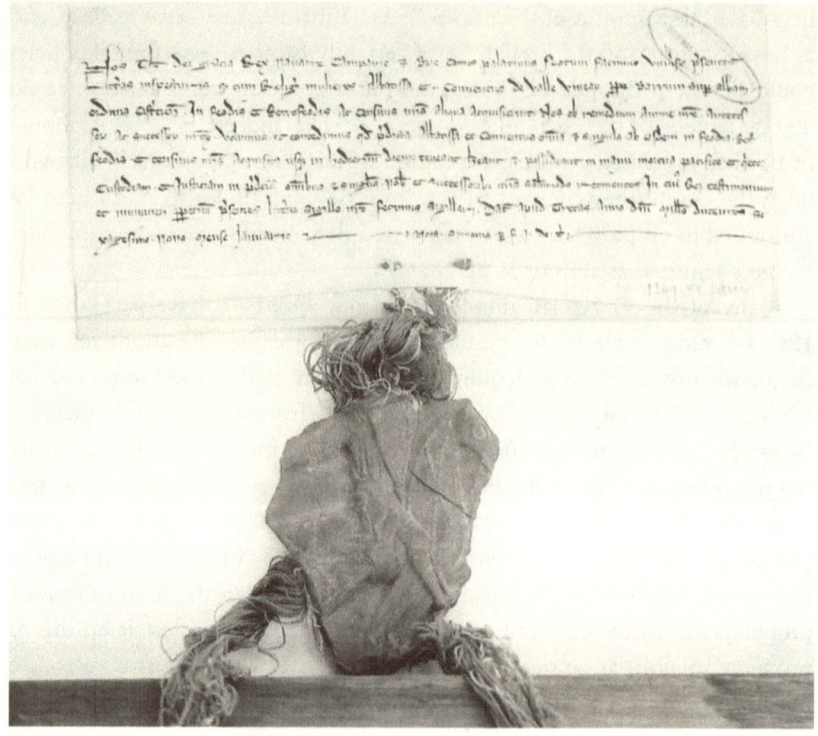

FIGURE 10. Amortization for Val-des-Vignes from Thibaut V, count of Champagne, king of Navarre. AD Aube, 3 H 4011 (January 1269). Photo by the author.

support a crusade or after 1285 the war with Aragon—but they also openly acknowledged that fiefs were alienated, and by the 1260s more often sold, to religious houses on a regular basis. The rise in sales certainly reflected the need on the part of the lesser aristocracy for cash to fund their crusade ambitions. Selling fiefs, parts of fiefs, and rents from fiefs was a way to do this, and the counts needed to approve such transfers to support this larger aim. That the counts for the most part appear not to have taxed the Cistercian nunneries when they granted amortizations and that such grants likewise applied to future acquisitions that the nunneries might make are indicative of their spiritual ideals and the recognition that the Cistercian convents were poorer houses, which the counts clearly favored.

Strikingly, the policy of amortization also further altered the social and topographical landscape of the county and in particular the suburban spaces that the nunneries occupied. Many of the fiefs the nuns acquired came from lands near their own abbeys, that is, lands and rents paid in *cens* and customary dues from the areas surrounding the fair towns and the main roadways of Champagne. What had once been fiefs were now properties and incomes controlled by the nuns in effect as allodial lands. The counts retained only the rights to high justice and occasionally the obligations of castle guard. The translation of fiefs back into allods also promoted the rise of social groups, particularly the urban bourgeoisie, who could take part in the purchasing and repurchasing of such lands after they had been donated—with comital approval—to the nuns. The sale of fiefs, year after year, little by little as documented in the Cistercian convent archives is powerfully indicative of the downward social mobility that affected the lesser aristocracy and even what some scholars have called a "crisis of the knightly class."[98] That such social changes are represented vividly within the nuns' archives demonstrates how vital these institutions had become within the social fabric of the county.

A Space Apart

The incremental accumulation of properties and rents over the course of the thirteenth century integrated the Cistercian convents of Champagne into the landscape of the county as permanent institutions. Nunneries founded just outside the fair towns or along the vital arteries and roadways of the county amassed estates made up of suburban land and urban rents and in turn cultivated a space set apart from the urban fray but still deeply dependent on the social and economic forces shaping the county. As the economy constricted by the close of the thirteenth century, many communities of Cistercian nuns became reliant on their connections with the urban bourgeoisie with whom they bought and sold property, and leased out old fiefs, and who they accepted into their communities as nuns and *conversae*. In doing so these convents amassed a patrimony along the margins of the county's urban centers. But by virtue of their social and religious functions such as caring for the sick

---

98. The failing fortunes of the Jaucourt family offer a clear illustration of this process. In 1269 Erard of Jaucourt assigned 40 *l. provinois* as well as several measures of grain to be paid to the nuns at the time of his death. By 1272 it may have been difficult for his widow Agnes and her sons to make this payment. In a charter recognizing Erard's donation, they also sold arable lands and fields totaling 60 *l.*, perhaps to cover the costs of his donations; AD Aube, 3 H 4038 (April 1272). Other sales of arable land were made in April 1273 and July 1274 (AD Aube, 4118). On the changing status of knights and esquires in the first part of the thirteenth century in Champagne, see Theodore Evergates, "The Aristocracy of Champagne in the Mid-Thirteenth Century: A Quantitative Description," *Journal of Interdisciplinary History* 5 (1974): 1–18. On the notion of "crisis," see Edmund King, "Large and Small Landowners in Thirteenth-Century England," *Past and Present* 47 (1970): 26–50; P. R. Cross, "Sir Geoffrey de Langley and the Crisis of the Knightly Class in Thirteenth-Century England," *Past and Present* 68 (1975): 3–34; and the response by D. A. Carpenter, "Was There a Crisis of the Knightly Class in the Thirteenth-Century? The Oxfordshire Evidence," *English Historical Review* 95 (1980): 721–52.

and praying for the dead, the Cistercian nuns made the margins integral to the shape of the social and religious landscape of Champagne.

This creation was not unintended but deliberate. Donors, prelates, and the nuns themselves constructed the margins as a necessary zone of salvation, which allowed the center—the public squares, taverns, brothels, and other places of profit, conspicuous consumption, corruption, and sin—to hold, to persist. Like the small cells belonging to penitents that encircled many of the towns of northern Italy or like the beguine houses of the urban centers of Flanders, the Cistercian nunneries of Champagne had become fixed points animating the social and religious world. In this way, over the course of the thirteenth century, the women's religious movement was successfully institutionalized and integrated into the fabric of the county. The hundreds of documents that shaped this process speak to the vital and varied support provided to these religious women and the ideals they upheld. Moreover, as the charters make clear, layers of social connections joined the nuns with patrons, local deans, officials, counts, kings, and bishops in constructing a religious reform. It was these relationships that made the Cistercian convents into permanent institutions.

Epilogue

A Deplorable and Dangerous State: Crisis, Consolidation, and Collapse

The crisis began almost imperceptibly. Inflation had persisted steadily through the second half of the thirteenth century. Taxes for crusade expeditions became a regular burden. Sometime in the mid-1280s the price of grain began to rise. A few nunneries borrowed money or put more lands to lease to cope with these conditions and to purchase enough food for the year. It is likely that they did so with the hope, perhaps even the conviction, that prices would drop and the values of their rents would return to what they had been the year before.[1] Yet by the end of the thirteenth century the twin pressures of inflation and population growth began to exert themselves, eroding the economic stability of Champagne and its Cistercian convents.[2] Some nunneries attempted to counteract fiscal shortcomings with better accounting and administration, but none of these measures became routine practice. Rather for most small houses the goal remained solvency.

---

1. See G. Fourquin, *Les campagnes de la région parisienne à la fin du Moyen Âge, du milieu du XIIIe siècle au début du XVIe siècle* (Paris, 1964), who shows that the price of cereal doubled between 1287 and 1303 in the region of St.-Denis. See also Guy Bois, *Crise de féodalisme: Économie rurale de démographie en Normandie orientale du début du 14e siècle au milieu du 16e siècle* (Paris, 1976); in English, *The Crisis of Feudalism: Economy and Society in Eastern Normandy c. 1300–1550* (Cambridge, 1984); Gérard Sivéry, *L'économie du royaume de France au siècle de Saint Louis (vers 1180—vers 1315)* (Lille, 1984); Philippe Contamine et al., *L'économie médiévale*, 3rd ed. (Paris, 2004), 251–383; and Steven A. Epstein, *An Economic and Social History of Later Medieval Europe, 1000–1500* (Cambridge, 2009).

2. Bois, *Crise de féodalisme*, 263–70.

EPILOGUE

Political changes in the county sharpened the effects of economic constriction. In 1284 Champagne was formally joined to the kingdom of France through the marriage of Countess Jeanne to Philip the Fair, the future king of France. At first the union seemed to have little effect on the county. From the middle of the thirteenth century the counts had frequently been absent from the region, in the kingdom of Navarre, on crusade, or increasingly in residence in Paris. Immediately after 1284 only aspects of the highest level of the county's administration seemed to change. Taxes collected by the *bailli* and *prévôts* of the county were paid into the royal treasury. The high court of Champagne, the Jours de Troyes, came to be staffed by royal officials who heard cases in Troyes and in Paris in the name of the king. And, as Abbess Alice of St.-Jacques knew and others soon learned, it was now possible to appeal a case up from Troyes to Paris.[3] On the whole the mechanisms of fiscal and judicial administration as experienced by individuals living in Champagne remained little altered. But just as the courts were made subject to Paris, the economy of the county suffered in the 1290s when Philip the Fair debased the currency of the kingdom to cover the costs of war with the English. In 1305 he reversed his original triple debasement, an act that plunged the kingdom further into economic crisis.[4] In Champagne this was felt even more acutely, for the economic engine of the county—its annual round of fairs—began to wane. Merchants preferred to sell in Paris, and Italian creditors and bankers relocated closer to the source of new profits and debtors: to Flanders, where the cloth they financed and purchased was produced, and to Paris, where deeper pockets of wealth accrued alongside more cosmopolitan habits of consumption.[5]

For Cistercian nunneries, like other religious institutions, the burdens of crusade taxation compounded the growing fiscal crisis. In 1245 the papacy and the Cistercian order began negotiations regarding the payment of a crusade tax. The papacy had granted a special crusade tithe to Louis IX to support his first expedition to Egypt, and the levy was intended to affect churches throughout France. In 1248, to preserve the order's privilege of tithe exemption, the General Chapter volunteered the payment of a fixed sum of

---

3. For a general overview, see John F. Benton, "Philip the Fair and the *Jours de Troyes*," reprinted in his *Culture, Power and Personality in Medieval France*, ed. Thomas Bisson (London, 1991), 191–254.

4. See Joseph Strayer, *The Reign of Philip the Fair* (Princeton, 1980), 151–52, 394–96; idem, "Italian Bankers and Philip the Fair," reprinted in his *Medieval Statecraft and the Perspectives of History* (Princeton, 1971), 239–47; and R. Cazelles, "Quelques réflexions à propos des mutations de la monnaie royale française (1295–1360)," *Le Moyen Âge* 72 (1966): 83–105, 251–78.

5. Robert-Henri Bautier, "Les foires de Champagne: Recherches sur une evolution historique," in *La Foire* (Brussels, 1953), 97–147; and Sivéry, *L'économie du royaume de France*, 199–246, esp. 238–45.

money to aid the king. In the following years the sum was augmented to support the expeditions of Charles of Anjou, who sought the kingdom of Sicily in the 1260s, and for Louis IX's second crusade expedition in 1270. Crusade taxation of the clergy continued throughout the 1270s and 1280s, to support smaller ventures in the East and failed attempts to salvage what remained in Western hands or to aid the besieged city of Acre.[6] The General Chapter continued to negotiate fixed payments that the order would contribute to the crown in times of financial necessity. The sums were collected from all houses in the order, including its nunneries. In 1285, as the king prepared to embark on a crusade against Aragon, the order agreed to the payment of 75,000 *l. tournois,* of which the nunneries were to pay 2000 *l.* By this point, however, many communities, and nunneries in particular, began to default on their payments.[7]

The tax assessments did not end. In 1289 Philip the Fair began to raise money again in the name of a crusade, this time intended for the Holy Land. Many houses of the order chafed under the tax and simply did not pay.[8] In turn, papal legates circulated to investigate firsthand those who claimed the strain of severe poverty. The royal demands proved too much to bear for the nuns of Notre-Dame-des-Prés. In the same year, with the aid of the deans of the Benedictine houses of St.-Martin and St.-Loup and the procurer of the Franciscans of Troyes, the women wrote to the cardinal legate to plead their case for poverty and to ask for exemption from the tax. In the letter, as was standard practice, the nuns submitted a brief account of their finances. They explained that the income they held from property and rents was only enough to sustain themselves and no more. The charter lists the totals collected from rents, houses, *tailles, cens,* arable land, and vineyards. On the bottom of the page was noted the total value of their annual income: 78 *l.* and 12 *s. tournois.*[9] They supported forty-one persons, including nuns, *conversae,*

---

6. See Xavier Hélary, "Les rois de France et la terre sainte, de la croisade de Tunis à la chute d'Acre (1270–1291)," *Annuaire-Bulletin de la Société de l'histoire de France* 118 (2005): 21–104.

7. Daniel S. Buczek, "Medieval Taxation: The French Crown, the Papacy and the Cistercian Order, 1190–1320," *Analecta Cisterciensia* 25 (1969): 42–106; and Joseph Strayer, "The Crusade against Aragon," in his *Medieval Statecraft,* 107–22. In 1285 La Cour Notre-Dame-de-Michery defaulted on payment of the tax. See William Chester Jordan, "The Cistercian Nunnery of La Cour Notre-Dame de Michery: A House That Failed," *Revue bénédictine* 95 (1985): 311–20.

8. Buczek, "Medieval Taxation," 69–72.

9. "summa totius septuaginta octo libri et duodecem solidi tournois"; AD Aube, 23 H 14 (9 November 1289). When the nunnery of La Cour Notre-Dame-de-Michery underwent an investigation before the papal legate in 1286 for defaulting on its payment, it was determined that the nuns were supporting a community of more than sixty persons on an income of 295 *l.* 7 *s.* 10 *d.* The degree of poverty may have been worse at Notre-Dame-des-Prés than at La Cour. For La Cour, see the figures in Jordan, "Cistercian Nunnery of La Cour Notre-Dame de Michery," 315.

and scholars on this meager sum. Matters had become desperate, and the nuns did their best to make that clear.

Although fiscal crises of this magnitude affected all religious communities, male and female alike, in 1298 the situation was made acutely more difficult for the nunneries. In that year Pope Boniface VIII promulgated the bull *Periculoso,* demanding total claustration for all professed nuns. He seems to have done so in response to mounting reports of nuns leaving their cloisters to beg for alms and in search of any possible remedy to their growing financial hardships. *Periculoso* closed nuns off from business transactions outside the cloister, from dispute resolution, and from litigation. It affected a kind of paralysis of administration for many convents. Moreover, it provided a legal means through which to prosecute the nuns in order to enforce claustration.[10] The Cistercian order seems to have taken the bull very seriously, and the General Chapter disseminated its contents to the nunneries under its care. In 1298 the nuns of Val-des-Vignes received a copy of the bull in the hand of a brother of Clairvaux (fig. 11).[11] This charter had been tailored to fit the community specifically. It reiterated the basic stipulation of *Periculoso* and specified that the nuns were expressly forbidden from engaging in public mendicancy. To ensure the financial solvency of the house, the number of nuns was limited to twenty.

The situation worsened as the fourteenth century dawned. Here the silence of the archives says a great deal. The number of charters in the nuns' collections simply drops off after the first decade of the fourteenth century. There are one or two documents, typically reconfirmations of property holdings or alms in the name of the king, but rarely do we find charters of donation and sale, and never in the numbers that had accrued during the 1260s. It was as if all business but the barest day-to-day necessities had stopped. This was probably the case. From 1314 to 1322 famine descended on northern Europe. As the archival record dried up, the rains began to fall and did not stop until they were replaced by devastating drought, initiating a corrosive cycle that persisted for seven years. Famine wiped out the income of monastic houses in northern France and Flanders in particular.[12] One is left to imagine its detrimental effects on the Champagne convents.

---

10. The bull has been edited and analyzed by Elizabeth Makowski, *Canon Law and Cloistered Women: Periculoso and Its Commentators, 1298–1545* (Washington, DC, 1997).

11. AD Aube, 3 H 4003 (1298).

12. William Chester Jordan, *The Great Famine: Northern Europe in the Early Fourteenth Century* (Princeton, 1996), esp. 63–77.

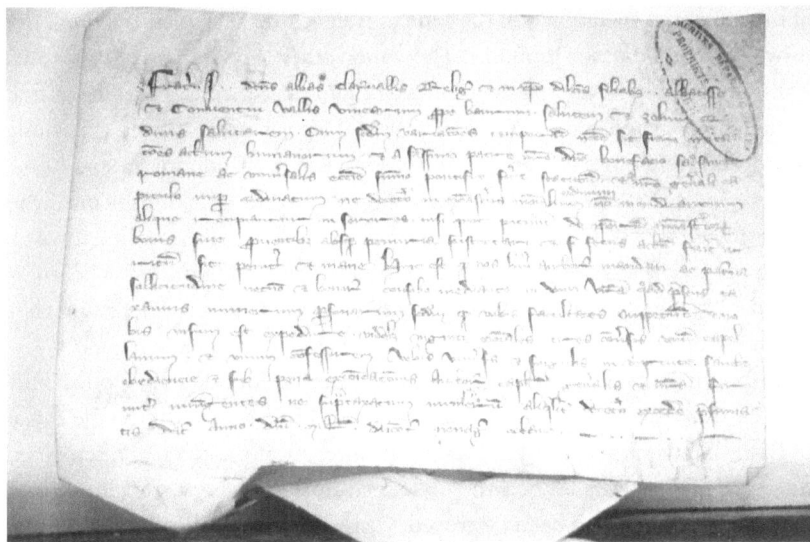

FIGURE 11. Charter from the abbot of Clairvaux to the nuns of Val-des-Vignes concerning Boniface VIII's *Periculoso*. AD Aube, 3 H 4003 (1298). Photo by the author.

Fifteen years after crop yields began to recover to what they had been in the late thirteenth century, long-held animosities between the French and the English came to fruition in war. Nine years after the death of the last direct Capetian male heir in 1328, the king of England, Edward III, claimed the throne of France through his mother, Isabelle of France, daughter of Philip IV. The English claim ignited a conflict that would not meet an end for well over one hundred years. The war that followed was fought largely on French soil.[13] Lawless marauding and pillaging aggravated the conflict, all of which wrought devastation upon the landscape of northern France and Champagne.

The French accounts of the effects of the war—which came to be called the Hundred Years' War (1337–1453)—vary in their detail, but they convey the same story of ruin and despair. Male and female religious communities probably suffered equally, though many of the nunneries did not have the resources to return to or sustain a monastic life after the fighting had subsided. In the ecclesiastical provinces of Sens and Reims, those that encompass Champagne, most

---

13. See Edouard Perroy, *La guerre de cent ans* (Paris, 1945); in English, *The Hundred Years War*, trans. David C. Douglas (London, 1962); Michael Jones, "War and Fourteenth-Century France," in *Arms, Armies and Fortifications in the Hundred Years War*, ed. Anne Curry and Michael Hughes (Woodbridge, 1994), 103–20; and Nicholas Wright, *Knights and Peasants: The Hundred Years War in the French Countryside* (Woodbridge, 1998).

of the nunneries mentioned in the sources were left derelict, their buildings destroyed or burned to the ground.[14] Those monastic houses located outside town walls were simply razed, and the monks and nuns dispersed to beg alms or find habitation in the nearest town.[15] Hospitals and leper houses suffered grievously as well and were often turned over to the local parish for administration.[16] One gets the sense that the countryside was simply emptied of its inhabitants, who were either killed or to be found begging in the streets of the fortified towns.[17] Attempts to collect taxes from nunneries under these conditions grew pointless, and in 1339 the situation had become so dire that the Cistercian General Chapter exempted the nuns of the order from collection altogether.

In Provins, the Clarissan nuns of St.-Catherine founded by Count Thibaut IV were forced to abandon their house in 1367, driven out by the threat of English pillaging. They retreated to the interior of the town and remained there for fifteen years. When they returned to the nunnery, the church and monastic buildings had been destroyed. Only in 1382 did they receive a papal indulgence to begin reconstruction.[18] The convent buildings and church of the Paraclete founded by Abelard and Heloise were likewise razed to the ground in the 1360s and the nuns dispersed. Only in 1366 did the bishop of Troyes give them permission to return.[19] Although it took time, several of the Champagne convents did eventually recover. The Paraclete, Notre-Dame-aux-Nonnains, Foissy, Argensolles, and Notre-Dame-des-Prés were rebuilt, and slowly the communities of nuns were reconstituted.

By contrast, for the most part the Cistercian communities on the margins of the towns, in their small chapels and *domus-Dei*, never recovered from the compounded crises of debt and war. As the fourteenth century closed, some of the nuns, in an attempt to begin the monastic life again, sought to establish more permanent residences in cities. In 1363, when it was clear that the effects of the war would leave their community outside Reims "destroyed and demolished," the women of Clairmarais retreated inside the city's walls.[20] In the same year, King Jean of Valois (r. 1350–1364) granted them formal

---

14. See Henri Denifle, *La désolation des églises, monastères et hopitaux en France pendant la guerre de cent ans*, 2 vols. (Paris, 1897–99; reprint, Brussels, 1965).

15. See Denifle, *Désolation des églises*, 1:23, no. 77, and 472, no. 970.

16. Ibid., 1:471–42, no. 969.

17. On the significant population decline in Champagne during this period, see ibid., 2:594–95.

18. Ibid., 2:723.

19. Ibid., 2:241–42; also "Cartulaire de l'Abbaye du Paraclet," in Charles Lalore, ed. *Collection des principaux cartulaires du diocese de Troyes*, 7 vols. (Paris, 1875–90), 2:xxii.

20. "quod cum propter factum guerrarum nostrarum omnia aedificia monialium monasterii de Claro-marisco Cisterciensis ordinis, prope Remis, adeo destructa et demolita fuerint"; *GC* 10:68, instr. 73.

permission to relocate to a house inside the urban enceinte with an adjacent courtyard garden, which the women had purchased from a townsman, Thomas Jupin. They were allowed to have an oratory or small church constructed in the precinct of the house. Under these circumstances the nunnery was much reduced from the numbers it had known in the mid-thirteenth century, but the community persisted. In contrast, other houses without ties to urban centers like Reims tried to amass enough capital to initiate the process of repair and rebuilding.[21] For many of the nunneries, however, despite their attempts, a return to the life they had known was never possible; they had neither enough money nor a sufficient number of nuns to sustain communal life.

In 1399 the Cistercian General Chapter took up a new policy toward failing female communities. The monks decreed that all houses with fewer than twelve persons were to be converted into cells or male priories of the order.[22] The Cistercian convent of Les Isles outside of Auxerre served as the model for a process that reduced the number of Cistercian nunneries in the region by half. Les Isles, it was decided, was to be "consolidated, incorporated and annexed by the monastery of Pontigny, to be maintained as a grange or cell for the monks."[23] The abbess, nuns, and other religious persons still in residence at Les Isles were dispersed among other convents within the order better able to provide for them. The statute emphasized that the nuns and all other women living with them, whomever they may be, should be expelled from the nunnery, even with the aid of the secular arm if needed. The suppression of Les Isles became a template for the consolidation of other convents in the same year. In the next statute from 1399, in identical language, the Cistercian nunnery Mont-Notre-Dame outside of Provins was suppressed and given over to the monks of Preuilly as a grange and the nuns were dispersed. Four other nunneries in Champagne met with the same fate, among them the women of Benoîtevaux and Val-des-Vignes.[24]

The suppression of Cistercian convents continued along these lines well into the fifteenth century. Neither the small plots of suburban vineyards and arable land, nor the rents from houses in Bar or Troyes, nor alms once donated by the counts proved sufficient to sustain the Cistercian nuns through

---

21. See Josephus-Mia Canivez, *Statuta Capitulorum Generalium Ordinis Cisterciensis ab anno 1116 ad annum 1786,* 8 vols. (Louvain, 1933–41), 3:(1396)29, (1397)15, and (1398)13.

22. "quodque minora monasteria tam monachorum quam monialium, in quibus non possent congrue sustentari duodecim monachi vel moniales ibidem assidue residentes, ut per omnia possent communia statuta Ordinis observare, patres abbates committerent aliis monasteriis et unirent." Ibid., 3:(1399)36.

23. Ibid.

24. Ibid., 3:(1399)37–41; also references in Anne Bondeelle-Souchier, "Les moniales cisterciennes et leurs livres manuscrits dans la France d'ancien régime," *Cîteaux* 45 (1994): 193–337.

this period. It was less a matter of mismanagement than of compounded and unforeseen exigencies that provoked the collapse of the nunneries. The close of the fourteenth century saw the end of a particular religious way of life for women in the county at an institutional level. Yet it would be wrong to see this development as the end of the women's religious movement. Rather, as is definitive of movements, it continued in protean forms. The women of Clairmarais are a good example. They lived in fewer numbers inside the city of Reims, praying together in their small house-church, eating communal meals, and tempering their ideas of labor and charity as the profound necessities of fourteenth-century life demanded. Those nuns sent out to other houses would have lived in much the same manner: in towns, in small communities, and in a world of changing devotion. Food would almost always be scarce for the remainder of the century. Patronage as they had known it in the thirteenth century was no longer available, and the ideals of religious practice and devotions were changing as well. A new emphasis on private prayer with personal Psalters and devotional books became more common. A culture of local preaching and book production held greater influence. And increasingly women in Champagne, like women in most parts of Europe, would turn to more open and self-defined interpretations of the common religious life. Although a life outside of strict regulation would still draw concern and scrutiny, the institutional mechanisms of episcopal oversight, aristocratic patronage, and monastic discipline would never be in place as forcefully as they had been during the thirteenth century.[25] As for the lepers and the sick and poor whom these women served within an institutional setting, their care increasingly moved—of necessity and convenience—into the hands of local parish networks, under the auspices of individual charity and smaller domestic poor houses.[26]

In the face of such pressures and changes, memory, history, and paper became tightly bound. As the convents were suppressed, what remained of their claustral complexes passed to the nearest male house of the order. This transfer also saw the charters the nuns had amassed during the thirteenth century subsumed into male hands. Beginning in the early fifteenth century, Cistercian monks sat with the parchment records of these nunneries, diligently organized them according to the geography of each convent's holdings, and

---

25. See Robert Lerner, *The Heresy of the Free Spirit in the Later Middle Ages* (Notre Dame, 1972); and John Van Engen, *Sisters and Brothers of the Common Life: The Devotio Moderna and the World of the Later Middle Ages* (Philadelphia, 2008).

26. See Sharon Farmer, *Surviving Poverty in Medieval Paris: Gender, Ideology, and the Daily Lives of the Poor* (Ithaca, 2002).

copied them into paper cartularies. It was a conscious act of recovery and reproduction meant to record a new beginning. The charters and their ordered copies were useful to the monks as new owners of a patrimony that they needed to administer. There may also have been a sense that such records, particularly those that described the ties between female communities and the aristocracy, offered a sense of the history of the order and its longevity and influence. By contrast, the nunneries of the thirteenth century and the women who had once created them—through the arc and aggregate of spiritual ideals and economic sufficiency—seemed to dissolve into the early modern topography of France and into the common habits of oblivion.

Appendix

Cistercian Convents and *Domus-Dei* of Champagne

The appendix presents a list of Cistercian convents in northern France and Champagne and lists those connected to or affiliated with leper houses, hospitals, or *domus-Dei*. It is organized chronologically by date of foundation and incorporation. Significant familial burials in the convents are also indicated.

Convent	Foundation date	Leper house or domus-Dei	Diocese/location	Bishop	Early/significant patrons
Montreuil-les-Dames	Filiation with La Tart from 1136		Laon	Bartholomew of Jura (1113–1151)	Jacques de Troyes, later Pope Urban IV, donated a relic of the Holy Face (1249)
Fervaques	Founded 1140; filiation to Montreuil, incorporated 1235		Noyon	Nicolas de Roie (1228–1240)	Reinier, seneschal of Vermandois, and his wife, Elisabeth; their daughter was first abbess
Épagne	1178		Amiens	Theobald III d'Heilly (1169–1204)	Enguerrand des Fontaines, seneschal Ponthieu
Lézinnes	1184; incorporated 1237		Langres	Manasses of Bar (1179–1193); incorporated into the Cistercian order under Robert of Thourotte	William I, lord of Lézinnes
Benoîtevaux	ca. 1194–1200	In 1240 received the leprosarium of Reynel	Langres	Garner de Rochefort (ca. 1193–1195) [In 1240, Robert of Thourotte]	Guyard de Reynel and wife, Ermengarde; 1290 Alix de Reynel, wife of Jean de Joinville, was buried there
St-Antoine-des-Champs	1198		Paris	Eudes of Sully (1196–1208)	Following preaching campaign of Fulk of Neuilly
Willencourt	1199		Amiens	Theobald III d'Heilly (1169–1204)	William, count of Ponthieu
L'Abbaye-aux-Bois	1202		Noyon	Stephen of Nemours (1188–1221)	Jean of Nesle and Eustachie of St.-Pol, his wife (burial)
Porrois or Port-Royal-des-Champs	1204 (recognized 1224)		Paris	Eudes of Sully (1196–1208); William of Seignelay (1220–1223)	Mathilde of Garlande, widow of Matthieu, lord of Marly
Les Clairets	1204 (Cistercian in 1213)		Chartres	Reginald of Bar (de Monçon) (1182–1217)	Geoffroy IV and Mathilda of Brunswick, count and countess of Perche
Parc-aux-Dames	1205		Senlis	Gaudfrid II (1185–1213)	Eleanor, countess of St.–Quentin and King Philip Augustus
Voisins	1213		Orléans	Manasses III of Seignelay (1207–1221)	Transferred from original location in Bucy by Manasses III de Seignelay

La Barre-Dieu	1213 as Augustinian nunnery; 1240 becomes Cistercian		Soissons	Haymard of Provins (1208–1219)	Guido de la Barre, chaplain of St.-Thibaut near Château-Thierry; Blanche of Navarre, initially founded as a house for the poor
Pentémont	1217 (incorporated as Cistercian 1221)		Beauvais	Philip of Dreux (1175–1217); Milo de Châtillon-Nateuil (1217–1234)	Philip of Dreux and his brother Milo
Lieu Notre-Dame	1218–1222		Orléans	Manasses III of Seignelay (1207–1221); Philip de Joui (1221–1234)	Isabelle, countess of Chartres
Le Paraclet	1219		Amiens	Evrard (1212–1222)	Enguerrand, lord of Bowes and his wife, Ada; daughter Margaret was first abbess
Les Isles	1219–20	Given hospital of Appoigny	Auxerre	William of Seignelay (1207–1220); Henry of Villeneuve (1220–1234)	Gérard Baleine, canon of Auxerre; Seignelay family (burials), Hugh de Malliaco, a knight, as well as Guy and Mathilda, count Forez, Auxerre, Tonnerre, and Nevers
Villiers-aux-Nonnains	1220–1225		Sens	Peter II of Corbeil (1200–1222)	Bono de St.-Antoine, chaplain (Dominican) in Paris; Amicie, widow of Jean, lord of Berteuil
Clairmarais	1222		Reims	William of Joinville (1219–1226)	Briard (goldsmith), citizen of Reims and his wife, Agnes
La Grâce-Notre-Dame	1223		Troyes	Robert of Troyes (1223–1233)	Lords of Bergères; Jean, count of Chartres, Mathew of Montmirail; Guy de Nully, Enguerrand of Coucy, and Agnes de Noyers
Argensolles	1222–1224		Soissons	Jacques de Bazoches (1219–1242)	Blanche of Navarre, countess of Champagne
Ste.-Hoïde	1225–1229		Toul	Otto de Sorcy (1219–1228)	Henry, count of Bar in his castle at Putil; Jeanne de Dampierre, countess of Bar (daughter of Marguerite of Flanders buried there; d. 1239)

(Continued)

(Continued)

Convent	Foundation date	Leper house or domus-Dei	Diocese/location	Bishop	Early/significant patrons
Pont-aux-Dames	1226	Founded in domus-Dei (on the bridge of Couilly or Pont-de-Couilly)	Meaux	Peter III of Cuisy (1223–1255)	Hugh of Châtillon, count of St.-Pol (burial)
La Cour Notre-Dame-de-Michery	1225; incorporated 1226	Attached to leprosarium at Viluis	Sens	Gautier Cornut (1222–1241)	Anseau of Traînel, Geoffroy of Sergines
L'Eau-lès-Chartres	1226		Chartres	Gautier of Chartres (1219–1234)	Jean and Isabelle, count and countess of Chartres
St-Dizier	1227		Châlons	William II of Perche (1215–1226)	William of Dampierre (burial) and his wife, Margaret of Flanders
Le Sauvoir	1228; incorporated 1239		Laon	Anselme de Mauny (1215–1238); Garnier (1238–1248)	Anselme de Mauny
La Piété-Dieu	1229; incorporated 1233	Began as Filles-Dieu; 1236 given hospital of St.-Jean and domus-Dei of Ramerupt	Troyes	Robert (1223–1233)	Philip of Mécringes, Erard of Brienne
Jardin-lès-Pleurs	1229		Troyes	Robert (1223–1233)	Marie, countess of Brienne, wife of Gauthier IV of Brienne
Notre-Dame-des-Prés	1231; incorporated 1235	Began as Filles-Dieu; 1239 given domus-Dei of St.-Julien at Mergey	Troyes	Robert (1223–1233); Nicholas de Brie (1233–1269)	Stephen of Champguyon, citizen of Troyes; Hugh of St.-Maurice and his wife
La Joie-lès-Nemours	1230; incorporated 1236	Given the domus-Dei at Malay-le-Roi	Sens	Gautier of Cornut (1222–1241)	Philip of Nemours
Val-des-Vignes	1232; incorporated 1236	Began as Filles-Dieu; near leper house of Bar-sur-Aube	Langres	Robert of Thourotte (1232–1239)	Family of Peter of Jancourt (burial)

L'Amour-Dieu	1232; incorporated 1237	Began in *domus-Dei* at Troissy	Soissons	Jacques de Bazoches (1219–1242)	Hugh de Châtillon, count of St.-Pol, and Phillip de Mécringes
St.-Jacques de Vitry	1233–1234	Began in *domus-Dei* of Count Thibaut IV at Vitry	Châlons	Philip II de Merville (1228–1237)	Count Thibaut IV of Champagne
La Joie-Notre-Dame	1234; incorporated 1240	Founded in the leprosarium of Berneuil	Soissons	Jacques de Bazoches (1219–1242)	Jacques de Bazoches; King Louis IX
Beauvoir	1234		Bourges	Philip Berruyer (1234–1260)	Robert and Mathilde of Courtenay
St.-Loup	1235	Began as *Filles-Dieu*	Orléans	Philip Berruier (1234–1236); Guillaume de Bucy (1237–1258)	King Louis IX
Baiche-lès-Péronne	1235; incorporated 1236		Noyon	Nicolas de Roye (1228–1240)	Peter Quercus, a canon, and Fursy Botte, burgher of Péronne
Mont Notre-Dame-lès-Provins	1236	Initial community of *Filles-Dieu*	Sens	Gautier Cornut (1222–1241)	Jean Bouvier, cleric in Provins
Consolations-les-Mazures	1239		Reims	Henry de Dreux (1227–1240)	Pierre and Giles de Montcornet
Monchy-Humières	1239; incorporated 1241		Beauvais	Robert of Cressonsacquisart (1237–1248)	Philip of Dreux (bishop, 1175–1217); Matthew de Roye, a knight
Marcilly	1239	Transferred to the leprosarium of Cerces in 1256	Autun/Sens	Gautier Cornut (1222–1241); Guy de Vergy (1224–1245)	Bure de Prey and his wife, Marie d'Anglure; (burial of the lords of Noyers)
Maubuisson	1239–1240		Rouen	Peter II de Colmieu (1237–1245)	Blanche of Castile (burial)
Les Rosiers	1240		Reims	Henry de Dreux (1227–1240)	Baldwin II, lord of Autry
Belleau	1242		Troyes	Nicholas de Brie (1233–1269)	Mathew, lord of Montmirail and Oisy
Le Lys	1244		Sens	Giles Cornut (1244–1254)	Blanche of Castile and Capetian family

Bibliography

Primary Sources

Manuscripts

PARIS

Bibliothèque nationale de France (Paris)
    Cartulary of Countess Blanche of Navarre, lat. 5993
    Cartulary of St.-Maclou, nouv. acq. lat. 110
    Cartulary of St.-Étienne, lat. 17098
    Collection Champagne, vols. 151–54
    Collection Duchesne, vol. 4

AUXERRE

Archives départementales de l'Yonne
    Cartulary of La Cour Notre-Dame-de-Michery, H 787
    Charters of La Joie Notre-Dame-de-Nemours, H 211

CHÂLONS-SUR-MARNE

Archives départementales de la Marne
    Charters of L'Amour-Dieu, 69 H
    Charters of Argensolles, 70 H
    Charters of St.-Dizier, 71 H
    Charters of St.-Jacques de Vitry, 71 H

CHAUMONT

Archives départementales de la Haute-Marne
    Charters of Benoîtevaux, 25 H

ÉPERNAY

"Life of Ida of Argensolles." Bibliothèque municipale, MS 55

TROYES

Médiathèques de l'Agglomération Troyenne:
    Cartulary of the Paraclete, MS 2284
    Sermon Collection, MS 228
    Sermon Collection, MS 1082
    Sermon Collection, MS 1100
    Jacques de Vitry, Exempla Collection, MS 1750

Archives départementales de l'Aube
>   Charters of Clairmarais 3 H 3701
>   Charters of Clairvaux 3 H
>   Cartulary of Clairvaux 3 H 9 and 3 H 10
>   Charters of the Priory of Foissy (Fontevraud), 27 H
>   Charters of Notre-Dame-aux-Nonnains, 22 H
>   Charters of Notre-Dame-des-Prés, 23 H
>   Cartulary of Notre-Dame-des-Prés, 23 H 5
>   Charters of the Paraclete, 24 H
>   Charters of Val-des-Vignes, 3 H 4001
>   Charters of the bishop of Troyes, series G

Printed Sources

L'Abbaye du Pont-aux-Dames (ordre de Cîteaux) assise en la paroisse de Couilly, châtellenie de Crécy, election et diocese de Meaux-en-Brie, 1226–1790. Ed. Claude H. Berthault. Meaux: Le Blondel, 1878.

Abelard, Peter. "Abelard's Rule for Religious Women." Ed. T. P. McLaughlin. *Mediaeval Studies* 18 (1956): 241–92.

———. *Historia calamitatum*. Ed. Jacques Monfrin. Paris: J. Vrin, 1978.

———. "The Letter of Heloise on the Religious Life and Abelard's First Reply." Ed. J. T. Muckle. *Mediaeval Studies* 17 (1955): 240–81.

———. *The Letters of Abelard and Heloise*. Trans. Betty Radice and Michael T. Clanchy. New York: Penguin, 2003.

———. "The Personal Letters between Abelard and Heloise." Ed. J. T. Muckle. *Mediaeval Studies* 15 (1953): 47–94.

Acta sanctorum quotquot toto orbe coluntur. Ed. Jean Bollandus et al. Antwerp, 1643–present.

Anecdotes historiques, légends et apologues, tirés du recueil inédit d'Étienne de Bourbon, Dominicain du XIIIe siècle. Ed. A. Lecoy de la Marche. Paris: Librarie Renouard, 1877.

Apolda, Dietrich von. *Vita S. Elysabeth*. In *Das Leben der heiligen Elisabeth*. Ed. Monika Rener. Marburg: Elwert, 2007.

Aubry of Trois-Fontaines. "Chronicon." Ed. Paul Scheffer-Boichorst. In *MGH SS*, 23:621–950. Hannover: Hahn, 1874.

Auvray, Lucien, ed. *Les registres de Grégoire IX: Recueil des bulles de ce pape publiées ou analysées d'après les manuscrits originaux du Vatican*. 3 vols. Paris: A. Fontemoing, 1896–1910.

Becquart, Noël. "Notre-Dame-des-Prés abbaye cisterciennes au diocèse de Troyes." Thesis. École nationale des Chartes, 1945.

Benton, John F., Michel Bur, and Dominique Devaux, eds. *Recueil des actes d'Henri le Libéral, comte de Champagne, 1152–1181*. Vol. 1. Paris: Académie des inscriptions et belles lettres, 2009.

Bernard of Clairvaux. "Liber ad milites templi: De laude novae militiae." In *Sancti Bernardi Opera* 3:213–39.

———. *In Praise of the New Knighthood: A Treatise on the Knights Templar and the Holy Places of Jerusalem*. Trans. M. Conrad Grennia. Cistercian Fathers Series 19B. Kalamazoo, MI: Cistercian Publications, 2000.

———. *On the Song of Songs III*. Trans. Killian Walsh and Irene M. Edmonds. Kalamazoo, MI: Cistercian Publications, 1979.
———. *Sancti Bernardi Opera*. 8 vols. Ed. Jean Leclercq, H.-M. Rochais, and C. Talbot. Rome: Editiones Cistercienses, 1957–77.
Beugnot, A., ed. *Les Olim ou registres des ârrets rendus par la cour du roi*. Paris: Impr. Royale, 1839.
Bevegnati, Giunta. *Legenda de vita et miraculis Beatae Margaritae de Cortona*. Ed. Fortunato Iozzelli. Grottaferrata: Editiones Collegii S. Bonaventurae ad Claras Aquas, 1997.
Caesarius of Heisterbach. *The Dialogue on Miracles*. 2 vols. Trans. H. von E Scott and C. C. Swinton Bland. New York: Harcourt, 1929.
———. *Dialogus Miraculorum*. Ed. Joseph Strange. Cologne: Heberle, 1851.
———. *Vita Sancte Elyzabeth*. In *Das Leben der heiligen Elisabeth und andere Zeugnisse*. Ed. Ewald Könsgen. Marburg: N. G. Elwert, 2007.
———. *Vita sante Elyzabeth langravie*. In "Des Cäsarius von Heisterbach Schriften über die hl. Elisabeth von Thüringen." Ed. Albert Huyskens. *Annalen des Historischen Vereins für den Niederrhein* 86 (1908): 1–59.
Canivez, Josephus-Mia. *Statuta Capitulorum Generalium Ordinis Cisterciensis ab anno 1116 ad annum 1786*. 8 vols. Louvain: Bureaux de la Revue, 1933–41.
Le cartulaire de l'Abbaye Cistercienne d'Obazine (XIIe–XIIIe siècle). Ed. Bernadette Barrière. Clermont-Ferrand: Institute d'Études du Massif Central, 1989.
Cartulaire de l'Abbaye de Porrois aux diocèse de Paris plus connue sous son nom mystique Port-Royal. Ed. A. de Dion. Paris: Picard, 1903.
"Cartulaire de l'Abbaye du Paraclet." In Lalore, *Collection des principaux cartulaires du diocèse de Troyes*, vol. 2.
Cartulaire de l'église Notre-Dame de Paris. 4 vols. Ed. B. Guérard. Paris: Crapelet, 1850.
"Cartulaire de Montier-la-Celle." In Lalore, *Collection des principaux cartulaires du diocèse de Troyes*, vol. 4.
Les chansons de croisade. Ed. J. Bédier and P. Aubry. Paris: H. Champion, 1909.
"Chartes de la commanderie de Beauvoir de l'ordre teutonique." In Lalore, *Collection des principaux cartulaires du diocese de Troyes*, vol. 3, 177–328.
Chrétien de Troyes. *Authurian Romances*. Trans. Carleton W. Carroll. New York: Penguin, 1991.
———. *Les romans de Chrétien de Troyes: IV, Le chevalier au Lion (Yvain)*. Edited from the copy of Guiot (BNF fr. 794). Ed. Mario Roques. Paris: Honoré Champion, 1982.
Clare of Assisi: Early Documents. Ed. and trans. Regis J. Armstrong. New York: Paulist Press, 1988.
Coq, Dominique, ed. *Chartes en langue française antérieures à 1271 conservées dans les départements de l'Aube, de la Seine-et-Marne, et de l'Yonne*. Documents linguistiques de la France, série française 3. Paris: Éditions du CNRS, 1988.
Couvret, Anne-Marie. "Charte de Jean de Dampierre pour l'Abbaye Notre-Dame de Saint-Dizier." *Cahier Haut-Marnais: Revue de sciences, de lettres et d'art* 131 (1977): 157–59.
D'Avray, David L. *Medieval Marriage Sermons: Mass Communication in a Culture without Print*. Oxford: Oxford University Press, 2001.

Decrees of the Ecumenical Councils. Ed. Norman P. Tanner. 2 vols. Washington, DC: Georgetown University Press, 1990.
The Deeds of Pope Innocent III by an Anonymous Author. Trans. James M. Powell. Washington, DC: Catholic University of America Press, 2004.
Denifle, Henri. *La désolation des églises, monastères et hopitaux en France pendant la guerre de cent ans.* 2 vols. Paris: Picard, 1897–99; reprint, Brussels: Culture et civilization, 1965.
Les deux vies de Robert d'Arbrissel, fondateur de Fontevraud: Légendes, écrits et témoignages. Ed. and trans. Jacques Dalarun, Geneviève Giordanengo, Armelle Le Huërou, Jean Longère, Dominque Poirel, and Bruce L. Venarde. Disciplina Monastica 4. Turnhout: Brepols, 2006.
Documents linguistiques de la France (série française). Chartes en langue française antérieures à 1271 conservées dans le département de la Haute-Marne. 2 vols. Ed. Jean-Gabriel Gigot. Paris: Éditions du Centre national de la recherché scientifique, 1974.
Epistolae duorum amantium: Briefe Abaelards und Heloises? Ed. Ewald Könsgen. Mittellateinische Studien und Texte 8. Leiden: E. J. Brill, 1974.
"Extràits de la chronique attribuée à Baudoin d'Avesnes." In *RHGF,* 21.
Flamare, H. de, ed. and trans. "La charte de depart pour la Terre-Sainte de Gaucher de Châtillon." *Bulletin de la Société Nivernaise* 13 (1886–89): 174–82.
Gautier, Cornut. "De susceptione coronae spineae Jesu Christi." In *RHGF,* 22:27–33.
Gilbert of Tournai. *Collectio de scandalis ecclesiae.* In P. Autbertus Stroick, "Collectio de scandalis ecclesiae. Nova editio," *Archivum Franciscanum Historicum* 24 (1931): 33–62.
Goswin of Bossut. *Send Me God: The Lives of Ida the Compassionate of Nivelles, Nun of La Ramée, Arnulf, Lay Brother of Villers, and Abundus, Monk of Villers.* Trans. Martinus Cawley. Turnhout: Brepols, 2003; reprint, University Park: Pennsylvania State University Press, 2006.
Griesser, P. B., ed. "Registrum Epistolarum Stephani de Lexinton abbatis de Stanlegia et de Savigniaco." *Analecta Sacri Ordinis Cisterciensis* 2 (1946): 1–118, and 8 (1952): 181–378.
Guignard, Philippe. *Les monuments primitifs de la règle Cistercienne.* Dijon: Imprimerie Darantiere, 1878.
Guillaume de Saint-Pathus. *Vie de Saint Louis.* Ed. H.-Franois Delaborde. Paris: A. Picard, 1899.
Harmond, M. "Notice historique sur la léproserie de la ville de Troyes." *MSA* 7–8 (1847–48): 429–669.
Hartigan, François X. *The Accounts of Alphonse of Poitiers, 1243–1248: A Quantitative Edition.* New York: University Press of America, 1984.
Henninges, Diodorus, ed. "Vita S. Elisabeth, Landgraviae Thuringiae." *Archivum Franciscanum Historicum* 2 (1909): 240–68.
Henriquez, Chrysostomo. *Quinque Prudentes Virgines sive B. Beatricis de Nazareth, B. Aleydis de Scharenbecka, B. Idea de Nivellis, B. Idea de Lovanio, B. Idea de Levvis, Ordinis Cisterc. Praeclara gesta, ex antiquis M.S. eruta.* Antwerp, 1630.
Herman of Tournai. *De miraculis S. Mariae Laudunensis.* In *PL* 156, cols. 961–1018.

Humbert of Romans. *De eruditione religiosorum praedicatorum.* Vol. 25 of *Maxima bibliotheca veterum patrum et antiquorum scriptorum ecclesiasticorum.* Ed. Marguerin de la Bignes. Lyon: Anisson, 1677.
Huyskens, Albert, ed. *Quellenstudien zur Geschichte de hl. Elisabeth, Landgräfin von Thüringen.* Marburg: Elwert, 1908.
"Institutes of the Paraclete." In *PL* 178, cols. 313–26.
Jacques de Vitry. *The Exempla or Illustrative Stories from the Sermones Vulgares of Jacques de Vitry.* Ed. Thomas Frederick Crane. London: D. Nutt, 1890; reprint, New York: Franklin, 1971.
———. *The Historia Occidentalis of Jacques de Vitry: A Critical Edition.* Ed. John Frederick Hinnebusch. Spicilegium Friburgense 17. Fribourg: University Press, 1972.
———. *Lettres de Jacques de Vitry (1160/70–1240).* Ed. R. B. C. Huygens. Leiden: Brill, 1960.
Jean de Joinville. *Vie de Saint Louis.* Ed. Jacques Monfrin. Paris: Dunod, 1995.
Lalore, Charles, ed. *Collection des principaux cartulaires du diocèse de Troyes.* 7 vols. Paris: E. Thorin, 1875–90.
———. "Documents sur l'Abbaye de Notre-Dame-aux-Nonnains de Troyes," *MSA* 38 (1874): 5–236.
———. *Le trésor de Clairvaux du XIIe au XVIIIe siècle.* Paris: Ernest Thorin, 1875.
Layettes du trésor des chartes. 5 vols. Ed. Alexandre Teulet et al. Paris: Imprimerie Nationale, 1863–1909.
Legenda sanctae Clarae. In *AASS,* 12 August, 2:739–68.
Libellus de diversis ordinibus et professionibus qui sunt in aecclesia. Ed. and trans. Giles Constable and Bernard S. Smith. Oxford: Oxford University Press, 2003.
Longère, Jean. "Quatre sermons ad religiosas de Jacques de Vitry." In Parisse, *Les religieuses en France au XIIIe siècle,* 215–300.
Longnon, Auguste, ed. *Documents relatifs au comté de Champagne and Brie (1172–1361).* 3 vols. Paris: Imprimerie Nationale, 1901–14.
Lucet, Bernard. *La codification cistercienne de 1202 et son évolution ultérieure.* Rome: Editiones Cistercienses, 1964.
———. *Les codifications cisterciennes de 1237 et de 1257.* Paris: CNRS, 1977.
Mansi, J. D., ed. *Sacrorum conciliorum nove et amplissima collectio.* 53 vols. Venice, Florence, and Paris, 1759–89.
Vita de B. Joanne de Monte Mirabili. In *AASS,* September, 8:186–255.
Vita Margaret of Cortona. In *AASS,* February, 3:304–462.
Martène, Edmond, and Ursin Durand. *Thesaurus novus anecdotorum.* 3 vols. 1717; reprint, New York: B. Franklin, 1968.
Nusse, C. "Charte de fondation d'un Hôtel-Dieu à la Barre." *Annales de la Société historique et archéologique de Chateau-Thierry* (1874): 191–92.
Peter of les Vaux-de-Cernay. *The History of the Albigensian Crusade: Peter of les Vaux-de-Cernay's Historia Albigensis.* Trans. W. A. Sibly and M. D. Sibly. Woodbridge: Boydell, 1998.
Philip the Chancellor. *In Psalterium Davidicum CCXXX sermones.* Paris, 1523.
Philip Mouskes. *Chronique rime de Philippe Mouskes.* Ed. Frédéric de Reiffenberg. 2 vols. Brussels: M. Hayez, 1836–38.

Pipon, Brigitte. *Le chartrier de l'Abbaye-aux-Bois (1202–1341): Étude et édition*. Paris: École des Chartes, 1996.
Poncelet, Edouard. "Chartes du Prieuré d'Oignies de l'ordre de Saint Augustin." *Annales de la Société archéologique de Namur* 31 (1913): 1–104.
Poquet, Alexandre-Eusèbe. "L'Abbaye de Barre et son recueil de chartes." *Mémoires de la Société historique et archéologique de Chateau-Thierry* (1884): 117–77.
Praecepta Recta Vivendi. In *PL* 162, cols. 1083–86.
Quantin, Maximilien, ed. *Cartulaire général de l'Yonne: Recueil de documents authentiques pour servir à l'histoire des pays qui forment ce déparatement*. 2 vols. Auxerre: Perriquet, 1854–60.
———, ed. *Recueil de pièces pour faire suite au cartulaire général de l'Yonne (XIIIe siècle)*. Auxerre: Société des sciences historiques et naturelle de l'Yonne, 1873.
Regula Benedicti. Ed. Adalbert de Vogüé. In *La règle de saint Benoît*. 7 vols. Sources chrétiennes. 181–87. Paris: Éditions du Cerf, 1971–72.
Regulae sanctimonialium Fontis Ebraldi. In *PL* 162, cols. 1079–82.
Rôles des fiefs du comté de Champagne sous le règne de Thibaud le Chansonnier (1249–52). Ed. Auguste Longnon. Paris: H. Menu, 1877.
Souancé, Vicomte Hector de. *Abbaye royale de Notre-Dame des Clairets: Histoire et cartulaire, 1202–1790*. Nogent-le-Rotrou: Hamard, 1894.
Speculum virginum. Ed. Jutta Seyfarth. Corpus Christianorum. Continuatio Mediaevalis, 5. Turnhout: Brepols, 1990.
Swan, Carolyn T., *The Old French Prose Legend of Saint Julian the Hospitaller*. Beihefte zur Zeitschrift für romanische Philologie, 160. Tübingen: Max Niemeyer, 1977.
Testaments saint-quentinois du XIVe siècle. Ed. Pierre Desportes. Paris: CNRS, 2003.
Thomas Aquinas. *Commentary on the Epistles. In omnes S. Pauli Apostoli Epistolas commetaria*. 5th ed. Turin, 1917.
Thomas of Cantimpré. *Bonum universale de apibus*. Douai, 1627.
———. *Vita Margarete de Ypres*. Ed. G. Meersseman. In "Les frères prêcheurs et le mouvement dévot en Flandre aux XIIIe s." *Archivum Fratrum Praedicatorum* 18 (1948): 106–30.
Thomas of Celano. "Life of Saint Francis." *Vita Prima*. In *Analecta Franciscana*, 10, fascs. 1–3. Quarrachi: Collegium S. Bonaventurae, 1926–28.
Thomas of Froidmont. *Hodoeporicon et pericula Margarite Iherosolimitane*. In P. G. Schmidt, "'Peregrinatio periculosa.' Thomas von Froidmont über de Jerusalemfahrten seiner Schwester Margareta." In Stache, Maaz, and Wagner, *Kontinuität und Wandel*, 461–85.
Villefosse, E. Héron de, ed. "Vie manuscrite de la bienheureuse Ide, première abbesse du monastère d'Argensoles (Marne)." *Revue de Champagne*, 2nd ser., 1 (1889): 481–98.
Waddell, Chrysogonus, ed. and trans. *Narrative and Legislative Texts from Early Cîteaux*. Studia et documenta 9. Cîteaux: Commentarii cistercienses, 1999.
———, ed. *The Paraclete Statutes Institutiones Nostrae: Troyes, Bibliothèque Municipale, MS 802, ff. 89r–90v*. Cistercian Liturgy Series 20. Trappist, KY: Gethsemani Abbey, 1987.
———. *Twelfth-Century Statutes from the Cistercian General Chapter*. Ed. Chrysogonus Waddell. Studia et documenta 12. Brecht: Cîteaux, Commentarii cistercienses, 2002.

Waquet, Jean, Jean-Marc Roger, and Laurent Veyssière, eds. *Recueil des chartes de l'Abbaye de Clairvaux au XIIe siècle.* Paris: C.T.H.S., 2004.

Secondary Sources

Actes du 111e Congrès national des sociétés savantes, Poitiers, 1986, Section d'histoire médiévale et de philologie, t. 2: Entre Loire et Gironde au Moyen Âge: Histoire religieuse; onomastique. Paris: Éditions du CTHS, 1987.
Adaine, Jean-Luc. "Le domaine de Maubuisson." In Pressouyre, *L'espace cistercien,* 554–67.
Adelson, Howard L., ed. *Studies in Medieval and Renaissance History.* Vol. 8. Lincoln: University of Nebraska Press, 1971.
Ahlers, Gerd. *Weibliches Zisterziensertem im Mittelalter und seine Klöster in Niedersachsen.* Studien zur Geschichte, Kunst und Kulture der Zisterzienser, 13. Berlin: Lukas, 2002.
Alberzoni, Maria Pia. *Clare of Assisi and the Poor Sisters in the Thirteenth Century.* Saint Bonaventure, NY: Franciscan Institute Publications, 2004.
Andrea, Alfred. "Adam of Persigne and the Fourth Crusade." *Cîteaux* 36 (1985): 21–37.
Arbois de Jubainville, Henri d'. "Études sur les documents antérieurs à l'année 1285, conservés dans les archives des quatre petits hôpitaux de la ville de Troyes." *MSA* 21 (1857): 49–116.
——. *Histoire de Bar-sur-Aube sous les comtes de Champagne, 1077–1284.* Paris: A. Durand, 1859.
——. *Histoire des ducs et des comtes de Champagne.* 7 vols. Paris: Durand, 1859–69.
——. "Les premiers seigneurs de Ramerupt." *BEC* 22 (1861): 440–58.
Assistance et assistés jusqu'à 1610. Actes du 97e Congrès National des Sociétés Savantes Nantes, 1972. Paris: Bibliothèque Nationale, 1979.
Aubert, Marcel. *L'architecture cistercienne en France.* 2 vols. Paris: Les Éditions d'art et d'histoire, 1953.
Avril, Joseph. *Le gouvernement des évêques et la vie religieuse dans le diocese d'Angers (1148–1240).* 2 vols. Paris: Cerf, 1984.
——. "Le IIIe concile de Latran et les communautés de lépreux." *Revue Mabillon* 60 (1981): 21–76.
Baker, Derek, ed. *Medieval Women.* Studies in Church History, Subsidia. Oxford: Blackwell, 1978.
——, ed. *Sanctity and Secularity, The Church and the World.* Studies in Church History, 10. Oxford: Blackwell, 1973.
Baldwin, John. *Aristocratic Life in Medieval France. The Romances of Jean Renart and Gerbert de Montreuil, 1190–1230.* Baltimore: Johns Hopkins University Press, 2000.
——. *The Government of Philip Augustus: Foundations of French Royal Power in the Middle Ages.* Berkeley: University of California Press, 1986.
——. *Masters, Princes and Merchants: The Social Views of Peter the Chanter and His Circle.* Princeton: Princeton University Press, 1970.
Barber, Malcom. *The New Knighthood: A History of the Order of the Temple.* Cambridge: Cambridge University Press, 1994.

Barret, Sébastien, and Gert Melville, eds. *Oboedientia. Zu Formen und Grenzen von Macht und Unterordnung im mittelalterlichen Religiosentum.* Vita Regularis 27. Münster: LIT, 2005.

Barrière, Bernadette. "The Cistercian Monastery of Coyroux in the Province of Limousin in Southern France in the Twelfth and Thirteenth Centuries." *Gesta* 31 (1992): 76–82.

Barrière, Bernadette, and Marie-Elizabeth Henneau, eds. *Cîteaux et les femmes.* Paris: Créaphis, 2001.

Barrow, Julia, Charles Burnett, and David Luscombe. "A Checklist of the Manuscripts containing the Writings of Peter Abelard and Heloise and Other Works Closely Associated with Abelard and His School." *Reuve d'histoire des textes* 14–15 (1984–85): 183–302.

Bautier, Robert-Henri. "Les aumônes du Roi aux maladreries, maisons-Dieu et pauvres établissements du royaume: Contribution à l'étude du réseau hospitalier et de la fossilisation de l'administration royale de Philippe Auguste à Charles VII." In *Assistance et assistés jusqu'à 1610,* 37–105.

———. "L'authentification des actes privés dans la France médiévale: Notariat public et juridiction gracieuse." In *Notariado público y documento privado,* 2:281–304.

———. *Chartes, sceaux et chancelleries: Études de diplomatique et de sigillographie médiévales.* 2 vols. Paris: Écoles des chartes, 1990.

———. "L'exercice de la juridiction gracieuse en Champagne du milieu du XIIIe siècle à la fin du XVe." Reprinted in Bautier, *Chartes, sceaux et chancelleries,* 1:359–436.

———. "Les foires de Champagne: Recherches sur une evolution historique." In *La Foire,* 97–147.

———. "Les registres des foires de Champagne à propos d'un feuillet récemment découvert." Reprinted in Bautier, *Chartes, sceaux et chancelleries,* 1:157–88.

Beauvoir, Simone de. *Le deuxiéme sexe.* Paris: Gallimard, 1949.

———. *The Second Sex.* Trans. H. M. Parshley. New York: Vintage, 1989.

Bedos-Rezak, Brigitte. "Diplomatic Sources and Medieval Documentary Practices: An Essay in Interpretive Methodology." In Van Engen, *The Past and Future of Medieval Studies,* 313–43.

———. "Medieval Identity: A Sign and a Concept." *American Historical Review* 105 (2001): 1489–1533.

———. "Women, Seals, and Power in Medieval France, 1150–1350." In Erler and Kowaleski, *Women and Power in the Middle Ages,* 61–82.

Bell, David N. "The Cistercians and the Practice of Medicine." *Cîteaux* 40 (1989): 139–73.

Bellenger, Yvonne, and Danielle Quéruel, eds. *Les champenois et la croisade: Actes des quatrièmes journées rémoises, 27–28 novembre 1987.* Paris: Aux amateurs de livres, 1989.

Benton, John F. "The Accounts of Cepperello da Prato for the Tax on *Nouveaux Acquêts* in the Bailliage of Troyes." Reprinted in Benton, *Culture, Power and Personality in Medieval France,* 255–74.

———. "The Court of Champagne as a Literary Center." *Speculum* 36 (1961): 551–91. Reprinted in Benton, *Culture, Power and Personality in Medieval France,* 3–43.

———. *Culture, Power and Personality in Medieval France.* Ed. Thomas N. Bisson. London: Hambledon Press, 1991.

———. "Philip the Fair and the Jours de Troyes." Reprinted in Benton, *Culture, Power and Personality in Medieval France*, 191–254.
Benvenuti Papi, Anna. *"In Castro poenitentiae": Santità e società femminile nell'Italia medievale*. Italia Sacra 45. Rome: Herder, 1991.
———. "Mendicant Friars and Female Pinzochere in Tuscany: From Social Marginality to Models of Sanctity." In Bornstein and Rusconi, *Women and Religion*, 84–103.
———. "Pubblica assistenza e marginalità femminile." In Benvenuti, *"In Castro poenitentiae,"* 656–58.
Berger, Jutta Maria. *Die Geschichte der Gastfreundschaft im Hochmittelalterlichen Mönchtum: Die Cistercienser*. Berlin: Akademie Verlag, 1999.
Bériou, Nicole. *L'avènement des maîtres de la Parole: La prédication à Paris au XIIIe siècle*. 2 vols. Collection des études augustiniennes. Série Moyen Âge et Temps Moderns 31–32. Paris: Institut d'études augustiniennes, 1998.
———. "Les lépreux sous le regard des prédicateurs d'après les collections des sermons *ad status* du XIIIe siècle." In Bériou and Touati, *Voluntate Dei leprosus*, 35–80.
———. "La prédication au béguinage de Paris pendant l'année liturgique 1272–1273." *Recherches Augustiniennes* 13 (1978): 105–229.
Bériou, Nicole, and François-Olivier Touati, eds. *Voluntate Dei leprosus: Les lépreux entre conversion et exclusion aux XIIème et XIIIème siècles*. Spoleto: Centro Italiano di Studi sull'Alto Medioevo, 1991.
Berkhofer, Robert F. *Day of Reckoning: Power and Accountability in Medieval France*. Philadelphia: University of Pennsylvania Press, 2004.
Berlow, Rosalind Kent. "The Development of Business Techniques at the Fairs of Champagne from the End of the Twelfth Century to the Middle of the Thirteenth Century." In Adelson, *Studies in Medieval and Renaissance History*, 8:3–31.
Berman, Constance H. "Abbeys for Cistercian Nuns in the Ecclesiastical Province of Sens: Foundation, Endowment and Economic Activities of the Earlier Foundations." *Revue Mabillon* 69 (1997): 83–113.
———. "Buildings in Wood, Brick, Stone, Tiles: Vestiges of the Architecture for Cistercian Nuns in Southern France." In Lillich, *Cistercian Nuns and Their World*, 23–59.
———. *The Cistercian Evolution: The Invention of a Religious Order in Twelfth-Century Europe*. Philadelphia: University of Pennsylvania Press, 2000.
———. "Cistercian Nuns and the Development of the Order: The Abbey of Saint-Antoine-des-Champs Outside Paris." In Elder, *The Joy of Learning and the Love of God: Studies in Honor of Jean Leclercq*, 121–56.
———. "Cistercian Women and Tithes." *Cîteaux* 49 (1998): 95–127.
———. "Dowries, Private Income, and Anniversary Masses: The Nuns of Saint-Antoine-des-Champs (Paris)." *Proceedings of the Western Society for French History* 20 (1993): 3–12.
———. "Fashions in Monastic Patronage: The Popularity of Supporting Cistercian Abbeys for Women in Thirteenth-Century Northern France." *Proceedings of the Annual Meeting of the Western Society for French History* 17 (1990): 36–45.
———. "The 'Labours of Hercules,' the Cartulary, Church and Abbey for Nuns of La Cour-Notre-Dame-de-Michery." *Journal of Medieval History* 26 (2000): 33–70.
———. "Were There Twelfth-Century Cistercian Nuns?" *Church History* 68 (1999): 824–64.

Berthault, Claude-Hyacinthe. *L'Abbaye de Pont-aux-Dames, ordre de Cîteaux; Assise en la paroisse de Couilly, châtellenie de Crécy, élection et diocèse de Meaux-en Brie, 1226–1790.* Meaux: Libraire Le Blondel, 1878.

Bertrand, Paul. *Commerce avec dame pauvreté: Structures et fonctions des couvents mendiants à Liège (XIIIe–XIVe s.).* Liège: Bibliothèque de la faculté de philosophie et lettres de l'Université de Liège, 2004.

Biller, Peter. *The Measure of the Multitude: Population in Medieval Thought.* Oxford: Oxford University Press, 2000.

Biller, Peter, and A. J. Minnis, eds. *Handling Sin: Confession in the Middle Ages.* York Studies in Medieval Theology. Woodbridge: York Medieval Press, 1998.

Bird, Jessalynn. "Innocent III, Peter the Chanter's Circle and the Crusade Indulgence: Theory, Implementation, and Aftermath." In Sommerlechner, *Innocenzo III: Urbs et Orbis,* 1:503–24.

———. "The Religious's Role in a Post-Fourth-Lateran World: Jacques de Vitry's *Sermones ad Status* and *Historia Occidentalis.*" In Muessig, *Medieval Monastic Preaching,* 209–39.

Biver, Paul, and Marie-Louise. *Abbayes, monastères, couvents de femmes: À Paris des origines à la fin du XVIIIe siècle.* Paris: Presses Universitaires de France, 1975.

Blumenfeld-Kosinski, Renate, and Timea Szell, eds. *Images of Sainthood in Medieval Europe.* Ithaca: Cornell University Press, 1991.

Bois, Guy. *Crise du féodalisme: Économie rurale de démographie en Normandie orientale du début du 14e siècle au milieu du 16e siècle.* Paris: Presses de la fondation nationale des sciences politiques, 1976.

———. *The Crisis of Feudalism: Economy and Society in Eastern Normandy c. 1300–1550.* Cambridge: Cambridge University Press, 1984.

Boitel, Alexandre Clemet. *Histoire du bienheureux Jean, surnommé l'humble, seigneur de Montmirail-en-Brie.* Paris: H. Vrayet de Surcy, 1859.

Bolton, Brenda M. "Daughters of Rome: All One in Christ Jesus!" Reprinted in Bolton, *Innocent III: Studies on Papal Authority and Pastoral Care,* 101–15.

———. *Innocent III: Studies on Papal Authority and Pastoral Care.* Aldershot: Ashgate, 1995.

———. "Mary of Oignies: A Friend to the Saints." In Mulder-Bakker, *Mary of Oignies: Mother of Salvation,* 199–220.

———. "*Mulieres Sanctae.*" In Baker, *Sanctity and Secularity,* 77–99.

———. "*Vitae Matrum:* A Further Aspect of the *Frauenfrage.*" In Baker, *Medieval Women,* 253–73.

Bondeelle-Souchier, Anne. "Les moniales cisterciennes et leurs livres manuscrits dans la France d'ancien régime." *Cîteaux* 45 (1994): 193–337.

Bonis, Armelle, and Monique Wabont. "Cisterciens et cisterciennes en France du nord-ouest: Typologie des fondations, typologie des sites." In Barrière and Henneau, *Cîteaux et les femmes,* 151–75.

Bonnardot, Hippolyte. *L'Abbaye royale de Saint-Antoine-des-Champs de l'ordre de Cîteaux étude topographique et historique.* Paris: Féchoz et Letouzey, 1882.

Bonnassie, Pierre, ed. *Fiefs et féodalité dans l'Europe méridionale: Italie, France du Midi, Péninsule Hispanique du Xe au XIIe siècle.* Toulouse: CNRS, Université de Toulouse–Le Mairail, 2002.

Bornstein, Daniel, and Roberto Rusconi, eds. *Women and Religion in Medieval and Renaissance Italy.* Trans. Margaret J. Schneider. Chicago: University of Chicago, 1996.
Bouchard, Constance B. *Holy Entrepreneurs: Cistercians, Knights, and Economic Exchange in Twelfth-Century Burgundy.* Ithaca: Cornell University Press, 1991.
———. "Monastic Cartularies: Organizing Eternity." In Kosto and Winroth, *Charters, Cartularies, and Archives: The Preservation and Transmission of Documents in the Medieval West*, 22–32.
Bouter, Nicole, ed. *Les religieuses dans le cloître et dans le monde des origines à nos jours.* Actes du deuxième colloque international du C.E.R.C.O.R., Poitiers, 29 septembre–2 octobre 1988. Saint-Étienne: Université de Sainte-Étienne, 1994.
Boutiot, Théophile. *Histoire de la ville de Troyes et de la Champagne méridionale.* 5 vols. Troyes: Dufey-Robert, 1870–74.
Bouton, Jean de la Croix. *Les moniales cisterciennes.* 4 vols. Grignan: Abbaye N.D. d'Aiguebelle, 1986–89.
Bozoky, Edina. *La politique des reliques de Constantin à Saint Louis: Protection collective et légitimation du pouvoir.* Paris: Beauchesne, 2006.
Brasher, Sally Mayall. *Women of the Humiliati: A Lay Religious Order in Medieval Civic Life.* New York: Routledge, 2003.
Britnell, Richard, ed. *Pragmatic Literacy East and West, 1200–1300.* Woodbridge: Boydell, 1997.
———. "Pragmatic Literacy in Latin Christendom." In Britnell, *Pragmatic Literacy East and West, 1200–1300*, 3–24.
Brodman, James William. *Charity and Religion in Medieval Europe.* Washington, DC: Catholic University of America Press, 2009.
Brody, Saul N. *Disease of the Soul: Leprosy in Medieval Literature.* Ithaca: Cornell University Press, 1974.
Brooke, Rosalind B. *The Image of Saint Francis: Responses to Sainthood in the Thirteenth Century.* Cambridge: Cambridge University Press, 2006.
Brouette, E. "Philip de La Charmoye." In *Dictionnaire des auteurs cisterciens* (1975 ed.), 557.
Brown, Elizabeth A. R. "Authority, the Family, and the Dead in Late Medieval France." *French Historical Studies* 16 (1990): 803–32.
———. "The Cistercians in the Latin Empire of Constantinople and Greece, 1204–1276." *Traditio* 14 (1958): 63–120.
———. "The Tyranny of a Construct: Feudalism and Historians of Medieval Europe." *American Historical Review* 79 (1974): 1063–88.
Brown, Peter. *The Rise of Western Christendom: Triumph and Diversity, 200–1000.* Oxford: Blackwell, 1996.
Bruno, Galland. "Les hommes de culture dans la diplomatie pontificale au XIIIe siècle." *Mélanges de l'école française de Rome* 108 (1996): 615–43.
Brussel, Nicholas, *Nouvel examen de l'usage général des fiefs en France pendant le XI, le XII, le XIII et le XIVe siècle.* 2 vols. 2nd ed. Paris: J. de Nully, 1750.
Buczek, Daniel S. "Medieval Taxation: The French Crown, the Papacy and the Cistercian Order, 1190–1320." *Analecta Cisterciensia* 25 (1969): 42–106.
Buhot, Jacqueline. "L'Abbaye normande de Savigny, chef d'ordre et fille de Cîteaux." *Le Moyen Âge* 46 (1926): 1–19, 104–21, 178–90, 249–72.

Bullough, David, and R. L. Storey, eds. *The Study of Medieval Records: Essays in Honor of Kathleen Major.* Oxford: Clarendon Press, 1971.

Bulst, Neithard, and Karl-Heinz Spieß, eds. *Sozialgeschichte Mittelalterlicher Hospitäler.* Vorträge und Forschungen 65. Ostfildern: Thorbecke, 2007.

Bur, Michel. *La Champagne médiévale: Recueil d'articles.* Langres: Dominique Guéniot, 2005.

Burr, David. *The Spiritual Franciscans: From Protest to Persecution in the Century After Saint Francis.* University Park: Pennsylvania State University Press, 2001.

Burton, Janet E., and Karen Stöber, eds. *Monasteries and Society in the British Isles in the Later Middle Ages.* Woodbridge: Boydell, 2006.

Bynum, Caroline Walker. "The Female Body and Religious Practice in the Later Middle Ages." In Bynum, *Fragmentation and Redemption,* 181–238.

———. *Fragmentation and Redemption: Essays on Gender and the Human Body in Medieval Religion.* New York: Zone Books, 1991.

———. *Holy Feast and Holy Fast: The Religious Significance of Food to Medieval Women.* Berkeley: University of California Press, 1987.

———. *Jesus as Mother: Studies in the Spirituality of the High Middle Ages.* Berkeley: University of California Press, 1982.

———. "Women Mystics in the Thirteenth Century: The Case of the Nuns of Helfta." In Bynum, *Jesus as Mother: Studies in the Spirituality of the High Middle Ages,* 170–262.

Caciola, Nancy. *Discerning Spirits: Divine and Demonic Possession in the Middle Ages.* Ithaca: Cornell University Press, 2003.

Cariboni, G. "Comunità religiose femminili legate ai Cistercensi a Piacenza e in Lombardia tra I pontificati di Innocenzo III e Alessandre IV." Ph.D. dissertation. Università Cattolica del Sacro Cuore, Milan, 1997.

Carolus-Barré, Louis. "L'Abbaye de La Joie-Notre-Dame à Berneuil-sur-Aisne (1234–1430)." In Chauvin, *Mélanges à la mémoire du Père Anselme Dimier,* 2:487–504.

———. "L'organisation de la juridiction gracieuse à Paris, dans le dernier tiers du XIIIe siècle: L'officialité et le Châtelet." *Le Moyen Âge* 69 (1963): 417–35.

Carpenter, D. A. "Was There a Crisis of the Knightly Class in the Thirteenth-Century? The Oxfordshire Evidence." *English Historical Review* 95 (1980): 721–52.

Carpenter, Jennifer. "Juette of Huy, Recluse and Mother (1158–1228): Children and Mothering in the Saintly Life." In *Power of the Weak: Studies on Medieval Women,* ed. Jennifer Carpenter and Sally-Beth MacLean, 57–93. Urbana: University of Illinois Press, 1995.

Casagrande, Carla, ed. *Prediche alle donne del secolo XIII.* Milan: Bompiani, 1978.

Casagrande, Giovanna, ed. *Donne tra Medioevo ed Età Moderna in Italia. Ricerche.* Perugia: Morlacchi Editore, 2004.

Cassidy-Welch, Megan. *Monastic Spaces and Their Meanings: Thirteenth-Century English Cistercian Monasteries.* Turnhout: Brepols, 2001.

Cazelles, Raymond. "La population de Paris avant la peste noire." *Comptes-Rendus des séances de l'académie des inscriptions et belles-lettres* 110 (1966): 539–50.

———. "Quelques réflexions à propos des mutations de la monnaie royale française (1295–1360)." *Le Moyen Âge* 72 (1966): 83–105, 251–78.

Chapin, Elizabeth. *Les villes de foires de Champagne: Des origines au début du XIVe siècle.* Paris: Champion, 1937.
Chaube, Fabienne. "Les *Filles-Dieu* de Rouen aux XIIIe–XVe siècle: Étude du process de regularization d'une communauté religieuse." *Revue Mabillon* n.s. 1 (1990): 179–211.
Chauvin, Benoît. "L'intégration des femmes à l'Ordre de Cîteaux au XIIe siècle, entre hauts de Meuse et rives du Léman." In Barrière and Henneau, *Cîteaux et les femmes,* 193–211.
———, ed. *Mélanges à la mémoire du Père Anselme Dimier.* 3 vols. in 6. Arbois: Pupillin, 1982–87.
———. "Morimond et la *conversio* des femmes au XIIe siècle: Belfays, abbaye cisterciennes feminine dans l'orbite de Morimond (vers 1130?–1393)." *Les Cahiers Haut-Marnais* 196–99 (1994): 55–106.
Chénon, E. "L'hérésie à La Charité-sur-Loire et les débuts de l'inquisition monastique dans la France du nord au XIIIe siècle." *Nouvelle revue historique de droit* 41 (1917): 299–345.
Chiaudano, Mario. "Il libro delle fiere di Champagne della compagnia degli Ugolini mercati senesi nella seconda metà del secolo XIII." In Mario Chiaudano, ed. *Studi e documenti per la storia del diritto commerciale italiano nel sec. XIII,* 143–208.
———, ed. *Studi e documenti per la storia del diritto commerciale italiano nel sec. XIII,* ser. 2, memoria 8. Torino: University of Torino, 1930.
Church, Stephen, and Ruth Harvey, eds. *Medieval Knighthood V: Papers from the Sixth Strawberry Hill Conference 1994.* Woodbridge: Boydell, 1995.
Clanchy, Michael. *From Memory to Written Record: England 1066–1307.* 2nd ed. Oxford: Blackwells, 1993.
Coakley, John. "Gender and the Authority of Friars: The Significance of Holy Women for Thirteenth-Century Franciscans and Dominicans." *Church History* 60 (1991): 445–60.
Cochelin, Isabelle. "Sainteté laïque: L'exemple de Juette de Huy (1158–1228)." *Le Moyen-Âge: Revue d'histoire et de philologie* 95 (1989): 397–417.
Cohen, Esther. "Patterns of Crime in Fourteenth-Century Paris." *French Historical Studies* 11 (1980): 307–27.
Cohen, Meredith. "An Indulgence for the Visitor: The Public at the Sainte-Chapelle of Paris." *Speculum* 83 (2008): 840–83.
Cole, Penny J. *The Preaching of the Crusades to the Holy Land, 1095–1270.* Cambridge, MA: Medieval Academy of America, 1991.
Collette, Florence, and Denise Méa. "Les établissements charitables dans l'ancien diocèse de Bourges à la fin du Moyen Âge." In *Actes du 111e Congrès national des sociétés savantes, Poitiers, 1986,* 79–110.
Constable, Giles. "The Ceremonies and Symbolism of Entering Religious Life and Taking the Monastic Habit, from the Fourth to the Twelfth Centuries." In *Segni e riti nella chiesa altomedievale occidentales, Spoleto, 11–17 aprile 1985* (Spoleto: Presso la sede del Centro, 1987). Reprinted in Constable, *Culture and Spirituality in Medieval Europe,* 771–834.
———. *Culture and Spirituality in Medieval Europe.* Aldershot: Ashgate, 1996.
———. *Monastic Tithes: From Their Origins to the Twelfth Century.* Cambridge: Cambridge University Press, 1964.

———. *The Reformation of the Twelfth Century*. Cambridge: Cambridge University Press, 2001.

———. "The Second Crusade as Seen by Contemporaries." *Traditio* 9 (1953): 213–79.

Contamine, Philippe, et al. *L'économie médiévale*. 3rd ed. Paris: Armand Colin, 2004.

Coomans, Thomas. "Moniales cisterciennes et mémoire dyanstique: Église funéraires princières et abbayes cisterciennes dans les anciens pays-bas médiévaux." *Cîteaux* 56 (2005): 87–145.

Cooper, Kate, and Jeremy Gregory, eds. *Elite and Popular Religion*. Studies in Church History 42. Woodbridge: Boydell, 2006.

Corbet, Patrick. "Les collégiales comtales de Champagne (v. 1150–v. 1230)." *Annales de l'Est* 29 (1971): 195–241.

Courtet, René. "Historie de l'Abbaye des Iles, anciennement de Celles." *Bulletin de la Société des sciences historiques et naturelles de l'Yonne* 120 (1988): 47–69.

Cross, P. R. "Sir Geoffrey de Langley and the Crisis of the Knightly Class in Thirteenth-Century England." *Past and Present* 68 (1975): 3–34.

Curry, Anne, and Michael Hughes, eds. *Arms, Armies and Fortifications in the Hundred Years War*. Woodbridge: Boydell, 1994.

Dalarun, Jacques. "*Capitula regularia magistri Roberti:* De Fontevraud au Paraclet." *Comptes-Rendus des séances de l'académie des inscriptions et belles-lettres* 147 (2003): 1601–36.

———. "Les plus anciens statuts de Fontevraud." In *Robert d'Arbrissel et la vie religieuse dans l'Ouest de la France: Actes du colloque de Fontevraud 13–16 décembre 2001*, ed. J. Dalarun, 139–72. Disciplina Monastica 1. Turnhout: Brepols, 2004.

———. *Robert of Arbrissel: Sex, Sin, and Salvation in the Middle Ages*. Trans. Bruce L. Venarde. Washington, D.C.: Catholic University of America, 2006.

Darrow, Margaret H. "French Volunteer Nursing and the Myth of War Experience in World War I." *American Historical Review* 101 (1996): 80–106.

Davis, Adam. *The Holy Bureaucrat: Eudes Rigaud and Religious Reform in Thirteenth-Century Normandy*. Ithaca: Cornell University Press, 2006.

———. "Preaching in Thirteenth-Century Hospitals." *Journal of Medieval History* 36 (2010): 72–89.

Davis, Michael T. "On the Threshold of the Flamboyant: The Second Campaign of Construction of Saint-Urbain, Troyes." *Speculum* 59 (1984): 847–84.

Deane, Jennifer. "*Geistliche Schwestern:* The Pastoral Care of Lay Religious Women in Medieval Würzburg." In Griffiths and Hotchins, *"Brothers and Sisters in Christ,"* forthcoming.

De Ganck, Roger. "The Integration of Nuns in the Cistercian Order Particularly in Belgium." *Cîteaux* 35 (1984): 235–47.

———. "Marginalia to Visitation Cards for Cistercian Nuns in Belgium." *Cîteaux* 40 (1989) 227–43.

Degler-Spengler, Brigitte. "The Incorporation of Cistercian Nuns into the Order in the Twelfth and Thirteenth Century." In Nichols and Shank, *Hidden Springs*, 1:85–134.

———. "'Zahlreich wie die Sterne des Himmels': Zisterzienser, Dominikaner und Franziskaner vor dem Problem der Inkorporation von Frauenklöstern." *Rottenburger Jahrbuch für Kirchengeschichte* 4 (1985): 37–50.

Derbes, Anne, and Mark Sandona. "'Ave charitate plena': Variations on the Theme of Charity in the Arena Chapel." *Speculum* 76 (2001): 599–637.

Dereine, Charles. "Vie commune, règle de Saint Augustin et channoines réguliers au XIe siècle." *Revue d'histoire ecclésiastique* 61 (1946): 365–406.
Dernbecher, Christine. *"Deum et virum suum diligens": Zur Rolle und Bedeutung der Frau im Umfeld der Kreuzzüge.* Sofie. Saarländische Schriftenreihe zur Frauenforschung 16. St. Ingbert: Röhrig, 2003.
Desmarchelier, Michel. "L'architecture des églises de moniales cisterciennes, essai de classement des différents types de plans (en guise de suite)." In Chauvin, *Mélanges à la mémoire du père Anselme Dimier*, 3:79–121.
Desportes, Pierre. *Reims et les rémois aux XIIIe et XIVe siècles.* Paris: Picard, 1979.
Dickson, Gary. *The Children's Crusade: Medieval History, Modern Mythistory.* Houndmills: Palgrave, 2008.
———. *Religious Enthusiasm in the Medieval West: Revivals, Crusades, Saints.* Aldershot: Ashgate, 2000.
Dictionnaire topographique du département de l'Aube. Ed. Théophile Boutiot and Émile Socard. Paris: Imprimerie Nationale, 1874.
Didier, Robert, and Jacques Toussaint. *Autour de Hugo d'Oignies.* Namur: Société archéologique de Namur, 2003.
Dijkhof, Eef. "Goatskin and Growing Literacy: The Penetration of Writing in the Former Counties of Holland and Zeeland in the Thirteenth Century in Relation to the Changes of the Internal and External Features of the Charters Issued." In Heidecker, *Charters and the Use of the Written Word*, 101–12.
Dimier, Anselme. "L'Abbaye du Sauvoir-sous-Laon." *MSM* 86 (1971): 121–31.
———. "L'architecture des églises de moniales cisterciennes." *Cîteaux* 25 (1974): 8–23.
———. *Saint Louis et Cîteaux.* Paris: Letouzey and Ané, 1954.
Dionnet, Alain-Charles. "La cassette reliquaire du Bienheureux Jean de Montmirail." *Revue française d'héraldique et de sigillographie* 65 (1995): 89–107.
Dollinger, Philippe. "Le chiffre de la population de Paris au XIVe siècle: 210,000 ou 80,000 habitants?" *Revue historique* 116 (1956): 35–44.
Domanda e consumi: Livelli e strutture (nei secoli XIII–XVIII). Atti della sesta Settimana di studio [27 aprile–3 maggio 1974]. Florence: L. S. Olschki 1978.
Domenico di Caleruega e la Nascita dell'ordine dei Frati Predicatori. Atti del XLI Convegno storico internazionale. Todi, 10–12 ottobre 2004. Spoleto: Fondazione Centro Italiano di Studi Sull'alto Medioevo, 2005.
Donnet, N. "La fondation de l'Abbaye d'Argensolles." *Cîteaux* 10 (1959): 212–18.
Dossat, Yves. "Alphonse de Poitiers et les clercs." In *Les évêques, les clercs et le roi (1250–1300)*, 361–91.
———. "L'hérésie en Champagne aux XIIe et XIIIe siècles." Reprinted in *Église et hérésie en France au XIIIe siècle*, by Y. Dossat, 57–63. London: Variorum, 1982.
Drossbach, Gisela. "Das Hospital—eine kirchenrechtliche Institution? (ca. 1150–ca. 1350)." *Zeitschrift der Savigny-Stiftung für Rechtsgeschichte-Kanonistische Abteilung* 87 (2001): 510–22.
———, ed. *Hospitäler im Mittelalter und Früher Neuzeit: Frankreich, Deutschland und Italien: Ein Vergleichende Geschichte. Hôpitaux au Moyen Âge et aux temps modernes: France, Allemagne et Italie: Une histoire comparée.* Pariser historische Studien 75. Munich: Oldenbourg, 2007.
Dubois, J. "Les ordres religieux au XIIe siècle selon la curie romaine." *Revue bénédictine* 78 (1968): 283–309.
Duchesne, André. *Histoire de la maison de Chastillon sur Marne.* Paris: Cramoisy, 1621.

Dufour, Jean, and Henri Platelle, eds. *Foundations et oeuvres charitables au Moyen Âge.* Paris: Éditions du CTHS, 1999.

Dufournet, Jean, ed. *Ami et Amile: une chanson de geste de l'amitié.* Paris: H. Champion, 1987.

Dunbabin, Jean. *France in the Making, 843–1180.* 2nd ed. Oxford: Oxford University Press, 2000.

Dutton, Marsha L. "Intimacy and Imitation: The Humanity of Christ in Cistercian Spirituality." In Sommerfeldt, *Erudition at God's Service,* 33–69.

Duval-Arnould, Louis. "Les aumones d'Aliénor dernière comtesse de Vermandois et dame de Valois (+ 1213)." *Revue Mabillon* 60 (1984): 395–453.

Edginton, Susan B., and Sarah Lambert, eds. *Gendering the Crusades.* New York: Columbia University Press, 2001.

Elder, E. Rozanne, ed. *The Joy of Learning and the Love of God: Studies in Honor of Jean Leclercq.* Cistercian Studies Series, 160. Kalamazoo, MI: Cistercian Publications, 1995.

Elliott, Dyan. "Alternative Intimacies: Men, Women and Spiritual Direction in the Twelfth Century." In Famous and Leyser, *Christina of Markyate: A Twelfth-Century Woman,* 160–83.

———. *Proving Woman: Female Spirituality and Inquisitorial Culture in the Later Middle Ages.* Princeton: Princeton University Press, 2004.

———. *Spiritual Marriage: Sexual Abstinence in Medieval Wedlock.* Princeton: Princeton University Press, 1993.

Elm, Kaspar. "Die Stellung der Frau in Ordenswesen, Semireligiosentum und Häresie zur Zeit der heiligen Elisabeth." In *Sankt Elisabeth: Fürstin Dienerin Heilige,* 7–28.

———. "*Vita religiosa sine regula,* Bedeutung, Rechtsstellung und Selbstverständnis des mittelalterlichen und frühneuzeitlichen Semireligiosentums." In Smahel, *Häresie und vorzeitige Reform im Spätmittelalter,* 239–73.

Elm, Kaspar, and Michel Parisse, eds. *Doppelkloster und andere Formen der Symbiose männlicher und weiblicher Religiösen im Mittelalter.* Berliner historische Studien 18, Ordensstudien 8. Berlin: Buncker and Humblot, 1992.

Epstein, Steven A. *An Economic and Social History of Later Medieval Europe, 1000–1500.* Cambridge: Cambridge University Press, 2009.

Erler, Mary C., and Maryanne Kowaleski, eds. *Gendering the Master Narrative: Women and Power in the Middle Ages.* Ithaca: Cornell University Press, 2003.

———, eds. *Women and Power in the Middle Ages.* Athens: University of Georgia Press, 1988.

Études d'histoire du droit canonique dédiées à G. Le Bras. Paris: Sirey, 1965.

Les évêques, les clercs et le roi (1250–1300). Cahiers de Franjeux 7. Toulouse: Privat, 1972.

Evergates, Theodore. *The Aristocracy in the County of Champagne, 1100–1300.* Philadelphia: University of Pennsylvania Press, 2007.

———. "The Aristocracy of Champagne in the Mid-Thirteenth Century: A Quantitative Description." *Journal of Interdisciplinary History* 5 (1974): 1–18.

———. "Aristocratic Women in the County of Champagne." In Evergates, *Aristocratic Women in Medieval France,* 74–110.

———, ed. *Aristocratic Women in Medieval France*. Philadelphia: University of Pennsylvania Press, 1999.
———, ed. *The Cartulary of Countess Blanche of Champagne*. Toronto: University of Toronto Press, 2010.
———. "The Chancery Archives of the Counts of Champagne." *Viator* 16 (1985): 159–79.
———, ed. and trans. *Feudal Society in Medieval France: Documents from the County of Champagne*. Philadelphia: University of Pennsylvania Press, 1993.
———. *Feudal Society in the Bailliage of Troyes under the Counts of Champagne, 1152– 1284*. Baltimore: Johns Hopkins University Press, 1975.
———, ed. *Littere Baronum: The Earliest Cartulary of the Counts of Champagne*. Toronto: University of Toronto Press, 2003.
———. "The Origin of the Lords of Karytaina in the Frankish Morea." *Medieval Prosopograpy* 15 (1994): 81–113.
Face, R. D. "Techniques of Business in the Trade between the Fairs of Champagne and the South of Europe in the Twelfth and Thirteenth Centuries." *Economic History Review* 10 (1958): 427–38.
———. "The *Vectuarii* in the Overland Commerce between Champagne and Southern Europe." *Economic History Review* 12 (1959): 239–46.
Famous, Samuel, and Henrietta Leyser, eds. *Christina of Markyate: A Twelfth-Century Woman*. London: Routledge, 2005.
Farmer, Sharon A. "The Leper in the Master Bedroom: Thinking through a Thirteenth-Century Exemplum." In Voaden and Wolfthal, *Framing the Family*, 79–100.
———. *Surviving Poverty in Medieval Paris: Gender, Ideology, and the Daily Lives of the Poor*. Ithaca: Cornell University Press, 2002.
Farmer, Sharon, and Carol Braun Pasternack, eds. *Gender and Difference in the Middle Ages*. Medieval Cultures 32. Minneapolis: University of Minnesota Press, 2003.
Farmer, Sharon, and Barbara H. Rosenwein, eds. *Monks and Nuns, Saints and Outcasts: Religion in Medieval Society: Essays in Honor of Lester K. Little*. Ithaca: Cornell University Press, 2000.
Feuchter, Jörg. *Ketzer, Konsuln und Büßer: Die städtischen Eliten von Montauban vor dem Inquisitor Petrus Cellani (1236–1241)*. Tübingen: Mohr Siebeck, 2007.
Field, Sean. *Isabelle of France: Capetian Sanctity and Franciscan Identity in the Thirteenth Century*. Notre Dame: University of Notre Dame Press, 2006.
Finot, Jules. "Héluyse de Joinville, soeur de l'historien Jean de Joinville (1264– 1312)." *BEC* 37 (1876): 528–40.
Fleureau, Basile. "Histoire de l'Abbaye de Villiers au diocèse de Sens." *Annales de la Société historique et archéologique du Gatinais* 11 (1893): 6–11.
Florival, M. de. "Un pèlerinage au XIIe siècle: Marguerite de Jérusalem et Thomas de Froidmont." *Bulletin de la Société académique de Laon* 26 (1882–1884): 35–69.
La Foire. Recueils de la Société Jean Bodin, vol. 5. Brussels: Éditions de la Librairie Encyclopedique, 1953.
Folkerts, Suzan. "The Manuscript Transmission of the *Vita Mariae Oigniacensis* in the Later Middle Ages." In Mulder-Bakker, *Mary of Oignies*, 221–41.

Fournier, Paul. *Les officialités au Moyen Âge: Étude sur l'organisation, la competence et la procédure des tribunaux ecclésiastiques ordinaries en France, de 1180 à 1328*. Paris: E. Plon, 1880.

Fourquin, Guy. *Les campagnes de la région parisienne à la fin du Moyen Âge, du milieu du XIIIe siècle au début du XVIe siècle*. Paris: Presses Universitaires de France, 1964.

———. *Le domaine royal en Gâtinais d'après la prisée de 1332*. Paris: S.E.V.P.E.N., 1963.

Foviaux, Jacques. "Les sermons donnés à Laon, en 1242 par le Chanoine Jacques de Troyes, futur Urbain IV." *Recherches augustinennes* 20 (1985): 203–56.

France, John, and William G. Zajac, eds. *The Crusades and the Sources: Essays Presented to Bernard Hamilton*. Aldershot: Ashgate, 1998.

Frederichs, Jules. *Robert le Bougre, premier inquisiteur général en France*. Ghent: H. Engelcke, 1892.

Freed, John B. "Urban Development and the *Cura Monialium* in Thirteenth-Century Germany." *Viator* 3 (1972): 311–27.

Frolow, Anatole. *La relique de la vraie croix: Recherches sur le développement d'un culte*. Paris: Insitut français d'études byzantines, 1961.

Galvin, M. "Credit and Parochial Charity in Fifteenth-Cetury Bruges." *Journal of Medieval History* 28 (2002): 131–54.

Gaposchkin, M. Cecilia. *The Making of Saint Louis: Kingship, Sanctity and Crusade in the Later Middle Ages*. Ithaca: Cornell University Press, 2008.

Geldsetzer, Sabine. *Frauen auf Kreuzzügen, 1096–1291*. Darmstadt: Wissenschaftliche Buchgesellschaft, 2003.

Génestal, Robert. *Rôle des monastères comme éstablissements de crédit étudié en Normandie du XIe à la fin du XIIIe siècle*. Paris: Librairie nouvelle de droit et de jurisprudence, 1901.

Gennaro, Clara. "Clare, Agnes, and Their Earliest Followers: From the Poor Ladies of San Damiano to the Poor Clares." In Bornstein and Rusconi, *Women and Religion*, 39–55.

Georgianna, Linda. "Any Corner of Heaven: Heloise's Critique of Monasticism." *Mediaeval Studies* 49 (1987): 221–53. Updated and reprinted in Wheeler, *Listening to Heloise*, 187–216.

Geremek, Bronislaw. "Paris, la plus grande ville de l'Occident médiéval." *Acta Poloniae Historica* 18 (1968): 18–37.

Gerish, Deborah. "Gender Theory." In Nicholson, *Palgrave Advances in the Crusades*, 130–47.

Gervers, Michael, ed. *The Second Crusade and the Cistercians*. New York: St. Martin's, 1992.

Gilchrist, Roberta. *Gender and Material Culture: The Archaeology of Religious Women*. London: Routledge, 1994.

Gill, Katherine. "Penitents, Pinzochere, and Pious Laywomen: Varieties of Women's Religious Communities in Central Italy, ca. 1300–1500." Ph.D. dissertation. Princeton University, 1994.

———. "*Scandala*: Controversies concerning *Clausura* and Women's Religious Communities in Late Medieval Italy." In Waugh and Diehl, *Christendom and Its Discontents*, 177–203.

Giugni, Marco, Doug McAdam, and Charles Tilly, eds. *How Social Movements Matter*. Minneapolis: University of Minnesota Press, 1999.

Goodich, Michael. "Contours of Female Piety in Later Medieval Hagiography." *Church History* 50 (1981): 20–32.
Goodson, Caroline, Anne E. Lester, and Carol Symes, eds. *Cities, Texts and Social Networks, 400–1500: Experiences and Perceptions of Medieval Urban Space.* Aldershot: Ashgate, 2010.
Gordon, Stewart, ed. *Robes and Honor: The Medieval World of Investiture.* New York: Palgrave, 2001.
Grandmottet, Odile. "Les officialités de Reims aux XIIIe et XIVe siècles." *Bulletin d'information de l'I.R.H.T.* 4 (1955): 77–106.
Graves, Coburn V. "English Cistercian Nuns in Lincolnshire." *Speculum* 54 (1979): 492–99.
Greven, Joseph. *Die Anfänge der Beginen: Ein Beitrag zur Geschichte der Volksfrömmigkeit und des Ordenwesens im Hochmittelalter.* Vorreformationsgeschichtliche Forschungen 8. Münster: Aschendorff, 1912.
——. "Der Ursprung des Beginenwesens." *Historisches Jahrbuch* 35 (1914): 26–58.
Griesser, P. B., ed. "Registrum Epistolarum Stephani de Lexinton abbatis de Stanlegia et de Savigniaco." *Annalecta Sacri Ordinis Cisterciensis* 2 (1946): 1–118; 8 (1952): 181–378.
——. "Stephan Lexington, Abt von Savigny, als Visitator der ihm unterstehendem Frauenklöster." *Cistercienserchronik* 67 (1960): 14–34.
Griffiths, Fiona J. "Brides and *Dominae:* Abelard's *Cura monialium* at the Augustinian Monastery of Marbach." *Viator* 34 (2003): 57–88.
——. "The Cross and the *Cura monialium:* Robert of Arbrissel, John the Evangelist, and the Pastoral Care of Women in the Age of Reform." *Speculum* 83 (2008): 303–30.
——. *The Garden of Delights: Reform and Renaissance for Women in the Twelfth Century.* Philadelphia: University of Pennsylvania Press, 2007.
——. "'Men's Duty to Provide for Women's Needs': Abelard, Heloise, and Their Negotiation of the *Cura Monialium.*" *Journal of Medieval History* 30 (2004): 1–24.
Griffiths, Fiona, and Julie Hotchin, eds. *"Brothers and Sisters in Christ": Men, Women, and the Religious Life in Germany, 1100–1500.* Turnhout: Brepols, forthcoming.
Griffiths, Quentin. "The Capetian Kings and St. Martin of Tours." *Studies in Medieval and Renaissance History* 9 (1987): 83–133.
——. "Les collégiales royales et leurs clercs sous le gouvernement capétien." *Francia* 18 (1991): 93–110.
——. "Royal Counselors and Trouvères in the Houses of Nesle and Soissons." *Medieval Prosopography* 18 (1997): 123–37.
——. "Saint Louis and the New Clerks of *Parlement.*" In Sommerfeldt, Syndergaard, and Elder, *Studies in Medieval Culture,* 2: 269–89.
Grundmann, Herbert. *Religiöse Bewegungen im Mittelalter.* Berlin: Ebering, 1935; 2nd ed., Darmstadt: Wissenschaftliche Buchgesellschaft, 1961.
——. *Religious Movements in the Middle Ages: The Historical Links between Heresy, the Mendicant Orders, and the Women's Religious Movement in the Twelfth and Thirteenth Century with the Historical Foundations of German Mysticism.* Trans. Steven Rowan. Notre Dame: University of Notre Dame Press, 1995.
Guébin, P. "Les amortissements d'Alphonse de Poitiers (1247–1270)." *Revue Mabillon* 15 (1925): 80–106, 133–44, 293–304; 16 (1926): 27–33.

Guest, Gerald B. "A Discourse on the Poor: The Hours of Jeanne d'Evreux." *Viator* 26 (1995): 153–80.
Guyotjeannin, Olivier. "Juridiction gracieuse ecclésiastique et naissance de l'officialité à Beauvais (1175–1220)." In Parisse, *À propos des actes d'évêques: Hommage à Lucie Fossier*, 295–310.
Guyotjeannin, Olivier, Laurent Morelle, and Michel Parisse, eds. *Les cartulaires: Actes de la table ronde organisée par l'école nationale des chartes et le G.D.R. 121 du C. N. R. S. (Paris, 5–7 décembre 1991)*. Paris: École des Chartes, 1993.
Haidu, Pierre. *The Subject Medieval/Modern: Text and Governance in the Middle Ages*. Stanford: Stanford University Press, 2004.
Hall, Edwin, and James Ross Sweeney. "An Unpublished Privilege of Innocent III in Favor of Montivilliers: New Documentation for a Great Norman Nunnery." *Speculum* 44 (1974): 662–73.
Hall, Jackie. "The Legislative Background to the Burial of Laity and Other Patrons in Cistercian Abbeys." *Cîteaux* 56 (2005): 363–71.
Hall, Jackie, Sheila Sneddon, and Nadine Sohr. "Table of Legislation." *Cîteaux* 56 (2005): 373–413.
Hamilton, Bernard. "The Cistercians in the Crusader States." Reprinted in *Monastic Reform, Catharism and the Crusades, 900–1300*, by B. Hamilton, 405–22. London: Variorum, 1979.
Haskins, Charles Homer. "The Heresy of Echard the Baker of Rheims." In Haskins, *Studies in Medieval Culture*, 245–55.
———. "The Inquisition in Northern France." In Haskins, *Studies in Medieval Culture*, 193–244.
———. *Studies in Medieval Culture*. New York: Frederick Ungar, 1929; reprint, 1965.
Hautcoeur, E. *Histoire de l'Abbaye de Flines*. Paris: J.-B. Dumoulin, 1874.
Heidecker, Karl, ed. *Charters and the Use of the Written Word in Medieval Society*. Turnhout: Brepols, 2000.
Hélary, Xavier. "Les rois de France et la terre sainte, de la croisade de Tunis à la chute d'Acre (1270–1291)." *Annuaire-Bulletin de la Société de l'histoire de France* 118 (2005): 21–104.
Henneau, Marie-Élisabeth. "Les Isles." In Kinder, *Les cisterciens dans l'Yonne*, 163–71.
Higonnet, Margaret R., Jane Jenson, Sonya Michel, and Margaret Collins Weitz, eds. *Behind the Lines: Gender and the Two World Wars*. New Haven: Yale University Press, 1989.
Higounet-Nadal, Arlette. "Les jardins urbains dans la France médiévale." In *Jardins et vergers en Europe occidentale (VIIIe–XVIIIe siècles)*, 115–44.
Hodgson, Natasha R. *Women, Crusading and the Holy Land in Historical Narrative*. Woodbridge: Boydell, 2007.
Hoffmann, Wesley J. "The Commerce of the German Alpine Passes during the Early Middle Ages." *Journal of Political Economy* 31 (1923): 826–39.
Hollywood, Amy. "Inside Out: Beatrice of Nazareth and Her Hagiographer." In Mooney, *Gendered Voices*, 79–98.
———. *The Soul as Virgin Wife: Mechthild of Magdeburg, Marguerite Porete, and Meister Eckhart*. Notre Dame: University of Notre Dame Press, 1995.

Howell, Martha C. "The Gender of Europe's Commercial Economy." *Gender and History* 20 (2008): 519–38.

———. *The Marriage Exchange: Property, Social Place and Gender in Cities of the Low Countries, 1300–1550*. Chicago: University of Chicago Press, 1998.

———. *Women, Production, and Patriarchy in Late Medieval Cities*. Chicago: University of Chicago Press, 1986.

Humbert, Jean. "La frontière occidentale du comté de Champagne du XIe au XIIIe siècle." In *Recueil de travaux offert à M. Clovis Brunel*, 2:11–30.

Imbert, Jean. *Les hôpitaux en droit canonique*. Paris: J. Vrin, 1947.

Jamroziak, Emilia, and Janet Burton, eds. *Religious and Laity in Western Europe, 1000–1400: Interaction, Negotiation, and Power*. Turnhout: Brepols, 2006.

Jansen, Katherine Ludwig. *The Making of the Magdalene: Preaching and Popular Devotion in the Later Middle Ages*. Princeton: Princeton University Press, 2000.

———. "Mary Magdalen as Model for Uncloistered Religious Women of Late Medieval Italy." In Casagrande, *Donne tra Medioevo ed Età Moderna in Italia. Ricerche*, 103–52.

Jardins et vergers en Europe occidentale (VIIIe–XVIIIe siècles). Auch: Centre culturel de l'Abbaye de Flaran, 1989.

Johnson, Penelope D. *Equal in Monastic Profession: Religious Women in Medieval France*. Chicago: University of Chicago Press, 1991.

Jones, Michael. "War and Fourteenth-Century France." In Curry and Hughes, *Arms, Armies and Fortifications in the Hundred Years War*, 103–20.

Jordan, Erin. "Patronage, Prayers and Polders: Assessing Cistercian Foundations in Thirteenth-Century Flanders and Hainaut." *Cîteaux* 53 (2002): 99–125.

———. *Women, Power, and Religious Patronage in the Middle Ages*. Houndmills: Palgrave, 2006.

Jordan, William Chester. "The Cistercian Nunnery of La Cour Notre-Dame de Michery: A House That Failed." *Revue bénédictine* 95 (1985): 311–20.

———. "Crusader Prologues: Preparing for War in the Gothic Age." *The Christian Culture Lecture*. Notre Dame, University of Notre Dame Press, 2009.

———. *From Servitude to Freedom: Manumission in the Sénonais in the Thirteenth Century*. Philadelphia: University of Pennsylvania Press, 1986.

———. *The Great Famine: Northern Europe in the Early Fourteenth Century*. Princeton: Princeton University Press, 1996.

———. *Ideology and Royal Power in Medieval France*. Aldershot: Ashgate, 2001.

———. "Isabelle of France and Religious Devotion at the Court of Louis IX." In Nolan, *Capetian Women*, 209–23.

———. "Jews, Regalian Rights, and the Constitution in Medieval France," *AJS Review* 23 (1998): 1–16. Reprinted in Jordan, *Ideology and Royal Power in Medieval France*, 9–14.

———. *Louis IX and the Challenge of the Crusade*. Princeton: Princeton University Press, 1979.

———. "The Representation of the Crusades in the Songs Attributed to Thibaud, Count Palatine of Champagne." *Journal of Medieval History* 25 (1999): 27–34.

———. "The Rituals of War: Departure for Crusade in Thirteenth-Century France." In Noel and Weiss, *The Book of Kings: Art, War, and the Morgan Library's Medieval Picture Bible,* 99–105.

———. *Unceasing Strife, Unending Fear: Jacques de Thérines and the Freedom of the Chruch in the Age of the Last Capetians.* Princeton: Princeton University Press, 2005.

———. *Women and Credit in Pre-Industrial and Developing Societies.* Philadelphia: University of Pennsylvania Press, 1993.

Karras, Ruth Mazo. *From Boys to Men: Formations of Masculinity in Late Medieval Europe.* Philadelphia: University of Pennsylvania Press, 2002.

Kedar, B. Z., ed. *The Horns of Hattin: Proceedings of the Second Conference of the SSCLE Jerusalem and Haifa, 2–6 July 1987.* London: Variorum, 1992.

Kerr, Julie. "Cistercian Hospitality in the Later Middle Ages." In Burton and Stöber, eds. *Monasteries and Society in the British Isles in the Later Middle Ages,* 25–39.

———. *Monastic Hospitality: The Benedictines in England, c. 1070–c. 1250.* Studies in the History of Medieval Religion 32. Woodbridge: Boydell, 2007.

Keyser, Richard. "The Transformation of Traditional Woodland Management: Commercial Sylviculture in Medieval Champagne." *French Historical Studies* 32 (2009): 352–84.

Kienzle, Beverly Mayne. *Cistercians, Heresy and Crusade in Occitania, 1145–1229.* Woodbridge: York Medieval Press, Boydell, 2001.

Kinder, Terryl. "Blanche of Castile and the Cistercians: An Architectural Re-evaluation of Maubuisson Abbey." *Cîteaux* 27 (1976): 161–188.

———, ed. *Les cisterciens dans l'Yonne.* Pontigny: Les Amis de Pontigny, 1999.

King, Edmund. "Large and Small Landowners in Thirteenth-Century England." *Past and Present* 47 (1970): 26–50.

King, Margot. "The Desert Mothers Revisited: The Mothers of the Diocese of Liège." *Vox Benedictina* 5, no. 4 (1988): 325–54.

Klaniczay, Gábor. *Holy Rulers and Blessed Princesses: Dynastic Cults in Medieval Central Europe.* Trans. Éva Pálmai. Cambridge: Cambridge University Press, 2000.

———. "Religious Movements and Christian Culture: A Pattern of Centripetal and Centrifugal Orientations." In Klaniczay, *The Uses of Supernatural Power,* 28–50.

———. *The Uses of Supernatural Power: The Transformation of Popular Religion in Medieval and Early-Modern Europe.* Ed. Karen Margolis. Trans. Susan Singerman. Princeton: Princeton University Press, 1990.

Kleinman, Arthur. "'Everything That Really Matters': Social Suffering, Subjectivity, and the Remaking of Human Experience in a Disordering World." *Harvard Theological Review* 90 (1997): 315–35.

Knox, Lezlie. *Creating Clare of Assisi: Female Franciscan Identities in Later Medieval Italy.* Leiden: Brill, 2008.

Koslin, Désirée. "Robes of Simplicity: Initiation, Robing and Veiling of Nuns in the Middle Ages." In Gordon, *Robes and Honor,* 255–74.

Kosto, Adam J., and Anders Winroth, eds. *Charters, Cartularies, and Archives: The Preservation and Transmission of Documents in the Medieval West.* Toronto: Pontifical Institute of Medieval Studies, 2002.

Koudelka, Vladimir J. "Le 'Monasterium Tempuli' et la fondation dominicaine de San Sisto." *Archivum Fratrum Praedicatorum* 31 (1961): 5–81.

Krenig, Ernst Günther. "Mittelalterliche Frauenklöster nach den Konstitutionem von Cîteaux." *Annalecta Sacri Ordinis Cisterciensis* 10 (1954): 1–105.
Kuhn-Rehfus, Marne. "Cistercian Nuns in Germany in the Thirteenth Century: Upper-Swabian Cistercian Abbeys under the Paternity of Salem." In Nichols and Shank, *Hidden Springs,* 1:135–58.
Kupfer, Marcia. *The Art of Healing: Painting for the Sick and the Sinner in a Medieval Town.* University Park: Pennsylvania State University Press, 2003.
———. "Symbolic Cartography in a Medieval Parish: From Spatialized Body to Painted Church at Saint-Aignan-sur-Cher." *Speculum* 75 (2000): 615–67.
Kwanten, A. "L'Abbaye Notre-Dame d'Argensolles." *MSM* 84 (1969): 75–85.
———. "L'Abbaye Saint-Jacques de Vitry-en-Perthois." *MSM* 81 (1966): 93–109.
Ladurie, Emmanuel Le Roy. *Montaillou: The Promised Land of Error.* Trans. Barbara Bray. New York: George Braziller, 1978.
———. *Montaillou, village Occitan de 1294 à 1324.* Paris: Gallimard, 1975.
Lambert, Sarah. "Crusading or Spinning." In Edginton and Lambert, *Gendering the Crusades,* 1–15.
Lauer, Phillipe, ed. *Collections manuscrits sur l'histoire des provinces de France.* 2 vols. Paris: Leroux, 1905–1911.
Laurenceau, André. *Essai historique sur l'Abbaye royale de Saint-Loup-lez-Orléans.* Orléans: A. Laurenceau, 1974.
Lauwers, Michel. "Expérience béguinale et récit hagiographique: À propos de la "Vita Mariae Oigniacensis" de Jacques de Vitry (vers 1215)." *Journal des Savants* (1989): 61–103.
———. *La mémoire des ancêtres, le souci des morts: Morts, rites et société au Moyen Âge (Diocèse de Liège, XIe–XIIIe siècles).* Paris: Bauchesne, 1997.
———. *"Noli me tangere:* Marie Madeleine, Marie d'Oignies et les penitents de XIIIe siècle." *Mélanges d'école française de Rome: Moyen Âge* 104 (1992): 209–68.
Lawrence, C. H. "Stephan Lexington and Cistercian University Studies in the Thirteenth Century." *Journal of Ecclesiastical History* 11 (1960): 164–78.
Le Blévec, Daniel. *La part du pauvre: L'assistance dans les pays du Bas-Rhône du XIIe siècle au milieu du XVe siècle.* 2 vols. Collection de l'école française de Rome 265. Rome: École française de Rome, 2000.
Lees, Clare A., ed. *Medieval Masculinities: Regarding Men in the Middle Ages.* Medieval Cultures Series 7. Minneapolis: University of Minnesota Press, 1994.
Lefèvre, Jean A., and Bernard Lucet. "Les codifications cisterciennes au XIIe et XIIIe siècles d'après les traditions manuscrites." *Analecta Sacri Ordinis Cisterciensis* 15 (1959): 3–22.
———. "L'ère des grandes codifications cisterciennes (1202–1350)." In *Études d'histoire du droit canonique dédiées à G. Le Bras,* 249–62. Paris: Sirey, 1965.
Lefèvre, Jean-Baptiste. "Le cadre religieux." In Didier and Toussaint, *Autour de Hugo d'Oignies,* 21–36.
Le Goff, Jacques. "Merchant's Time and Church's Time in the Middle Ages." Reprinted in Le Goff, *Time, Work, and Culture in the Middle Ages,* 29–42.
———. *Saint Louis.* Paris: Gallimard, 1996.
———. *Saint Louis.* Trans. Gareth Evan Gollrad. Notre Dame: University of Notre Dame Press, 2009.

———. *Time, Work, and Culture in the Middle Ages.* Trans. Arthur Goldhammer. Chicago: University of Chicago Press, 1990.
Le Grand, Leon. "Les maisons-Dieu et léproseries du diocese de Paris au milieu du XIVe, d'après le register de visites du délégué de l'évêque (1351–1369)." *Mémoires de la Société de l'histoire de Paris et de l'Île-de-France* 24 (1897): 61–365.
———. "Les maison-Dieu et léproseries du diocese de Paris au milieu du XIVe siècle." *Mémoires de la Société de l'histoire de Paris et de l'Île-de-France* 25 (1898): 47–178.
———. *Statuts d'hôtels-Dieu et de léproseries: Recueil de textes du XIIe au XIVe siècle.* Paris: Picard, 1901.
Lehmijoki-Gardner, Maiju. *Worldly Saints: Social Interaction of Dominican Penitent Women in Italy, 1200–1500.* Bibliotheca Historica 35. Helsinki: Suomen Historiallinen Seura, 1999.
———. "Writing Religious Rules as an Interactive Process: Dominican Penitent Women and the Making of Their *Regula.*" *Speculum* 79 (2004): 660–87.
Lekai, Louis. *The Cistercians: Ideals and Reality.* Kent, OH: Kent State University Press, 1977.
Lemarignier, Jean-François. *Recherches sur l'hommage en marche et les frontières féodales.* Lille: Bibliothèque Universitaire, 1945.
Lerner, Robert E. *The Heresy of the Free Spirit in the Later Middle Ages.* Notre Dame: University of Notre Dame Press, 1972.
———. "Vagabonds and Little Women: The Medieval Netherlandish Dramatic Fragment *De Truwanten.*" *Modern Philology* 65 (1968): 301–6.
Lester, Anne E. "Cares beyond the Walls: Cistercian Nuns and the Care of Lepers in Twelfth- and Thirteenth-Century Northern France." In Jamroziak and Burton, *Religious and Laity in Western Europe,* 197–224.
———. "Cleaning House in 1399: Disobedience and the Demise of Cistercian Convents in Northern France at the End of the Middle Ages." In Barret and Melville, *Oboedientia. Zu Formen und Grenzen von Macht und Unterordnung im mittelalterlichen Religiosentum,* 423–44.
———. "Lost But Not Yet Found: Medieval Foundlings and Their Care in Northern France, 1200–1500." *Proceedings of the Western Society for French History* 35 (2007): 1–17.
———. "Making the Margins in the Thirteenth Century: Suburban Space and Religious Reform between the Low Countries and the County of Champagne." *Parergon* 27 (2010): 59–87.
Lester, Anne E., and William Chester Jordan, "La Cour Notre-Dame de Michery: A Response to Constance Berman." *Journal of Medieval History* 27 (2001): 43–54.
Lewis, Patricia. "Mortgages in the Bordelais and Bazadais." *Viator* 10 (1979): 23–38.
Lex, Léonce. "Martyrologe et chartes de l'Abbaye Notre-Dame du Jardin-lez-Pleurs (Marne)." *MSA* 21 (1884): 365–93.
Lillich, Meredith Parsons, ed. *Cistercian Nuns and Their World.* Vol. 6 of Studies in Cistercian Art and Architecture. Kalamazoo: Cistercian Publications, 2005.
Lock, Peter. *The Franks in the Aegean, 1204–1500.* London: Longman, 1995.
Longnon, Jean. *Les compagnons de Villehardouin: Recherches sur les croisés de la quatrième croisade.* Geneva: Droz, 1978.
Lot, Ferdinand. "L'état des feux de 1328." *BEC* 90 (1929): 51–107, 256–315.

Lower, Michael. *The Barons' Crusade: A Call to Arms and Its Consequences.* Philadelphia: University of Pennsylvania Press, 2005.

———. "The Burning at Mont-Aimé: Thibaut of Champagne's Preparations for the Baron's Crusade of 1239." *Journal of Medieval History* 29 (2003): 95–108.

Luscombe, David. "From Paris to the Paraclete: The Correspondence of Abelard and Heloise." *Proceedings of the British Academy* 74 (1988): 247–83.

Lusse, Jackie. "Les religieuses en Champagne jusqu'au XIIIe siècle." In Parisse, *Les religieuses en France aux XIIIe siècle,* 11–26.

Maas, Walther. *Les Moines-Défricheurs: Études sur les transformations du paysage au Moyen-Âge aux confines de la Champagne et de la Lorraine.* Moulins: Imprimerie du Progrés de l'Allier, 1944.

Maccarrone, Michele. "Le costituzioni del IV Concilio lateranense sui religiosi." In Maccarrone and Lambertini, *Nuovi studi su Innocenzo III,* 1–45.

———. *Studi su Innocenzo III.* Studi e documenti di storia ecclesiastica 17. Padua: Italia Sacra, 1972.

Maccarrone, Michele, and Roberto Lambertini, eds. *Nuovi studi su Innocenzo III.* Nuovi studi storici 25. Rome: Nella sede dell'Instituto, 1995.

Mackay, Dorothy-Louise. *Les hôpitaux et la charité à Paris aux XIIIe siècle.* Paris: Champion, 1923.

Mahn, Jean-Berthold. *L'ordre cistercien et son gouvernement: Des origines au milieu du XIIIe siècle (1098–1265).* 2nd ed. Paris: Éditions E. de Boccard, 1982.

Maier, Christoph T. "Crisis, Liturgy and the Crusade in the Twelfth and Thirteenth Centuries." *Journal of Ecclesiastical History* 48 (1997): 628–57.

———. *Crusade Propaganda and Ideology: Model Sermons for the Preaching of the Cross.* Cambridge: Cambridge University Press, 2000.

———. "Mass, the Eucharist and the Cross: Innocent III and the Relocation of the Crusade." In Moore, *Pope Innocent III and His World,* 351–60.

———. *Preaching the Crusades: Mendicant Friars and the Cross in the Thirteenth Century.* Cambridge: Cambridge University Press, 1994.

———. "The Roles of Women in the Crusade Movement: A Survey." *Journal of Medieval History* 30 (2004): 61–82.

Makowski, Elizabeth. *Canon Law and Cloistered Women: Periculoso and Its Commentators, 1298–1545.* Washington, DC: Catholic University of America Press, 1997.

———. "*Mulieres Religiosae,* Strictly Speaking: Some Fourteenth-Century Canonical Opinions." *Catholic Historical Review* 85 (1999): 1–14.

———. *"A Pernicious Sort of Woman," Quasi-Religious Women and Canon Lawyers in the Later Middle Ages.* Washington, DC: Catholic University of America Press, 2005.

Mansfield, Mary. *The Humiliation of Sinners: Public Penance in Thirteenth-Century France.* Ithaca: Cornell University Press, 1995.

Martin, Robert. "Aux sources de l'Abbaye de Pont-aux-Dames." *Bulletin de la Société littéraire et historique de la Brie* 40 (1984): 17–36.

Marx, Jacques, ed. *Propagande et contre-propagande religieuses.* Brussels: Éditions de l'Universitaire, 1987.

Mathieu, Jean-Noël. "A propos des châtelains de Châtillon-sur-Marne." *MSM* 107 (1992): 7–27.

Mathieu, M. R. *Montmirail en Brie: Sa seigneurie et son canton*. Paris: Librairie A. Deruelle, 1975.

McDonnell, Ernst W. *The Beguines and Beghards in Medieval Culture: With Special Emphasis on the Belgian Scene*. New Brunswick, NJ: Rutgers University Press, 1954.

McGuire, Brian Patrick. "The Cistercians and the Transformation of Monastic Friendships." *Analecta Cisterciensia* 37 (1981): 1–63. Reprinted in Brian McGuire, *Friendship and Faith: Cistercian Men, Women, and Their Stories, 1100–1250*. Aldershot: Ashgate, 2002.

McLaughlin, Mary Martin. "Heloise the Abbess: The Expansion of the Paraclete." In Wheeler, *Listening to Heloise*, 1–18.

McNamara, Jo Ann. "*De Quibusdam Mulieribus*: Reading Women's History from Hostile Sources." In Rosenthal, *Medieval Women and the Sources of Medieval History*, 237–58.

——. "The *Herrenfrage*: The Restructuring of the Gender System, 1050–1150." In Lees, *Medieval Masculinities*, 3–29.

——. "The Need to Give: Suffering and Female Sanctity in the Middle Ages." In Blumenfeld-Kosinski and Szell, *Images of Sainthood in Medieval Europe*, 199–221.

——. *Sisters in Arms: Catholic Nuns through Two Millennia*. Cambridge: Harvard University Press, 1996.

McNamer, Sarah. *Affective Meditation and the Invention of Medieval Compassion*. Philadelphia: University of Pennsylvania Press, 2010.

Meersseman, G. "Les frères prêcheurs et le mouvement dévot en Flandre aux XIIIe s." *Archivum Fratrum Praedicatorum* 18 (1948): 69–130.

Mellinkoff, Ruth. *Outcasts: Signs of Otherness in Northern European Art of the Late Middle Ages*. 2 vols. Berkeley: University of California Press, 1993.

Melville, Gert. "'Diversa sunt monasteria et diversas habent institutiones.' Aspetti delle molteplici forme organizzative dei religiosi nel Medioevo." In *Chiesa e società in Sicilia. I secoli XII–XVI*, 323–45.

——. "Ordensstatuten und Allgeneines Kichenrecht: Eine Skizze zum 12/13 Jahrhundert." In Landau and Mueller, *Proceedings of the Ninth International Congress of Medieval Canon Law*, 691–712.

Mercier, Jean. "L'Abbaye du Val-des-Vignes à Ailleville." *MSA* 115 (1990): 135–52.

Mesqui, Jean. "Le palais des comtes de Champagne à Provins (XIIe–XIIIe siècles)." *Bulletin monumental* 151 (1993): 321–55.

Mews, Constant J. "Hildegard, the *Speculum virginum* and Religious Reform in the Twelfth Century." In Reverchon, *Hildegard von Bignenin ihrem historischen Umfeld*, 237–67.

——, ed. *Listen, Daughter: The "Speculum virginum" and the Formation of Religious Women in the Middle Ages*. New York: Palgrave, 2001.

——. *The Lost Love Letters of Heloise and Abelard: Perceptions of Dialogue in Twelfth-Century France*. New York: St. Martin's, 1999.

——. "Negotiating the Boundaries of Gender in Religious Life: Robert of Arbrissel and Hersende, Abelard and Heloise." *Viator* 37 (2006): 113–48.

Mignardot, Andrée, and Maurice Mignardot. *Histoire d'un village du nord-Sénonais, Michery*. Sens: Chevillon, 1996.

Miller, Tanya Stabler. "Now She Is Martha, Now She Is Mary: Beguine Communities in Medieval Paris (1250–1470)." Ph.D. dissertation, University of California at Santa Barbara, 2007.
Miramon, Charles de. *Les donnés au Moyen Âge: Une forme de vie religieuse laïque (v. 1180–v. 1500)*. Paris: Cerf, 1999.
Mollat, Michel. "L'hôpital dans la ville au Moyen Âge en France." *Bulletin de la Société française d'histoire d'hôpitaux* 47 (1983): 6–17.
Mooney, Catherine M., ed. *Gendered Voices: Medieval Saints and Their Interpreters*. Philadelphia: University of Pennsylvania Press, 1999.
———. "*Imitatio Christi* or *imitatio Mariae*? Clare of Assisi and Her Interpreters." In Mooney, *Gendered Voices*, 52–77.
Moore, John C., ed. *Pope Innocent III and His World*. Aldershot: Ashgate, 1999.
Moore, Robert I. *The Formation of a Persecuting Society: Authority and Deviance in Western Europe, 950–1250*. Oxford: Blackwell, 1987; 2nd ed., 2007.
Morin, Louis. "Recherches sur la fabrication des cartes à jouer à Troyes." *Annuaire de l'Aube* 62, 2nd ser. (1899): 67–124.
Mousnier, Mireille. *L'Abbaye cistercienne de Grandselve et sa place dans l'économie et la société méridionales (XIIe–XIVe siècles)*. Toulouse: CNRS/Université de Toulouse–Le Mirail, 2006.
Mueller, Joan. *The Privilege of Poverty: Clare of Assisi, Agnes of Prague, and the Struggle for a Franciscan Rule for Women*. University Park: Pennsylvania State University Press, 2006.
Muessig, Carolyn. *The Faces of Women in the Sermons of Jacques de Vitry*. Toronto: Peregrina, 1999.
———, ed. *Medieval Monastic Preaching*. Leiden: Brill, 1998.
Mulder-Bakker, Anneke B. *Lives of the Anchoresses: The Rise of the Urban Recluse in Medieval Europe*. Trans. Myra Heerspink Scholz. Philadelphia: University of Pennsylvania Press, 2005.
———, ed. *Mary of Oignies: Mother of Salvation*. Trans. Margot King and Hugh Feiss. Turnhout: Brepols, 2006.
———, ed. *Sanctity and Motherhood: Holy Mothers in the Middle Ages*. New York: Garland, 1995.
Neff, Amy. "The Pain of *Compassio:* Mary's Labor at the Foot of the Cross." *Art Bulletin* 80 (1998): 254–73.
Neils, H. "Les doyens de chrétienté: Étude de diplomatique sur leurs actes de juridiction gracieuse en Belgique au XIIIe siècle." *Revue Belge de philologie et d'histoire* 3 (1924): 59–74.
Newman, Barbara. *From Virile Woman to WomanChrist: Studies in Medieval Religion and Literature*. Philadelphia: University of Pennsylvania Press, 1995.
———. "The Heretic Saint: Guglielma of Bohemia, Milan, and Brunate." *Church History* 74 (2005): 1–38.
———. "Possessed by the Spirit: Devout Women, Demoniacs, and the Apostolic Life in the Thirteenth Century." *Speculum* 73 (1998): 733–70.
Newman, Martha G. *Boundaries of Charity: Cistercian Culture and Ecclesiastical Reform, 1098–1180*. Stanford: Stanford University Press, 1996.
———. "Crucified by the Virtues: Monks, Lay Brothers, and Women in Thirteenth-Century Cistercian Saints' Lives." In Farmer and Pasternack, *Gender and Difference in the Middle Ages*, 182–209.

———. "Real Men and Imaginary Women: Engelhard of Langheim Considers a Woman in Disguise." *Speculum* 78 (2003): 1184–1213.

Newman, William Mendel. *Les seigneurs de Nesle en Picardie (XIIe–XIIIe siècle), leurs chartes et leur histoire: Étude sur la noblesse régionale ecclésiastique et laïque.* 2 vols. Philadelphia: American Philosophical Society, 1971.

Nichols, John A., and Lillian Thomas Shank, eds. *Hidden Springs: Cistercian Monastic Women.* 2 vols. Kalamazoo, MI: Cistercian Publications, 1995.

Nicholson, Helen J., ed. *Palgrave Advances in the Crusades.* New York: Palgrave, 2005.

———. "Women on the Third Crusade." *Journal of Medieval History* 23 (1997): 335–49.

Nieus, Jean-François. "Un example précoce de repertoire féodale: Le livre des fiefs de la châtellenie d'Encre (nord de la France, ca. 1245)." *Bulletin de la commisson royale d'histoire* 168 (2002): 1–70.

———. *Un pouvoir comtal entre Flandre et France: Saint-Pol, 1000–1300.* Brussels: De Boeck, 2005.

Noël, Albert. "L'Abbaye de l'Amour-Dieu de l'ordre de Cîteaux (1232–1802)." *Revue de Champagne et de Brie* 1 (1876): 144–53.

Noel, William, and Daniel Weiss, eds. *The Book of Kings: Art, War, and the Morgan Library's Medieval Picture Bible.* London: Third Millennium, 2002.

Nolan, Kathleen, ed. *Capetian Women.* New York: Palgrave, 2003.

Notariado público y documento privado. 7ème Congrès international de diplomatique, Valence, 1986. 2 vols. Valencia: Generalitat Valencia, 1989.

Oberste, Jörg. *Die Dokumente der Klösterlichen Visitationen.* Typologie des sources du moyen âge occidental, facs. 80. Turnhout: Brepols, 1999.

Oliva, Marilyn. *The Convent and the Community in Late Medieval England: Female Monasteries in the Diocese of Norwich, 1350–1540.* Woodbridge: Boydell, 1998.

Olson, David R., and Nancy Torrance, eds. *Literacy and Orality.* Cambridge: Cambridge University Press, 1991.

Osheim, Duane J. "Conversion, *Conversi,* and the Christian Life in Late Medieval Tuscany." *Speculum* 58 (1983): 368–90.

Ostrowitzki, Anja. *Die Ausbreitung der Zisterzienserinnen im Erzbistum Köln.* Cologne: Böhlau, 1993.

The Oxford Illustrated History of the Crusades. Ed. Jonathan Riley-Smith. Oxford: Oxford University Press, 1995.

Paden, William D. "*De monachis rithmos facientibus:* Hélinant de Froidmont, Bertran de Born and the Cistercian General Chapter of 1199." *Speculum* 55 (1980): 669–85.

Parat, Alexandre. "L'Abbaye de Marcilly." *Bulletin de la Société des sciences historiques et naturelles de l'Yonne* 79 (1925): 339–57.

Paravy, Pierrette, and Nicole Bouter, eds. *Les mouvances laïques des ordres religieux: Actes du troisième colloque international du C.E.R.C.O.R. en collaboration avec le Centre International d'Études Romanes, Tournus, 17–20 juin 1992.* Saint-Étienne: L'Université de Saint-Étienne, 1996.

Parisse, Michel, ed. *À propos des actes d'évêques: Hommage à Lucie Fossier.* Nancy: Presses Universitaires de Nancy, 1991.

———, ed. *Les religieuses en France aux XIIIe siècle.* Nancy: Presses Universitaires de Nancy, 1985.

Pegg, Mark Gregory. *A Most Holy War: The Albigensian Crusade and the Battle for Christendom*. Oxford: Oxford University Press, 2008.
Pellegrini, Luigi. "Female Religious Experience and Society in Thirteenth-Century Italy." In Farmer and Rosenwein, *Monks and Nuns, Saints and Outcasts*, 97–122.
Perroy, Edouard. *La guerre de cent ans*. Paris: Gallimard, 1945.
———. *The Hundred Years War*. Trans. David C. Douglas. London: Eyre and Spottiswoode, 1962.
———. "Social Mobility among the French *Noblesse* in the Later Middle Ages." In Yves Renouard, *Études d'histoire médiévale*, 2 vols. Vol. 1, 225–38. Paris: S.E.V.P.E.N., 1968.
Peters, Edward. "Restoring the Church and Restoring Churches: Event and Image in Franciscan Biography." *Franziskanische Studien* 68 (1986): 213–36.
Peterson, Ingrid. "Like a Beguine: Clare before 1212." In *Clare of Assisi: Investigations*, ed. Mary Francis Hone, 47–67. Saint Bonaventure, NY: Franciscan Institute, 1993.
Petrakopoulos, Anna. "Sanctity and Motherhood: Elizabeth of Thuringia." In Mulder-Bakker, *Sanctity and Motherhood: Holy Mothers in the Middle Ages*, 259–96.
Peyroux, Catherine. "The Leper's Kiss." In Farmer and Rosenwein, *Monks and Nuns, Saints and Outcasts*, 172–88.
Phillips, Jonathan. *The Second Crusade: Extending the Frontiers of Christendom*. New Haven: Yale University Press, 2007.
Picó, Fernando. "Membership in the Cathedral Chapter of Laon, 1217–1238." *Catholic Historical Review* 61 (1975): 1–30.
Pirenne, Henri. "La chancellerie et les notaries des comtes de Flandre avant le XIIIe siècle." In *Mélanges Julien Havet*. Paris: E. Leroux, 1895.
Pixton, Paul B. *The German Episcopacy and the Implementation of the Decrees of the Fourth Lateran Council, 1216–1245*. Leiden: Brill, 1994.
Powell, James. *Anatomy of a Crusade, 1213–1221*. Philadelphia: University of Pennsylvania Press, 1986.
———. "The Role of Women in the Fifth Crusade." In Kedar, *The Horns of Hattin*, 294–301.
Pressouyre, Léon, ed. *L'espace cistercien*. Paris: Comité des travaux historiques et scientifiques, 1994.
Prevenier, Walter, and Thérèse de Hemptinne, eds. *La diplomatique urbaine en Europe au Moyen Âge: Actes du congrès de la commission internationale de diplomatique, Gand, 25–29 août 1998*. Leuven: Garant, 2000.
Prévost, A. "Les champenois aux croisades." *MSA* 85 (1921): 109–86.
———. *Le diocèse de Troyes: Histoire et documents*. 3 vols. Dijon: Union typographique, 1923.
Proceedings of the Ninth International Congress of Medieval Canon Law. Ed. P. Landau and J. Mueller. Monumenta iuris canonici, series C, vol. 10. Vatican City: Biblioteca Apostolica Vaticana, 1997.
Purkis, William J. *Crusading Spirituality in the Holy Land and Iberia c. 1095–c. 1187*. Woodbridge: Boydell, 2008.
———. "Elite and Popular Perceptions of *imitatio Christi* in Twelfth-Century Crusade Spirituality." In Cooper, *Elite and Popular Religion*, 54–64.

Putter, Ad. "Knights and Clerics at the Court of Champagne: Chrétien de Troyes's Romances in Context." In Church and Harvey, *Medieval Knighthood V*, 243–66.

Queller, Donald E., Thomas K. Compton, and Donald A. Campbell. "The Fourth Crusade: The Neglected Majority." *Speculum* 49 (1974): 441–65.

Quéruel, Danielle, ed. *Jean de Joinville: De la Champagne aux royaumes d'outre-mer.* Langres: D. Guéniot, 1998.

Rawcliffe, Carole. *Leprosy in Medieval England.* Woodbridge: Boydell, 2006.

Recueil de travaux offert à M. Clovis Brunel. 2 vols. Paris: Société de l'École des Chartes, 1955.

Reverchon, Alexander, ed. *Hildegard von Bignenin ihrem historischen Umfeld: Internationaler wissenschaftlicher Kongreß zum 900 jährigen Jubiläum, 13.–19. September 1988, Bingen am Rheim.* Mainz: Philipp von Zabern, 2000.

Richard, Jean. *Les ducs de Bourgogne et la formation du duché du XIe et XIVe siècle.* Paris: Société des Belles Lettres, 1954.

Rigon, Antonia. "A Community of Female Penitents in Thirteenth-Century Padua." In Bornstein and Rusconi, *Women and Religion,* 28–38.

Riley-Smith, Jonathan. *The Crusades: A Short History.* New Haven: Yale University Press, 1987.

——. *The Crusades, Christianity, and Islam.* New York: Columbia University Press, 2008.

——. "Family Traditions and Participation in the Second Crusade." In Gervers, *The Second Crusade and the Cistercians,* 101–8.

——. *The First Crusaders: 1095–1131.* Cambridge: Cambridge University Press, 1998.

Riley-Smith, Jonathan, ed. *The Oxford Illustrated History of the Crusades.* New York: Oxford University Press, 1995.

Roisin, Simone. "L'efflorescence cistercienne et le courant feminine de piété au XIIIe siècle." *Revue d'histoire ecclesiastique* 39 (1943): 342–78.

——. *L'hagiographie cistercienne dans le diocèse de Liège au XIIIe siècle.* Louvain: Bibliothèque de l'Université, 1947.

Rolnick, J. Francois, R. Valde, and Warren E. Weber. "The Debasement Puzzle: An Essay on Medieval Monetary History." *Journal of Economic History* 56 (1996): 789–808.

Rosenthal, Joel T., ed. *Medieval Women and the Sources of Medieval History.* Athens: University of Georgia Press, 1990.

Roserot, Alphonse. *Dictionnaire historique de la Champagne méridonale (Aube) des origines à 1790.* 3 vols. Langres: Imprimerie Champenoise, 1942–48; reprint, Marseilles: Laffitte Reprints, 1983.

——. "Notice sur le prieuré de Foissy." *Annuaire de l'Aube* 49 (1886): 50–56.

Ross, Ellen. "'She wept and cried right loud for sorrow and pain': Suffering, the Spiritual Journey, and Women's Experience in Late Medieval Mysticism." In Wiethaus, *Maps of Flesh and Light,* 45–59.

Rousseau, Constance M. "Home Front and Battlefield: The Gendering of Papal Crusading Policy (1095–1221)." In Edginton and Lambert, *Gendering the Crusades,* 31–44.

Routledge, Michael. "Songs." In *The Oxford Illustrated History of the Crusades,* 91–111.

Rubin, Miri. *Charity and Community in Medieval Cambridge.* Cambridge: Cambridge University Press, 1987.

———. *Corpus Christi: The Eucharist in Late Medieval Culture.* Cambridge: Cambridge University Press, 1991.

Rubner, Heinrich. *Untersuchungen zur Forstverfassung des mittelalterlichen Frankreichs.* Wiesbaden: F. Steiner, 1965.

Rupp, Leila J., and Verta Taylor. "Forging Feminist Identity in an International Movement: A Collective Identity Approach to Twentieth-Century Feminism." *Signs* 24 (1999): 363–86.

Saint-Denis, Alain. *L'Hôtel-Dieu de Laon, 1150–1300: Institution hospitalière et société aux XIIe et XIIIe siècles.* Nancy: Presses Universitaires de Nancy, 1983.

Salmon, Jean. "L'Abbaye de Benoîtevaux, regard et évocation." *Bulletin de la Société historique et archéologique de Langres* 17 (1980): 321–27.

Sankt Elisabeth: Fürstin Dienerin Heilige. Sigmaringen: Jan Thorbecke, 1981.

Saunier, Annie. *"Le pauvre malade" dans le cadre hospitalier médiéval: France du nord, vers 1300–1500.* Paris: Éditions Arguments, 1993.

Savetiez, Charles. "Maison de Dampierre-Saint-Dizier." *Revue de Champagne et de Brie* 17 (1884): 10–12, 113–25, 210–20, 283–90, 361–68, 465–71; 18 (1885): 66–72.

Schlager, Bernard. "Foundresses of the Franciscan Life: Umiliana Cerchi and Margaret of Cortona." *Viator* 29 (1998): 141–66.

Schlotheuber, Eva. *Klostereintritt und Bildung: Die Lebenswelt der Nonnen im späten Mittelalter. Mit einer Edition des, Konventstagebuche' einer Zisterzienserin von Heilig-Kreuz bei Braunschweig (1484–1507).* Tübingen: Mohr Siebeck, 2004.

Schmidt-Chazan, Mireille. "Aubri de Trois-Fontaines, historien entre la France et l'Empire." *Annales de l'Est* 36 (1984): 163–92.

Schmitt, Jean-Claude. *Mort d'une hérésie: L'Église et les clercs face aux béguines et aux béghards du Rhin supérieurs du XIVe au XVe siècle.* Paris: ÉHÉSS, 1978.

Searle, John R. *The Construction of Social Reality.* New York: Free Press, 1995.

———. *Making the Social World: The Structure of Human Civilization.* Oxford: Oxford University Press, 2010.

Sée, Henri. "Étude sur les classes serviles en Champagne du XIe au XIVe siècle." *Revue Historique* 56 (1894): 225–52; 57 (1895): 1–21.

Selle, Xavier de la. *Le service des âmes à la cour: Confesseurs et aumôniers des rois de France du XIIIe au XVe siècle.* Paris: École des Chartes, 1995.

Siberry, Elizabeth. "The Crusading Counts of Nevers." *Nottingham Medieval Studies* 34 (1990): 64–70.

Simon, André. *L'ordre des pénitentes de Ste Marie-Madeleine en Allemagne au XIIIeme siècle.* Fribourg, 1918.

Simons, Walter. *Cities of Ladies: Beguine Communities in the Medieval Low Countries, 1200–1565.* Philadelphia: University of Pennsylvania Press, 2001.

Sivéry, Gérard. *L'économie du royaume de France au siècle de Saint Louis (vers 1180—vers 1315).* Lille: Presses Universitaires de Lille, 1984.

Smahel, Frantisek, ed. *Häresie und vorzeitige Reform im Spätmittelalter.* Munich: Oldenbour, 1998.

Smith, Bonnie G. "Gender and the Practices of Scientific History: The Seminar and Archival Research in the Nineteenth Century." *American Historical Review* 100 (1995): 1150–76.

Smith, Caroline. *Crusading in the Age of Joinville*. Aldershot: Ashgate, 2006.
Smith, Julie Ann. "Prouille, Madrid, Rome: The Evolution of the Earliest Dominican *Instituta* for Nuns." *Journal of Medieval History* 35 (2009): 340–52.
Smith, Katherine Allen. "Saints in Shining Armor: Martial Asceticism and Masculine Models of Sanctity, ca. 1050–1250." *Speculum* 83 (2008): 572–602.
Sommerfeldt, John R., ed. *Erudition at God's Service*. Studies in Medieval Cistercian History 9. Kalamazoo, MI: Cistercian Publications, 1987.
Sommerfeldt, John, Larry Syndergaard, and E. Rozanne Elder, eds. *Studies in Medieval Culture*. 2 vols. Kalamazoo: Medieval Institute Publications, Western Michigan University, 1974.
Sommerlechner, Andrea, ed. *Innocenzo III: Urbs et Orbis. Atti del Congresso Internazionale Roma, 9–15 settembre 1998*. 2 vols. Rome: Società romana di storia patria: Istitutostorico italiano per il Medio Evo, 2003.
Southern, Richard W. *Western Society and the Church in the Middle Ages*. New York: Penguin, 1970; reprint, 1979.
Spiegeler, Pierre de. *Les hôpitaux et l'assistance à Liège (Xe—XVe siècles): Aspects institutionnels et sociaux*. Paris: Société d'Éditions les Belles Lettres, 1987.
Stache, Ulrich, Justus Wolfgang Maaz, and Fritz Wagner, eds. *Kontinuität und Wandel: Lateinishe Poesie von Naevius bis Baudelaire: Franco Munari zum 65. Geburtstag*. Hildesheim: Weidmann, 1986.
Stathakopoulos, Dionysios. "Discovering a Military Order of the Crusades: The Hospital of St. Sampson of Constantinople." *Viator* 37 (2006): 255–73.
Stock, Brian. *The Implications of Literacy: Written Language and Models of Interpretation in the Eleventh and Twelfth Centuries*. Princeton: Princeton University Press, 1983.
———. "Medieval Literacy, Linguistic Theory, and Social Organization." *New Literary History* 16 (1984): 13–29.
Strayer, Joseph. "The Crusade against Aragon." In Strayer, *Medieval Statecraft and the Perspectives of History*, 107–22.
———. "Italian Bankers and Philip the Fair." In Strayer, *Medieval Statecraft and the Perspectives of History*, 239–47.
———. *Medieval Statecraft and the Perspectives of History*. Princeton: Princeton University Press, 1971.
———. *The Reign of Philip the Fair*. Princeton: Princeton University Press, 1980.
Swietek, Francis R., and Terrence M. Deneen. "The Roman Curia and the Merger of Savigny with Cîteaux: The Import of the Papal Documents." *Revue bénédictine* 112 (2002): 323–55.
Switten, Margaret. "Singing the Second Crusade." In Gervers, *The Second Crusade and the Cistercians*, 67–76.
Thompson, Augustine. *Cities of God: The Religion of the Italian Communes, 1125–1325*. University Park: Pennsylvania State University Press, 2005.
Thompson, Sally. "The Problem of Cistercian Nuns in the Twelfth and Early Thirteenth Centuries." In Baker, *Medieval Women*, 227–53.
———. *Religious Women: The Founding of English Nunneries after the Norman Conquest*. Oxford: Oxford University Press, 1991.
Tilly, Charles. "From Interactions to Outcomes in Social Movements." In Giugni, McAdam, and Tilly, *How Social Movements Matter*, 253–70.

Touati, François-Olivier. *Archives de la lèpre: Atlas des léproseries entre Loire et Marne au Moyen Âge*. Paris: Éditions du CTHS, 1996.

———. "*Domus judaeorum leprosorum:* Une léproserie pour les juifs à Provins au XIIIe siècle." In Dufour and Platelle, *Foundations et oeuvres charitables au Moyen Âge*, 97–106.

———. "François d'Assise et la diffusion d'un modèle thérapeutique au XIIIe siècle." *Histoire des sciences médicales* 16 (1982): 175–84.

———. "Les groupes de laïcs dans les hôpitaux et les léproseries au Moyen Âge." In Paravy and Bouter, *Les mouvances laïques des orders religieux*, 137–62.

———. *Maladie et société au Moyen Âge: La lèpre, les lépreux et les léproseries dans la province ecclésiastique de Sens jusqu'au milieu du XVIe siècle*. Brussels: De Boeck Université, 1998.

Traill, David A. "Philip the Chancellor and the Heresy Inquisition in Northern France, 1235–1236." *Viator* 37 (2006): 241–54.

Van Engen, John. "The Christian Middle Ages as an Historiographical Problem." *American Historical Review* 91 (1986): 519–52.

———. "From Canons to Preachers: A Revolution in Medieval Governance." In *Domenico di Caleruega e la Nascita dell'ordine dei Frati Predicatori*, 261–95.

———. "The Future of Medieval Church History." *Church History* 71 (2002): 492–522.

———, ed. *The Past and Future of Medieval Studies*. Notre Dame: University of Notre Dame Press, 1994.

———. "Professing Religion: From Liturgy to Law." *Viator* 29 (1998): 323–43.

———. *Sisters and Brothers of the Common Life: The Devotio Moderna and the World of the Later Middle Ages*. Philadelphia: University of Pennsylvania Press, 2008.

Vauchez, André. "Assistance et charité en occident, XIIIe–XVe siècles." In *Domanda e consumi: Livelli e strutture (nei secoli XIII–XVIII)*, 151–62.

———. *The Laity in the Middle Ages: Religious Beliefs and Devotional Practices*. Ed. Daniel E. Bornstein. Trans. Margery J. Schneider. Notre Dame: University of Notre Dame Press, 1993.

———. "Lay People's Sanctity in Western Europe: Evolution of a Pattern (Twelfth and Thirteenth Centuries)." In Blumenfeld-Kosinski and Szell, *Images of Sainthood in Medieval Europe*, 21–32.

———. "Proselytisme et action antihérétique en milieu feminine au XIIIe siècle: La Vie de Marie d'Oignies (d. 1213) par Jacques de Vitry." In Marx, *Propagande et contre-propagande religieuses*, 95–110.

———. *La sainteté en Occident aux derniers siècles du Moyen Âge*. Paris: École française de Rome, 1988.

———. *Sainthood in the Later Middle Ages*. Trans. Jean Birrel. Cambridge: Cambridge University Press, 1997.

Veissière, Michel. *Une communauté canoniale au Moyen Âge: Saint-Quiriace de Provins (XIe–XIIIe siècles)*. Provins: Société d'Histoire et d'Archéologie l'Arondissement de Provins, 1961.

Venarde, Bruce. *Women's Monasticism and Medieval Society: Nunneries in France and England, 800–1215*. Ithaca: Cornell University Press, 1997.

Veyssière, Laurent. "Cîteaux et tart, foundations parallèles." In Barrière and Henneau, *Cîteaux et les femmes*, 179–90.

Voaden, Roalynn, and Diane Wolfthal, eds. *Framing the Family: Narrative and Representation in the Medieval and Early Modern Periods.* Tempe: Arizona Center for Medieval and Renaissance Studies, 2005.

Waddell, Chrysogonus. "The Myth of Cistercian Origins: C. H. Berman and the Manuscript Sources." *Cîteaux* 51 (2000): 299–386.

Walker, David. "The Organization of Material in Medieval Cartularies." In Bullough and Storey, *The Study of Medieval Records: Essays in Honor of Kathleen Major,* 132–50.

Warnatsch-Gleich, Friederike. *Herrschaft und Frömmigkeit: Zisterzienserinnen im Hochmittelalter.* Studien zur Geschichte, Kunst und Kulture der Zisterzienser, 21. Berlin: Lukas, 2005.

Warr, Cordelia. "*De Indumentis:* The Importance of Religious Dress during the Papacy of Innocent III." In Sommerlechner, *Innocenzo III: Urbs et Orbis,* 489–502.

———. "Religious Habits and Visual Propaganda: The Vision of the Blessed Reginald of Orléans." *Journal of Medieval History* 28 (2002): 43–72.

Watson, Sethina. "City as Charter: Charity and the Lordship of English Towns, 1170–1250." In Goodson, Lester, and Symes, *Cities, Texts and Social Networks, 400–1500,* 235–62.

———. "The Origins of the English Hospital." *Transactions of the Royal Historical Society* 16 (2006): 75–94.

Waugh, Scott L., and Peter D. Diehl, eds. *Christendom and Its Discontents: Exclusion, Persecution, and Rebellion, 1000–1500.* Cambridge: Cambridge University Press, 1996.

Wehrli-Johns, Martina. "Voraussetzungen und Perspektiven mittelalterlicher Laienfrömmigkeit seit Innozenz III. Eine Auseinandersetzung mit Herbert Grundmanns 'Religiösen Bewegungen.'" *Mitteilungen des Instituts für Österreichische Geschichtsforschung* 104 (1996): 286–309.

Wheeler, Bonnie, ed. *Listening to Heloise: The Voice of a Twelfth-Century Woman.* New York: Palgrave, 2000.

Wiethaus, Ulrike, ed. *Maps of Flesh and Light: The Religious Experience of Medieval Women Mystics.* Syracuse: Syracuse University Press, 1993.

Willems, E. "Cîteaux et la Second Crusade." *Revue d'histoire ecclésiastique* 49 (1954): 116–52.

Wolbrink, Shelley. "Women in the Premonstratensian Order of Northwestern Germany, 1120–1250." *Catholic Historical Review* 89 (2003): 387–408.

Wolf, Kenneth Baxter. *The Poverty of Riches: St. Francis of Assisi Reconsidered.* Oxford: Oxford University Press, 2003.

Wright, Nicholas. *Knights and Peasants: The Hundred Years War in the French Countryside.* Woodbridge: Boydell, 1998.

Zito, G., ed. *Chiesa e società in Sicilia: I secoli XII–XVI.* Turin: Societa editrice internazionale, 1995.

Index

abbess and abbesses. *See under* Cistercians
Abelard, 86
account books, 173
Acre, 148, 203
administration: of alms to nunneries, 194–95; of convents or nunneries, 110–14, 173–80, 200, 204; and gender, 172–80; of hospitals, leper houses, and *domus-Dei,* 118, 125–34, 172, 206
Ailleville, 36, 104, 190
Aisne (river), 48
Alberzoni, Maria, 90
Alexander III (pope), 125
Alice of Schaerbeek, 169
allod, 63, 65, 190–91, 196, 198–99
alms, 66, 100–102, 104, 141, 186–87, 192–95, 204
Alphonse of Poitiers, 194, 197
Amiens: bishop of, 107; diocese of, 106
amortization, 195–99
annuities, 61–62, 66, 174
apostolic charity. *See* charity
apostolic life. See *vita apostolica*
archives, 11, 18, 104, 173, 180–85, 193, 195, 199, 204. *See also* charters; documents
Argensolles (Cistercian convent), 21, 28–33, 35, 66, 69, 97, 107, 112–13, 116, 175, 188–89, 194, 197, 206; foundation narrative, 28–29, 86, 142
aristocracy: 47, 69–70; identity, 104–5; lesser aristocracy, 46–47, 58, 67–70, 102; patronage by, 102–7, 153–62; stratification of, 49. See also *armiger*
Armançon (river), 48
armiger, 46, 49–50, 67–68, 192
Arnaud Amaury, 93
Arnulf of Villers, 28–29, 85, 142
asceticism, 24–26, 30, 34, 144, 169
Assisi, 25–27, 100
Aube: department of, xi; river of, 48, 68

Auberville (Cistercian monastery), abbots of, 105
Aubry of Trois-Fontaines, 37, 45–46, 80
Augustinian convents, 22
Aulne (Cistercian monastery), 110
Autun, bishop of, 133
Auxerre: bishop of, 49, 66; city of, 66, 112, 207; counts and countesses of (also with Tonnerre and Nevers), 48, 69; Notre-Dame-de-la-Cité, canons of, 65
Avril, Joseph, 125

Barbeaux (Cistercian monastery), 105
Bar-sur-Aube, 19, 36, 41, 45, 48, 51, 54, 62, 66, 100, 104, 160, 175, 183–85, 190
Bar-sur-Seine, 45
Beatrix, of St.-Remy (of Reims), donor, 1–4, 73, 102
Beauvais, diocese of, 148, 155
begging, 94–95, 101, 115–16, 141–42, 193, 204
béguinage, 24, 63
beguines, 4, 9, 23, 80, 139, 185, 200
Belfay (Cistercian convent), 83
Belleau (Cistercian convent), 19, 159
Benedictine convents, 22. *See also individual convent names*
Benoîtevaux (Cistercian convent), 133, 207
Bergères, lords of, 68
Berman, Constance, 7, 111
Bernard de Montcuq, 58–59
Bernard of Clairvaux, preaching of, 115, 145, 153–54, 167–68; on the *Song of Songs,* 145, 167
Berneuil, leper house of, 97, 130, 197
Béziers, 93
bishops: 11, 97, 125–26, 133; reform-minded, 88, 115, 126, 128–29. *See also* Episcopal; *names of individual bishops*
bizoke. See penitents

251

Blanche of Castile (queen of France), 21, 69, 97–98, 105–6, 112, 193
Blanche of Navarre (countess of Champagne), 21, 28–33, 41–42, 52, 65, 68–69, 85–86, 97, 107, 142, 160, 197
blindness, 121
Boniface VIII (pope), 204
Boulancourt (Cistercian monastery), 104; abbots of, 131
bourgeoisie: class, 46–47, 50, 142, 196, 199; patrons, 60–65, 102; women, 5. *See also* burgher class
Bouvines, battle of, 157–59
Boves, Enguerrand of, 106–7, 155; daughters of, 161
Breteuil, Amice of, 70
Bretonval, 36, 190
Briard of Reims (citizen), and wife, Agnes, 60–61, 101
Brie, county of, 31, 48
Brienne: Erard of (also lord of Ramerupt), 19, 31, 74, 122, 158, 166; Marie, countess of, 159; Sybille of, 74, 161
buildings, 94, 96–102, 105, 133, 191; destroyed, 205–7; rebuilding and restoration of, 97, 100–102, 191, 206–7
bureaucracy, 51–52, 180, 182
burgher class, 3, 18, 36, 180–85, 189–90, 195; burgher-artisans, 61–62, 76, 123, 182, 186; burgher-merchant class, 46–47, 57–72; women, 6, 47, 57–77
Burgundy: duchy of, 50, 67, 78; duke of, 49, 52
burial, 105, 152, 157, 160, 165–67
Bynum, Caroline Walker, 29–30

Caesarius of Heisterbach, 29, 137, 164
Cahor, 58
canonesses, 4, 21, 27, 86
canons, secular, 46, 49, 51–54. *See also* clerics; deans
captivity, by Muslims, 147–48, 164
Cardinal Sinibaldo Fieschi, 16–17. *See also* Innocent IV
caregiving for poor, sick, and leprous, 39–42, 69–70, 75–76, 109, 117–19, 122, 126–30, 132, 134–46, 159, 162, 168–69, 199–200
caritas, 119, 143–46. *See also* charity
Carta caritatis, 83, 110
cartularies, 32, 177, 209
Cassidy-Welch, Megan, 144
Cathars. *See* heresy

cens. See rents
Central Europe, 24
Cerce, leper house of, 133
"certain women," 15–18
Châlons: bishop of, 79, 132, 171–72; city of, 54, 188
Champagne: archives of, 6, 12; civil war, 30–32; counts and countesses (*see* individual names); county of, 19–21, 25, 28, 45, 47–50, 172; fairs of (*see* fair towns); landscape of, 48–49, 172, 182, 191, 194, 198–200, 201–3, 205–6. *See also* religious movements; women's religious movement
Champguyon, family of, 57–61, 64–65; Alice, 58; Andrea, 57–61; Guy, 58; Isabelle, 58, 73; John, 57–58; Marguerite, 58–59; Stephen, 15–16, 57–61, 73, 97, 102–3, 187
chancery, 51–53, 177, 180, 196; records of, 50
chapels, family, 67, 96–102. *See also* buildings
charity, 7, 69–70, 95, 117–46, 193–95, 208; charitable institutions, 120–24, 191–92
Charles of Anjou, 203
charters, 1–2, 33, 79–80, 133, 173–92, 197–99, 200, 208–9; by abbesses, 131; of franchise, 45–47. *See also* archives; documents
Chartres: bishop of, 94; countesses of, 69; diocese of, 91; Isabelle, countess of, 70; Jean, count of, 68; town of, 70, 154
Château-Thierry, *domus-Dei* of, 42, 65, 67, 97
Châtillon (Châtillon-sur-Marne), family of, 157–59; counts of, 21; Gaucher II, 157; Gaucher III, 157; Gaucher of Montjay, 158, 162; Guy III, 157; Guy IV, 157; Hugh V of Châtillon and St.-Pol, 41, 68, 112, 157–59, 166
Chaumont, 48, 104, 184, 189–90
Chauvin, Benoît, 83
Cheminon (Cistercian monastery), 163
Chichéry, 15–19, 34–35, 43–44, 57–60, 187
children, 23, 50, 57–61, 71, 159; education of, 93
Chrétien de Troyes, 55
Christ, 23, 69, 100, 102, 117; humanity of, 120, 144–45, 167–68; suffering for, 148, 150; suffering of, 7, 86, 120, 167. *See also imitatio Christi*
church. *See* buildings
Cistercian convents: and care of lepers, 129–34, 139–46; collapse of, 201–9; foundation of, 5–6, 8, 18–21, 24, 81–85, 91–116, 128–29, 154–62, 196, 200,

211–15; numbers of nuns, 75, 132, 173, 203–4, 207; profession in, 74–75; suppression of, 207–9

Cistercian order: 7–12, 81–116, 177, 204; affiliation with or house of, 1, 7, 91; annual statutes of, 6–8, 81, 84–85, 92–96, 98, 118, 160; of Argensolles, 32–33, 107, 112; daughter house, 83, 104; filiation, 110–14; General Chapter, 9, 81, 83, 91–97, 104, 160, 164, 165, 202–4, 207; imitation and emulation of, 42, 84, 95; incorporation, 7, 11, 17, 42–44, 60, 67, 81–82, 85, 87, 92–116, 129–30, 207; *Institutes*, 8, 83, 90–93, 96; of La Barre, 42; of La Cour Notre-Dame-de-Michery, 40, 112; of L'Amour-Dieu, 113; of La Piété, 130; legislation, 6, 10, 83, 86–87, 92–96, 107, 114; Le Paraclet, 106–7; liturgy, 83–84, 165; model or reform, 12; of Notre-Dame-des-Prés, 71, 104; of Notre-Dame La-Joie in Berneuil, 97, 130; number of, 96; *ordo Cisterciensis*, 2; petitions for, 95–96, 104–5, 160; of St.-Antoine-des-Champs, 111; of St.-Loup in Orléans, 36; tax or tithe exemption, 202–3, 206; of Val-des-Vignes, 41, 105, 160. *See also* visitation

Cistercians: abbess and abbesses, 111, 131, 133, 161, 173–80; abbot and abbots, 1–2, 32, 92–96, 104–7, 110–14, 158, 175–80, 205; *conversa* and *conversae*, 27–29, 39, 71, 73, 88, 110–14, 144, 148–49, 168, 199, 203; *conversus* and *conversi*, 11, 62, 75, 84–85, 94, 110, 112, 142, 174–75, 191; crusade preaching and support for, 153–54; customs and customary, 2, 11, 35, 37, 84, 86–92, 143–46; "customs of Cîteaux," 17, 21; friendship, 85; historiography of, 8–9, 114–16; monasteries, male houses, 67, 196; monks, 85–87, 94, 111, 113, 146, 175–77, 205–9; nuns, definition of, 6, 11, 87, 92–96, 131; preaching, 115; priories, 207–8; spirituality, 29–31, 85, 115, 168; spirituality, female, 109, 119, 134, 143, 154, 157, 160. *See also names of individual houses*

Cîteaux (Cistercian monastery), 12, 32–33, 82–83, 93, 111–13; abbots of, 107, 112, 131

civil war, 30–32

citizens (*cives*), 39, 47, 51, 62–63, 180–85

Clairmarais (Cistercian convent), 1–4, 20, 60–62, 71, 73, 101, 164, 191, 197, 206, 208

Clare of Assisi, 3–4, 12, 25, 76, 89–90, 100. *See also* Franciscans; Poor Clares

Clarivaux (Cistercian monastery) 12, 29–33, 82, 85–86, 111–12, 163, 166, 204; abbots of, 104, 107, 113, 131, 205; manuscripts from, 145

class: new social classes, 45–57. *See also* aristocracy; bourgeoisie; burgher class

claustration. *See* cloister

clerics, 51–54, 126, 174, 180–85; patronage of, 66–68. *See also* canons, secular

cloister, 8, 87–96, 98, 115, 177, 204

collective identity, 3–5

Cologne, 24, 27

Common Life, sisters and brothers of, 185

Compiègne, 63, 130

Compostella, 148

confession, 88, 127–28

Conrad of Marburg, 24

conversion, 22–23, 26–28, 34, 65, 76, 117–19, 135, 138, 140, 143–46, 148; *conversa* and *conversus*, 39, 62, 71, 73, 88–89; process of, 40

Corinthians, letters to, 125–26

Cortona, 26

Coucy, Engerrand of, 68

councils, ecclesiastical, 88, 126–29; legislation of, 124–28, 138

Courlandon, hospital of, 20

credit, 192, 202

crisis, fiscal, 201–9

crusade movement, 21, 149, 152, 160

crusades, 7, 51, 88, 103, 126, 128, 147–70, 192; Albigensian Crusade, 93, 153, 157, 159; against Aragon, 198, 203; Barons' Crusade, 79, 159; and Cistercians, 153–54; definition of, 150; departure for, 162–67, 194; Fourth Crusade, 58, 154–55, 159; Fifth Crusade, 106, 151, 155–56, 159; funding of, 151, 194–99; indulgence, 151; liturgy for, 164–65; Louis IX's second expedition, 192, 203; masses for, 165–66; Second Crusade, 150, 153, 157; songs, 163; taxes for, 132, 195–99, 201–3; Third Crusade, 147–48, 150, 156–59; vows, 150–52; women and, 149–52

cura monialium. *See* spiritual care and guidance

currencies, xix; debasement of, 202; *provinois*, xix; *tournois*, xix

Damietta, siege of, 155, 169

damoiselles (*domicellae*), 50, 67–68, 75

Dampierre, family of, 74, 156–57; Beatrix, 74, 161; Guy II, 156, 163; Helvide, 159, 167; Jean, 156–57; lords of, 122; William II, 98, 156–57, 166; William III, 156

daughter-house. *See* Cistercian order
daughters, 1–4, 47, 58–59, 72, 74–75, 143, 161, 175
deans, 174, 178, 180–85; deans of Christianity, 181–84
debt, 173, 184, 202, 206
Degler-Spengler, Brigitte, 113
devotion, 149, 152, 155, 157, 208
documents and documents of practice, xi–xiii, 18, 44, 134, 195, 200; production of, 46, 51–52, 174, 178–85. *See also* archives; charters; texts
Dominican order, 11–12, 70, 78, 89–91, 96, 105; tertiary sisters, 24. *See also* friars
Dominic of Guzman, 89
domus-Dei, 6, 19, 38–42, 65, 67–69, 97–100, 118, 123–24, 128–34, 161–62, 192, 211–15
dowery, 35, 50, 70–72
dress, penitential, 25, 42–43, 78–80. *See also* habits

Eberbach, 29, 85
Ecclesiastica officia, 83
Edward II (king of England), 205
eels, 106–7, 155
Egypt, 155, 202
Elizabeth of Hungary, 4, 24, 33, 39, 143
Elizabeth of Thuringia. *See* Elizabeth of Hungary
enclosure. *See* claustration
endowment, 94, 98, 102–7, 116, 134, 156–62
England, 147
Épernay, 30, 48, 66, 188–89
Episcopal: archives, xi–xiii; courts, 51, 181–84; jurisdiction, 115; officials, 51, 178, 188. *See also* bishops
Epistolae duorum amantium, 86
ergotism, 121
Eudes of Sully (bishop of Paris), 111
Eudes Rigaud (archbishop of Rouen), 114; register of, 173
Eugenius III (pope), 153
Evergates, Theodore, 46, 196
exempla collections, 27, 86, 120, 135–39
Exordium magnum, 83
Exordium parvum, 83

fair towns, 45–46, 48, 54–56, 67, 123; administration of, 54–55; culture of, 76. *See also* names of individual towns
family and kin, 57–61, 64; of crusaders, 149, 152–53, 156–62; renunciation of, 22–23
famine, 204
father, 23, 117, 178

feudal registers, 50, 68
fief, 48–50, 67–68, 70–71, 102, 105, 160, 180, 195–99; "culture of the fief," 49–50; purchase of, 196–99
Filles-Dieu, 5–6, 13, 17, 19, 25, 33–39, 68–69, 79, 81, 87, 100, 109
Flanders: countesses of, 32, 69; countess Margaret of, 98, 156–57, 166; counts of, 52; county of, 20, 22, 29–30, 157, 163, 181, 200, 202
Flines, 157, 163
Fontenay (Cistercian monastery), abbot of, 105
Fontevraud (Benedictine convent), 34, 86, 109, 194
forests (Ardennes, Der, Othe), 48, 106
foundation: contingencies, 1–6; monastic, 67–70, 98–100, 103, 155; process of, 65
foundlings, 121
Fourth Lateran Council, 5, 8, 85, 88, 119, 126–29; Canon 13, 10, 89; Canon 21, 127; Canon 22, 127
France: kingdom of, 155, 165, 172, 202–6, 209; kings and queens, 49, 166, 193 (*see also individual names*); northern, 22, 34–35, 69, 78–81, 88, 91, 96, 113–14, 117, 121, 125; ports of, 147; royal court, 24; royal domain, 47–48, 193; southern, 88, 169
franchise: effects of, 46; property, 65; urban, 45–47, 58–59. *See also* allod
Franciscans: convents of, 96; customs of, 89–91
Francis of Assisi, 3, 12, 26, 39, 100, 139; *vita prima*, 100
Frankish Morea, 58
friars, 9, 139, 160. *See also* mendicant orders
Froidmont (Cistercian monastery), 148
Fulk of Neuilly, 35–37

Garonne (river), 25
Gautier Cornut (archbishop of Sens), 66, 105
Génestal, Robert, 192
Genoa, 54, 151
Gerard of Larrivour (monk), 28–29
Germany: German Empire, 24, 50; Order of Penitent Sisters, 38; religious movements in, 4, 12
Gertrude of Dagsburg, 31
Gila (widow of Provins, "the abbess"), 78–81
Gilbert of Tournai, 80, 108, 136
Gosbert (lord of Aspermont), 98
Gospel texts, 120, 134; Gospel of Matthew, 39, 138
Gothic buildings, 101
grange (and farm buildings), 15–17, 40–41, 57, 67, 97–99, 100–102, 132, 186–88, 190; agriculture, 186

grapes, cultivation of. *See* vineyards
Gregorian Reform, 7, 21
Gregory VIII (pope), 164
Gregory IX (pope), 12, 16, 34, 78, 89–91, 97, 114
goldsmiths, 3, 57, 60, 76. *See also* patrons
"good women," 25
Gratian, 43
Grundmann, Herbert, 4, 9–10, 115

habits, monastic or religious, 17, 37; color of, 108; penitential habits, 79; white habits (Cistercian style), 15, 32, 42–44, 107–10, 117–18, 141, 145
hagiography, 4–5, 29–32, 76, 118, 135–36, 139–43. *See also* vitae *under individual names*
Hautvillers (Cistercian monastery), 97; monks of, 188
Hegan of Ervy, 123
Heisterbach (Cistercian monastery), 29
Heloise, 84, 86; letters of, 86
hen and chicks, 28–29
Henry I the Liberal (count of Champagne), 51–54
Henry II (count of Champagne), 31, 52
heresy, 10, 78, 88, 93, 126, 154; heretical imaginings and fear of, 25, 87, 115; heretics and heretical sects, 10, 25, 79–81
Holy Land, 31, 123, 147–50, 154–55, 164, 166, 203
home front (during crusades), 149, 154, 170
Honorius III (pope), 89–90
hospices and hospitals, 39–42, 65, 67, 97, 101, 123–34, 160, 178, 192. *See also domus-Dei*
hospitality, 118–20
hospitals (larger establishments), 121–22; Order of the Holy Spirit, 121
Hostiensis (cardinal bishop of Ostia), 43
Hugh of Floreffe, 118, 136
Hugh of St.-Maurice, and wife, Margaret, 71, 102–4, 187
Hugolino of Ostia. *See* Gregory IX
Humbert of Romans, 108, 136
humiliati, 28
humility, as an ideal, 108–9, 140–46
Hundred Years' War, 205
husband, 3, 24, 51, 69–71, 117, 138, 151, 154, 178
Huy, 23–24, 30; leprosarium of, 118

Ida (abbess of Argensolles, prioress of Val-Notre-Dame), 30–31, 142
Igny (Cistercian monastery), 1

imitatio Christi (imitation of Christ), 7, 22, 116, 134, 136–39, 144–46, 149, 152–53, 162, 165, 167–70
immigrants, 55–56, 62–63
incorporation. *See under* Cistercian order
infirmary, 120
inheritance, 23, 50, 70; partible, 46, 50, 173
Innocent III (pope), 8, 10, 31, 35, 88–92, 114, 126, 128, 150, 152, 165
Innocent IV (pope), 16n2, 186
inquisition, 78–81
Instituta generalis capituli, 83
institutionalization, process of, 2–4, 6, 10–12, 18, 37, 79, 81, 86, 96–97, 107, 121, 129, 185, 200. *See also* Cistercian order; reform
Isabelle of Colaverday (abbess of La Piété), 131
Isabelle (sister of Louis IX), 161n64
Isabelle of France (daughter of Louis IX), 180
Isabelle of France (daughter of Philip IV), 205
Italy: female foundations in, 90; ports of, 147; religious movements in, 4, 12, 25–27, 200

Jacques de Bazoches (bishop of Soissons), 97, 130
Jacques de Panteleon, 73–74
Jacques de Vitry, 4, 23, 69, 108, 136–38, 141, 145, 151, 163–64
Jardin-lès-Pleurs. *See* Le Jardin (Cistercian convent)
Jaucourt, family of, 104–5, 160, 199n98; Alice, 104; Alix, 161; Erard, 160, 166; lords of, 122; Peter, 104, 160, 166, 176, 189–91; Thomas, 104
Jeanne of Navarre (countess of Champagne), 172, 202
Jerusalem, 147, 150, 152–53, 168
Johanna of Marcilly, abbess, 133
Joinville, lords of: Geoffroy, 53; Jean, 37, 163; William (archbishop of Reims), 32
Jours de Troyes, 132, 171–72, 202
Julianna of Mont-Cornillon, 141, 177
Jully-les-Nonnains, 82
jurée, in Troyes, 46
juridical concerns, 87, 92, 94, 110–14

knights, and knightly class, 49, 68–70, 192. *See also armiger*
Knights Templar, 153–54
Kupfer, Marcia, 124

L'Abbaye-aux-Bois (Cistercian convent), 63, 92, 155
La Barre (Cistercian convent), 42, 65, 67–68, 97

La Biache-lès-Péronne (Cistercian convent), 65
labor, 108–9, 143–46, 208
La Celle (Cistercian convent), 112
La Cour Notre-Dame-de-Michery (Cistercian convent), 21, 40, 75, 95, 97, 99, 101, 112, 131–32, 186, 194
Lagny, town of, 48
La Grâce (Cistercian convent), 19, 35, 68, 159
La Ferté (Cistercian monastery), 32, 107
La Joie-lès-Nemours (Cistercian convent), 21, 104–5
La Joie Notre-Dame in Berneuil. *See* Notre-Dame La Joie
L'Amour-Dieu (Cistercian convent), 20, 41, 68, 70, 97, 112, 157–58, 178
Langres: bishops of, 49, 79, 104; diocese of, 48, 181, 184; town of, 36
language and legal formalism, 5–6, 52, 91–96, 136, 182, 207
Laon: bishops of, 79; city of, 61, 73–74, 148
La Piété, or La Piété-Dieu (Cistercian convent), 19, 35, 68, 74, 97, 130, 158–59, 167, 195
Larrivour (Cistercian monastery), 28–30, 85, 104, 142
La Tart, 83
law: canon, 43, 87; customary, 132; municipal, 71; Roman, 181
Lazarus, 136
L'Eau-lès-Chartres (Cistercian convent), 95
legates, papal, 5, 8, 20, 27, 88, 176, 203
Le Grand-Beaulieu in Chartres, 122
Le Jardin (Cistercian convent), 19, 35, 159
Lekai, Louis, 114
Le Lys (Cistercian convent), 20–21, 69, 112, 116
Le Paraclet (Cistercian convent), 106–7, 155, 161
lepers, 23–24, 40, 69–70, 97, 101, 117–44, 159
Le Popelin of Sens, 122
leprosarium, or leper house, 23, 36, 39–42, 65, 97, 100–101, 104, 118–19, 121–22, 124–34, 193
leprosy: care of, 39–42, 121, 135–39, 169; definition of, 123–24, 135; disease, 30, 119; and Gospels, 135–36; in Isaiah, 135; for Jews, 122; in Leviticus, 135–36. *See also* lepers; leprosarium
Le Sauvoir (Cistercian convent), 61, 74
Les Clairets (Cistercian convent), 70, 91, 154

Les Deux-Eaux (leprosarium in Troyes), 39–40, 122, 124
Les Isles (Cistercian convent), 65–66, 207
letters, 27–28, 86
Levant coast, 148
Lézinnes, William of, 58
libellus, of monks of Montier-la-Celle, 16–19, 43–44
Libellus diffinitionum, 93, 109. *See also* Cistercian order
Liège: bishop of, 31; city of, 27, 142; diocese of, 4, 23, 25, 28, 30, 109, 139
Longpont (Cistercian monastery), 159, 167
Louis IX (king of France), 36–37, 39, 63, 105–6, 139, 156–60, 162–65, 169, 180, 192–94, 196, 202–3; office for, 165
Low Countries, religious movements in, 4, 22, 28–33, 76, 139
Luc de Waudes, 58

Maier, Christoph, 148, 151–52, 164
Mainmort, 46, 195
Malay-le-Roy, 133; *domus-Dei* of, 133
Manichean, 79
Mansourah, battle of, 158
Marburg, 24
Marcilly (Cistercian convent), 134
Margaret of Beverley, 147–49, 168; *vita* of, 148–49
Margaret of Cortona, 26–27, 33
Margaret of Jerusalem. *See* Margaret of Beverley
Margaret of Ypres, 141
margins, 23–24; marginal populations, 120; of towns and cities, 100–101, 145, 199–200, 206
Marie de Esternay, 74
Marne (river), 19, 48, 68
marriage and married couples, 26, 31, 39–40, 50, 72, 88, 103, 126, 140, 156–62, 174, 202
martyr and martyrdom, 25, 169–70
Mary of Oignies, 4, 23, 31, 33, 38–39, 76, 141, 143, 169
masters (*magister*), 174, 183–84
Mathilda of Brunswick (countess of Perche), 70, 154
Mathilda of Courtenay (countess of Auxerre), 66
Mathilda of Garlande, 155
Matthew of Montmorency, 155
Maubuisson (Cistercian convent), 20, 69, 112, 116

INDEX

Meaux: bishops of, 79; city of, 41, 121; country of, 48
mendicancy. *See* begging
mendicant orders, 22
merchants, 28, 54–55, 60–70, 202; of Tyre, 147
Meuse (river), 48, 140, 181
mills, 56, 70, 188
Mira, 3, 6, 7
miracles, 137–38, 142, 159
Moha: count of, 30; county of, 31
Molesme, 82
monastic concerns: administration, 90; customs, 5; identity, 177; profession, 43. *See also* Cistercians: customs; rules
Moncel, abbot of, 172
Mont-Aimé, burning of heretics at, 79–81
Mont-Cornillon, leper house of, 177
Montepulciano, 28
Montier-la-Celle, 15–18, 43–44, 160
Montmirail, 68; Elizabeth, 143, 161; Jean, 143, 159, 167; Jean II, 159; lady of, 70; leper house of, 132, 159, 161, 171–72; Matthew (of Oisy), 68, 159
Mont-Notre-Dame (lès-Provins) (Cistercian convent), 36, 66, 81, 194, 207
Montpellier, 93, 120
Montreuil-les-Dames (Cistercian convent), 83, 148–49
moral theology, 88, 128–29
Morimond (Cistercian male abbey), 32, 83
mothers and motherhood, 1–4, 23, 38, 69, 71–72, 74–75, 117, 140
movement and mobility, 11, 17, 28, 48, 54–56, 115–16, 121; social mobility, 57–60, 64, 172, 199
muliercula(e), 5, 79–81, 95, 115
mulieres religiosae, 5, 17, 19, 34, 47, 81. *See also Filles-Dieu;* religious women
Muslims, 153

Narbonne, bishop of, 93
Navarre, kingdom of, 46, 180, 202
necropolis. *See* burial
neighborhoods, 55–56, 62–63
Nesle, lords of: Jean I, 63; Jean II, 155
Nesle, town of, 63
networks: administrative, 174–85; familial and kin, 47, 68, 76; social, 47, 56–72, 107, 180–85, 189; spiritual, 28–33, 69, 71, 85, 110–14, 139, 208; women's, 28, 47
Newman, Martha, 85, 146
Nicholas of Brie (bishop of Troyes), 102, 131

nobility. *See* aristocracy
Normandy, duchy of, 113, 192
Notre-Dame-aux-Nonnains (Benedictine convent), 109, 160, 206
Notre-Dame-des-Prés (Cistercian convent), 19, 35, 57–61, 62, 70–71, 73–74, 97, 102–4, 133, 164, 174–76, 186–88, 191–92, 194–97, 203, 206; abbess Isabelle of, 176
Notre-Dame La-Joie (in Berneuil) (Cistercian convent), 97, 130, 197
Noyon, diocese of, 65
nuns (*moniales*), 17, 36, 73, 88, 95, 108. *See also under* Cistercians

obedience, 110–14; disobedience, 116. *See also* administration
oblation, 43
officials (*officiales*). *See under* Episcopals
Oise (river), 48
Order of the Poor Ladies of the Spoleto Valley, 89
Orléans: bishops of, 79; city of, 120–21; *Filles-Dieu* of, 36
Ormont (Cistercian convent), 20, 74
ovens, 56, 58, 188

papacy, 87–92, 202–4
Paraclete (Benedictine convent, of Abelard and Heloise), 86, 108–9, 160, 173, 177, 206; Marie (sister of Eudes Rigaud), abbess of, 173
Parc-aux-Dames (Cistercian convent), 92, 116
Paris: bishop of, 111; city of, 19–21, 28, 35, 63, 110, 120–21, 132, 163, 172, 180, 202; diocese of, 51; *Filles-Dieu* of, 37; masters of, 150, 171–72; schools, 88, 128–29; St.-Lazar leper hospital, 37
parish and parochial rights, 16, 121, 178
Parlement of Paris, 132, 171–72
Passion relics, 166
patronage, of Cistercian convents, 47, 57–74, 102–7, 152
pauperes Christi, 123–24, 135, 141, 146, 162
Peloponnese, 58, 153–54
penance, 15, 33–35, 118, 143–46, 150, 152, 154–55, 162
penitential piety, 6, 33–36, 39–42, 117–19, 124, 134, 143, 152, 161–62, 167–70; theology, 128
penitents and penitent sisters, 4, 9, 25–28, 33–39, 43, 75, 88–91, 123, 200; Dominican penitents, 11; Order of Penitent Sisters of Blessed Mary Magdalene, 38, 90

258   INDEX

Perche: Geoffrey IV, count of, 70, 154; Mathilda of Brunswick, countess of, 70, 154
Periculoso, 204
Péronne, town of, 63, 65
Peter the Chanter, 128, 150
Philip II Augustus (king of France), 31, 157–59, 197
Philip IV the Fair (king of France), 172, 197, 202–3
Philip of Mécringes, 35, 41, 68–69, 112–13, 158–59
Philip of Nemours, 105–6
Philippa (daughter of Count Henry II of Champagne), 31
Philip the Chancellor (of University of Paris), 78–81
Picardy, 54, 181
pilgrims and pilgrimage, 48, 67, 147–48, 150
pinzochere. *See* penitents
Pipon, Brigitte, 155
Pont-aux-Dames (Cistercian convent), 21, 41, 157–58, 166
Ponthieu, count of, 42
Pontigny (Cistercian monastery), 32–33, 107, 123, 160, 207
poor, 65, 67, 69, 116, 123–24, 133, 141, 158. *See also* women: poor
Poor Clares, 4, 12, 26
pope. *See individual names*
population growth, 120–21, 202; populations of cities, 121
portable altar, 166
Portiuncula (near Assisi), church of, 100
Port-Royal (Cistercian convent), 63, 92, 110, 116, 155
poverty: 95, 119, 176, 203; poverty movement, 56, 177; "Privilege of Poverty," 90; as a religious ideal, 11, 26, 102, 106, 108–9, 115, 120, 141–42, 172
prayer, 15, 118, 142, 152, 162–67, 208; for the dead, 101, 105, 162–67, 200
preachers and preaching, 69, 95, 108, 139, 163, 169
prebend, 49, 53, 174
Premonstratensian order, 11, 86, 118, 172
Preuilly (Cistercian monastery), 207; abbot of, 105
prévôts, 182–83, 202
priests, 114, 122, 131, 133, 174
processions, 163–65
profit, 56, 76, 116, 177, 202; profit economy, 11, 54, 141

property: "female property," 72; landed, 50, 134; rural and suburban, 71–72, 174, 185–92; sales and purchases of, 187–99; urban, 60–70
prostitutes, repentant, 34–38, 75
Prouille (Dominican female convent), 89–90
Provins, 21, 28, 36, 45, 48, 51, 54, 66, 78–81, 122, 206–7; May fair of, 55; Jewish leper house, 122
Prudentibus virginibus (papal bull), 91
Psalter, 15, 148, 208

quedam mulieres, 17, 19. *See also* "certain women"
Quia maior, 150–51
Quincy, 33; abbot of, 105

Ramerupt, 19, 31, 35, 122, 158; *domus-Dei* of, 68, 97, 130; leprosarium of, 130–31; lords of, 74. *See also* Brienne
rebellion, 32–33
rebuilding. *See under* buildings
recluse, 23–24, 48, 122
reform: Cistercian reform, 8, 89–92; of hospitals and hospices, 119, 124–34; of religious movements, 2, 6, 10; religious reform, 5, 35–36, 78–116, 200. *See also* institutionalization
Reims: archbishop of, 49, 79; archdiocese of, 51, 120, 129, 181, 205–6; city of, 3, 20, 36, 54, 62, 101, 164, 178, 206–8; court of, 1, 181, 184; hospital of, 71
religious movements, 10; in Champagne, 3–6; definition of, 3–6. *See also* women's religious movement
religious orders, 9; historiography of, 8; "new" orders, 11
religious women, 15, 17–19, 42–44, 79–82, 88–92
remembrance, 164–67. *See also* prayer: for the dead
rents, 1, 46, 63, 71, 103–7, 115, 134, 172, 174, 177–78, 191–92, 199; declining value, 201–9; income from, 185–92, 203; rental lists or rent books, 62, 177–78; rental market, 55, 187
restoration. *See* buildings
Reynel, leper house of, 133
Rhine river and Rhine valley, 24, 47
Rhône river, 25
Richard I (king of England), 148
Riley-Smith, Jonathan, 161
Robert le Bougre, 78–81

INDEX

Robert of Arbrissel, 34
Robert of Thourotte (bishop of Langres), 104
Rôles des fief, 71
Rome: city of, 26, 125, 148; diocese of, 88
Rouen: city of, 120; *Filles-Dieu* of, 38
royal patronage, 105–6, 116, 192–97. *See also* France *and names of individual sovereigns*
Royaumont (Cistercian monastery), 165
rules: monastic, 5, 10, 77; *Rule of Augustine*, 21, 89, 91; *Rule of Benedict*, 83, 89–92, 108, 167

Saint Clare. *See* Clare of Assisi
Saint Dominic, 89
Saint Francis. *See* Francis of Assisi
Saint Julian the Hospitaller, legend of, 136–37
Saint Louis. *See* Louis IX
Saint Margaret of Antioch, shrine to, 147–48
saints lives. *See* hagiography; vitae *under individual names*
Saladin, 147–48, 150
Salzburg, 137
San Damiano, 12, 25, 100; order of, 89–90
San Pietro (near Assisi), 100
San Sisto (nunnery in Rome), 89–91
Sara (daughter of Beatrix of St.-Remy and nun of Clairmarais), 1–4
Savigny (Cistercian monastery), abbot of, 113
scapular, 108–9. *See also* habits
Schönau, 29, 86
seals: of officials (deans and prévots), 180–85; of women, 50, 70–71, 173, 175
Seine river and Seine valley, 19, 48
semi-religious women. *See* beguines; penitents; religious women
Semphringham, order of, 89
Senlis, diocese of, 92
Sénonais, 48
Sens: archbishop of, 48, 66, 70, 95, 105, 205–6; archdiocese of, 16, 78–81, 111, 120, 129; city of, 40, 101, 121
serfs, freed, 54, 56
sermons, 27, 108, 120, 137, 144–45, 150
Sézanne, 68, 137
Siena, 12, 54
Sicily, 203
silence, vow of, 113
Simon, André, 38
sin, 127–28
singing, 15
single women, 38, 71, 75

sisters, biological, 3, 47, 143
Sisters, Devout, 76
social networks. *See under* networks
"social striving," 22
Soissons: bishops of, 79, 112, 130; diocese of, 30, 48, 97
Somme (river), 181
soul, 127, 162–67
Southern, Richard, 114
Speculum virginum, 86
spiritual care and guidance of women, 29–30, 67, 82–87, 94, 110–14, 174; of lepers and the sick, 124, 131; prohibitions against, 95
stability, 96–102
St.-Aignan, 36
St.-André (parish). *See under* Troyes
St.-Antoine-des-Champs (Cistercian convent), 21, 35–37, 63, 75, 111–12, 116, 163; customs of, 112
St.-Ayoul in Provins, 55
St.-Catherine, female convent of (Franciscan order), 21, 206
St.-Denis: abbey of, 163; abbot of, 49
St.-Dizier (Cistercian convent), 98, 156 57, 166
St.-Donatian of Bruges, 52
Stephan of Lexington, 113
Stephen of Bourbon, 138
St.-Étienne, canons of, 49, 51, 58, 73, 177
St.-Florentin (comital town), 45
St.-Jacques de Vitry (Cistercian convent), 41, 97, 132, 197; Alice, abbess of, 132, 171–72, 202
St.-Jacques in Provins, 16
St.-Julien in Mergey, leper house of, 133
St.-Lazare, leper houses of: Blois, 122; Meaux, 122; Orléans, 122; Paris, 122; Pontoise, 122
St.-Leonard, hospital of, 30
St.-Loup (Benedictine monastery in Troyes), 176, 203
St.-Loup (Cistercian convent), 36
St.-Maclou, canons of, 52, 66, 177
St.-Martin (Benedictine monastery in Troyes), 176, 203
St.-Martin of Tours, 52
St.-Pierre of Troyes, 44; canons of, 130, 175
St.-Pol: Elizabeth, 157; Eustachie, 155. *See also* Châtillon: Hugh V
St.-Quentin: countess of, 92; town of, 63
St.-Quiriace: canons of, 49, 51, 196; Garias, provost of, 175

INDEX

Strasbourg, 24
St.-Urbain, canons of, 74
suburbs, 18, 58–65, 97, 121, 124, 172. *See also* margins
suffering, 128, 136–39, 144–46, 152; on crusade, 148, 170. *See also* Christ: suffering for
sufficiency, 95–96, 101–7, 115–16, 172–73, 178, 209
suspicion, 80–81
Syria, 155

taille. See rents
taxation: 177, 195–99; royal, 172, 195–99, 202–3. *See also* franchise
testament, last will and, 101, 158, 160, 162–64, 181, 185, 192–95
texts, 4–5; manuscripts, 145. *See also* charters; documents; hagiography
Thibaut II (count of Champagne), 31; and leper of Sézanne, 137
Thibaut IV (count of Champagne), 21, 30–32, 41, 46, 52, 58, 65, 79, 97, 153, 180, 188–89, 196, 206
Thibaut V (count of Champagne), 59, 122, 180, 191, 195–98
Third Lateran Council, 119, 125–26, 128
Thomas Aquinas, 80
Thomas Becket, 147
Thomas of Cantimpré, 29, 137, 169
Thomas of Celano, 100
Thomas of Froidmont, 147–48, 150
tithes, 104–6, 115, 131–32, 186, 189–90; tithing, 130
Touati, François-Olivier, 122
towns. *See* fair towns; *towns by name*
townsmen and women. *See* burgher class
trade and trade routes, 28, 49
transubstantiation, 88
travel: between Flanders and Champagne, 29, 142; of ideals, 27; of people, 28, 67, 123. *See also* movement and mobility
Trinitarians, order of, 160
Troissy, *domus-Dei* of, 21, 41, 68, 112, 157–58
Troyes: bishop of, 79, 100, 102, 131, 176, 206; cathedral of, 73; diocese of, 97, 158, 181; drapery of, 63; fairs of, 54–55; Franciscans of, 59, 176, 203; leper house (*see* Les Deux-Eaux); parish of St.-André, 15, 57–60; parish of St.-Jean, 57; parish of St.-Savine, 57–60; rue des Lorgnes, 57–58; suburbs of, 18, 57–58, 175; tannery, 61; town of, 16–21, 28, 35, 45, 48, 51, 70, 73–74, 97, 121–23, 164

True Cross, 166
Tuscany, 89–90

University of Paris, 35, 37, 51, 63, 78–81; masters of, 51
urban, self-government, 46. *See also* franchise
Urban IV (pope), 73–74
usury, 88, 126, 128

Val-des-Vignes (Cistercian convent), 19, 36, 41, 62, 66, 72, 75, 100, 160, 166, 175, 189–92, 194–97, 204, 207
Val-Notre-Dame (near Huy), 30–31, 35, 142
Val Regis, 1
Van Engen, John, 76n133
Vauclair (Cistercian monastery), 167
Vaux-de-Cernay (Cistercian monastery), abbot of, 105, 111
veil. *See* habits
vernacular texts, 53–54
Vertus, 188
Villehardouin, family of, 164; Geoffrey of, 58
Villemaur (comital town), 45
Villeneuve-l'Archévêque, 40
villeneuves, 49, 56
Villers (Cistercian monastery), 28–29, 85, 110
Villiers (Cistercian nunnery), 70
Viluis, 40, 97, 132, 186
vineyards, 32, 36, 48, 58, 62, 66, 103, 182, 186, 189–90, 203, 207
Virgin Mary, devotion to, 149, 168–70
visitation and oversight, 8, 73, 89–91, 110–14, 173–75, 185
vita(e), 24, 27, 34; of Liège, 4, 139–43
vita apostolica, 6, 19, 21–24, 42–44, 56, 75–76, 102, 115–16, 119, 177
Vitry, 41, 48
Vitry-le-Franois, 35
Vivi, 6, 11, 17
vows: crusade, 69–70; lepers, 122; monastic, 42–44; penitential, 69, 118

widows, 1, 24, 47, 51, 71, 73, 75, 78–80, 117, 182
will and testament. *See* testament
William of Auvergne, 37–38
William of Joinville (archbishop of Reims), 32
Willencourt (Cistercian convent), 42
wives, 38, 69, 71, 117
woods (Argonne, Beaumont, Boissicant, Clairvaux), 48. *See also* forests
women: actions of, 4, 11, 15–17, 42–44; aristocratic, 50–51, 69–71, 143; bourgeois, 51;

patronage of, 67–77; pregnant, 121; poor, 38, 79–80, 193; townswomen, 71–78
women's religious movement, 3–5, 12, 21–28, 33, 56, 89, 200; in Champagne, 18–21, 38–40, 42–44, 47, 185

Yonne (river), 48, 66
Yvette of Huy, 23–24, 31, 33, 38–39, 42, 76, 109, 117–19, 140–43, 169; *vita* of, 136, 140–41

zoccoli. See penitents